CHRIST
IN HIS MYSTERIES

CHRIST
IN HIS MYSTERIES

by
The Right Rev. Dom Columba Marmion, O.S.B.
Abbot of Maredsous Abbey

THE CENACLE PRESS
AT SILVERSTREAM PRIORY

Christ in His Mysteries was first published in French in 1919. First published in English in 1924 (translated from the French by Mother M. St Thomas of Tyburn Convent), this Cenacle Press edition is based on the 9th edition of Sands and Co. The Sands edition bore the *Nihil Obstat* of R. Michael, *can., libr. cens.,* and the *Imprimatur* of J. Lecouvet, *vic. gen.* (Tornaci, 27a Maii 1939).

This revised edition, published in 2022 by The Cenacle Press at Silverstream Priory, provides translation of Latin texts left untranslated in the original English edition. It also incorporates some minor corrections to the text.

The translations introduced to this new edition are taken from the following sources: Aquinas translations are sourced from the *Opera Omnia* published by The Aquinas Institute. Patristic quotations appearing in the *Summa* have been taken from the same source. Used with permission.
All other translations are original and Copyright © 2022 by Silverstream Priory.

The Cenacle Press at Silverstream Priory
Silverstream Priory
Stamullen, County Meath, K32 T189, Ireland
www.cenaclepress.com

ppr ISBN 978-1-915544-18-6
cloth ISBN 978-1-915544-19-3

Interior layout by Kenneth Lieblich
Cover design by Silverstream Priory

Cover art: Detail from the great east window of Ampleforth Abbey church by Herbert Hendrie (Photo: Lawrence Lew, OP).

TO THE SACRED HEART OF JESUS
WHEREIN DWELLETH
ALL THE FULNESS OF THE DIVINITY,
ALL THE TREASURES
OF WISDOM AND KNOWLEDGE
WHICH IS FOR US
THE FOUNT OF LIFE AND HOLINESS.

LETTER OF HIS HOLINESS
BENEDICT XV TO THE AUTHOR

Dilecto Filio Columbae Marmion, O.S.B. Abbati Maredsolensi.
BENEDICTUS PP. XV.

Dilecte Fili, salutem et apostolicam benedictionem.

Binos tuos illos libros, quos Nobis perhumaniter obtuleras, quorum alter "Le Christ, Vie de l'Ame," alter "Le Christ dans ses Mysteres" inscribitur, cum his proximis diebus, quantum per occupationes licuit volveremus, facile cognovimus jure sane ac merito eos laudari, utpote ad excitandam alendamque in animis divinae caritatis flammam valde accommodatos. Etsi enim non hic omnia exponuntur quae in tuis ad sodales sermonibus de Jesu Christo, omnis sanctitatis et exemplari et effectore, explicaveris, his tamen eorum tamquam commentariis idonee foveri studium videtur Ejus imitandi de Ipsoque vivendi "qui factus est nobis sapientia a Deo, et justitia, et sanctificatio et redemptio."

Optimum igitur consilium fuit haec in lucem dari volumina, unde non modo sodales tui sed multo plures ad omnem virtutem proficerent: lateque jam, ut audimus, vel laicorum manibus versantur. Itaque cum gratias tibi agimus, tum etiam gratulamur: atque auspicem caelestium munerum, apostolicam benedictionem tibi, dilecte Fili, paterna cum benevolentia impertimus.

Datum Romae apud Sanctum Petrum die X mensis octobris MCMXIX, Pontificatus Nostri anno sexto.

BENEDICTUS PP XV.

**To Our beloved Son Columba Marmion, O.S.B. Abbot of Maredsous
BENEDICT XV. Pope.**

Beloved Son, health and the Apostolic Benediction.

Having recently perused, as far as Our occupations permitted, the two books: "Christ, the Life of the Soul" and "Christ in His Mysteries," which you have kindly sent Us, We readily appreciate their praiseworthiness as being singularly conducive to excite and maintain the flame of Divine love in the soul. For although these pages do not contain the whole of the discourses you have made to your spiritual sons concerning Jesus Christ, the Exemplar and Cause of all sanctity, nevertheless these commentaries, so to speak, on the matter of your teaching, show clearly how this doctrine is capable of fostering the desire to imitate Christ and to live by Him "Who of God is made unto us wisdom, and justice, and sanctification, and redemption."

It was therefore a most happy inspiration to publish these works so that not only your own spiritual children but many others should be helped in the way of perfection. We are told that these works are already in the hands of many even among the laity. Therefore thanking you, We at the same time congratulate you and, as a pledge of heavenly reward, We impart to you, beloved Son, the Apostolic Benediction.

Given at St. Peter's, Rome, October 10th, 1919, the sixth year of Our Pontificate.

BENEDICT XV. Pope.

FOREWORD TO THE 1ST EDITION

I N   A L L O W I N G   the publication of the conferences "Christ the Life of the Soul," the author had only in view to show forth the fundamental character of the Christian life, according to the Gospel, the Epistles of St Paul, and the conclusions of theological teaching. The Christian life is essentially supernatural, and can only be found in Christ, the supreme Model of perfection, the infinite Treasure of grace and the efficient Cause of all holiness.

The conferences that compose the present volume are the logical continuation of those of the preceding volume.

The life of Christ, the divine and at the same time the accessible Exemplar of the Christian life, is manifested to us by the states and mysteries, the virtues and actions of the Sacred Humanity. Human in its outward expression, the life of the Word Incarnate is altogether divine in its origin.

Thus the mysteries of the God-Man are not only models which we must consider: they contain moreover within themselves treasures of merit and grace. By His almighty virtue, Christ Jesus, ever-living, produces the inward and supernatural perfection of His states in those who are moved by the desire of imitating Him and placing themselves in contact with Him by faith and love.

It is in the light of these truths that the author has set forth the principal mysteries of Jesus.

The plan is simple.

A double preliminary conference shows how much Christ's mysteries are ours, and how, in a general manner, we can come in contact with them and assimilate the fruits of them.

We shall only well understand the transcendent value of these mysteries, their wonderful splendour, their logical connection, the profound unity that knits them together, if we first of all consider the One Who lived them for us. This is why, in the first part, the attempt has been made to sketch in outline the essential traits of the *Person* of Jesus, the Eternal Word—made Flesh—Who comes to redeem the world by His Sacrifice.

The second part is devoted to the contemplation of the *mysteries* of the God-Man. Taking for his basis the records of the Gospel and the liturgical texts, the author has sought to establish the reality at once human and divine of these mysteries, to mark their meaning, and point out their application for the faithful soul. As to the choice of these mysteries, it has been thought best to dwell upon those which the Church proposes to us in her liturgical cycle. Indeed, who better than the Church knows the secret of her Bridegroom, and possesses the art of distributing the Gospel? Who better than she knows how to lead us to the Saviour?

The extremely kind welcome that the public has deigned to give to the volume "Christ, the Life of the Soul," has not only been a precious encouragement for the author. It is besides one of the most consoling symptoms in the sorrows and anxieties of a particularly troubled time. It shows that, under the pressure of events, many souls, docile to God's voice, have entered into themselves; hungering for salvation, peace and light, they have turned towards the One Who alone is the Infallible Way, the Truth that enlightens every man here below, the Life that saves from death.

It is "in Him" that, according to the words of St Paul, all things must be restored: *Omnia instaurare in Christo.* For, according to the thought of the same Apostle, except on this divine foundation, nothing is stable nor lasting. All the ambition of the author, in permitting the publication of these conferences, is to contribute, for his small part, to this great work of Christian reconstruction.

May Christ vouchsafe to bless these pages! Written for Him, they speak only of Him. May they further reveal to souls the secret of the love of a God who appeared amongst us! May they lead souls to drink more often at the fountains of living water which have sprung up, for our salvation and joy, from the pierced Heart of Jesus! *Haurietis aquas in gaudio de fontibus Salvatoris.*[1]

D.C.M.

Feast of the Annunciation.
March 25, 1919.

---

[1] "Thou shall draw waters with joy out of the Saviour's fountains," Isa. xii, 3.

INDEX OF CONFERENCES

FACTUS EST HOMO QUI ERAT DEUS, ACCIPIENDO QUOD NON ERAT NON AMITTENDO QUOD ERAT: ITA FACTUS EST HOMO DEUS, IBI HABES ALIQUID PROPTER INFIRMITATEM TUAM: IBI HABES ALIQUID PROPTER PERFECTIONEM TUAM. ERIGAT TE CHRISTUS PER ID QUOD HOMO EST; DUCAT TE PER ID QUOD DEUS-HOMO EST; PERDUCAT TE AD ID QUOD DEUS EST.

HE WHO WAS GOD WAS MADE MAN, IN TAKING THAT WHICH HE WAS NOT, BUT WITHOUT LOSING THAT WHICH HE WAS: THUS GOD BECAME MAN, HEREIN THOU HAST THAT WHICH IS NEEDFUL TO THY WEAKNESS, AND THOU HAST THAT ALSO WHICH IS NEEDFUL TO THY PERFECTION. MAY CHRIST RAISE THEE BY HIS "BEING" AS MAN: MAY HE GUIDE THEE BY HIS "BEING" AS GOD-MAN: MAY HE BRING THEE EVEN TO HIS "BEING" AS GOD!

S. Augustine. *In Joan.* XXIII, 6.

PRELIMINARY CONFERENCES

THE MYSTERIES OF CHRIST ARE OUR MYSTERIES

OUR CONTACT WITH THE MYSTERIES OF JESUS

THE MYSTERIES OF CHRIST
ARE OUR MYSTERIES

SUMMARY.—I. How St. Paul dwells upon the mystery of Christ.—II. How much God desires that this mystery should be known.—III. Such knowledge is the true basis of piety and a source of joy.—IV. Threefold reason whereby Christ's mysteries are ours:—Christ lived them for us; in them He shows Himself to us as our Exemplar; in them He unites us with Himself as the members of His Body.—V. The virtue of these mysteries is ever actual.

WHEN we study attentively the Epistles of St Paul, it is evident that for him all is summed up in the practical knowledge of the mystery of Christ.

He writes to the Ephesians: "According to revelation, the mystery has been made known to me, as I have written above in a few words; as you reading may understand my knowledge in the mystery of Christ...to me the least of all the saints, is given this grace, to preach among the Gentiles, the unsearchable riches of Christ, and to enlighten all men, that they may see what is the dispensation of the mystery which hath been hidden from eternity in God."[1]

It is of this mystery, although ineffable, that I intend, with God's grace, to speak. I will presently show to what an intimate degree this mystery is ours: it is the very subject of this first conference.

First it will be useful for us to consider for a few moments how St. Paul spoke of this important and fruitful truth of which Christ in person appointed him the herald. And from whom better than from him can we

---

1 Ephes. III, 3–4, 8–9.

learn how vital the knowledge of this mystery is for our souls!

I

As you know, it is on the morrow of his conversion that St. Paul receives the mission of making known the name of Jesus. From this moment, he has nothing more at heart than to fulfil this mission. If he undertakes numerous and perilous voyages,[1] if he preaches without intermission in the synagogues, at the Areopagus, before the Jews, before the learned men of Athens and before the Roman procurators; if, even in prison, he writes long letters to the faithful; if he suffers a thousand persecutions,[2] it is in order that he may carry the name of Christ "before Gentiles, and kings, and the children of Israel."[3]

It is above all from his preaching to the pagan nations of whom he was constituted the apostle, that we grasp most vividly with what intensity St. Paul lives by this mystery. He comes before the pagan world so as to regenerate, renew and save it. And what does he bring to this corrupted society whose utter depravity he describes in such terrible terms?[4] Does he bring the advantages of birth? the wisdom of philosophers? the knowledge of the learned? the strength of conquerors?

The Apostle has none of these things. He declares that he is "as one born out of due time"[5]; he writes to the Corinthians: "I was with you in weakness and in fear and in much trembling...."[6] He reminds the Galatians that it was in infinity of the flesh that he preached the Gospel to them heretofore.[7] Thus he brings neither an attractive appearance, nor the prestige of learning, nor the authority of natural wisdom, nor splendour of eloquence, nor charm of human language; all this he disdains: *Non in sublimitate sermonis aut sapientiae...non in persuasibilibus humanae sapientiae verbis...non in sapientia hominum.*[8]

What then does he bring? Nothing but Christ, and Him crucified: *Non enim judicavi me scire aliquid inter vos nisi Jesum Christum, et hunc*

---

1 II Cor. i, 5 sq.   2 Ibid. xi, 26.   3 Act. ix, 15.   4 Rom. i, 24–32.
5 I Cor. xv, 8.   6 I Cor. ii, 3.   7 Gal. iv, 13.
8 "Not in loftiness of speech or of wisdom...not in the persuasive words of human wisdom...not on the wisdom of men," I Cor. ii, 1, 4–5.

crucifixum.[1] He sums up all his preaching in this knowledge; all his doctrine is contained in this mystery.

He is so penetrated with it that he makes it the one object of his prayer for his disciples: "For this cause I bow my knees to the Father of our Lord Jesus Christ...that He would grant you...to be strengthened by His Spirit with might unto the inward man, that...you may be able to comprehend, with all the saints, what is the breadth, and length, and height, and depth [of the mystery of His Son]; to know also the charity of Christ, which surpasseth all knowledge, that you may be filled [by Christ] unto all the fulness of God."[2]

What a wonderful prayer! How it makes us realise the Apostle's innermost conviction and the ardour of his soul to make this conviction shared by others!

Moreover, this prayer is unceasing. "We...cease not to pray for you, and to beg that you may be filled with the knowledge of His will, in all wisdom, and spiritual understanding": *In omni sapientia et intellectu spirituali.*[3]

Why, then, does St. Paul constantly revert to this subject to the point of making it the one doctrinal theme of his preaching? Why does he offer to God such earnest and continuous supplications for his Christians? Why does he burn with longing to see the mystery of Christ not only known but experienced by all Christians? For notice that he does not address his epistles only to a few of the initiated, but to all the faithful of the Churches that he has founded. These lines are intended to be read publicly in the Christian assemblies. What is his underlying motive in all this?

The Apostle himself reveals it in his letter to the Colossians: "I would have you know what manner of care I have for you...that [your] hearts may be...instructed in charity, and unto all riches of fulness of understanding, unto the knowledge of the mystery of God the Father and of Christ Jesus, in Whom are hid all the treasures of wisdom and knowledge."[4]

This last phrase shows us how convinced St. Paul is that we have all things in Christ: *Quomodo non etiam cum illo omnia nobis donavit?*[5] that

---

1 "For I judged not myself to know anything among you but Jesus Christ, and him crucified," Ibid. ii, 2.
2 Ephes. iii, 14, 16, 18–19.   3 Col. i, 9.   4 Ibid. ii, 1–3.
5 "How hath he not also, with him, given us all things?" Rom. viii, 32.

in Him "nothing is wanting" to us: *Ita ut nihil vobis desit in ulla gratia*[1]; and this Christ Who was "yesterday," is "to-day, and the same for ever."[2]

To raise the fallen world, St. Paul brings only one means:—Christ, and Christ crucified. It is true that this mystery is a stumbling block for the Jews and foolishness for the Grecian sages,[3] but it contains the virtue of the Divine Spirit,[4] Who alone can renew the face of the earth."[5]

In Christ alone can be found all the "wisdom, and justice, and sanctification, and redemption"[6] of which souls have need in all ages. And this is why St. Paul makes the whole formation of the inward man consist in the practical knowledge of the mystery of Jesus.[7]

II

Moreover, in this, the Apostle, instructed by Christ Himself,[8] is only the faithful echo of His Divine Master.

In that ineffable prayer after the Last Supper,[9] in which our Saviour allows all the tenderness of His blessed soul to overflow before His enraptured disciples, at the supreme moment of His earthly existence, we hear these words: "Father...this is eternal life: that they may know Thee, the only true God, and Jesus Christ, whom Thou hast sent": *Haec autem vita aeterna: ut cognoscant te solum Deum verum et quem misisti Jesum Christum.*[10]

We thus learn, from the lips of Jesus Himself, from the infallible Truth, that all Christian life—of which eternal life is but the regular unfolding

---

1 "So that nothing is wanting to you in any grace," I Cor. i, 7.
2 Hebr. xiii, 8.   3 I Cor. i, 23.   4 Ibid. ii, 4, 12.
5 Ps. ciii, 30.   6 I Cor. i, 30.
7 Cf. Ephes. iii, 16–18 and Col. i, 27–25. "How often we lose our time in barren speculations, in laborious roundabout ways, while in Christ we have at our disposal so simple a means of going straight to God and of living in habitual union with Him....And when the authorised messengers of the Eternal Word, instead of giving Christ, "the Resurrection and the Life," to souls,...give them the insipid dilutions of human thought and literature, powerless to satisfy their hunger and thirst, we cannot refrain from asking with the Apostle St. Paul: "Where are the faithful dispensers of the Gospel?" Hic jam quaeritur inter dispensatores ut fidelis quis inveniatur (Here now it is required among the dispensers that a man be found faithful) I Cor. iv, 2. Cardinal D. J. Mercier, Devotion to Christ and to His Blessed Mother.
8 Gal. i, 16–18.   9 Joan. xvii, 1–26.   10 Ibid. xvii, 3.

and natural term—is summed up in the practical knowledge of God and of His Son.

You will at once say that we do not see God: *Deum nemo vidit unquam.*[1] That is true. We shall know God perfectly only when we see Him face to face in eternal beatitude.

But, here below, God manifests Himself to our faith through His Son Jesus. Christ, the Incarnate Word, is the great revelation of God to the world: *Ipse illuxit in cordibus nostris...in facie Christi Jesu.*[2] Christ is God appearing amongst men, conversing with them, under the skies of Judea, and showing them by His human life how a God lives among men, in order that men may know how they ought to live so as to be pleasing to God.

It is, then, upon Christ that all our gaze ought to be concentrated. Open the Gospel: you will there see that three times only does the Eternal Father cause His voice to be heard by the world. And what does this Divine Voice say to us? Each time the Eternal Father tells us to contemplate His Son, to listen to Him, that He may be thereby glorified: "This is my beloved Son in Whom I am well pleased. Hear ye Him": *Hic est Filius meus dilectus...ipsum audite.*[3] All that the Father asks of us is to contemplate Jesus, His Son, to listen to Him, so as to love and imitate Him, because Jesus, being His Son, is equally God.

And we ought to contemplate Him in His Person, in all the actions of His life and death, in all the states of His glory. Our Lord, being God, the least circumstances of His life, the least features of His mysteries, are worthy of attention. Nothing is little in the life of Jesus. The Eternal Father looks upon the smallest action of Christ with more delight than He looks upon the whole universe. Before Christ's coming, God makes all converge towards Him: after His Ascension, God makes all revert to Him. All was foreseen and prophesied concerning Christ; all the more important particulars of His life, all the details of His death were marked out by Eternal Wisdom and announced by the Prophets long before their realisation.

Why, then, did God take care to prepare for the coming of His Son so long in advance? Why did Christ leave us so many divine teachings? Why did the Holy Spirit inspire the sacred writers to note so many details of

---

1 "No man hath seen God at any time," Joan. i, 18.
2 "[He] hath shined in our hearts...in the face of Christ Jesus," II Cor. iv, 6.
3 Matth. iii, 17 and xvii, 5; Joan. xii, 28.

seeming insignificance? Why did the Apostles write such long and urgent epistles to their churches?

Was it in order that these teachings should remain buried, like a dead letter, in the depths of the Holy Scriptures? Certainly not, but so that we should search out, as St. Paul desires, the mystery of Christ; that we should contemplate His Person, and study His actions; His actions reveal to us His virtues and His will. We ought to contemplate Him, not by means of a merely intellectual study—such study is often dry and sterile—but in *omni sapientia et intellectu spirituali,* in a spirit full of heavenly wisdom, which will cause us to seek in the Divine Gift for the truth that will enlighten our lives. We ought to contemplate Him so as to conform our lives to this Model Who renders God accessible to us, to draw divine life from Him in order that our thirst may be fully quenched: *Haec est autem vita aeterna.*[1]

III

This knowledge acquired by faith, in prayer, under the inspiration of the Holy Spirit, is truly the fountain of living water springing up unto everlasting life: *Fons aquae salientis in vitam aeternam.*[2] For—and here is a great truth upon which more light will be thrown in the course of these conferences—the Eternal Father has placed in Christ Jesus, all the grace, all the gifts of sanctification that He destines for souls. We can only go to the Father by Christ: *Nemo venit ad Patrem, nisi per me*[3]; without Christ, we have nothing, but with Him we have everything, we "can do all things"[4]; "for in Him dwelleth all the fulness of the Godhead corporeally."[5] Whosoever understands the mystery of Christ, and lives by it, has found the pearl of great price of which the Gospel speaks[6]; the treasure that alone is worth all other treasures: for with it eternal life is gained.

The more we know Christ, the more we enter deeply into the mysteries of His Person and of His life, the more we study, in prayer, the circumstances and details that Revelation has given to us,—the more also will

---

1 "Now this is eternal life," Joan. xvii, 3. 2 Joan. iv, 14.
3 "No man cometh to the Father, but by me," Ibid. xiv, 6.
4 Philipp. iv, 13. 5 Col. ii, 9. 6 Matth. xiii, 46.

our piety be true and our holiness real.[1]

Our piety must be based upon faith and upon the knowledge that God has given to us of supernatural and divine things. Piety that is only founded upon sentiment is as fragile and as ephemeral as the sentiment that serves for its base: it is a house built upon the sand which falls at the least shock. On the contrary, when our piety is based upon convictions which themselves result from a deep knowledge of the mysteries of Jesus, the only true God with His Father and their common Spirit, it is like an edifice built upon the rock, that is to say, it cannot be shaken: *Fundata enim erat super petram.*[2]

This knowledge is for us a never failing source of joy.

Joy is the sentiment that is born in a soul, conscious of the good it possesses. The good of our intelligence is truth; the more this truth is abundant and luminous, the deeper is our inward joy.

Christ brings us truth, He is the Truth itself,[3] truth full of sweetness showing us the munificence of our Heavenly Father; from the bosom of the Father where He ever dwells, Christ reveals to us the divine secrets[4] which we possess by faith. What a feast, what satisfaction, what joy for the faithful soul to contemplate God, the Infinite and ineffable Being, in the Person of Christ Jesus; to hear God speaking in the words of Jesus; to discover what are God's sentiments, if I may thus speak, in the sentiments of the Heart of Jesus; to contemplate the Divine actions, to penetrate into their mystery, in order to drink therefrom, as from the source, the very life of God: *Ut impleamini in omnem plenitudinem Dei!*[5]

O Christ Jesus, our God and our Redeemer, Revelation of the Father, our Elder Brother and our Friend, grant that we may know You! Purify the eyes of our heart so that we may contemplate You with joy; silence

---

1 *Vitam Domini Jesu die ac nocte tamquam pretiosissimam margaritam in arca pectoris tui reconditam habe. Hanc ubique tecum circumfer, hanc internis oculis progrediens quiescensque amanter inspice, secundum Dei donum quod sese cordi tuo insinuaverit.* (Day and night, hold the life of the Lord Jesus as a most precious pearl hidden in the treasury of your heart. Bear it everywhere with you, going forth and resting, lovingly gaze upon it with the eyes of your soul, according to the gift of God which he has placed in your heart.) Blosius, *Canon Vitae Spiritualis,* C. 19.

2 Matth. vii, 25.   3 Joan. xiv, 6.   4 Ibid. i, 18.

5 "So that you might be filled unto all the fulness of God," Ephes. iii, 19.

the noise of creatures that we may follow You unimpeded. Reveal Yourself to our soul as You did to the disciples of Emmaus, while expounding to them the sacred pages which spoke of Your mysteries, and we shall feel "our hearts burn within us"[1] with the longing to love and attach ourselves to You!

IV

In the following conferences we shall have the joy of lingering over each of the principal mysteries of Jesus, of contemplating His actions, of gathering up His words. We shall see how inexpressibly divine and profoundly human are all the actions of the Incarnate Word; we shall see that each of these mysteries contains its own teaching, bears its special light, and is for our souls the source of a particular grace of which the object is "to form Jesus within us."

The mysteries of Jesus have this characteristic that they *are ours as much as they are His.*

We have here a fundamental truth upon which we can never meditate enough, and of which we must never lose sight, for it is singularly fruitful for our supernatural life.

It is an inexhaustible source of confidence for a soul that loves Jesus to know that He Himself unites her intimately with each of His mysteries. This truth gives rise to acts of gratitude and love which yield the soul entirely to Him who so generously wills to give Himself and unite Himself to her.

But is not this truth a dream, a chimera? Is it truly a reality? Yes, it is a reality, a divine reality; but faith alone receives it as love alone has given it: *Et nos...credidimus caritati.*[2]

How is it that Christ's mysteries are our mysteries? For a threefold reason.

First of all, because Christ lived them for us.

Undoubtedly, love for His Father was the underlying motive power of every act in the life of the Incarnate Word. At the moment of complet-

---

1 Luc. xxiv, 32.
2 "And we have believed the charity [which God hath to us]," I Joan. iv, 16.

8

ing His work, Christ declares to His Apostles that it is because He loves His Father that He is about to deliver Himself up: *Ut cognoscat mundus quia diligo Patrem.*[1] In that wonderful prayer which He then makes, Jesus says that He has accomplished His work which was to glorify His Father upon earth: *Ergo te clarificavi super terram; opus consummavi quod dedisti mihi ut faciam.*[2] Indeed at each instant of His life, He could say in all truth that He only sought the good pleasure of His Father: *Quae placita sunt ei facio semper.*[3]

But His love for the Father is not the only love with which Christ's Heart beats; He loves us too and in an infinite manner. It was veritably for us that He came down from Heaven, in order to redeem us and save us from death: *Propter nos et propter nostram salutem*; it was to give us life: *Ego veni ut vitam habeant, et abundantius habeant.*[4] He had no need to satisfy and to merit for Himself, for He is the very Son of God, equal to His Father, at Whose right hand He is seated in the heights of Heaven; but it was for us that He bore everything. For us He became Incarnate, was born at Bethlehem, and lived in the obscurity of a life of toil; for us He preached and worked miracles, died and rose again; for us He ascended into Heaven and sent the Holy Spirit; He still remains in the Eucharist for us, for love of us. Christ, says St. Paul, loved the Church, and delivered Himself up for her, that He might purify and sanctify her and win her to Himself.[5]

So then, Jesus lived all His mysteries for us, in order to give us to be one day where He is, by right, in the glory of His Father. Yes, each of us can say with St. Paul: *Dilexit me, et tradidit semetipsum* PRO ME.[6] Christ Jesus "loved me, and delivered Himself up for me." And His immolation was but the crowning point of the mysteries of His earthly life; it was for me, because He loved me, that He accomplished all things.

Thanks be to Thee, O my God, for this unspeakable Gift that Thou didst make to us in the Person of Thy Son, our Salvation and our Redemption: *Gratias Deo super inenarrabili dono ejus!*[7]

Another reason whereby the mysteries of Jesus belong to us is that *in all of them Christ shows Himself to us as our Exemplar.*

---

1 Joan. xiv, 31. 2 Ibid. xvii, 4. 3 Ibid. viii, 29.
4 Ibid. x, 10. 5 Ephes. v, 27. 6 Gal. ii, 20. 7 II Cor. ix, 15.

He has come to be our Model. It is not only to announce salvation to us and to work out in principle our redemption that the Word becomes Incarnate; it is also to be the ideal of our souls. Christ Jesus is God living in our midst;—God appearing amongst us, rendered visible and tangible, and showing us by His life as well as by His words the way of holiness. We have no need to seek elsewhere than in Him for the model of our perfection. Each of His mysteries is a revelation of His virtues. The humility of the manger, the labours and self-effacement of His hidden life, the zeal of the public life, the depths of His immolation, the glory of His triumph, are virtues which we ought to imitate, sentiments we ought to share, or states in which we ought to participate. At the Last Supper, after having washed the feet of His Apostles, thus giving to the Twelve an example of humility, Christ their Lord and Master said to them: "I have given you an example, that as I have done to you, so you do also."[1] He might have said the same of all that He did.

He said moreover: "I am the Way": *Ego sum via*[2]; but He is the way only in order to go before us: "He that followeth me, walketh not in darkness, but shall have the light of life."[3] Jesus, through His mysteries, has, so to speak, marked out all the stages which, in the supernatural life, we must follow after Him; or rather, He Himself draws the faithful soul with Him in the way that He runs as a giant: *Exsultavit ut gigas ad currendam viam.*[4] "I created souls in My image and likeness," said our Lord to St. Catherine of Siena[5]; "even more, in taking human nature, I made Myself like to one of you. Consequently, I do not cease working to make your souls like to Me, as far as they are capable of it, and I endeavour to renew in them, when they are tending towards heaven, all that took place in My Body."

This is why the contemplation of Christ's mysteries is so profitable for the soul. The life, death and glory of Jesus are the example of our life,

---

1 Joan. xiii, 15.   2 Ibid. xiv, 6.   3 Ibid. viii, 12.   4 Ps. xviii, 6.
5 Life by Bl. Raymund of Capua. It was to the same Saint that the Eternal Father vouchsafed to say: "Know well, my daughter, that all the mysteries, all the actions accomplished in this world by my Truth, whether with the disciples, or apart from them, were representative of what passes in the inmost soul of my servants and of all men. You may draw from these facts a lesson and a rule of life. They should be meditated upon in the light of reason, and the most uncultured minds as well as the most subtle, ordinary intellects as well as the highest, can derive profit from them; each can take part in them, if he will." Dialogue.

death and glory. Never forget this truth: the Eternal Father accepts us only inasmuch as He sees in us a resemblance to His Son. Why is this? Because it is to this very resemblance that, from all eternity, He predestinated us.[1] There is no other form of holiness for us than that which Christ showed to us; the measure of our perfection is fixed by the degree of our imitation of Jesus.

There is, finally, a third reason, deeper and more intimate, which makes Christ's mysteries our own. Not only did Jesus live them for us, not only are they examples for us, but furthermore *in His mysteries, Christ makes but one with us*. There is no truth upon which St. Paul insisted more strongly than upon this, and my most ardent wish is that you should understand all its depth.

We make one with Christ *in the divine thought*.

It is *in Him* that God the Father chose us: *Eligit nos in ipso*[2]; not apart from Him. God does not separate us from His Son Jesus; if He predestinates us to be conformable to the image of His Son, it is in order that His Son may be "the Firstborn amongst many brethren": *Praedestinavit in multis fratribus*.[3]

This union which God wills to realise between His Son Jesus and the elect is so intimate that St. Paul compares it to that which exists between the members and the head of the same body. The Church, says the great Apostle, is the body of Christ, and Christ is its Head[4]; united, they form what St. Augustine calls the "whole Christ": *Totus Christus, caput et corpus est*; *caput unigenitus Dei Filius et corpus ejus Ecclesia*.[5] Here we have truly the divine plan: *Deus omnia subjecit sub pedibus ejus*; *et ipsum dedit caput supra omnem Ecclesiam*.[6] Christ is the Head of this mystical body which He forms with the Church, because He is its Chief and the source of life for all its members. The Church and Christ are, so to speak, one and the same being: *Membra sumus corporis ejus, de carne ejus et de ossibus ejus*.[7]

---

1 Rom. vii, 29.   2 Ephes. i, 4.   3 Rom. viii, 29.

4 I Cor. xii, 12 sq.; Ephes. v, 23.

5 "The whole Christ is head and body; the head is the only begotten Son of God and the body is his church," *De Unitate Eccles.* 4.

6 "And he hath subjected all things under his feet and hath made him head over all the church," Ephes. i, 22.

7 "Because we are members of his body, of his flesh and of his bones," Ephes. v, 30.

God the Father unites the elect to His Divine Son in such a manner that all Christ's mysteries were lived by Him as Head of the Church.

See how explicit St. Paul is on this point: "God," he says, "who is rich in mercy, for His exceeding charity wherewith He loved us, even when we were dead in sins, hath quickened us together in Christ....And hath raised us up *in Him,* and hath made us sit *together* in the heavenly places, *with* Jesus Christ; that He might show in the ages to come the abundant riches of His grace, in His bounty towards us in Christ Jesus."[1] This thought is repeated more than once under the pen of the Apostle: God has buried us together with Christ: CONsepulti enim sumus CUM ILLO[2]; He wills us to be one with Christ in His Resurrection and in His Ascension: CONresuscitavit nos, CONsedere fecit nos in ILLO.[3]

Nothing is more certain than is this union of Christ with His chosen ones in the Divine thought; what makes Christ's mysteries ours is, above all, because the Eternal Father saw us with His Son in each of the mysteries lived by Christ and because Christ accomplished them as Chief of the Church. I might even say that, on account of this, the mysteries of Christ Jesus are more our mysteries than they are His. Christ, inasmuch as He is the Son of God, would not have undergone the abasements of the Incarnation, the sorrows and sufferings of the Passion; He would have had no need of the triumph of the Resurrection, which succeeded the ignominy of His death. He went through all this as Head of the Church; He took upon Himself *our* miseries and *our* infirmities: *vere languores* NOSTROS *ipse tulit*[4]; He willed to pass through what we ourselves must

---

1 Ibid. ii, 4–7.   2 Rom. vi, 4.

3 "And hath raised us up TOGETHER and hath made us sit TOGETHER in [Him]," Ephes. ii, 6.

4 Isa. liii, 4.—For the development of these ideas, we refer the reader to the conference The Church, the Mystical Body of Christ, in our preceding volume, *Christ, the Life of the Soul.*—*Habeant licet singuli quique vocatorum ordinem suum et omnes Ecclesiae filii temporum sint successione distincti, universa tamen summa fidelium, fonte orta baptismatis, sicut cum Christo in passione crucifixi, in resurrectione resuscitati, in ascensione ad dexteram Patris collocati, ita cum ipso sunt in hac nativitate congeniti* (Although every individual is called in his own turn, and all the Church's sons are separated from one another by intervals of time, yet the entire body of the faithful, born in the baptismal font, is born with Christ in His nativity, just as all are crucified with Him in His passion, raised again in His resurrection, and set at the Father's right hand in His ascension). S. Leo, *Sermo* xxvi, *In Nativit. Domini,* vi, 2.

pass through, and He merited for us the grace to follow after Him in each of His mysteries.

For neither does Christ Jesus separate us from Himself in anything that He does. He declares that He is the Vine and we are the branches.[1] What closer union can there be than that, since it is the same sap, the same life which circulates in the root and in the shoots? Christ unites us so closely to Himself that all that is done to whomsoever it may be who believes in Him, it is to Himself that it is done: *Quamdiu fecistis uni ex his fratribus meis minimis, mihi fecistis.*[2] He wills that the union which, by grace, attaches Him to His disciples, should be the same as that which, by nature, identifies Him with His Father: *Ut unum sint, sicut tu, Pater, in me, et ego in te.*[3] This is the sublime end to which He wills to lead us through His mysteries.

Moreover, all the graces that He merited by each of His mysteries, He merited them in order to distribute them to us. He received the fulness of grace from His Father: *Vidimus eum plenum gratiae*; but He did not receive it for Himself alone; for St. John at once adds that it is of this fulness we have all received: *Et de plenitudine ejus nos omnes accepimus*[4]; it is from Him that we receive it, because He is our Head and His Father has made all things subject to Him: *Omnia subjecit sub pedibus ejus; et ipsum caput supra omnem Ecclesiam.*

So His wisdom, His justice, His holiness, His strength have become *our* wisdom, *our* justice, *our* strength: *[Christus] factus est* NOBIS *sapientia a Deo, et justitia, et sanctificatio, et redemptio.*[5] All that He has is ours; we are rich with His riches, holy with His holiness. "O man," says Ven. Louis de Blois, "if thou dost truly desire to love God, behold thyself rich in Christ, however poor and destitute thou art of thyself. For thou mayest humbly appropriate to thyself that which Christ did and suffered for thee."[6]

Christ is truly our own, for we are His mystical body. His satisfac-

---

1 Joan. xv, 5.
2 "As long as you did it to one of these my least brethren, you did it to me," Matth. xxv, 40.
3 "That they all may be one, as thou, Father, in me, and I in thee," Joan. xvii, 21.
4 Ibid. i, 16.
5 "[Christ] of God is made unto us wisdom and justice and sanctification and redemption," I Cor. i, 30.
6 *Canon Vitae Spiritualis*, c. 37.

tions, His merits, His joys, His glories are ours.... O ineffable condition of the Christian, associated so closely with Jesus and with His states! O surprising greatness of the soul to whom nothing is lacking of the grace merited by Christ in His mysteries! *Ita ut nihil nobis desit in ulla gratia!*[1]

V

It is true that in their historical, material duration, the mysteries of Christ's terrestrial life are now past; but *their virtue remains,* and the grace which gives us a share therein is always operating.

In His glorious state, Christ no longer merits; He could merit only during His mortal life until the hour when He drew forth his last breath upon the cross. But the merits that he had acquired, He never ceases to make ours. Christ was yesterday, He is to-day, He lives throughout the ages: *Christus heri, et hodie, ipse et in saecula.*[2] Never let us forget that Christ Jesus *wills* the holiness of His mystical body: all His mysteries are to bring about this holiness: *Dilexit Ecclesiam et seipsum tradidit pro ea,* UT *illam sanctificaret.*[3] But what is the Church? The small number of those who had the privilege of seeing the God-Man living upon earth? Assuredly not. Our Saviour did not come only for the inhabitants of Palestine who lived in His time, but for men of all times: *Pro omnibus mortuus est Christus.*[4] The gaze of Jesus, being divine, fell upon every soul; His love extended to each one of us; His sanctifying will remains as sovereign, as efficacious as on the day when He shed His Blood for the salvation of the world.

If the time of meriting has ceased for Him, the time of communicating the fruit of His merits endures and will endure until the last of the elect is saved. Christ is ever living: *Semper vivens ad interpellandum pro nobis.*[5]

Let us raise our thoughts up to Heaven, up to the sanctuary whither Christ ascended forty days after His Resurrection; and there let us behold our Lord ever before the face of His Father: *Introivit in caelum, ut*

---

1 "So that nothing is wanting to you in any grace," I Cor. i, 7.   2 Hebr. xiii, 8.
3 "Christ also loved the Church and delivered himself up for it: that he might sanctify it," Ephes. v, 25–26.
4 II Cor. v, 15.   5 "Always living to make intercession for us," Hebr. vii, 25.

appareat NUNC *vultui Deo pro nobis.*[1] Wherefore does Christ ever stand before the face of His Father?

Because He is His Son, the Only-begotten Son of God. "He thought it not robbery to be equal with God,"[2] since He is the true Son of God. The Eternal Father looks upon Him and says to Him: *Filius meus es tu, ego hodie genui te.*[3] Now, at this very moment, Christ is there before His Father, and He says to Him: *Pater meus es tu*[4]: "Thou art My Father," I am truly Thy Son. And inasmuch as He is the Son of God, He has the right of beholding His Father face to face, of treating with Him as equal with equal, as He has the right of reigning with Him for ever and ever.

But St. Paul adds that it is *for us* that He uses this right; it is for us that He stands before His Father. What does this signify but that Christ stands before the face of His Father, not only by right of being His Only-begotten Son, the object of the divine complacency, but as our Mediator. He is called Jesus, that is to say Saviour; this name is Divine, because it comes from God, it was given by God.[5] Christ Jesus is in Heaven, at the right hand of His Father as our Representative, our High-Priest, and our Mediator. It was in this capacity that, here below, He did the Father's will unto the last iota and in all its details, and that He lived all His mysteries; it is in this capacity that He now lives at the right hand of God, presenting to Him His merits and unceasingly communicating the fruit of His mysteries to our souls, in order to sanctify them: *Semper vivens ad interpellandum pro nobis.*

What a powerful motive of confidence it is to know that the Christ Whose life we read in the Gospels, Whose mysteries we celebrate, is ever living, ever interceding for us; that the virtue of His Divinity is ever operating; that the power possessed by His Sacred Humanity (as the instrument united to the Word) of healing the sick, consoling the afflicted and giving life to souls, is ever the same. As in the past, Christ is still the infallible Way that leads to God, the Truth that enlightens every man coming into this world, the Life that saves from death: *Christus heri, et*

---

1 "He entered into heaven, that he may now appear in the presence of God for us," Hebr. ix, 24.
2 Philipp. ii, 6.
3 "Thou art my son, this day have I begotten thee," Ps. ii, 7.
4 Ps. lxxxviii, 27.   5 Matth. i, 21.

HODIE, *ipse et in saecula.*

I believe, Lord Jesus, but increase my faith! I have full confidence in the reality and plenitude of Your merits, but strengthen this confidence! I love You, O Jesus, You Who have manifested Your love in all Your mysteries, *in finem,* but make my love ever greater.

OUR CONTACT WITH THE MYSTERIES OF JESUS

SUMMARY.—I. We associate ourselves with Christ's mysteries in meditating on the Gospel, and, above all, in uniting ourselves, in the Liturgy, to the Church, the Bride of Jesus.—II. Variety and fruitfulness of the grace contained in the mysteries set before us in the Liturgy.—III. The dispositions that we ought to have in order to derive full benefit from the contemplation of these mysteries are faith, adoration, love.

THE mysteries that Christ Jesus, the Incarnate Word, lived here below were lived for us; in them, He shows Himself as our Model, but, above all, He wills to make only one with our souls as being the Head of one mystical body of which we are the members.

Such even is the virtue of these mysteries that it is always active and efficacious; from Heaven, where He is seated at the right hand of God His Father, Christ continues to communicate the fruit of His states to souls so as to realise in them a divine resemblance to Himself.

Participation in the mysteries of Jesus requires the co-operation of the soul.

If God reveals the secrets of His love towards us, it is in order that we may accept them, that we may enter into His views and designs, and adapt ourselves to the Eternal Plan, apart from which neither holiness nor salvation are possible. If Christ opens to us the unfathomable treasures of His states and mysteries, it is that we may draw from them and make them bear fruit, on pain of being, at the last day, cast out of the kingdom into the outer endless darkness, like the negligent servant in the Gospel.

But we do not seek for what we do not know; the will does not attach itself to a good that the intelligence does not set before it: *Ignoti nulla cupido.*[1]

How then, now that Christ has taken His sensible presence away from us, are we to know His mysteries, their beauty, harmony, virtue and power? Above all, what are we to do in order to be put into life-giving contact with them and thereby to reap the fruits which will transform our souls and effect in them union with Christ, the indispensable condition for being numbered among His disciples?

This is what remains for us to see so as to complete the exposition of this truth that the mysteries of Jesus are ours as much as they are His.

I

The knowledge of Jesus and of His states is to be derived first of all from the Gospel.

These sacred pages, inspired by the Holy Spirit, describe the life of Jesus upon earth and contain His teachings. It is sufficient for us to read these pages, so simple and so sublime—but to read them with faith—in order to see and hear Christ Himself. The soul who, in prayer, often has recourse to this unrivalled book, comes little by little to the knowledge of Jesus and of His mysteries, penetrates into the secrets of His Sacred Heart and understands that magnificent revelation of God to the world which is Jesus: *Qui videt me, videt et Patrem.*[2] For this book is inspired; light and power go out from it to enlighten and strengthen souls that are upright and sincere. Happy are they who open it every day! They drink at the very well-spring of living waters.

Another way of knowing the mysteries of Jesus is by associating ourselves with the Church in her liturgy.

Before ascending into heaven, Christ said to the Apostles upon whom He founded His Church: "All power is given to me in heaven and in earth....[3] As the Father hath sent me, I also send you....[4] He that heareth you, heareth me...."[5] And this is why the Church is like an extension, throughout the ages, of the Incarnation; she replaces Jesus with us; she

---

1 "I desire nothing which is unknown."
2 "He that seeth me seeth the Father also," Joan. xiv, 9.
3 Matth. xxviii, 18.   4 Joan. xx, 21.   5 Luc. x, 16.

has inherited the divine tenderness of her heavenly Bridegroom; from Him she has received as dowry, with the power of sanctifying souls, the riches of grace acquired by Jesus upon the Cross on the day of their mystical espousals.

We can then say of the Church, all proportion guarded, what her Bridegroom said of Himself: she is for us the way, the truth and the life.—The way, because we only come to God through Christ Jesus, and we can only be united to Christ by being incorporated (in fact or in desire) in the Church, by baptism.—The truth, because with all the authority of her Founder, she has the custody of the truths brought to us by Revelation which she proposes to our belief.—Finally, the life, because by the public worship which she alone has the right of organising, by the sacraments which she alone administers, she distributes the life of grace to souls and maintains it within them.

You at once see that we sanctify ourselves according to the measure in which we allow ourselves to be taught and guided by the Church, for, says Jesus to His Bride, "He that heareth you, heareth me"; and to hear Jesus, is not that to go to the Father?

We know that it is especially by the liturgy that the Church brings up the souls of her children in order to make them like unto Jesus and thus perfect that image of Christ which is the very form of our predestination.[1]

Guided by the Holy Spirit, who is the Spirit of Jesus Himself, the Church unfolds before the eyes of her children, every year from Christmas to the Ascension, the complete cycle of Christ's mysteries, sometimes greatly abridged, sometimes in their exact chronological order, as during Holy Week and Paschal time. She thus makes each mystery of her Divine Bridegroom to be lived over again by an animated living representation; she makes us pass through each phase of His life. If we let ourselves be guided by her, we shall infallibly come to know the mysteries of Jesus and above all enter into the thoughts and feelings of His Divine Heart. Why is this?

The Church, knowing the secret of her Bridegroom, takes from the Gospel the pages which best place each of these mysteries in relief; then, with perfect art, she illustrates them with passages of the psalms, proph-

---

1 Rom. viii, 29.

ecies, the epistles of St. Paul and the other Apostles, and quotations from the Fathers of the Church. She thus places the teachings of the Divine Master, the details of His life, and the substance of His mysteries in a clearer and fuller light.

At the same time, by the choice of readings from the Holy Scriptures and sacred authors, by the aspirations that she suggests to us, by her symbolism and ritual, she places our souls in the attitude demanded by the meaning of these mysteries, she fosters in our hearts the requisite dispositions in order that we may assimilate the spiritual fruit of each mystery in the greatest possible measure.

II

For although it is always the same Saviour, the same Jesus, pursuing the same work of our sanctification, each mystery, however, is a fresh manifestation of Christ for us; each has its special beauty, its particular splendour, as likewise its own grace. The grace that flows for us from the Feast of the Nativity has not the same character as that which the celebration of the Passion brings us; we ought to rejoice at Christmas, to feel sorrow for our sins when we contemplate the unspeakable sufferings whereby Christ expiated them. In the same way, the inward joy that floods our souls at Easter arises from another source and has another splendour than that which thrills us when we celebrate the coming of our Saviour upon earth.

The Fathers of the Church speak more than once of what they call the *vis mysterii*,[1] the virtue and signification of the mystery which is being celebrated. In each of Christ's mysteries we may apply to Christians what St. Gregory of Nazianzen said of the faithful at the feast of Easter: *Nihil autem daturus est tantum, quantum si se ipse obtulerit hujus mysterii rationem probe intelligentem,* "We cannot offer a gift more pleasing to God than to offer ourselves with a perfect understanding of the mystery."

Some there are who see nothing in the celebration of Christ's mysteries beyond the perfection of the ceremonies, the beauty of the music and liturgical ornaments, the harmony of the ritual. There is all this; and that is excellent.

---

1 S. Gregory Nazian., *Orat. I in Sanct. Pascha* iv.

First of all because the Church, Christ's Bride, having herself regulated all the details of the worship of her Bridegroom, their perfect observance honours God and His Son Jesus. "It is an established law for all the mysteries of Christianity, that to reach our intelligence they must first be placed before our senses. This had to be so in order to honour Him Who, being invisible by nature, willed to appear under a sensible form for love of us."[1]

Next, it is a psychological law of our nature—matter and spirit—that we should pass from the visible to the invisible. The outward elements of the celebration of the mysteries serve as rungs in a ladder whereby our souls may rise to the contemplation and love of heavenly and supernatural realities. This is, moreover, as we sing at Christmas, the dispensation of the Incarnation itself: *Ut dum visibiliter Deum cognoscimus,* PER HUNC *in invisibilium amorem rapiamur.*[2]

These outward elements, therefore, have their use, but we must not exclusively stop at them; they are but the fringe of Christ's garment; the virtue of the mysteries of Jesus is above all interior, and it is this virtue that we must seek before all. Holy Church asks of God more than once as the fruit of Communion itself to give us the right apprehension of the virtue proper to each mystery so that we may be penetrated by it and live thereby: *Ut mysteria quae solemni celebramus officio, purificatae mentis intelligentia consequamur.*[3] This is to know Christ "in all wisdom, and

---

1 Bossuet, Sermon upon the Word of God.

2 "So that as we recognize God made visible, we are drawn to love what is invisible," Preface of the Nativity. The Holy Council of Trent expressly teaches us as follows, on the subject of the rites of the Mass, the primordial act of the Liturgy: *Cum natura hominum ea sit ut non facile queat sine adminiculis exterioribus ad rerum divinarum meditationem sustolli, propterea pia mater Ecclesia ritus quosdam…instituit, ceremonias item adhibuit quo mentes fidelium per haec visibilia religionis et pietatis signa ad rerum altissimarum… contemplationem excitarentur* (Whereas such is the nature of man, that, without external helps, he cannot easily be raised to the meditation of divine things, therefore pious mother Church has instituted certain rites; she has likewise employed ceremonies whereby the minds of the faithful might be excited, by those visible signs of religion and piety, to contemplation). Sess. xxii, 2, 5. This doctrine can be perfectly applied to the whole liturgy.

3 Postcommunion of the Epiphany and Transfiguration. See also the Postcommunion for the Octave of the Epiphany: *Ut mysterium…et puro cernamur intuitu et digno percipiamus affectu* (So that we might discern the mystery with a pure regard and perceive it with a worthy disposition).

spiritual understanding."[1]

Christ's mysteries are truly not only examples, and subjects of contemplation; they are likewise sources of grace.

It is said of Jesus that when He was upon earth "virtue went out from Him, and healed all": *Virtus de illo exibat et sanabat omnes.*[2] Christ Jesus is ever the same; if, with faith, we contemplate His mysteries, either in the Gospel or in the liturgy that the Church sets before us, the grace that He merited for us when He lived these mysteries is produced within us. In this contemplation we see how Jesus, our Exemplar, practised virtue; we share the particular dispositions of His Divine Heart in each of these states; but above all we find in Him the special graces that He then merited for us.

The mysteries of Jesus are states of His Sacred Humanity; all His graces came from His Divinity in order to be communicated to His Humanity, and, through His Humanity, to each member of His mystical body: *Secundum mensuram donationis Christi.*[3] In taking a human nature from our race, the Word, so to speak, espoused all humanity to Himself, and every soul shares—in a measure known to God, and proportioned, in what regards ourselves, to the degree of our faith—in the grace that inundates Christ's blessed soul.

Each of Christ's mysteries, representing a state of the Sacred Humanity, thus brings to us a special participation in His Divinity. For example, at Christmas we celebrate the Birth of Christ upon earth; we sing that "wonderful exchange,"[4] which was made in Him between the Divinity and Humanity. He takes a human nature from us so as to make us partakers of His Divine nature, and each Christmas, worthily celebrated, is for the soul, by a more abundant communication of grace, like a new birth to divine life. Upon Calvary, we die to sin with Christ; Jesus gives us the grace to detest more deeply all that offends Him. During Paschal time, we participate in that liberty of soul, in that more intense life for God, of which He is the model in His Resurrection. On the day of His Ascension, we ascend with Him to Heaven to be like Him, by faith and desire, with the Heavenly Father, *in sinu Patris,*[5] in the intimacy of the divine sanctuary.

---

1 Col. i, 9.   2 Luc. vi, 19.

3 "According to the measure of the giving of Christ," Ephes. iv, 7.

4 Antiphon for the office of the Circumcision.

5 "In the Bosom of the Father," Joan. i, 18.

Following Christ Jesus in this manner in all His mysteries, uniting ourselves to Him, we share, little by little, but surely, and each time more fully and deeply, in His divinity and in His divine life.[1] According to the beautiful words of St. Augustine, that which was formerly brought to pass in a divine reality, is spiritually received in fervent souls by the repeated celebration of these mysteries: *Quod semel factum in rebus veritas indicat, hoc saepius celebrandum in cordibus piis solemnitas renovat.*[2]

It is then true to say that when we contemplate Christ's different mysteries, in their successive order, we do so not only in order to evoke the remembrance of events wrought for our salvation, and to glorify God for them by our praise and thanksgiving; it is not only to see how Jesus lived and strive to imitate Him, but furthermore that our souls may participate in each special state of the Sacred Humanity and draw forth from it the proper grace that the Divine Master attached to it, in meriting this grace as Head of the Church for His mystical body.

This is why the Sovereign Pontiff Pius X, of glorious memory, was able to write that "the active participation of the faithful in the sacred mysteries and in the public and solemn prayer of the Church is *the first and indispensable source of the Christian spirit.*"[3]

On this subject there is in fact a truth of great importance too often forgotten or even sometimes unknown.

Man can imitate Christ, our Model, in two ways. He can strive to imitate Him by purely natural efforts, as when one aims at reproducing a human ideal presented by some hero or other personage whom one loves or admires. There are people who think it is in this manner that we must imitate our Lord and reproduce in ourselves the traits of His adorable Person.

This is to lose sight of the truth that Christ is a divine model. His

---

1 We dwelt on these ideas more at length in the conference *Vos Sponsae* in our preceding volume *Christ, the Life of the Soul.*

2 *Sermo ccxx, In Vigil. Paschae* ii.

3 This is what the Vicar of Christ says: "Our keenest desire being that the true Christian spirit should flourish again in every way and be maintained in all the faithful, it is necessary, before all things, to see the holiness and dignity of the place where the faithful assemble precisely in order to find therein this spirit at its first and indispensable source, namely: the active participation in the sacred mysteries and in the public and solemn prayer of the Church." Pius X, *Motu proprio* of Nov. 23rd 1903.

human beauty and virtues have their roots in His Divinity and thence derive all their splendour. We can, and assuredly must, with the help of grace, make every effort to comprehend Christ and to model all our virtues and actions upon His, but the Holy Spirit alone—*Digitus paternae dexterae*[1]—is capable of reproducing within us the true image of the Son, because our imitation must be of a supernatural order.

Now this work of the Divine Artist is wrought above all in prayer based upon faith and enkindled by love. While, with the eyes of faith and the love that yearns to give itself, we contemplate Christ's mysteries, the Holy Spirit, Who is the Spirit of Christ, acts within our inmost soul and fashions it, by His sovereignly efficacious touches, in such a way as to reproduce within it, as by a sacramental virtue, the traits of the Divine Model.

This is why the contemplation of the mysteries of Jesus is so fruitful in itself; this is why the essentially supernatural contact with the states of her Spouse, into which the Church, guided by the Holy Spirit, places us in the liturgy is so vital for us. There is no surer way nor more infallible means for making us one with Christ.[2]

III

This contemplation of the mysteries of Jesus will only produce such great fruit in us if we bring thereto certain dispositions which can be summed up into three: *faith, reverence and love.*

Faith is the primordial disposition for placing us in vital contact with Christ.

We celebrate mysteries, that is to say human and visible signs of a divine and hidden reality. To comprehend, to touch this reality, faith is needed. Christ appears as both man and God in each of these mysteries; often even, as in the Nativity, and in the Passion, the divinity is more than ordinarily hidden; in order to grasp it, to pierce the veil and reach to it, to see God in the Child lying in the manger, or in the One Who was "made a curse for us"[3] hanging on the gibbet of Calvary, or again under the Eucharistic

---

1 "The right finger of God."
2 See, at the end of this conference, a quotation, too long to be given here, from one of the masters of the spiritual life.
3 Gal. iii, 13.

appearances, faith is needed: *Praestet fides supplementum sensuum defectui.*[1]

Without faith we shall never penetrate into the depths of the mysteries of Jesus; but with it, we have no need to envy Christ's contemporaries. We do not see Our Lord as those who lived with Him, but it is given to us by faith to contemplate Him, to dwell with Him, and be united to Him in a no less efficacious way than it was for those who were His contemporaries. We sometimes say: Oh, if I had lived in His time, if I might have followed Him with the multitude, with the disciples; if I might have served Him like Martha, or knelt listening to His words like Magdalen! But He has said: BEATI *qui non viderunt et crediderunt,*[2] "Blessed are they that have not seen, and have believed." If we have faith, we can remain as united to Jesus as could those who saw Him with their eyes or touched Him with their hands.

I will even add this: it is the measure of this faith that, for our part, determines the degree of our participation in the grace of Jesus contained in His mysteries. See what took place during His terrestrial life: those who lived with Him, who were in material contact with Him, like the Shepherds and Wise Men at the manger, the Apostles and all who sought Him during the years of His public life, St. John and St. Mary Magdalen at the foot of the Cross, the disciples who saw Him risen and ascending to Heaven, all received grace according to the degree of their faith. It is always to faith that He grants the miracles asked of Him; every page of the Gospel shows us that He made faith an indispensable condition for receiving His grace.

We cannot now see Jesus with bodily sight. Christ has ascended to Heaven. But faith takes the place of flight; and the degree of this faith, as was the case with Christ's contemporaries, is, with love, the degree of our union with Him. Let us never forget this important truth: Christ Jesus without Whom we can do nothing, and of Whose fulness we must all receive, will only give us a share in His grace according to the measure of our faith. St. Augustine says it is not in walking that we approach Christ, but it is in believing: *Non enim ad Christum ambulando currimus, sed credendo.*[3]

Thus the stronger and deeper is our faith in Jesus, the Incarnate Word,

---

1 "Faith for all defects supplying where the feeble senses fail," Hymn *Pange Lingua.*
2 Joan. xx, 29.   3 Tract. in Joan. xxvi, 3.

the Son of God, the nearer we approach Christ.

Moreover faith gives birth within us to two other sentiments which must enter into the attitude of the soul in the presence of Christ. These are reverence and love.

We must approach Christ with inexpressible *reverence.* For Christ Jesus is God, that is to say the Almighty; the Infinite Being Who possesses all wisdom, all justice, all perfections; the Sovereign Master of all things; the Creator of all that is and the Last End of all that exists; the source of all beatitude. Wherever He may be, Jesus is always God. Even when He gives Himself with the most benignity and liberality, He ever remains the One before Whom the highest angels veil their faces: *Adorant Dominationes, tremunt Potestates.*[1] In the manger, He allows Himself to be touched; the Gospel tells us that the multitude thronged Him on every side[2]; during His Passion, He lets Himself be struck in the face, smitten and insulted; but He is ever God. Even when He is scourged, and spat upon, when He dies upon the Cross it is ever He Who created heaven and earth by His power and governs them by His wisdom; and therefore, whatever be the page of the Gospel that we read, or the mystery of Jesus that we celebrate, we must adore Him.

When we have a living faith, this reverence is so deep that it makes us fall at the feet of this God-Man to adore Him. Tu es Christus, Filius Dei vivi[3]: "Thou art Christ, the Son of the Living God"; *et procidens adoravit eum.*[4]

Adoration is the first impulse of the soul drawn to Christ by faith: *Love* is the second.

Love underlies all Christ's mysteries. The humility of the manger, the obscurity of the hidden life, the fatigues of the public life, the torments of the Passion, the glory of the Resurrection, all is due to love: *Cum dilexisset suos, in finem dilexit eos.*[5] It is love, above all, that is revealed and shines out in the mysteries of Jesus. And it is above all by love that we understand

---

1 "Dominations adore, Powers tremble."
2 Marc. v, 31.   3 Matth. xvi, 16.
4 "And falling down, he adored him," Joan. ix, 38.
5 "Having loved his own, he loved them unto the end," Joan. xiii, 1.

them: *Et nos credidimus caritati.*

If we want our contemplation of Christ's mysteries to be fruitful, we must contemplate them with faith, with reverence, but above all with love—the love that seeks to give itself, to yield itself up to the divine good pleasure in order to accomplish it.

It is then that the contemplation of the mysteries of Jesus bears fruit. *Qui autem diligit me...manifestabo ei meipsum.*[1] "If any one love Me," says our Lord, "I will manifest Myself to him." What does that mean? If any one loves Me in faith, contemplates Me in My Humanity, in the different states of My Incarnation, to him I will discover the secrets of My Divinity.

Happy, thrice happy, is the soul in whom so magnificent a promise is fulfilled! Christ Jesus will reveal "the gift of God"[2] to her; by His Spirit "Who searcheth...the deep things of God,"[3] He will make this soul penetrate into the sanctuary of this *sacramentum absconditum*[4] which His mysteries are; He will open to her those "storerooms" of the King[5] of which the Canticle of Canticles speaks, where she will be inebriated with truth and joy. Doubtless, this intimate manifestation of Jesus to the soul, while she is here below, will not reach to the Beatific Vision, which remains the privilege of the blessed in heaven; but it will fill her with divine enlightenment, fortifying her in her ascension towards God: *Scire supereminentem scientiae caritatem Christi* UT IMPLEAMINI IN OMNEM PLENITUDINEM DEI.[6]

This is truly the fountain of living water springing up for us unto life everlasting: *Fons aquae salientis in vitam aeternam;* for is not everlasting life to know God and His Divine Son, to confess with our lips and our lives that Jesus is the beloved Son in Whom the Father has placed all His delight, and in Whom He wills that we should find all things?

NOTE I

Extract from *Catechism of Christian Doctrine published by order of His Holiness Pius X.* (1913).

---

1 Ibid. xiv, 21.   2 Ibid. iv, 10.   3 I Cor. ii, 10.
4 "Hidden mystery," Ephes. iii, 9.   5 Cant. i, 3.
6 "To know also the charity of Christ, which surpasseth all knowledge that you may be filled unto the fulness of God," Ephes. iii, 19.

"The feasts (of the Church) were instituted in order that we may render in common to God the supreme worship of adoration, praise, thanksgiving and reparation. All has been so well arranged and adapted to circumstances—the ceremonies, words, music, the outward observance in every detail—*as to cause the mysteries, truths, or facts which we celebrate to penetrate deeply into our minds and lead us to corresponding sentiments and acts. If the faithful* were well instructed in this matter and *celebrated the feasts in the spirit that the Church willed in instituting them, a notable renewal and increase of faith, piety, religious instruction would be obtained, and, consequently, the inward life of Christians would thereby be reanimated and made better.*"

"Let every good Christian, by the help of sermons or of some appropriate book, strive *to understand and to make the spirit of each feast his own,* considering its object and special end, meditating upon the truth, virtue, miracle, or benefit therein especially commemorated, seeking in every way to derive personal improvement from it. He will thus better know God, Our Lord Jesus Christ, the Blessed Virgin and the Saints, and will love them more fervently; he will love the sacred Liturgy, the preaching of the Word of God, and Holy Church, and will even seek to promote this love in others. *Every feast should hence be for him a Lord's Day, a true feast which will rejoice, restore, and fortify his soul and fill him with fresh vigour for bearing the sufferings and daily struggles of the week.*"

NOTE II

"...The great secret for leading this free, pure and already almost superhuman Christian life, [of which the life of Jesus upon earth at His coming forth from the tomb is the very real type and to the imitation of which Baptism obliges us], is not so much to consider the vanity of the world, the fragility and baseness of this present life, our own personal misery and passions, all those evils into which, without the help of grace, we should so easily fall, and our faults and sins, which we ought, however, to hate and deplore: (all that is useful, all that is indispensable; everyone who is wise will remember and think of it at certain hours; but it is not always the hour for thinking of it, and it is not, at all events, what is the most efficacious for us), *What is most efficacious, here as everywhere, the most decisive, the most triumphant, is, as far as one can, and habitually, to look upwards; it is to consider God and Jesus;* the perfections of God, His rights, His attributes, His appeals, His provocations, His patient waiting, His designs, His promises; *the mysteries of Jesus and the divine graces flowing from what he said, did, ordained and suffered. It is ever to remember that He is personally the point of departure and the Chief of the Christian life; that the great virtue of baptism is to incorporate us in Him, to give us His life, to make us of His race, and to pour forth His Spirit within us,* that is to say a light and a strength whereby we are enabled, and so remain, not only to avoid sin, as St. John expressly says, but moreover to judge all things, to discern our way and to follow it, and ascending from light to light, from liberty to liberty, to reach the inward state of him who said: "I live, now not I; but Christ liveth in me."

Mgr Gay, *Elevations upon the Life and Doctrine of our Lord Jesus Christ.* 91 st. Elev.

I
THE PERSON OF CHRIST

IN SINU PATRIS

SUMMARY.—Christ is above all the Son of God.—I. Dogma of the Divine fecundity: God is Father.—II. "Functions" of the Word in the Trinity: the Word, the Son of God, acknowledges that all comes to Him from the Father; He is the Father's image; His relation to the Father by love.—III. We must imitate the Divine Word in His "states."—IV. How Christ is the means established by God for making us participants in the Sonship of His Word.—V. Practical consequence of these doctrines: to remain united to the Incarnate Word, by faith, works, and the Sacrament of the Eucharist.—VI. These truths, sublime as they are, constitute the very foundation of Christianity and the substance of all sanctity.

C HRIST'S mysteries are ours. The union that Christ wishes to contract with our souls is such that all is common between Him and us. With divine liberality, He wishes to give us a share in the inexhaustible graces of salvation and sanctification that He merited for us by each of His mysteries, in order to communicate to us the spirit of His states and thus to realise in each one of us a likeness to Himself, the infallible pledge of our eternal predestination.

Christ has passed through divers states. He has been a Child, a Youth, a Doctor of the truth, a Victim upon the Cross, He has been glorious in His Resurrection and His Ascension: in thus traversing all the successive stages of His earthly existence, He has sanctified all human life.

But there is one essential state which He never leaves: He is always "the Only-begotten Son Who is in the bosom of the Father": *Unigenitus Filius qui* EST *in sinu Patris.*[1]

---

1 Joan. i, 18.

Christ is the Incarnate Son of God, the Word-made-Flesh. Before becoming man, Christ was God; in becoming man, He did not cease to be God: *Quod fuit permansit.*[1] Whether we consider Him as a little Infant in the manger, toiling in the workshop of Nazareth, preaching in Judea, dying upon Calvary, manifesting to His apostles His triumphant victory over death, or ascending to Heaven, He is always and above all the Only-begotten Son of the Father.

It is, then, His Divinity that we must first of all contemplate before speaking of the mysteries which proceed from the Incarnation itself; all the mysteries of Jesus are based upon His Divinity; from it they derive all their splendour; in it they find all fecundity.

The beginning of St. John's Gospel is very different from that of the other Evangelists who open their narrative by drawing up the human genealogy of Jesus in order to show how He was descended from the royal race of David. But St. John, who is reluctant to dwell upon earth, first rises, like an eagle, with a marvellous flight, to the highest heavens and tells us what takes place in the sanctuary of the divinity.

Before relating the life of Jesus, this Evangelist tells us what Christ was before His Incarnation. And in what terms does he speak? "In the beginning was the Word, and the Word was with God, and the Word was God": *In principio erat Verbum et Verbum erat apud Deum et Deus erat Verbum....* And to reassure us as to the weight of his testimony, He at once adds: "No man hath seen God at any time: the Only-begotten Son Who is in the bosom of the Father, He hath declared Him": *Deum nemo videt unquam; Unigenitus Filius qui est in sinu Patris* IPSE *enarravit.*

In fact, during three years, Jesus explained the divine secrets to His disciples; on the eve of His death, He recalled these secrets to them, saying that this was a mark of friendship which He gave only to them and to those who coming after them should believe in His words: *Vos dixi amicos: quia omnia quaecumque audivi a Patre meo nota feci vobis.*[2]

In order to know what Jesus is, what He was, we have then only to listen to the disciple who relates His words; or rather we have only to listen to Jesus Himself. But let us listen to Him with faith, with love, with adora-

---

1 "That which he was, he remained," Antiphon for the Office of the Circumcision.
2 "I have called you friends because all things whatsoever I have heard of my Father, I have made known to you," Joan. xv, 15.

tion; for He Who reveals Himself to us is the very Son of God.

The words that He brings to us are not words to be apprehended merely with bodily ears; they are altogether heavenly words of eternal life: *Verba quae ego locutus sum vobis spiritus et vita sunt.*[1] Only a humble and faithful soul can understand them.

Neither let us be astonished in that these words reveal profound mysteries to us: Jesus Himself willed it to be so. He has spoken these words to us in order to bring about our union with Him; He willed that they should be gathered up by the sacred writers; He sends His Holy Spirit Who "searcheth the deep things of God,"[2] to recall them to our minds,[3] so that "in all wisdom and spiritual understanding" we may savour the mysteries of the innermost life of God.[4] Does not participation in this divine life constitute the very basis of Christianity and the substance of all holiness?

I

Faith reveals to us this truly astonishing mystery that the power and act of fecundity is one of the divine perfections.

God is the plenitude of being, the shoreless ocean of all perfection and of all life. The images of which we often make use to depict Him, the ideas that we apply to Him by analogy in speaking of what is best in creatures, are powerless to represent Him. We shall never rise to a conception that does not belie God's Infinity by merely extending, even indefinitely, the limits of created being; we must recognise, in the most positive manner, that there are no limits where God is concerned. He is Very Being, the necessary Being, subsisting of Himself, and possessing the plenitude of all perfection.

Revelation teaches us this marvel of God's fecundity; there is in Him an altogether spiritual and ineffable paternity; He is Father, the principle of all the Divine Life in the Trinity.

Being Infinite Intelligence, God perfectly comprehends Himself; in a single act, He sees all that He is, all that is in Him. He comprehends, as it were, in a single glance, the plenitude of His perfections, and, in one

---

1 Joan. vi, 64.   2 I Cor. ii, 10.   3 Joan. xiv, 26.   4 Col. i, 9.

thought, in one word that exhausts all His knowledge, He expresses this infinite knowledge to Himself. This thought conceived by the eternal intelligence, this utterance whereby God expresses Himself is the Word. Faith tells us that this Word is God: *Et Deus erat Verbum,* because the Word has (or rather, He is) with God one and the same divine nature.

And because the Father communicates to this Word a nature not only like unto His own, but identical with it, Holy Scripture tells us that He begets the Word, and it calls the Word, *the Son.* The inspired books repeat the ineffable exclamation of God contemplating His Son and proclaiming the beatitude of His eternal Fatherhood: From the bosom of My Divinity, before the creation of the light, I communicated life to Thee: *Ex utero, ante luciferum, genui te*[1]; "Thou art My Son, My beloved Son, in Whom I am well pleased": *Tu es Filius meus dilectus, in te complacui mihi.*[2] Because this Son is indeed perfect, He possesses with the Father all the divine perfections saving the property of "being Father"; so perfect is He that He is the equal of His Father by the unity of nature. A creature can only give to another creature a nature *like* to his own: *simile sibi*; but God begets God and gives to Him His own nature. It is God's glory to beget the Infinite and to contemplate Himself in another Himself, Who is His equal. So equal is the Son to the Father that He is the Only-begotten, for there is only one Divine nature and the Son exhausts the eternal fecundity: *Unigenitus Dei, Filius*; therefore He is one with His Father: *Ego et Pater unum sumus.*[3]

Finally this beloved Son, equal to the Father, although distinct from Him, and, like Him, a Divine Person, does not leave the Father. The Word ever dwells in the infinite Intelligence that conceives Him; the Son ever dwells in the bosom of the Father Who begets Him: *Unigenitus Dei Filius qui* EST *in sinu Patris.* He dwells there by unity of nature. He also dwells there by the love which they mutually bear to one another and whence proceeds, as from one principle, the Holy Spirit, the substantial love of the Father and of the Son.

You see what is the mysterious order of the ineffable communication of the intimate life of God in the Trinity.—The Father, plenitude of all life, begets a Son; from the Father and the Son, as from one principle,

---

1 Ps. cix, 3.   2 Luc. iii, 22; Marc. i, 11.   3 Joan. x, 30.

proceeds the Spirit of Love. All Three have the same eternity, the same infinity of perfection, the same wisdom, the same power, the same sanctity, because the Divine nature is one for the Three Persons.

But each Person possesses exclusive properties—"to be Father, to be Son, to proceed from the Father and the Son"—which establishes ineffable relations between them and distinguishes them from each other. There is an order of origin, without there being either priority of time, or superiority of hierarchy, or relation of dependance.

Such is the language of Revelation; we could not have attained to a knowledge of these things unless they had been unveiled for us; but Christ Jesus has willed, for the exercise of our faith and the joy of our souls, to give us this knowledge.[1] When in eternity, we shall contemplate God, we shall see that it is essential to infinite life, that it is natural to the Divine Being, to be one in Three Persons. The true God Whom we must know so as to have eternal life,[2] is He of Whom we adore the Trinity of Persons in the unity of nature.

Come! let us adore this marvellous fellowship in the Unity, this wonderful equality of perfection in the distinction of Persons. O God, Father of incommensurable majesty, *Patrem immensae majestatis,* I adore Thee; I adore Thy Son, for He, like Thee, is worthy of all reverence, being Thy True and Only-begotten Son, God like Thyself: *Venerandum tuum verum et unicum Filium*; O Father, O Son, I adore Your common Spirit, Your eternal bond of love: *Sanctum quoque Paraclitum Spiritum.* Blessed Trinity, I adore Thee!...

---

1 "Wherefore plunge into those abysses? Wherefore has Christ Jesus disclosed them to us? Wherefore does He return to them so often? And so as not to forget the sublimity of the Christian doctrine ought we not to dwell on these truths? But we must do so in trembling, we must do so in faith; we must, whilst listening to Jesus Christ, and His altogether Divine words, believe that these words come from One Who is God; and we must also believe, at the same time, that this God whence they come comes Himself from God, and that He is Son; and at every word that we hear Him speak, we must rise as high as the source, contemplating the Father in the Son, and the Son in the Father." Bossuet, Meditations upon the Gospel. The Last Supper. 1st part, 86th day.
2 Joan. xvii, 3.

II

Let us now turn the eyes of our faith upon the Word, the Son, in order that we may know and admire some of His properties. It is this Son Who, born eternally of the Father, is born in time of a Virgin so as to become the God-Man and bring the mysteries of our salvation into effect. How shall we imitate Him, how shall we remain united with Him, without first knowing Him?

In the Holy Trinity, the Son is distinguished from the Father by His property of "being Son."

When we speak of a man as being someone's son, we affirm two different things: his individual human nature, and his condition of son. It is not so in the Trinity. The Son is really identified with the divine nature (which He possesses in an indivisible manner with the Father and the Holy Spirit); what distinguishes Him from the Person of the Father, what properly speaking constitutes His personality is not being God, but being Son; and inasmuch as He is a Divine Person, He is only Son, entirely Son, and that uniquely; He is, if I may thus express myself, a living filiation; He is entirely in relation to the Father.

And in the same way as the Father proclaims His ineffable fecundity: *Filius meus es tu, ego hodie genui te,*[1] the Son acknowledges that He is Son, that the Father is His principle, His source, and that all comes from the Father: this is, so to speak, the first "function" of the Word.

Open the Gospels, especially that of St. John, and you will see that the Incarnate Word is constantly laying stress upon this property. Christ loves to declare that, in His quality of Only-begotten Son, He receives everything from His Father. "I live by the Father".... He says to His Apostles: "My doctrine is not Mine, but His that sent Me...; the Son cannot do anything of Himself, but what He seeth the Father doing; for what things soever He doth, these the Son also doth in like manner...; I cannot of Myself do anything. As I hear, so I judge, and My judgment is just; because I seek not My own will, but the will of Him that sent Me,...I do nothing of Myself, but as the Father hath taught Me, these things I speak."[2]

What does Our Lord wish to make us understand by these mysteri-

---

1 "You are my son, this day have I begotten you," Ps. ii, 7.
2 Joan. vi, 58; vii, 16; v, 19, 30; viii, 28.

ous words, if not that in His quality of Son, He holds all things from the Father, while yet being equal to Him? Throughout, in all the remarkable circumstances of His life, as for example at the resurrection of Lazarus, Christ Jesus brings forward the ineffable relations that make of Him the Only-begotten Son of the Eternal Father.

Read above all the discourse and prayer of Jesus at the Last Supper, where, before consummating the series of His mysteries by His sacrifice upon the Cross, He raises a corner of the veil which hides the Divine life from our sight, and you will see with what insistence He dwells again and again upon the eternal Sonship and the properties that are its privilege: "Father, the hour is come, glorify Thy Son, that Thy Son may glorify Thee...glorify Thou Me, O Father, with Thyself, with the glory which I had, before the world was, with Thee. I have manifested Thy name to the men Whom Thou hast given Me out of the world....Now they have known, that all things which Thou hast given Me, are from Thee....And all My things are Thine, and Thine are Mine....That they all may be one, as Thou, Father, in Me, and I in Thee...Father, I will that where I am, they also whom Thou hast given Me may be with Me; that they may see My glory which Thou hast given Me, because Thou hast loved Me before the creation of the world."[1]

What a wonderful revelation of the Father and of the Son, of their incomprehensible relations, these words open out to us! Truly, as St. John says at the beginning of his Gospel, not that we have seen God; but "the Only-begotten Son Who is in the bosom of the Father, He hath declared Him." I believe, Lord Jesus, that Thou art the Only-begotten Son of the Father, God like unto Him. I believe, but increase my faith!

The second "function" of the Word is to be, as St. Paul says, the image of the Father: *Imago Dei invisibilis.*[2]

Not some vague image, but a perfect living image. The Word is the splendour of the Father's glory, the figure of His substance, the reflection of His eternal light: *Splendor gloriae et figura substantiae ejus.*[3] He is, as the Greek term indicates, the "character," the adequate expression of God, and like the impression of the seal upon the wax. The Eternal Father, in

---

1 Joan. xvii.   2 Col. i, 15.   3 Hebr. i, 3.

looking upon the Son, sees in Him the perfect reproduction of His divine attributes; the Son perfectly reflects, like a spotless mirror, *speculum sine macula*,[1] all that the Father gives Him.

And this is why the Father, in contemplating His Son, sees in Him all His own perfections; and ravished at this sight, He declares to the world that this Son is the object of all His dilection: *Filius dilectus in quo mihi* BENE *complacui*.[2]

Thus when He becomes incarnate, the Word reveals to us the Father, manifests God to us. When at the Last Supper, Our Lord spoke of His Father in such touching terms, the apostle Philip says to Him: "Lord, show us the Father and it is enough for us." And what does Christ Jesus answer? "Have I been so long a time with you, and have you not known Me?" "Philip, he that seeth Me, seeth the Father also": *Qui videt me, vivet et Patrem*.[3] What an amazing revelation is this! It is enough for us to see Jesus, the Incarnate Word, in order to know the Father of Whom He is the image. Christ translates all the Father's perfections into human actions, in language accessible to our minds. Let us often recall these words: *Qui videt me, videt et Patrem*.

We will presently study the principal mysteries of Jesus. He Whom we shall contemplate is God, the Infinite, Almighty and Supreme Being. This Infant lying in a manger and adored by the shepherds and magi, He is God. This Youth toiling as an obscure artisan in a poor workshop, He is God. This Man who heals the sick, multiplies the loaves, forgives sinners and saves souls, He is God. He is God, this Prophet persecuted by His enemies; God, He Who agonises beneath the weight of fear and sadness, Who is condemned to die upon a Cross; this Host kept in the tabernacle, and that I am about to receive at the Holy Table, contains God: *Qui videt me, videt et Patrem*.

And all the perfections which the states and mysteries of Jesus manifest: that wisdom which none can confound, that power which astonishes and enraptures the multitude, that unheard of mercy towards sinners, that untiring goodness which bears every injury, that ardent zeal for justice, that unalterable patience under insult, that generous and self-surrender-

---

1 Sap. vii, 26.
2 "This is my beloved Son, in whom I am well pleased," Matth. xvii, 5.
3 Joan. xiv, 8–9.

ing love, these are the perfections of a God, of our God: for he who sees Jesus, sees the Father, contemplates God.

At the end of His sacerdotal prayer, Christ said to His Father: "I have made known Thy name to [My disciples], and I will make it known; that the love wherewith Thou hast loved Me, may be in them, and I in them..."[1] O Jesus, by Thy mysteries, show us Thy Father, His perfections, His greatness, His rights, His will; reveal to us what He is for Thee, what He is for us, so that we may love Him, and He love us,—and we ask for nothing more: *Ostende nobis Patrem, et sufficit nobis.*

The third "function" of the Word is His constant relation by love to His Father.

In the Blessed Trinity, the love of the Son for the Father is infinite. If He proclaims that He holds all from His Father, He likewise refers all to Him with love, and from this movement of dilection which meets that of the Father, proceeds that Third Person Whom Revelation calls by a mysterious name: the Holy Spirit, Who is the substantial love of the Father and of the Son.

Here below, the love of Jesus for His Father shines out in an ineffable manner. All Christ's life, all His mysteries are summed up in those words which St. John relates: *Diligo Patrem,*[2] "I love the Father." Our Lord gave His disciples the infallible criterion of love. "If you keep My commandments, you shall abide in My love." And He at once gives an example: "As I also have kept My Father's commandments, and do abide in His love."[3] Jesus has ever remained in the love of the Father, because He has ever done His will. St. Paul expressly declares that the first movement of the Word-made-Flesh was a movement of love: "Behold I come that I should do Thy will, O God."[4] In this first glance of His earthly existence, the soul of Jesus saw the whole succession of His mysteries, the humiliations, the fatigues, the sufferings of which they were formed; and, by an act of love, He accepted to fulfil all these things.

This movement of love towards His Father has never ceased. Our Lord could say: *Quae placita sunt ei facio semper,*[5] "I do always the things that please Him." He fulfils everything to the last iota; He accepts all that His

---

1 Joan. xvii, 26. 2 Ibid. xiv, 31. 3 Joan. xv, 10. 4 Hebr. x, 7.
5 Joan. viii, 29.

Father requires of Him even to the bitter chalice of His agony: *Non mea voluntas, sed tua fiat*[1]; even to the ignominious death of the Cross, *Ut cognoscat mundus quia diligo Patrem, sic facio.*[2] And when all is consummated, the last beat of His Heart and His last thought are for the Father: "Father, into Thy hands, I commend My spirit."[3]

The love of Jesus for His Father underlies all His states and explains all His mysteries.

III

This Divine Word is our Model, the very form of our predestination. For, even after the Incarnation, He remains what He is: the Word co-eternal with the Father. This is why our imitation of Christ ought to extend not only to His human virtues, but likewise to His Divine Being.

Like Jesus and with Him, we ought first of all to confess and declare that all comes to Him from the Father.

When, at the Last Supper, Jesus prays to His Father for His Apostles, what reason does He bring forward in commending them to Him? "Father...the men whom Thou hast given Me...have known, that all things which Thou hast given Me, are from Thee...and they have known that I came out from Thee, and they have believed that Thou didst send Me. I pray for them..." The Incarnate Word has it at heart that we should acknowledge that He receives everything from His Father; how often He repeats this to His disciples: *It is therefore pleasing to Him that we should declare it with Him.*

It is likewise pleasing to the Father. At this Last Supper, Jesus said to His Apostles, "The Father Himself loveth you..." What words could be more sweet or give rise to greater confidence? Were they not spoken by Him Who knows the secrets of the Father? "The Father Himself loveth you..." And what reason does He give for this. "Because you have loved Me, and have believed that I came out from God."[4] To believe—with a practical faith which yields us up to Him that we may serve Him—that Jesus, the

---

1 "Not my will, but thine be done," Luc. xxii, 42.

2 "But that the world may know that I love the Father, so do I," Joan. xiv, 31.

3 Luc. xxiii, 46.   4 Joan. xvi, 27.

Incarnate Word came out from the Father, is the best way of pleasing God.

Let us often repeat, with deep reverence, especially after Communion, the words of the *Credo,* saying to Christ Jesus: Thou art "the only-begotten Son of God, born of the Father before all ages. God of God, Light of Light; true God of true God; begotten not made; consubstantial with the Father, by Whom all things were made." Grant me the grace that what I proclaim by my words, I may also proclaim by my deeds.[1]

We ought next to acknowledge that, *we too,* receive all from the Father, and that by a double title: as creatures and as children of God.

As creatures.—It is true to say that the creation is the work of the entire Trinity. But, as you know, it is especially attributed to the Father.[2] Why is this? Because in the intimate life of God, the Father is the principle of the Son and, with the Son, the principle of the Holy Spirit. Therefore the outward works wherein the character of origin is especially seen are particularly attributed to the Father: "I believe in God the Father Almighty, Creator of heaven and earth." The whole creation came forth from the hands of the Father, not by an emanation of His nature, as the pantheists would have it, but in that it was produced from nothing by virtue of the Divine Omnipotence.

It is very useful for us to acknowledge this dependence, and to praise God for it. Doubtless, God has no need of our praises; but it is meet and fitting that we should proclaim our condition as creatures by acts of thanksgiving to Him Who gave us life and being. "Thy hands have made me, and fashioned me wholly round about": *Manus tuae fecerunt me totum in circuitu.*[3] All that I have: body, soul, intelligence, will, health, I have from Thee, Thou Who art my principle, I adore and thank Thee; in return, I yield myself wholly up to Thee to do Thy will.

But it is above all because we are God's children that we ought to keep ourselves in this sense of dependence and gratitude. To the divine filiation, necessary and eternal, of His Only-begotten Son, the Father willed to add,

---

1 We have explained at more length this doctrine of appropriation in the conference The Holy Spirit, in our volume *Christ, the Life of the Soul.*

2 We have explained at more length this doctrine of appropriation in the conference The Holy Spirit, in our volume *Christ, the Life of the Soul.* [TRANSCRIBER'S NOTE: the text references footnote "2" twice; I have numbered the second one as reference "3" and repeated footnote 2 here.]

3 Job. x, 8.

by an act of love, infinitely free, a filiation of grace: He adopts us as His children, to the point that one day we shall share in the beatitude of His inmost life. This is an inexplicable mystery; but faith tells us that when a soul receives sanctifying grace at baptism, it participates in the divine nature: *Divinae consortes naturae.*[1] This soul becomes truly the child of God, *Dii estis et filii excelsi omnes.*[2] St. John speaks of a divine birth: *Ex Deo* NATI *sunt,*[3] not in the proper sense of the word, by nature, as the Word is begotten in the bosom of the Father, but by something analogous: *Voluntarie* GENUIT *nos verbo veritatis.*[4]

In a very real, very true sense, we are divinely begotten by grace. With the Word, we can say: "O Father, I am Thy son, I came out from Thee." The Word says it necessarily, by right, being essentially God's own Son; we only say it by grace, as adopted sons;—the Word says it from all eternity; we say it in time, although the decree of this predestination is eternal;— for the Word, this language denotes a relation of origin with the Father; for us, there is added a relation of dependance. But for us, as for Him, there is a true sonship: we are, by grace, God's children. The Father wills that despite our unworthiness, we should give Him the name of "Father." *Quoniam estis filii, misit Deus Spiritum Filii sui in corda vestra clamantem: abba, Pater.*[5] "God hath sent the Spirit of His Son" for that. This cry pleases our Heavenly Father. It is ineffable, but it is the truth. "Behold," says St. John, "what manner of charity the Father hath bestowed upon us, that we should be called, and should be the sons of God": *Videte qualem cantatem dedit nobis* PATER *ut filii Dei nominemur et* SIMUS.[6]

And in order to assure this decree of adoption, in order that this filiation of love should be wrought in us, God, with magnificent profusion, multiplies heavenly favours along our path; the Incarnation, the Church, the Sacraments,—especially the Eucharist,—the inspirations of His Spirit. So that every gift that raises us up to Him, every grace that leads us to perfection, "is from above, coming down from the Father of lights":

---

1 II Petr. i, 4.
2 "You are gods and sons of the most High," Ps. lxxxi, 6; Joan, x, 34.
3 Ibid. i, 13.
4 "For of his will hath he begotten us by the word of truth," Jac. i, 18.
5 "And because you are sons, God hath sent the Spirit of his Son into your hearts, crying: Abba, Father," Gal. iv, 6.
6 I Joan. iii, 1.

Omne datum optimum et omne donum perfectum desursum est, descendens a Patre luminum.[1]

This thought fills the soul with great confidence, but also with profound humility. If I may thus express myself, we ought to make all our activity proceed from God; to lay down at His feet all our own thoughts, all our own judgment, our self-will so as no longer to think, judge, will or act save as He wills. Was it not thus that Jesus acted? "The Son cannot do anything of Himself, but what He seeth the Father doing,"[2] the Incarnate Word said of Himself. All proportion guarded, it ought to be the same with us. We ought to immolate to God whatever is ill-regulated in the need we experience of being something of ourselves and of relying only on ourselves. And for this, before all that we do, let us implore the help of our Father in Heaven, as Jesus did. This is the practical homage whereby we acknowledge our dependance upon our Father Who is likewise our God, and whereby we proclaim, like Jesus, that all that we have is from the Father: *Omnia quae dedisti mihi abs te sunt.*[3]

Again we ought to imitate the Word inasmuch as He is the image of the Father. Holy Scripture tells us that God created us to His image and likeness. We bear within us, as creatures, vestiges of the divine power, wisdom and goodness.

But it is above all by sanctifying grace that we become like unto God. As St. Thomas says, this grace is a participated similitude of the divine nature: *Participata similitudo divinae naturae.*[4] To employ a theological word, grace is *deiform* because it places in us a divine similitude. When He contemplates His Word, the Father exclaims on beholding the perfection of His Son Who, begotten of Him, so adequately reflects His own perfection: "Thou art My beloved Son in Whom I am well pleased." Something analogous comes to pass in regard to a soul adorned with grace: the Father is well pleased with this soul. "If any one love Me," said Jesus, "My Father will love him, and we will come to him, and will make our abode with him."[5]

Sanctifying grace is the first and fundamental element of the divine similitude in us. But we must likewise be the image of our Father by our

1 Jac. i, 17.   2 Joan. v, 19.   3 Ibid. xvii, 7.
4 *Summa Theologiae* III, q. lxii, a. 1.   5 Joan. xiv, 23.

virtues. Christ Jesus Himself said: "Be ye therefore perfect, as also your heavenly Father is perfect."[1] Imitate His goodness, His mildness, His mercy: it is thus that you will reproduce His features in you. "Be ye therefore followers of God," St. Paul repeats after Jesus, "as most dear children."[2]

Undoubtedly this resemblance is not visible to bodily eyes, although it is revealed outwardly by works of holiness; it is in the soul that this resemblance is formed and perfected. Here below its beauty is hidden, its splendour is veiled. But the day will come when it will blossom forth and be manifested to the eyes of all. When we shall see God "we shall be like to Him," because on that day we shall be clear mirrors reflecting the divinity: *Similes ei erimus; quoniam videbimus eum sicuti est.*[3]

Finally, like the Word, we must refer ourselves entirely to our Heavenly Father through love. All in us comes from God by grace, all in us ought to return to our Father by a movement of love. God must be not only the principle, but also the end of all our works.

In order for our works to be pleasing to our Heavenly Father, they must be animated by love. In all that we do, great or small, known to men or hidden from sight, we ought to seek only the glory of our Father, act only in view of hallowing His name, extending His kingdom and doing His will. All the secret of holiness lies in this.

IV

The marvels of divine adoption are so great that human language cannot exhaust them. It is a wonderful thing that God should adopt us as His children; but the means that He has chosen to realise and establish this adoption is more wonderful still. And what is this means? It is His own Son: *In dilecto Filio suo.*[4] I have exposed this truth elsewhere,[5] but it is so vital that I cannot forbear returning to it.

God created us by His Word. After having said: "In the beginning... the Word was God," St. John adds: "All things were made by Him: and without Him was made nothing that made." What do these words sig-

---

1 Matth. v, 48.   2 Ephes. v, 1.   3 I Joan. iii, 2.   4 Ephes. i, 6.
5 Our Divine predestination in Christ Jesus. § iv, in the volume *Christ, the Life of the Soul.*

nify? In the Holy Trinity, the Word is not only the expression of all the perfections of the Father but moreover of all possible creatures. These have their prototype and exemplar in the divine essence. When God creates, He produces beings that will realise one of His thoughts. Then He creates all things by the power of His word: "He spoke and they were made: He commanded and they were created": *Ipse dixit, et facta sunt.*[1] This is why Holy Scripture says that the Father created all thing by His Word.

You already see what close and intimate relations with the Word the creation establishes in us. From the sole fact of our creation, we correspond to a divine idea, we are the fruit of an eternal thought contained in the Word. God knows His essence perfectly; expressing this knowledge, He begets His Word; He beholds in His Word the Exemplar of all creation. Thus each one of us represents a divine thought, and our individual holiness consists of carrying into effect this thought which God conceived of us before our creation.

In one sense, then, we proceed from God by the Word; and we ought to be, like the Word, the pure, perfect expression of God's thought for us. What hinders the realisation of this thought is when we impair God's work: for *to impair the divine* is truly the work that *is our own* in the creation,—our own, that is to say that belongs to us alone, God excluded. Thus all that comes from us and is in disaccord with the Divine will: sin, infidelities, resistances to inspirations from above, views that are merely human and natural; these are so many things whereby we spoil the divine idea in us.

But this relation with the Word, the Son, goes much further still in the work of our adoption.

The Apostle St. James tells us that every gift, every grace, comes down to us from our Heavenly Father; and he at once adds: "Of His own will hath He begotten us by the word of truth": *Voluntarie genuit nos verbo veritatis.* The divine adoption by grace which makes us children of God is wrought by the Son, by the Word.

This truth is one of those to which St. Paul returns most often. Like St. James, he declares that all blessings come from the Father and that they are all related to the decree of our adoption in Jesus Christ, His beloved

---

1 Ps. cxlviii, 5.

Son. In the eternal plan, we become God's children only in Jesus Christ, the Incarnate Word: *Elegit nos in ipso.*[1] The Father will only recognise us as His children if we bear in us the features of His Son Jesus: *Praedestinavit [nos]...conformes fieri Filii sui.*[2] So that it is only as joint-heirs with Christ that we are one day to be *in sinu Patris.*

Such is the divine decree. Let us now see the realisation, in time, of this eternal design, or rather the manner wherein the divine plan, which was crossed by Adam's sin, has been restored.

The Eternal Word is made flesh. The Psalmist says of the Word that He "hath rejoiced as a giant to run the way": *Exsultavit ut gigas ad currendam viam.* "It is from the heights of heaven that He comes forth": *A summo caelo egressio ejus;* "and it is to this sublime summit that He ascends": *Et occursus ejus usque ad summum ejus.*[3] This *egressio a summo caelo,* is the eternal birth in the bosom of the Father: *Exivi a Patre*; His return is His ascension towards the Father: *Relinquo mundum, et vado ad Patrem.*[4]

But He does not ascend alone. This giant came to seek lost humanity; He has regained it; and, in an embrace of love, He bears it away with Himself in His course to place it near Him *in sinu Patris*: "I ascend to My Father Who is also your Father, and I go to prepare a place for you in My Father's house."

Such is the work of the Divine Giant: to lead back fallen humanity into the bosom of the Father, the source of all beatitude whilst restoring to this humanity the grace of adoption by His life and His sacrifice.

Oh! let us say with the Apostle: " Blessed be the God and Father of our Lord Jesus Christ, Who hath blessed us with spiritual blessings" through His Son, in His Son, and hath made us sit with Him in those heavenly splendours where, in the midst of eternal felicity, He begets the Son of His dilection! *Consedere fecit nos in caelestibus.*[5] Yes, blessed be God! And blessed be the Divine Word Who was made flesh for us, Who by the shedding of His Blood has restored to us the heavenly inheritance. O Jesus, beloved Son of the Father, to You be all praise and all glory!

1 Ephes. i, 3–4.
2 "He predestined [us] to be conformable to his Son," Rom. viii, 29.
3 Ps. xviii, 6–7.
4 "I came forth from the Father....I leave the world and I go to the Father," Joan. xvi, 28.
5 "He hath made us sit in the heavenly places," Ephes. ii, 6.

V

Now what are for us the *practical consequences* of these doctrines?

If the Eternal Father has decreed that we should be His children, but only so in His Son Jesus: *Praedestinavit nos in adoptionem filiorum* PER JESUM CHRISTUM[1]; if He has made us partakers of the heritage of His beatitude only through His Son,—we can realise this divine plan and consequently assure our salvation, only by remaining united to the Son, to the Word. Never let us forget this: there is no other way for us to go to the Father: *Nemo venit ad Patrem, nisi per me!*[2] No man, *nemo*, can hope to come to the Father otherwise than by the Son. And to go to the Father, to reach Him, is not that all salvation and all holiness?

Now, how are we to remain united to the Word, to the Son?

First of all *by faith*. "In the beginning was the Word, and the Word was with God, and the Word was God…All things were made by Him… He was in the world, and the world was made by Him, and the world knew Him not. He came unto His own, and His own received Him not. But as many as received Him, He gave them power to be made the sons of God, to them that believe in His name," and thus "are born…of God."

The Eternal Father presents His Word to the world: "This is My beloved Son…Hear ye Him." If we receive Him by faith, that is to say if we believe that He is the Son of God, the Word makes us partakers of the best that He has: His Divine Sonship; He shares with us His condition of Son, He gives us the grace of adoption: *Dedit eis potestatem filios Dei fieri;* He gives us the right of calling God our Father.

All our perfection consists in our faithful imitation of the Son of God. Now, St. Paul tells us that all paternity comes from God: *Ex quo omnis paternitas nominatur.*[3] We can say too of the Son: *Ex quo omnis filiatio nominatur.* It is the Son alone Who, by His Spirit, teaches us how we may be sons: *Quoniam estis filii, misit Deus spiritum* FILII SUI *in corda vestra clamantem:* ABBA, PATER.[4]

We are to receive the Son Himself; to see ever in Him, whatever be

---

1 Ibid. i, 5.   2 "No one comes to the Father, except through me!" Joan. xiv, 6.
3 Ephes. iii, 15.
4 "And because you are sons, God hath sent the Spirit of his Son into your hearts, crying: Abba, Father," Gal. iv, 6.

the state wherein we contemplate Him, the Word co-eternal with the Father. Then we are to receive His teachings, His doctrine. He is in the bosom of the Father: and by His words He reveals to us that which He knows: *Ipse enarravit.* Faith is the knowledge that we have, through the Word, of divine mysteries. Whatever be the page of the Gospel that we read or that the Church sets before us in the course of the celebration of the mysteries of her Bridegroom, let us say to ourselves that these words are those of the Word: *Verba Verbi,* of Him Who expresses the thoughts, the desires, the will of our Father in Heaven: *Ipsum audite.*[1] Let us sing *Amen* to all that we hear from the Word, to each page that, in her liturgy, the Church detaches from the Gospel to propose to our faith. Let us say to God: O Father, I do not know Thee, since I have never seen Thee; but I accept all that Thy Divine Son, Thy Word, reveals to me of Thee.

This prayer is excellent; and often, when it is made with faith and humility a ray of light comes down from on high[2] which throws a light upon those texts that we read and makes us penetrate into their depths so that we find therein principles of life.

For the Word is not only the expression of the perfections of His Father, but, moreover, of all that the Father wills. All that the Word commands us in His Gospel or by His Church is the expression of the adorable will and desires of our Father in Heaven. And if we fulfil, above all through love, the precepts that Jesus gives us, we shall remain united to Him and, through Him, to the Father: *Si praecepta mea servaveritis,* MANEBITIS *in dilectione mea....Qui autem diligit me, diligetur a Patre...*[3]

Here is all the formula of holiness: to adhere to the Word, to His doctrine, to His precepts, and, through Him, to the Father Who sends Him and gives to Him the words that we are to receive.[4]

Lastly, we remain united to the Word above all by the Sacrament of union, the Eucharist. It is the Bread of Life, "the children's Bread."[5] Under the Eucharistic species, lies really hidden the Word, He Who is eternally begotten in the bosom of the Divinity. What a mystery! He Whom I receive in Communion is the Son begotten from all eternity, the be-

---

1 "Listen to him," Matth. xvii, 5; Luc. ix, 35.   2 Cf. Jac. i, 17.
3 "If you keep my commandments, you shall abide in my love....He that loveth me shall be loved of my Father," Joan. xv, 10; xiv, 21.
4 Cf. Joan. xvii, 8.   5 Sequence *Lauda Sion.*

loved Son to Whom the Father communicates His life, His Divine life, the fulness of His Being and His infinite beatitude. How much reason had Our Lord to say: "As the Living Father hath sent Me, and I live by the Father, so He that eateth Me the same also shall live by Me": *Et qui, manducat me, et ipse vivet propter me,* he..."abideth in Me, and I in him": *In me manet et ego in illo.*[1]

If we ask Our Lord what we can do that is most pleasing to His Sacred Heart, it is certain that He will tell us, before all else, to be like Him, the child of God. If then we want to please Him, let us receive Him every day in the Eucharistic Communion, and say to Him: "O Jesus, You are the Son of God, the perfect, adequate image of Your Father; You know Your Father, You are wholly His, You behold His Face; increase within me the grace of adoption which makes me the child of God; teach me to be, by Your grace and by my virtues, like You and in You, a worthy child of the Heavenly Father." It is certain that if we ask this grace with faith, the Word will give it to us.

He has told us: "The Son cannot do anything of Himself, but what He seeth the Father doing: for what things soever He doth, these the Son also doth in like manner."[2] He wills only what the Father wills. Hence the Son enters fully into the views of His Father, and when He gives Himself to us, it is in order to establish, preserve, and augment the grace of adoption within us. All His Divine personal life is to be *ad Patrem*; in giving Himself to us, He gives Himself as He is, seeking in all things His Father and the glory of His Father; and so our entire turning towards the Father is wrought when we receive the Word with faith, confidence and love. What we ought to ask and constantly seek after is that all our thoughts, all our aspirations, all our desires, all our activity, should tend, by the grace of our filiation and by love, to our Heavenly Father in His Son Jesus: *Viventes Deo in Christo Jesu.*[3]

VI

These truths are indeed elevated, this state is indeed sublime. And yet I have only reminded you of what the Word Himself revealed to us, and

---

1 Joan. vi, 57–58.   2 Ibid. v, 19.   3 Rom. vi, 11.

what St. John and St. Paul have repeated after Jesus. These are not dreams but realities, divine realities.

And these realities form the substance of Christianity. We shall understand nothing, I do not say merely of perfection, but even of simple Christianity, if we do not grasp that its most essential basis is constituted by the state of child of God, participation, through sanctifying grace, in the eternal filiation of the Incarnate Word. All the teachings of Christ and of the Apostles are summed up in this truth, all the mysteries of Jesus tend to establish its wonderful reality in our souls.

Never let us forget that all Christian life, all holiness, is being by grace what Jesus is by nature: the Son of God. It is this that makes the sublimity of our religion. The source of all the greatness of Jesus, the source of the value of all His states, of the fruitfulness of all His mysteries, is His Divine generation and His quality of Son of God. In the same way, the saint who is the highest in heaven is the one who here below was most perfectly a child of God, who made the grace of supernatural adoption in Jesus Christ fructify the most.

This is why all our spiritual life ought to be based upon this fundamental truth, all the work of perfection ought to consist in faithfully safeguarding our participation in the Divine Sonship of Jesus and in developing it in the greatest possible measure.

And do not let us say that this life is too high, that this programme is unrealisable. It is true that for our nature left to itself, this life is above the exigencies, the rights, the powers of our being, and that is why we call it supernatural.

But our Father in Heaven "knoweth what is needful"[1] for us. If He calls us, He likewise gives us the grace to come to Him. He gives us His Son in order that His Son may be our Way, that He may bring us Truth, and communicate Life to us. It suffices that we remain united to this Son by grace and by our virtues for us one day to be partakers of His glory *in sinu Patris*.

What did Jesus say to Magdalen, after His Resurrection? *Ascendo ad Patrem meum*: "I ascend to my Father"; and He adds: "And to your Fa-

---

1 Matth. vi, 8.

ther," *Et Patrem vestrum.*[1] And he goes "to prepare a place" for us: *Vado parare vobis locum,* for in His Father's house "there are many mansions."[2]

He has ascended to His Father, but as our Forerunner: *Praecursor pro nobis introivit Jesus.*[3] He has gone before us, but so that we may follow Him thither, for our life here below is only a passage, a probation: "In the world you shall have distress,"[4] said Jesus. There will be inward contradictions to be suffered, temptations to be borne from the prince of this world, disappointments arising from the course of events; for "the servant is not greater than his Master."[5] But, He added: "Let not your heart be troubled," do not be discouraged. "Believe in God, believe also in Me,"[6] Who am likewise God. "I am with you all days even to the consummation of the world."[7] "Your sorrow shall be turned into joy."[8] The hour will arrive when "I will come again, and will take you to Myself, that where I am you also may be" in My Father's kingdom: *Accipiam vos ad meipsum ut ubi sum ego et vos sitis.*[9]

O divine promise, given by the Uncreated Word, by the Word in person, by the infallible Truth; promise full of sweetness: "I will come Myself!..." We shall belong to Christ, and through Him to the Father, in the bosom of beatitude. "In that day," says Jesus, "you shall know"—no longer *in umbra fidei,* in the shadows of faith, but in the full radiance of eternal light, *in lumine gloriae*—"you shall know that I am in My Father, and you in Me, and I in you."[10] You shall see My glory as the Only-begotten Son,[11] and this vision shall be for you an ever living source of ineffable joy.

---

1 Joan. xx, 17.   2 Ibid. xiv, 2.   3 Hebr. vi, 20.   4 Joan. xvi, 33.
5 Ibid. xv, 20.   6 Ibid. xiv, 1.   7 Matth. xxviii, 20.
8 Joan. xvi, 20.   9 Ibid. xiv, 3.   10 Ibid. xiv, 20.   11 Ibid. i, 14.

...AND THE WORD
WAS MADE FLESH

SUMMARY.—I. Christ is perfect God and perfect Man: ineffable union of the divine and human in our Saviour's life.—II. Manner of union: the two natures are united in one same Divine Person. Consequence of this doctrine: infinite value of all the actions of Jesus; why He is so pleasing to His Father.—III. Our duties towards the Incarnate Word: to acknowledge Him first of all as God, by faith, adoration and submission.—IV. By adoration and absolute confidence, to acknowledge the reality of His Humanity united to the Word: *Fatigatur per quem fatigati recreantur.*[1]

I N T H E beginning was the Word, and the Word was with God, and the Word was God....And the Word was made flesh, and dwelt among us."

Christ is the Incarnate Word. Revelation teaches us that the second Person of the Holy Trinity, the Word, the Son, took a human nature in order to unite Himself personally to it. This is the mystery of the Incarnation.

Let us pause for a few seconds to consider this dogma of a God-Man, a dogma at once so amazing and so touching. It is the fundamental mystery upon which all the other mysteries of Jesus rest. Their beauty, their splendour, their virtue, their strength, their value are derived from this ineffable union of the Humanity with the Divinity. We shall only understand these mysteries properly if we first consider this one in itself and in the general consequences which proceed from it. Jesus is God and Man; if we want to know His Person, and to share in His states, we must try to understand not only that He is the Word, but also that He is the Word-

---

1 "He is wearied through whom the wearied are restored."

made-Flesh; if we would know Him worthily, it is as necessary for us to acknowledge the reality of His human nature as it is to adore the Divinity to which this nature is united.

Faith teaches us that there are two natures in Christ: the Human nature and the Divine nature; Christ is both perfect God and perfect Man.

Moreover these two natures are united in so close a manner that there is only one single Person, that of the Divine Word in Whom the Humanity subsists. From this ineffable union results the infinite value of Jesus' acts, of His states and of His mysteries.

Let us contemplate these truths. From this contemplation, made with humility and love, will spring forth quite naturally the sentiments which should animate us in regard to this mystery.

I

Christ is perfect God and perfect Man.

When He shows Himself to us in the manger at Bethlehem, in the workshop of Nazareth, upon the roads of Judea, preaching in the synagogues, nailed to the Cross, or ascending glorious into Heaven, He manifests Himself at the same time as God and as man.

He is perfect God. In taking our human nature, the Word remains what He was: *Quod fuit permansit:*[1] God, the Eternal Being, possessing in their plenitude all life, all perfection, all sovereignty, all power and all beatitude.

Let us hear the Incarnate Word Himself proclaim His Divinity: "As the Father hath life in Himself, so He hath given to the Son also to have life in Himself [eternal divine life]...."[2] My Father and I are one...."[3] Whatsoever He [the Father] doth, these [works] the Son also doth in like manner...."[4] All My things are Thine, and Thine are Mine."[5] As you see there is identity of perfections, equality of rights, because there is unity of nature.

Christ is the Son and consequently God Himself. The Pharisees acknowledged that God alone can remit sins; in their presence, in order to show that He is God, Jesus forgives the paralytic man and with a miracle emphasizes the grace given.[6] He declares that He is the Bread of Life

---

1 Antiphon for the Feast of the Circumcision.
2 Joan. v, 26. 3 Ibid. x, 30. 4 Ibid. v, 19. 5 Ibid. xvii, 10.
6 Marc. ii, 7–12.

come down from Heaven, the Bread that gives eternal life[1]; He only, by His own power, ascends into Heaven, because He alone came down from Heaven.[2] Also He asks His Father that the Humanity which He has taken may be glorified with that eternal glory which He had as the Word, as God, before the world was.[3] He treats with God as equal to equal, because He is the very Son of God.

Perfect God, Christ is likewise perfect Man: *Et verbum caro factum est.*[4] He took from us a human nature which He made His own in uniting Himself to it physically, substantially, personally, by ineffable bonds: *Quod non erat assumpsit.*[5]

This Eternal God, the Being necessarily subsisting by Himself, is born in time, of a woman: *Factum ex muliere.*[6] Christ has like us a human nature, complete, integral in its constitutive elements: *Debuit per omnia fratribus similari.*[7] Like us, Christ has a created soul, endowed with faculties like unto ours; His body is a true body, formed of the most pure blood of His Mother. In the early days of the Church, there were some heretics who affirmed that the Word took only the appearance of a human body; but they were condemned by the Church. Christ is authentically one of us, of our race. As the Gospel shows, He really suffered hunger, thirst, weariness; He shed tears, and sufferings weighed upon Him, body and soul, as truly as they weigh upon us. Even after His Resurrection, He keeps this human nature; He has it at heart that His incredulous disciples should verify its reality: *Palpate et videte*[8]: "Handle and see, for a spirit hath not flesh and bones, as you see Me to have." As they still doubt, He says to them: "Have you here anything to eat?" And they offer Him a piece of broiled fish and honeycomb which He takes and eats before them.

All that is ours He has made His own,—excepting sin: Absque peccato.[9] Christ knew neither sin nor that which is the source or moral consequence of sin: concupiscence, error, ignorance. His flesh is subject to suffering, because He comes to expiate sin by suffering; but sin itself has no hold

---

1 Joan. vi, 51–52.   2 Ibid. iii, 13.   3 Ibid. xvii, 5.
4 "And the Word was made flesh."
5 "That which he was not, he assumed."   6 Gal. iv, 4.
7 "It behoved him in all things to be made like unto his brethren," Hebr. ii, 17.
8 Luc. xxiv, 39 sq.   9 Hebr. iv, 15.

upon Him: "Which of you shall convince Me of sin?"[1] This challenge made to the Jews still remains unanswered; and, in order to condemn Christ to death, it was necessary to have recourse to false witnesses. He is man, but of a stainless purity, as befits the dignity of a God-Man: *Sanctus, innocens, impollutus, segregatus a peccatoribus.*[2]

Christ, then, possesses Divine nature and human nature. He is at once God and Man, perfect God and perfect Man.

Open the Gospel and on each page you will see that in all that He does the Incarnate Word shows Himself as God and man[3]; everywhere the Divinity and Humanity are manifested, each according to its nature and properties.

Christ is born of a woman, but He wills that His Mother shall be a Virgin and shall so remain;—in the manger, He is an infant Who needs a little milk to nourish Him, but the Angels celebrate His coming as that of the Saviour of the world;—He is laid upon straw in a stable, but a marvellous star leads the Eastern Magi to His feet;—like every Jewish boy, He undergoes circumcision, but at the same time He receives a name that comes from Heaven and marks a divine mission;—He grows in age and wisdom, but at twelve years old He throws the doctors of the Law themselves into admiration by His wonderful answers;—He wills to receive baptism from John the Precursor as if He needed to do penance, but at that same moment the heavens open, and the Eternal Father attests that He is His beloved Son;—in the desert, He is hungry, but the angels come to minister to Him;—during His journeys throughout Palestine, He suffers weariness, thirst and want, but, by His own authority, He makes the paralytics walk, cures the lame and halt, and multiplies the loaves to feed the multitude;—upon the Lake of Genesareth, sleep closes His eyelids while His disciples struggle against the tempest, but, the next

1 Joan. viii, 46.
2 "Holy, innocent, undefiled, separated from sinners," Hebr. vii, 26.
3 *Semper hoc egit Christus dictis et factis suis, ut Deus credatur et homo, Deus qui nos fecit, homo qui nos quaesivit...sic esse Christum hominem factum ut non destiterit Deus esse; manens Deus accepit hominem qui fecit hominem* (Christ always did this in his words and deeds, that He should be believed to be God and man, God who made us, man who sought us...Christ became man in such a way that He ceased not to be God; remaining God, He who made man took on manhood). S. Augustine, Tract. in Joan. xxviii.

instant, awakened by the terrified apostles, He stills the furious waves with a single gesture;—at the tomb of Lazarus, He is moved, He sheds tears, true human tears, but, with a word, He raises to life His friend who had been dead four days;—in the Garden of Gethsemani, after an agony full of weariness, distress and anguish, He allows Himself to be taken by His enemies, but the declaration that He is Jesus of Nazareth is sufficient to make them fall to the ground;—upon the Cross, He dies like the last of men, but all nature proclaims by the upheaval it undergoes that it is a God Who dies.

Thus, according to St. Leo's beautiful words,[1] "majesty is allied to lowliness, power to weakness, that which is mortal to that which is eternal... an inviolable nature to a passible nature....The true God is born in the integral and perfect nature of a true man, entirely with all that is His, entirely too with all that is ours": *Totus in suis, totus in nostris.*

Everywhere, from the entering of Jesus into this world, the union of the Divinity and Humanity is manifested in Him; a union which takes away nothing of the divine perfections and leaves intact the reality of the human nature: the Incarnation is an ineffable union.[2]

O Eternal Wisdom, how deep are Thy thoughts, how wonderful Thy works!

I I

That which further makes this mystery ineffable is the way wherein the union of natures is realised.

The divine nature and the human nature are united in one Person, the Eternal Person of the Word, of the Son.

In us, the soul and body united together form a human person. In Christ, it is not the same. The human nature, altogether integral, altogether perfect in its essence, in its constitutive elements, has, however, existence only through the Word, in the Divine Person of the Word. The Word gives

---

1 *Epistola 28 Dogmatica ad Flavian.*
2 *Agnosce mediatorem Dei et hominem qui ab ipso nativitatis suae exordio divinis humana sociat, ima summis* (Acknowledge the mediator of God and man, who from the very beginning of His birth, unites the human to the divine, the lowest to the highest). S. Bernard, *Sermo I de Circumcisione.*

to the human nature its reality of existence, which, in this case, means its personal "subsistence." There is then in Jesus but one Person, that of the Only-begotten Son of God.

Yet, as you know, however intimately they be united, the two natures keep their particular energies and their specific operations; there is neither blending nor confusion between them: *Non commixtionem passus*; inseparably united in the one Person of the Word, each preserves its own activity.

In fine, the human nature is rooted in the divinity. It is a human activity, truly human and authentic, which is manifested in Jesus; but it has its ultimate principle in the divinity. The Divine Person of the Word is the source of all Christ's perfections. In the Holy Trinity, the Word expresses the perfections of the Father by an infinitely simple act; in uniting Himself to the Sacred Humanity, the Word expresses through this Humanity all these perfections by manifold and varied acts conformed to human nature. It is thus that a ray of light in passing through a prism emerges in a variety of different shades of colours. The virtues of the Sacred Humanity of Jesus: His patience, sweetness, goodness, meekness, His kindness, zeal and love, are virtues accomplished by His human nature, but which are deeply rooted in the divinity, and at the same time manifest the perfections of the invisible God to our earthly gaze. Human in its outward expression, the life of Jesus is Divine in its source and principle.

What is the consequence of this doctrine? You know it, but it is extremely useful to return to it.

It is that all the actions of Jesus are the actions of a God. The actions of the Sacred Humanity are finite actions, bounded by time and space, in the same way as human nature is bounded.

But the moral value of these actions is divine. Why is this? Because every action, although it be accomplished by such or such a faculty of nature, is attributed to the person. In Christ, it is always God *Who* acts, but sometimes *through* His divine nature, sometimes *through* His human nature. It is then true to say that it is a God Who toiled, Who wept, Who suffered, Who died,—although all these actions were accomplished through the human nature. All Jesus Christ's human actions, however small they may be in their physical reality, have a divine value.[1]

And this is why Christ's whole life is so pleasing to His Father. The Father finds in Jesus, in His person and in His acts, in His most humiliating states as in His most glorious mysteries, all His delight, because He ever sees the Person of His Only-begotten Son. The Father sees Christ Jesus as no creature can ever see Him. If I may thus speak, He alone can appreciate the value of all that His Son does. As our Lord Himself said: "No one knoweth the Son, but the Father."[2] We may raise our souls and meditate upon the mysteries and states of Jesus, but we shall never arrive at appreciating them as they deserve. Only God can worthily know and recognize that which a God does. But in the Father's sight, the least acts of the Humanity of Jesus, the least movements of His Sacred Heart were a source of delight.

Another reason the Father has for contemplating the soul of Christ with complacency is that it is full of all grace. After having proclaimed the Divinity of the Word and the reality of the Incarnation, St. John immediately adds: "And we saw His glory...full of grace": *Et vidimus eum plenum gratiae.*

What is this fulness of grace that St. John admired in Jesus and of which he said that "of His fulness we all have received, and grace for grace"?

In Christ, there is first of all, as you know, the grace of union: *gratia unionis,* in virtue of which a human nature is substantially united to a Divine Person. Through this grace is wrought the union which constitutes the Incarnation. It is a grace unique of its kind, one which has only been given to Jesus Christ.

Furthermore the soul of Jesus, created like ours, was endowed with the fulness of sanctifying grace. Through the grace of union, the humanity in Jesus became the humanity of a God; through sanctifying grace, the soul of Jesus was rendered worthy of being and acting as befitted a soul united to God by a personal union. This sanctifying grace was given to Jesus in all its plenitude. To us it is given in a greater or lesser measure according to God's designs and our co-operation. To Jesus, it was conferred in its

---

1 In theological terms these actions are called theandric, from two Greek words which signify: human and divine.

2 Matth. xi, 27; Luc. x, 22.

fulness, on account of His personal quality of Son of God as well as on account of His title of Head of the mystical body to which He distributes it: *Secundum mensuram donationis Christi.*[1]

Finally, the Humanity of Jesus is holy because in an incomparable degree it possesses all those virtues which are compatible with His dignity as the Only-begotten Son of God;—because it is adorned, in a unique measure, with the gifts of the Holy Spirit.[2]

Nothing is wanting then to the Humanity of Jesus in order for it to be worthy of the Word to Whom it is united; it has indeed the fulness of all grace: *Et vidimus eum plenum gratiae.* It is without measure that "all the treasures of wisdom and knowledge"[3] are stored up in Jesus. In all things He holds the primacy "because in Him, it hath well pleased the Father that all fulness should dwell,"[4] and should remain with Him for ever. So that, says St. Paul, who in this is the echo of St. John, we "are filled in Him, Who is the head of all principality and power": *In ipso inhabitat* OMNIS PLENITUDO *divinitatis corporaliter: et estis in illo* REPLETI, *qui est* CAPUT *omnis principatus et potestatis.*[5]

III

What ought to be our soul's attitude in presence of this fundamental mystery of the God-Man?

The first attitude that we should have is one of faith. I have already said so, but this truth is of capital importance and therefore I do not hesitate to return to it.

At the beginning of his Gospel, after having extolled the glory of the Divine Word, St. John says that the Word came into this world, and that this world which He had created, which was His domain, which was "His own," received Him not. But, he adds, all such receive Him as believe in His name: *Quotquot autem receperunt eum...qui credunt in nomine ejus...* We receive the Incarnate Word, by faith; by faith, we accept the Divinity of Jesus: "Thou art the Christ, the Son of the living God."[6]

---

1 Ephes. iv, 7. 2 Joan. iii, 34. 3 Col. ii, 3. 4 Ibid. i, 18–19.
5 "In him dwelleth all the fulness of the Godhead corporeally. And you are filled in him, who is the head of all principality and power," Ibid. ii, 9–10.
6 Matth. xvi, 16; Joan. xi, 27.

Such is the attitude that the Eternal Father requires of us. "This is His commandment," says the same St. John, "that we should believe in the name of His Son Jesus Christ": *Et hoc est* MANDATUM *ejus: ut credamus in nomine Filii ejus Jesu Christi.*[1] He has Himself told us so: "This is My beloved Son...hear ye Him."[2] These words which were heard on Thabor, when the splendour of the Divinity filled the Sacred Humanity of Jesus with its rays, are but the echo, in the created world, of the words that the Heavenly Father utters in the heavenly sanctuary, *in splendoribus sanctorum,*[3] "Thou art My Son, this day have I begotten Thee."

Thus we are very pleasing to our Heavenly Father when, accepting His testimony, we profess that Jesus is His own Son, that He is co-eternal with the Father and shares with Him the Divine glory: *Tu solus altissimus Jesu Christe...in gloria Dei Patris...*

The mystery of the self-abasement of the Word-made-Flesh plunges St. Paul in such admiration that he can scarcely find terms wherewith to express the glory that, according to the very thoughts of God, these abasements will procure to Jesus. Listen to what he says: "Who being in the form of God, thought it not robbery to be equal with God; but emptied Himself, taking the form of a servant, being made in the likeness of men, and in habit, found as a man. He humbled Himself, becoming obedient unto death, even the death of the cross. For which cause God also hath exalted Him, and hath given Him a name which is above all names. That in the name of Jesus every knee should bow, of those that are in heaven, on earth and under the earth; and that every tongue should confess that the Lord Jesus Christ is in the glory of God the Father." *Et omnis lingua confiteatur quia Dominus Jesus Christus in gloria est Dei Patris.*[4]

We ought often to unite ourselves in mind and heart with the will of the Eternal Father to glorify His Son: *Clarificavi et iterum clarificabo.*[5] Before opening the Gospel or preparing ourselves to celebrate the mysteries of Jesus, let us first enter into God's views, confessing, by an act of intense faith, that this Christ Whom we are about to contemplate, He to Whom we would pray and unite ourselves, is God like the Father and the Holy Spirit.

---

1 I Joan. iii, 23.   2 Matth. xvii, 5; Marc. ix, 6; Luc. ix, 35.
3 Ps. cix, 3.   4 Philipp. ii, 6–11.
5 "I have glorified it and will glorify it again," Joan. xii, 28.

This attitude of soul is extremely profitable to us, for it raises us to the divine level and makes us pleasing to the Father: *Pater amat vos...quia credidistis quia ego a Deo exivi.*[1] St. Leo so well says that the faith "which justifies the impious, and from sinners makes saints, is that faith which believes that in one and the same Lord Jesus Christ are the true Divinity and the true Humanity. The Divinity whereby before all ages He is equal to the Father, having with Him the same eternal nature; the Humanity whereby, in these latter times, He has united Himself to us in taking upon Himself the form of a servant."[2]

This act of faith in the Divinity of Jesus should be the source of our adoration. Often, in the Gospel, we see the homage of adoration accompany the act of faith. It is the homage of the Magi,[3] of Peter after the miraculous draught of fishes[4], of the disciples who saw Jesus walking upon the water[5], of the man born blind when his sight had been restored to him: *Credo, Domine. Et procidens, adoravit eum.*[6]

By this act of adoration, the soul surrenders itself wholly to the Divine Word. When Our Lord dwells in our heart, especially after Holy Communion, we ought, according to the counsel of St. Francis of Sales, to cast all our faculties down at His feet in order to listen to Him and promise Him fidelity.

This is to imitate the Sacred Humanity of Jesus. This Sacred Humanity belonged and was so absolutely yielded up to the Word, that it had no proper personality: this is one of the essential aspects of the mystery of the Incarnation.

All proportion being kept, it ought to be so with us, for Jesus Christ is our Model in all things. His Humanity only acted as subject to the Word in Whom it subsisted, to the Word Who gave this Humanity existence. Let there be no movement in us that does not come from God, no desire that is not according to the Divine good pleasure, no action that does

---

1 "The Father loveth you, because...you have believed that I came out from God," Ibid. xvi, 27.

2 *Hoc enim est quod justificat impios, hoc quod ex peccatoribus facit sanctos, si in uno eodemque Domino nostro Jesu Christo et vera Deitas et vera credatur humanitas: Deitas qua ante omnia saecula in forma Dei aequalis est Patri: humanitas qua novissimis diebus in forma servi unitus est homini.* S. Leo, *Sermo 4 de Epiphan.*

3 Matth. ii, 11.　　4 Luc. v, 8.　　5 Matth. xiv, 33.

6 "I believe, Lord. And falling down, he adored him," Joan. ix, 38.

not tend to serve as an instrument to His glory. A soul that is in such dependance of love, of will and of action upon God can say in all truth: "The Lord ruleth me," *Dominus regit me.*

And the sacred writer adds: *Et nihil mihi deerit*[1] "And I shall want nothing." And so it is that because this soul is wholly given up to the Word, the Word says to His Father: "This soul is Mine, it is therefore also Thine, O Father," *Mea omnia tua sunt.* The Word gives this soul to the Father in order that the Father may send His most perfect gifts down upon it.

IV

Christ is God and Man. The faithful soul does not only confess the Divinity of Jesus but wills also to honour His Sacred Humanity.

There are some who think that they do better in their spiritual life not to occupy themselves with Christ's Humanity but only to contemplate His Divinity. This was for a time the error of St. Teresa. The great contemplative afterwards recognised this error. In what bitter terms she deplored it! How earnestly she warned her daughters, and others through them, against this opinion which she declared to be "a delusion," and one which she never recalled to mind without being seized with sorrow. For she says "I had taken a detestable path" and "it seemed to me that I had been guilty of the blackest treachery." To tell the truth it was "ignorance."

According to the saint, such an illusion has for its cause "a certain want of humility, so secret and hidden that we do not observe it." For we ought to account ourselves "exceedingly rich" to be able to stay near to the Humanity of Jesus in His mysteries. This want of humility she says "greatly hinders any progress in contemplation."

Another result of the error that the saint points out is that it leaves the soul without support. "We are not angels," she says, "we have a body....In the midst of business, of persecutions, of trials...in times of dryness, Christ is our best Friend. We see Him a man like ourselves, we contemplate Him in infirmity, in suffering....It is very advantageous for us, as long as we are in this life, to consider God-made-Man." Is it not indeed the very law of our nature to come to the invisible through visible things? Now

[1] Ps. xxii, 1.

65

the Incarnation is the most divine application of this psychological law.

The Bride in the Canticle of Canticles says: "I sat down under His shadow, Whom I desired": *Sub umbra illius quem desideraveram sedi*. This *umbra* is the Sacred Humanity whereby our gaze is permitted to contemplate the Divinity thus revealed to us.

The Saint concludes: "God is extremely pleased to see a soul humbly place His Divine Son as the Mediator between herself and Him."[1]

And what is the innermost reason of this?

It is that the Incarnation is a *Divine* mystery; it is the masterpiece of Eternal Wisdom and Infinite Love. Why not enter into God's views and designs? Why refuse to submit our limited and finite wisdom to Infinite Wisdom? Are then God's resources so inefficacious that we should have to improve them by our human calculations? If God has thus willed to effect our salvation and holiness by means of a humanity united to His Word, to His Son, why do we not take this means? Therein God's wisdom is as wonderful as His condescension.

When reading the Gospel, or celebrating the mysteries of Jesus, do not let us fear to contemplate the man in Christ. This Humanity is the Humanity of a God. This Man, Whom we see acting and living in the midst of men so as to draw them to Himself by sensible marks of His love, is God, our God.

Above all do not let us fear to render to this Humanity itself all the homage due to it.

Our adoration in the first place. It is true that this Humanity is a created humanity like unto our own. We do not adore it for its own sake; we must, however, adore it *in* itself, *on account of its union* with the Son of God. Our adoration goes to His Humanity, but the Divine Person to Whom it is substantially united is the term of this adoration.

Next, absolute confidence. God has willed to make Christ's Humanity the instrument of grace. It is through His Humanity that grace flows into us. It is not of the Word in the bosom of the Father, but truly of the Incarnate Word that St. John speaks when he says that He was "full of grace...and of His fulness we have all received."

During His earthly life, Our Lord, being God, could have wrought

---

1 Life by Herself, Chapter xxii. All this admirable chapter should be read.

all His miracles and given grace to men simply by an act of His Divine will. Each time that the sick were brought to Jesus to be healed or the dead to be raised to life, He could, by a single interior act of His Eternal will, have wrought the miracle demanded. But He did not do so. Read the Gospel and you will see that He willed to touch the eyes of the blind, the ears of the deaf, the tongue of the dumb; that He willed to touch the bier of the son of the widow of Naim, to take the daughter of Jairus by the hand, to give the Holy Ghost to His Apostles by breathing upon them. It was, then, by the contact of His Sacred Humanity that Christ performed miracles and gave grace: the Humanity served as the instrument united to the Word. And this wonderful and touching law is observed in all the mysteries of Jesus.

Now this order, willed by God Himself, always subsists because the union of natures in Jesus Christ remains indissoluble. Hence, when we read the pages of the Gospel or follow the Church in her liturgy, when we unite ourselves to the Sacred Humanity of Jesus by an act of faith, when, above all, we receive His Body in the Eucharist, this Sacred Humanity, inseparable from the Divine Word, serves as the instrument of grace for our souls.

"It is quite evident to me," writes St. Teresa, "that in order to please God, and receive great graces from Him, it is needful, and such is His will, that they should pass through the hands of this Sacred Humanity, wherein, as He Himself declared, He was well pleased. I have seen a number of times that this is the door whereby we must enter if we wish His Majesty to reveal high secrets to us....One walks with safety along this path."

And if you reflect, you will agree that all the economy of the spiritual life is based upon this truth. The Church, the Sacraments, the Holy Sacrifice, the preaching of the Word of God: these are so many means whereby God leads us to Himself.[1]

We see how important and necessary it is for us to remain united to the Sacred Humanity of Jesus: in it dwells the very plenitude of the Divinity, and it is from the Word, through the instrumentality of the Humanity, that we receive every grace: *Verbum caro factum est...et vidimus eum ple-*

---

1 See the development of this idea in the conference, The Church the Mystical Body of Christ, § ii, in our preceding volume, *Christ, the Life of the Soul.*

num gratiae et de plenitudine ejus nos omnes accepimus.[1] The Humanity of Jesus is the divinely established means for transmitting grace to souls.

It is also the means whereby souls come to the Divinity. This is a no less important truth which we ought never to forget. We ought not to stop at the Sacred Humanity as at the final term. In fact, you might say: "As for me, all my devotion consists in giving myself to Christ Jesus, in yielding myself up to Him." That is good, it is excellent, nothing is better than to give ourselves up to Christ. But what is it to give ourselves to Our Lord? It is to unite our will to His. Now the will of Jesus is to bring us to His Father. In that lies all His work; the Father is the term. "I am the way," said Christ Himself in speaking of His Humanity. This Humanity is the one way, it is true, but only a way. The supreme end to which this way leads is the Eternal Father: *Nemo venit* AD PATREM *nisi per me.*[2] By the Humanity we come to the Word, and by the Word to the Father.

This is what St. Paul said to the Christians of his time: *Omnia vestra sunt, vos autem Christi, Christus autem Dei.*[3] By these simple words the great Apostle expressed the degrees of the Divine work upon earth: "For all things are yours...and you are Christ's, and Christ is God's."

By the Humanity of Jesus we belong to the Word, to the Son; by the Son, we go to the Father. Christ thus leads us *in sinu Patris.*[4] This is, in what concerns us, the intimate reason of the ineffable mystery of the God-Man.

St. John tells us that at the outset of Our Divine Saviour's public life, when He was passing through Samaria, He came to a city called Sichar, near Jacob's well. Among the details of this scene carefully noted by the Evangelist, there is one that especially moves our hearts: *Jesus ergo fatigatus ex itinere, sedebat sic supra fontem*[5]: "Jesus therefore being wearied with His journey, sat thus on the well." What a touching revelation of the reality of the Humanity of Jesus!

We ought to read the wonderful commentary which St. Augustine[6] has given of these details, with that opposition of ideas and terms of which

---

1 "And the Word was made flesh...and we saw him full of grace...and of his fulness we have all received," Joan. i, 14, 16.
2 "No one comes to the Father except through me," Joan. xiv, 6.
3 I Cor. iii, 22–23.   4 Joan. i, 18.   5 Ibid. iv, 6.
6 Tract. in Joan. xv.

he has the secret, especially when he wants to place in relief the union and the contrast of the divine and the human in Jesus. "He is weary, He Who refreshes those who are weary; He Whose absence fills us with weariness, He Whose presence strengthens us": *Fatigatur per quem fatigati recreantur; quo deserente fatigamur, quo praesente firmamur.* "It is for you that Jesus is wearied on His journey. We find Jesus full of strength and of weakness. Why full of strength? Because He is the Eternal Word and all things were created by His wisdom and power. Why full of weakness? Because this Word was made flesh and dwelt amongst us. The strength of Christ created you; the weakness of Christ re-created you." *Fortitudo Christi te creavit; infirmitas Christi te recreavit.*

And the saint concludes: *Infirmus in carne Jesus; sed noli tu infirmari; in infirmitate illius tu fortis esto!* Jesus is weak in His Humanity; but as for you, take care not to remain in your weakness; go rather to draw strength from Him Who, being by nature Almighty, willed to become weak for love of you.

SAVIOUR AND HIGH PRIEST

SUMMARY.—Necessity of contemplating the work and mission of the Word-made-Flesh in order better to understand His Person; the names of the Incarnate Word declare His mission and characterise His work: "Jesus Christ" is the Son of God, Supreme High Priest Who by His sacrifice saves humanity.— I. Christ is established High Priest in His Incarnation.—II. How as soon as He enters into this world Christ inaugurates His sacrifice.—III. Diversity of the acts of the offering made by Jesus Christ.— IV. Perpetuity of Christ's priesthood and oblation in Heaven.—V. How upon earth the sacrifice of the Cross is renewed; the Church does not celebrate any of Christ's mysteries without offering the Eucharistic Sacrifice.

CHRIST Jesus is the Incarnate Word appearing in the midst of us, at once God and Man, true God and true Man, perfect God and perfect Man. In Him two natures are inseparably united in one Person, the Person of the Word.

These traits constitute the very being of Jesus. Our faith and piety adore Him as our God while confessing the touching reality of His Humanity.

If we would penetrate deeper into the knowledge of the Person of Jesus, we must begin by contemplating, for a few moments, His mission and His work. The Person of Jesus gives value to His mission and work; His mission and work complete the revelation of His Person.

And it is most noteworthy that the names which designate the very Person of the Incarnate Word declare at the same time His mission and characterise His work. These names are not, as is too often the case with ours, lacking in significance. They come from Heaven and are rich in meaning. What are these names? They are many, but the Church, following St. Paul in this, has especially retained two of them: that of Jesus,

71

and that of Christ.

As you know, Christ means one who is anointed, sacred, consecrated. Formerly, under the Ancient Alliance, kings were frequently anointed, prophets more rarely, and the high priest always. The name of Christ, like the mission of king, prophet and pontiff which it designates, was given to several personages in the Old Testament before being given to the Incarnate Word. But none save Himself could fulfil its signification in all its fulness. He is the Christ, for He alone is the King of Ages, the Prophet preeminently, the one supreme and universal High Priest.

He is King. He is so by His Divinity, *Rex Regum et Dominus dominantium*[1]; He rules over all creatures brought out of nothing by His almighty power: *Venite adoremus, et procidamus ante Deum....*[2] *Ipse fecit nos et non ipsi nos.*[3]

He will be so likewise as the Incarnate Word. The sceptre of the world had been foretold to Jesus by His Father. The Messias says: "I am appointed king by Him over Sion, His holy mountain, preaching His commandment. The Lord hath said to Me: Thou art My Son, this day have I begotten Thee. Ask of Me, and I will give Thee the Gentiles for Thine inheritance, and the utmost parts of the earth for Thy possession."[4]

The Word became Incarnate in order to establish "the Kingdom of God." This expression often occurs in the preaching of Jesus. In reading the Gospel you will have remarked an entire group of parables,—the pearl of great price, the hidden treasure, the sower, the grain of mustard seed, the murderous vine-dressers, the guests invited to the wedding-feast, the tares, the servants awaiting their Master, the talents, etc.,—which group is intended to show the greatness of this kingdom, its origin, its development, its extension to the pagan nations after the reprobation of the Jews, its laws, its conflicts, its triumphs. Christ organises this kingdom by the election of the Apostles, and the foundation of the Church to which He entrusts His doctrine, His authority, His sacraments. It is a wholly spiritual kingdom wherein is nothing temporal or political such as was dreamt of by the carnal minds of most of the Jews; a kingdom into which

---

1 "King of kings and Lord of lords," Apoc. xix, 16.
2 "Come let us adore and fall down before God," Ps. xciv, 6.
3 "He made us and not we ourselves," Ibid. xcix, 3.   4 Ibid. ii, 8.

every soul of good will enters; a wonderful kingdom of which the final splendour is altogether heavenly and the beatitude eternal.

St. John extols the magnificence of this Kingdom. He shows us the elect falling prostrate before their Divine Head, Christ Jesus, and proclaiming that He has redeemed them in His Blood, out of every tribe, and tongue, and people, and nation, and has made of them a kingdom to the glory of His Father: *Et fecisti nos Deo nostro regnum.*[1]

Christ is to be Prophet. He is the prophet preeminently, because He is the *Word* in person, the "Light of the World" Who alone can truly enlighten every man here below. "God...spoke in times past...by the prophets," St. Paul said to the Hebrews, but "in these days [God] hath spoken to us by His Son."[2] He is not a prophet who announces from afar off, to a small portion of the human race and under symbols, sometimes obscure, God's still hidden designs. He it is Who living in the bosom of the Father alone knows the divine secrets and makes the wondrous revelation of these secrets to mankind: *Ipse enarravit.*[3]

You know that from the beginning of His public life, Our Saviour applied to Himself the prophecy of Isaias declaring "the Spirit of the Lord is upon Me. Therefore He hath *anointed* Me to preach the Gospel to the poor...to preach deliverance to the captives, and sight to the blind...to preach the acceptable year of the Lord, and the day of reward."[4]

He is, then, the One sent, God's Legate Who proves, by miracles wrought by His own authority, the divinity of His mission, of His work, and Person. Thus we hear the multitude, after the miracle of the multiplication of loaves, cry out: "This is of a truth the prophet, that is to come into the world.[5]"

It is above all in His capacity of *High Priest* and Mediator, supreme High Priest and universal Mediator, that the Word Incarnate realises the signification of this name of Christ.

But here we must unite the name of *Jesus* to that of *Christ*. The name of Jesus means Saviour: "Thou shalt call His name Jesus," says the Angel

---

1 Apoc. v, 9–10. 2 Hebr. i, 1–2. 3 "He hath declared him," Joan. i, 18.
4 Luc. iv, 18–19; cf. Isa. lxi, 1. 5 Joan. vi, 14.

to Joseph, "for He shall save His people from their sins."[1] This is His essential mission: *Venit salvare quod perierat.*[2] Truly Jesus only fully realises the signification of His Divine name by His Sacrifice, in fulfilling His work as High Priest: *Venit Filius hominis dare animam suam redemptionem pro multis.*[3] The two names therefore complete each other and are henceforward inseparable. "Christ Jesus" is the Son of God, established as the Supreme Pontiff Who, by His Sacrifice, is the Saviour of all humanity.

That is why we must contemplate Christ's Priesthood and Sacrifice in order to understand, as far as is possible, the adorable Person of the Incarnate Word.

We are about to see that it is indeed by the Incarnation itself that Jesus was consecrated Pontiff, and that it was from the moment of His entrance into this world that He inaugurated His Sacrifice. All His existence bears the reflection of His mission of Pontiff and is marked with the characters of His Sacrifice.

Thus we shall better grasp both the greatness and the order of Christ's mysteries; we shall see what a profound unity knits them together: the sacrifice of Jesus, because it is His essential work, is the culminating point towards which all the mysteries of His earthly life converge, and the source whence all the states of His glorious life derive their splendour. We shall see too of what abundant graces He is the principle for every soul that comes to Him in order to drink at the Fountain of Life and Joy.

I

It is especially in his Epistle to the Hebrews that St. Paul sets forth in broad and strong terms the ineffable greatness of Christ as High Priest: *De quo nobis grandis sermo, et ininterpretabilis ad direndum.*[4] We herein see His mission of Mediator, the transcendency of His priesthood and sacrifice above the priesthood of Aaron and the sacrifices of the Old Testament: the unique sacrifice, consummated on Calvary, of which the offering is

---

1 Matth. i, 21.
2 "He is come to save that which was lost," Ibid. xviii, 11; cf. Luc. xix, 10.
3 "The Son of man is come to give his life for the redemption of many," Cf. Matth. xx, 28; Marc. x, 45.
4 "Of whom we have much to say and hard to be intelligibly uttered," Hebr. v, 11.

continued with inexhaustible efficacy in the sanctuary of heaven.

St. Paul reveals to us this truth that Christ Jesus possesses His Priesthood from the very moment of His Incarnation.

What is a priest? A mediator between man and God, says the Apostle. The priest offers the homage of the creature to God, and gives God, "the Holy One," to men, "*sacrum dans.*" Hence the name of *sacerdos*.

He is taken from among men, consecrated to God, in order to be mediator: *Omnis pontifex ex hominibus assumptus, pro hominibus constituitur in iis quae sunt ad Deum.*[1] In times past, this consecration was ordinarily made by a special "anointing" signifying that the Spirit of the Lord was upon the one who was chosen and thus marking him out in a particular manner for his sacerdotal mission. In the human priesthood, this sacerdotal character is a quality added as it were to the person of the man.

But in Christ, this character is wholly transcendent, as the mediation which He took upon Himself is unique. Jesus became High Priest from the moment of His Incarnation and by reason of His Incarnation.

Only faith can penetrate into this profound mystery, for human understanding is confounded before such greatness. Let us transport ourselves to Nazareth so as to be present at the heavenly colloquy which took place between the Angel and the Virgin. God's messenger says to Mary in explanation of the wonderful thing that is about to be accomplished in her: "The Holy Spirit shall come upon thee, and the power of the Most High shall overshadow thee. And therefore also the Holy which shall be born of thee shall be called the Son of God." The Virgin replies: "Behold the handmaid of the Lord; be it done to me according to thy word."[2]

At this moment, the Word is made flesh. The Word is for ever united, by an ineffable union, to our humanity. Through the Incarnation, the Word enters into our race, He becomes authentically one of ourselves, like unto us in all things, excepting sin. He can, then, become High Priest and Mediator, since being God and Man He can bind man to God: *Ex hominibus assumptus.*

In the Holy Trinity, the Second Person, the Word, is the Infinite glory of the Father, His essential glory: *Splendor gloriae et figura substantiae*

---

1 "Every high priest taken from among men is ordained for men in the things that appertain to God," Hebr. v, 1.
2 Luc. i, 35–38.

ejus.[1] But, as Word, before the Incarnation, He does not offer sacrifice to His Father. Why is this? Because sacrifice supposes homage, adoration, that is to say the acknowledgment of our own abasement in presence of the Infinite Being; the Word being in all things equal to His Father, being God with Him and like Him, cannot then offer Him sacrifice. Christ's Priesthood could only begin at the moment when the Word was made flesh. At that moment when the Word became Incarnate, He united in Himself two natures: the divine nature whereby He was able to say: *Ego et Pater unum sumus*[2]: "I and the Father are one," one in the unity of the Divinity, one in equality of perfections; the other, the human nature by reason of which He said: *Pater major me est*: "The Father is greater than I."[3] It is therefore inasmuch as He is God-Man that Jesus is Pontiff.

Learned authors derive the word "pontiff" from *pontem facere:* "to establish or build a bridge." Whatever be the value of this etymology the idea is just as applied to Christ Jesus. In The Dialogue of St. Catherine of Siena, we read that God the Father, vouchsafed to explain to her how, by the union of the two natures, Christ threw a bridge over the abyss that separated us from heaven: "I would that thou shouldst look at the Bridge that I have built for thee in My Only-begotten Son, and that thou shouldst see the greatness thereof for it reaches from heaven to earth, that is, the greatness of the Divinity is joined to the earth of your humanity.... That was necessary in order to restore the road which was broken and make it possible for man to pass through this world's bitterness and attain (eternal) life; but the bridge could not be made of earth large enough to span the abyss and reach eternal life, since the earth of human nature was incapable of itself to satisfy for sin and remove the stain of Adam's sin which has corrupted and infected the whole human race. It was, then, necessary to join human nature with the height of My nature, the Eternal Deity, so that it might satisfy for the whole human race. It was necessary that the human nature should bear the punishment and that the Divine nature, united with the human, should make acceptable the sacrifice that My Son offered to Me in order to destroy death and restore life to you. So the height of the Divinity, humbled to the earth of your humanity, built the Bridge and made the road....But in order that you should have life, it

---

1   "The brightness of his glory and the figure of his substance," Hebr. i, 3.

2   Joan. x, 30.   3   Ibid. xiv, 28.

is not enough that My Son should have become the Bridge, unless you pass over by this Bridge."[1]

Moreover it is through the Incarnation itself that the Humanity of Jesus was "consecrated," "anointed."[2] Not with an outward anointing, as is done for simple creatures, but with an entirely spiritual unction. By the action of the Holy Spirit, Whom the liturgy calls *spiritalis unctio,*[3] the Divinity is poured out upon the Human nature of Jesus, like an "oil of gladness": *Unxit te Deus oleo laetitiae prae consortibus tuis.*[4] This unction is so penetrating, the Humanity is so closely consecrated to God that no closer consecration could be possible, for this human nature has become the very Humanity of a God, of the Son of God.

This is why at the moment of the Incarnation whereby the first Priest of the New Alliance was consecrated, a cry resounded in Heaven: *Tu es sacerdos in aeternum,*[5] "Thou art a priest for ever." St. Paul, whose gaze pierced so many mysteries, likewise reveals this one to us. Listen to what he says: "Neither doth any man take the honour (of priesthood) to himself, but he that is called by God...thus Christ also did not glorify Himself, that He might be made a high priest; but He that said unto Him: *Thou art My Son, this day have I begotten Thee.* As He saith also in another place: *Thou art a priest for ever...*"[6]

So then, by the Apostle's testimony, it was from the Eternal Father Himself that Christ received the supreme Priesthood, from this Father Who also said to Him: "Thou art My Son, this day have I begotten Thee."[7] Christ's Priesthood is a necessary and immediate consequence of

---

1 Dialogue. The image of the bridge is familiar to S. Catherine. It is found in many places of the Dialogue and in her Letters.

2 S. Augustine, *De Trinitate,* xv, 27.   3 Hymn *Veni Creator.*

4 "God hath anointed thee with the oil of gladness above thy fellows," Ps. xliv, 8.

5 Ps. cix, 4.

6 *Nec quisquam sumit tibi honorem, sed qui vocatur a Deo, sic et Christus non semetipsum clarificavit ut pontifex fieret; sed qui locutus est ad eum: Filius meus es tu, ego hodie genui te, quemadmodum et in alio loco dicit: Tu es sacerdos in aeternum* (Neither doth any man take the honour to himself, but he that is called by God. So Christ also did not glorify himself that he might be made a high priest: but he that said unto him: Thou art my Son: this day have I begotten thee. As he saith also in another place: Thou art a priest for ever). Hebr. v, 4–6.

7 Ps. ii, 7.

His Incarnation.

Let us adore this holy, immaculate High Priest, Who is God's own Son; let us cast ourselves down before this Mediator Who alone, because He is at once God and Man, can fully realise His mission of salvation and render to us God's gifts by the sacrifice of His Humanity; but let us likewise confide ourselves to His Divine virtue which, also alone, was powerful enough to reconcile us with the Father.

II

The sacrifice of this one Pontiff is on a par with His priesthood: it was likewise from the moment of His Incarnation that Jesus inaugurated it.

You know that in Christ, the soul, created like ours, was not however subject to the progressive development of the corporal organism for the exercise of the faculties proper to it, intelligence and will: His soul had, from the first moment of its existence, the perfection of its own life, as befitted a soul united to the Divinity.

Now, St. Paul reveals to us the first movement of the soul of Jesus at the instant of His Incarnation.

In one and the same glance, it beholds the ages past, the abyss wherein humanity lies powerless to liberate itself, the multiplicity and fundamental insufficiency of all the sacrifices of the Old Law; for no creature, however perfect, can worthily repair the injury committed by sin against the Creator. Christ beholds the programme of immolation that God demands of Him in order to work out the world's salvation.

What a solemn moment for the soul of Jesus! What a moment too for the human race.

With a movement of intense love, His soul yields itself to perfect the work, both human and divine, which alone can render glory to the Father in saving humanity. O Father "sacrifice and oblation Thou wouldst not," they are not sufficiently worthy of Thee, "but a body Thou hast fitted to Me": *Corpus autem aptasti mihi.* And wherefore hast Thou given it to me? Thou requirest that I should offer it to Thee in sacrifice. "Behold I come. In the head of the book [of my life] it is written of Me, that I should do Thy will, O God": *Ecce venio, in capite libri scriptum est de me ut faciam,*

Deus, voluntantem tuam.[1]

With a perfect will, Christ accepted that sum of sorrows which began with the lowliness of the manger only to be ended by the ignominy of the Cross. From His entrance into this world, Christ offered Himself as Victim: the first action of His life was a sacerdotal act.

What creature is able to measure the love that filled this sacerdotal act of Jesus? Who is able to know its intensity and describe its splendour? The silence of adoration can alone praise it in some degree.

Never has Christ Jesus retracted this act, nor withdrawn anything from this gift. All His life was ordered in view of His Sacrifice upon the Cross. Read the Gospel in this light and you will see how in every mystery and state of Jesus is found an element of sacrifice leading Him little by little to the height of Calvary, so much is the character of High Priest, Mediator and Saviour essential to His person. We shall never grasp the true physiognomy of the Person of Jesus unless we constantly have in view His redeeming mission by the sacrifice and immolation of Himself. This is why when St. Paul said that he summed up everything in the knowledge of the mystery of Jesus, he immediately added: "and Him crucified": *Non enim judicavi aliquid scire inter vos nisi Jesum Christum,* ET HUNC CRUCIFIXUM.[2]

Christ is born in the most absolute destitution; He has to flee to a strange land to escape from a tyrant's rage; He knows hard and hidden toil in the workshop of Nazareth; during His Public Life, He has nowhere to lay His head; He is exposed to the persecution of the Pharisees, His most deadly enemies; He suffers hunger, thirst, weariness. Furthermore, He burns to achieve His sacrifice: *Baptismo autem habeo baptizari, et quomodo* COARCTOR *usquedum perficiatur.*[3]

There is in Jesus, if we may so speak, a kind of enthusiasm for His Sacrifice. See again in the Gospel how our Divine Saviour begins to disclose to His apostles, gradually in order to spare their weakness, the mystery

---

1 Hebr. x, 5–7; cf. Ps. xxxix, 7–9.

2 "For I judged not myself to know anything among you, but Jesus Christ: and him crucified," I Cor. ii, 2.

3 "And I have a baptism wherewith I am to be baptized. And how I am straitened until it be accomplished," Luc. xii, 50.

of His sufferings. One day He tells them that He must go to Jerusalem, that He will suffer many things from His enemies, and will be put to death. Then Peter immediately taking Him aside says: "Lord, be it far from Thee." But Jesus answers: "Go behind me, Satan, thou art a scandal unto Me; because thou savourest not the things that are of God, but the things that are of men."[1] In the midst of the splendours of His Transfiguration upon Thabor of what did the Saviour speak with Moses and Elias? Of His coming Passion.

Christ thirsted to give to His Father the glory which His Sacrifice was to procure for Him: *Iota unum aut unus apex non praeteribit a lege, donec omnia fiant.*[2] He wishes to fulfil everything to the last iota, that is to say, to the least detail.

When, in His agony, anguish and sorrow gather in His soul, He feels them acutely. "My Father," He says, "if it be possible, let this chalice pass from me, nevertheless not as I will, but as Thou wilt."[3] Finally upon Calvary, He consummates His immolation, and is able to say, before drawing His last breath, that He has entirely fulfilled all that His Father had given Him to do: *Consummatum est.*[4] This last cry of the Divine Victim upon the Cross corresponds to the *Ecce venio* of the Incarnation in the Virgin's bosom.

III

The offering that Christ made of Himself was a plenary, total and continuous offering, but it comprised different acts.

Adoration, first of all.

In the Holy Trinity, the Son belongs entirely to His Father, referring to Him, so to speak, all that He is. From the moment that the Word is made flesh, the Humanity that is united to Him is drawn into this ineffable current that bears the Son towards His Father. But as the Humanity is created and is inferior to the Divinity, this movement is translated by

---

1 Matth. xvi, 21–23; Marc. viii, 32–33.
2 "One jot, or one tittle shall not pass of the law, till all be fulfilled," Matth. v, 18.
3 Ibid. xxvi, 39, cf. Marc. xiv, 36; Luc. xxii, 42.
4 "It is consummated," Joan. xix, 30.

adoration. And this adoration is intense, perfect. From the instant the Humanity was joined to the Word, this Humanity, in Jesus, was lost in profound adoration, in self-annihilation, before the Divine Majesty of the Eternal Word Whose infinite perfections it contemplated through the Beatific Vision.

Then *thanksgiving.*

It is certain that of all the graces, of all the mercies God can grant, the greatest, the most eminent, is that which was given to the Humanity of Jesus. God chose it, predestinated it from among all others *prae consortibus tuis,* to be the Humanity of His Son; to unite it, in an incomparable union to His Word. This is a unique grace, surpassing all that the human mind can imagine as to the communication of the Divinity with the creature.

Thus the soul of Jesus filled, by this union, with the delights of the Divinity itself, overflows in thanksgiving. If at times we ourselves know not how to express the abundance of our gratitude to our Heavenly Father, what must have been the gratitude of the soul of Jesus for the ineffable grace given to it, for all the incomparable privileges which were to proceed from its union with the Word?

Expiation is likewise to be found.

The race wherefrom the Word takes a human nature so as to unite it to Himself, is a sinful, fallen race; the Word espoused a body made "in the likeness of sinful flesh," *in similitudinem carnis peccati.*[1]

Certainly sin never touched Him personally: *Tentatum autem per omnia pro similitudine, absque peccato.*[2] He is the Christ, that is to say the High Priest pre-eminently; "for it was fitting," says St. Paul, "that we should have such a high priest, holy, innocent, undefiled, separated from sinners, and made higher than the heavens."[3] But His Father laid upon Him the sins of all mankind: *Posuit in eo iniquitatem omnium nostrum.*[4] Jesus became, according to the energetic expression of St. Paul, "sin for us."[5] Thereby the offering that Jesus made of Himself to His Father, at the moment of His Incarnation, embraced the poverty of the manger,

---

1 Rom. viii, 3.
2 "But one tempted in all things like as we are, without sin," Hebr. iv, 15, cf. 11, 17.
3 Ibid. vii, 26.   4 Isa. liii, 6.   5 II Cor. v, 21.

the lowliness of the Hidden Life, the fatigues and conflicts of the Public Life, the terrors of the Agony, the ignominies of the Passion, the torments of a bitter Death: *Semetipsum exinanivit formam servi accipiens...humiliavit semetipsum, factus obediens usque ad mortem, mortem autem crucis.*[1] Although He was God, Christ did not eagerly cling to His equality with God; but He humbled Himself in taking, through the Incarnation, the condition of a created nature, in becoming like unto men; and in showing Himself under the aspect of a man, He further humbled Himself "becoming obedient...even to the death of the cross."

This death upon Calvary was an expiation of infinite value because Christ was God, but also because His abasements reached the utmost limit of humiliation. The dying Christ upon the Cross accepted to become for us "the reproach of men, and the outcast of the people": *Opprobrium hominum et abjectio plebis*[2]; and this unheard of abasement, into which He was to descend in order to expiate sin, was willed by the soul of Jesus from the moment of His Incarnation with all that was brought with it of humiliation, ignominy and suffering.

Finally, in this offering we find *impetration,* that is to say supplication.

The Gospel tells us nothing of Christ's prayer for us in the Incarnation, nor even during His public life, although it says that He passed whole nights in prayer: *Erat pernoctans in oratione Dei.*[3] But St. John has preserved the words of the prayer that Jesus made for His disciples and for us, at the Last Supper, at the moment of inaugurating His Passion and when about to complete His Sacrifice: it was the sacerdotal prayer of Jesus. The Gospel does not contain a more beautiful page. And can we doubt but that this prayer was the epitome and final echo of all those that Christ had addressed to His Father during His whole life?

"Father, the hour is come, glorify Thy Son, that Thy Son may glorify Thee. As Thou hast given Him power over all flesh, that He may give eternal life to all whom Thou hast given Him....I have manifested Thy name to the men whom Thou hast given Me....Now they have known that all things which Thou hast given Me, are from Thee....I pray for them...be-

---

1 "But emptied himself, taking the form of a servant....He humbled himself, becoming obedient unto death, even to the death of the cross," Philipp. ii, 7–8.
2 Ps. xxi, 7.   3 Luc. vi, 12.

cause they are Thine....Holy Father, keep them in Thy name whom Thou hast given me; that they may be one, as we also are....These things I speak in the world, that they may have my joy filled in themselves....I pray not that Thou shouldst take them out of the world, but that Thou shouldst keep them from evil....And for them do I sanctify myself, that they also may be sanctified in truth. And not for them only do I pray, but for them also who through their word shall believe in Me; that they all may be one, as Thou, Father, in Me, and I in Thee....Father, I will that where I am, they also whom Thou hast given Me may be with Me; that they may see My glory which Thou hast given Me, because Thou hast loved Me before the creation of the world."[1]

What a wonderful prayer! And rising up from what a Heart! From the Heart of Jesus, the supreme High Priest of all humanity, our Pontiff, when He is about to make Himself our Victim! Why then do we so often doubt Christ's power? Why are we discouraged, when Jesus, true God as well as true Man, offers such a prayer to His Father when He is on the point of glorifying Him with an infinite glory and immolating Himself for our sins?

O Christ Jesus, often repeat for us this prayer: Father, keep those whom Thou hast given Me from evil...that they may have My joy...that they may have it in its fullness...that they may share in My glory...that they also may be one in Us!...

IV

The prayer of Jesus has been granted; the immolation by which it was followed merited for the whole human race abundant graces of pardon, justification, union, life, joy and glory.

After saying that Christ was established supreme High Priest of the human race from the moment of His Incarnation, St. Paul immediately adds: "Who in the days of His flesh, with a strong cry and tears, offering up prayers and supplications to Him that was able to save Him from death, was heard for His reverence. And whereas He was the Son of God, He learned obedience by the things which He suffered; and being consum-

---

1 Joan. xvii.

mated, He became, to all that obey Him, the cause of eternal salvation."[1]

St. Paul also shows how our salvation proceeds from the oblation offered by Jesus at the moment of coming into this world; for this offering of Himself to the will of God, held in germ the immolation of Calvary: "In the which will, we are sanctified by the oblation of the body of Jesus Christ."[2]

So, as you see, every grace whatsoever, flows for us from the Cross: there is not one but is bought with the love and Blood of Jesus. The Priesthood of Christ makes Him our one Mediator Who is ever heard. This is why the Apostle exclaims in ardent conviction: "He that spared not even His own Son...how hath He not also, with Him, given us all things?" *Quomodo non etiam cum illo omnia nobis donavit?*[3] We are made so rich, says St. Paul again, that henceforward no grace is wanting to us: *Ita ut* NIHIL *nobis desit in* ULLA *gratia!*[4]

What absolute and unshaken confidence this revelation ought to give us! In Christ Jesus we find all, we possess all, and, if we will, in Him nothing is wanting to us: He is our Salvation, the source of all our perfection and of all our sanctification.

For so great is our Pontiff, so far-reaching His Priesthood that even now Christ fulfils this office of Mediator and continues His Sacrifice for our sanctification.

First of all He does this in Heaven.

It is there above all that the mystery is ineffable. The Eternal Priesthood of Christ Jesus contains hidden depths of which St. John and St. Paul give us glimpses, the one in his Apocalypse,[5] the other in the Epistle to the Hebrews.

St. Paul exalts the eternal Priesthood of Jesus in magnificent terms. "Jesus...now sitteth on the right hand of the throne of God."[6] We have in Him "a great High Priest that hath passed into the heavens."[7] Jesus "for that He continueth for ever, hath an everlasting priesthood...always living to make intercession for us...and made higher than the heavens."[8] "For Jesus is not entered into the holies made with hands, the patterns of the true: but into heaven itself, that He may appear now in the presence

---

1 Hebr. v, 7–9.   2 Ibid. x, 10.   3 Rom. vii, 32.   4 I Cor. i, 7.
5 Cf. v, 6–10.   6 Hebr. xii, 2.   7 Ibid. iv, 14.
8 Ibid. vii, 24–26.

of God for us."[1]

All these remarkable expressions show us that in heaven Christ Jesus eternally remains as High Priest, prolonging His oblation for us.

Doubtless, St. Paul does not forget that there is but one sacrifice of the Cross: UNA *enim oblatione, consummavit in sempiternum sanctificatos.*[2] There could not be any other; this sacrifice is unique and definitive.

But, he says, in the same way as each year in the Old Testament the high priest, after having offered the sacrifice in the first tabernacle of the Temple, entered alone with the blood of the victims into the second tabernacle, the Holy of Holies, and presenting himself before the Lord hence achieved his office of high priest,—so Christ, having offered His sacrifice upon earth, entered once for all by His own Blood, not into a tabernacle made by the hand of man, but into the sanctuary of the Divinity: *Per proprium sanguinem introivit semel in sancta...*[3] Hence He consummates in glory His divine office of Mediator: *Nunc autem semel in consummatione saeculorum, per hostiam suam apparuit.*[4]

What is it that Christ Jesus does in this sanctuary? What is His work?

He can no longer merit, it is true. The time of meriting ceased for Him at the moment He breathed forth His last breath upon the Cross; but the time of applying His merits to us ever endures.

And this is what our Lord does, He henceforward stands before the face of His Father to intercede for us: *Ut appareat* NUNC *vultui Dei pro nobis.*[5] There, "ever living," *semper vivens,* for "death shall no more have dominion over Him,"[6] He unceasingly offers to His Father for us His sacrifice already accomplished, but subsisting in His Person; He shows to His Father His Five Wounds of which He willed to keep the marks, those Wounds which are the solemn attestation and full pledge of His immolation upon the Cross. In the name of the Church of which He is the Head, He unites to His oblation our adoration and homage, our prayers and supplications, and our thanksgiving. We are constantly present in

---

1 Ibid. ix, 24.

2 "For by one oblation he hath perfected for ever them that are sanctified," Ibid. x, 14.

3 "By his own blood, He entered once into the Holies," Hebr. ix, 12.

4 "But now once, at the end of ages...he hath appeared for the sacrifice of himself," Ibid. 26.

5 Ibid. ix, 24.   6 Rom. vi, 9.

the thoughts of our compassionate High Priest, unceasingly He brings to bear for our sanctification His merits, His satisfactions, His Sacrifice.

Thus there is in Heaven, and will be until the end of time, a sacrifice celebrated for us by Christ in an eminent and sublime manner, but it is in perpetual continuity with His immolation upon the Cross: *Per hostiam suam apparuit.*

After having shown us something of the greatness and power of this Sacrifice, St. Paul gives us this exhortation: "Having therefore a great High Priest that hath passed into the heavens, Jesus, the Son of God, let us hold fast our confession." What confession? The confession of our faith in Jesus Christ, the supreme Mediator, faith in the infinite value of His merits, faith in the boundless extent of His Divine power with the Father.

The Apostle continues: "Let us go therefore with confidence, *Adeamus ergo cum fiducia,* to the throne of grace, that we may obtain mercy, and find grace in seasonable aid."[1]

Indeed what grace could be refused to us by this High Priest Who knows how to have compassion on our frailty, our infirmities, our sufferings, since, in order to be like unto us, He has experienced them all; this High Priest Who is so powerful, since being the Son of God, He deals with His Father as with His equal: VOLO *Pater*[2]; this High Priest Who wills to be united to us as, in the body, the head is united to the members? What graces of forgiveness, of perfection, of holiness may not be hoped for by a soul that truly seeks to remain united to Him by faith, confidence and love? Is He not the "High Priest of the good things to come"?[3] Is He not "able to do all things more abundantly than we desire or understand"?[4]

This is why, in all her worship, the Church, who better than anyone, knows her Bridegroom, addresses no prayer to the Heavenly Father, asks no grace, without marking her request with the sign of the cross, without invoking Jesus Christ, our Saviour and High Priest: *Per Dominum nostrum Jesum Christum.* This formula, in the Church's liturgy, is repeated daily and hourly. It is the ceaseless proclamation of Christ's universal mediation; but it is also the most explicit and most solemn confession of His Divinity, for the Church immediately adds: "Who liveth and reigneth with Thee in the unity of the Holy Spirit, world without end."

---

1 Hebr. iv, 16.   2 "Father, I will," Joan. xvii, 24.
3 Hebr. ix, 11.   4 Ephes. iii, 20.

V

In commenting, according to St. Paul, upon the work of Christ as Pontiff in Heaven, we have not exhausted the marvels of the priesthood of Jesus.

Heaven has its oblation, eminent and ineffable, continuous and altogether glorious. The Incarnate Word did not will to leave the earth without likewise bequeathing to it a sacrifice. This sacrifice is the Holy Mass which both recalls and reproduces, in a mystical manner, the immolation of Golgotha. As I have said, the Sacrifice of the Cross is the one and only Sacrifice; it suffices for all; but our Lord willed that it should be renewed in order to apply the fruit of it to souls. I will set forth this truth more in detail when we shall have to contemplate the mystery of the Eucharist. I would simply say here how our High Priest perpetuates His Sacrifice here below.

Christ chooses certain men to whom He gives a real participation in His priesthood. These are the priests whom the bishop anoints on the day of their ordination. Extending his hands over the head of the one whom he is about to consecrate, the bishop invokes the Holy Spirit, beseeching Him to descend upon that soul. At that moment the words that the Angel spoke to Mary might be repeated to the priest: *Spiritus Sanctus superveniet in te.*[1] The Holy Spirit envelops him, as it were, and effects within him so close a union and resemblance with Christ Jesus that he is, like Christ, a priest for all eternity. Christian tradition calls the priest "another Christ": he is, like Him, chosen to be, in the name of Christ, a mediator between heaven and earth. This is a supernatural reality. When the priest offers the Sacrifice of the Mass, which reproduces the Sacrifice of Calvary, he is identified with Christ. He does not say: "This is Christ's Body, this is Christ's Blood"; if he said this, there would not be sacrifice; but he says: "This is My Body, this is My Blood."

From this moment, the priest consecrated to God by the Holy Spirit becomes, like Christ, a pontiff and mediator between men and God, or rather, it is Christ's one mediation prolonged here below throughout the ages, by the ministry of priests. In the name of the faithful, the priest offers to God the Eucharistic Sacrifice upon the altar; from the altar he brings to the people the Holy Victim, the Bread of Life, and therewith

---

1 "The Holy Spirit shall come upon thee," Luc. i, 35.

every gift and every grace.

The altar is, on earth, the centre of the religion of Jesus, as Calvary is the summit of His life. All the mysteries of the terrestrial existence of Jesus converge, as I have said, towards His immolation upon the Cross; from the Cross all the states of His glorious life derive their splendour.

This is why the Church does not commemorate nor celebrate any of the mysteries of Jesus without offering the Holy Sacrifice of the Mass. All the public worship organised by the Church gravitates around the altar; all the lections, prayers, praises and homage of which the whole is called the Divine Office, and in which the Church exalts the Mysteries of her Divine Bridegroom and retraces them under the eyes of her children, were regulated by her only so as to enshrine the Eucharistic Sacrifice.

Whatever then be the mystery of Jesus that we celebrate, the best way to participate in it and to dispose ourselves to make the fruit of it our own is, after having meditated upon and contemplated it, to assist with faith and love at the Sacrifice of the Mass and to unite ourselves, by Holy Communion, to the Divine Victim, immolated for us upon the altar.

In the Life of Blessed Marie d'Oignies it is related that our Lord was accustomed, on the occasion of the different feasts, to show Himself to her in the Blessed Sacrament under a form in harmony with the mystery being celebrated.[1]

We have no need to envy this favour. By Holy Communion, Christ Jesus does not only show Himself to the soul; He comes within us, He communicates Himself entirely to us; He comes with His humanity as a compassionate High Priest, knowing our frailty, and with the virtue of His divinity which is able to raise us up to Himself at His Father's right hand. He comes within us, in order to pray to the Father in us, with us; to offer Him Divine homage and unite thereto our supplications; but above all to bring forth in our inmost souls, by His Spirit, the fruit of each of His mysteries.

You will have noticed that the thanksgiving which follows the holy Oblation and Communion, (Postcommunion) takes a different aspect according to the different mysteries. What does this indicate if not that

---

1 Father Faber, The Blessed Sacrament.

by Communion Christ wishes to make arise within us the thoughts and sentiments that He experienced when living the mystery that is being celebrated that day, and consequently wishes to apply to us the special fruits and graces proper to this mystery. This is what the Church asks at the Postcommunion on the feast of the Rosary wherein she honours the Mother of the Incarnate Word as united with all the mysteries of her Son Jesus. What does the Church beseech in the collect of the Mass? In her prayer to God, she brings forward the plea that "His only begotten Son has by His Life, Death and Resurrection merited for us the reward of eternal salvation." Then she asks "that in honouring these mysteries, we may imitate what they contain and obtain what they promise": *Concede... ut haec mysteria recolentes, et imitemur quod continent et quod promittunt assequamur.* A like thought inspires the Postcommunion of the feast: "Grant, o Lord, that we may obtain the virtues of the mysteries which we celebrate": *Ut mysteriorum quae recolimus virtus percipiatur.*

Thus, little by little, our identification with Jesus is realised: *Hoc enim sentite in vobis quod et in Christo Jesu.*[1] Is not that the very formula of our eternal predestination: *Conformes fieri imaginis Filii?*[2]

Such are the essential traits of the Person and the work of Christ Jesus. The Eternal Word—made Flesh for us—becomes, by His mysteries and His Sacrifice, our High Priest and our Mediator. A Mediator Who knows our needs, because He has been a man like unto us; an all-powerful Mediator, because He is God with the Father and the Holy Spirit; a Mediator Whose mediation is unceasing, in heaven by His eternal oblation, on earth by the Eucharistic Sacrifice.

And it is for us that Christ accomplishes this work: *pro nobis.* Christ saves us by His Sacrifice only in order to associate us with His glory.

O Lord, who shall be able to reveal how ineffable are the designs of Thy wisdom? Who shall celebrate the greatness of the gift Thou dost make to us? Who shall be able to render Thee thanksgiving worthy of it?

---

1 "For let this mind be in you, which was also in Christ Jesus," Philipp. ii, 5.
2 "To be made conformable to the image of his Son," Rom. viii, 29.

II
THE MYSTERIES OF CHRIST

DIVINE PREPARATION

(Time of Advent)

SUMMARY.—Why God willed to prolong the preparation for the Incarnation during so many centuries.—I. How Divine Wisdom, in recalling and specifying, by the voice of the prophets, the first promise of a Redeemer, prepared the souls of the just of the Old Covenant for the coming of the God-Man on earth.—II. St. John Baptist, the Forerunner of the Incarnate Word, sums up and surpasses all the prophets.—III. Although we live in "the fulness of time," the Church, under the guidance of the Holy Spirit, each year recalls the memory of these divine preparations. Threefold reason for this supernatural economy.—IV. Dispositions that we ought to have in order that Christ's coming may produce within our souls the plenitude of its fruits: purity of heart, humility, confidence and holy desires. To unite our aspirations to those of the Blessed Virgin Mary, Mother of Jesus.

ALL God's blessings that come down upon us have their source in the election that He made of our souls, throughout eternity, to make them "holy and unspotted in His sight."[1] In this divine decree so full of love is contained our adoptive predestination as children of God and all the favours thereto attached.

St. Paul says that it was through the grace of Jesus Christ, sent by God in the fulness of time, that this adoption was granted to us: *At ubi venit plenitudo temporis, misit Deus Filium suum factum ex muliere...ut adoptionem filiorum reciperemus.*[2]

---

1 Ephes. i, 4.
2 "But when the fulness of time was come, God sent his Son, made of a woman...that

God's eternal design of sending His own Son into the world to redeem the human race, broken and bruised by sin, and of restoring to it the children's inheritance and heavenly beatitude, this is the masterpiece of His wisdom and love. The views of God are not our views; all His thoughts are higher than ours as the heavens are higher than the earth; but it is especially in the work of the Incarnation and Redemption that the sublimity and greatness of the Divine ways shine forth. This work is so high, so closely united to the very life of the Most Holy Trinity, that it remained throughout long ages hidden in the depths of the divine secrets: *Sacramentum absconditum a saeculis in Deo.*[1]

As you know, God willed to prepare the human race for the revelation of this mystery during some thousands of years. Why did God chose to delay the coming of His Son amongst us for so many centuries? Why such a long period? We cannot, mere creatures as we are, fathom the depths of the reasons why God accomplishes His works under such or such conditions. He is the Infinitely Sovereign Being Who has no need of a counsellor.[2] But as He is likewise Wisdom itself that reacheth "from end to end mightily, and ordereth all things sweetly"[3] we may yet humbly seek to learn something of the appropriateness of the conditions of His mysteries.

It was fitting that men, having sinned by pride,—*Eritis sicut dii*[4]— should be obliged, by the prolonged experience of their weakness and the extent of their misery, to confess the absolute need they had of a Redeemer and to aspire after His coming with all the fibres of their nature.[5]

The idea of this future Redeemer fills all the Ancient Law; all the symbols, all the rites and sacrifices prefigure Him: *Haec omnia in figura contigebant illis*[6]; all desires converge towards Him. According to the beautiful expression of an author of the first centuries, the Old Testament bore Christ in its loins: *Lex Christo gravida erat.*[7] The religion of Israel was the expectation of the Messias.

Moreover, the greatness of the mystery of the Incarnation and the majesty of the Redeemer demanded that the revelation of Him to the

---

we might receive the adoption of sons," Gal. iv, 4–5.
1 Ephes. iii, 9.   2 Cf. Rom. xi, 34.
3 Sap. viii, 1; cf. Great antiphon *O Sapientia,* 17th Dec.
4 "You shall be as Gods," Gen. iii, 5.   5 Cf. S. Thom. iii, q. i, a. 5.
6 I Cor. x, 11.   7 Appendix to the works of St Augustine, Sermon cxcvi.

human race should only be made by degrees. Man, on the morrow of his fall, was neither worthy of receiving nor capable of welcoming the full manifestation of the God-Man. It was by a dispensation at once full of wisdom and mercy, that God disclosed this ineffable mystery only little by little, by the mouth of the prophets; when the human race should be sufficiently prepared, the Word, so many times announced, so often promised, would Himself appear here below to instruct us: *Multifariam multisque modis olim loquens patribus in prophetis...novissime locutus est nobis in Filio.*[1]

I will therefore point out some traits of these divine preparations for the Incarnation. We shall herein see with what wisdom God disposed the human race to receive salvation; it will be for us an occasion of returning fervent thanksgiving to "the Father of mercies"[2] for having caused us to live in "the fulness of time" which still endures and wherein He grants to men the inestimable gift of His Son.

I

You know that it was just after the sin of our first parents, in the very cradle of the already rebellious human race, that God began to reveal the mystery of the Incarnation. Adam and Eve, prostrate before the Creator, in the shame and despair of their fall, dare not raise their eyes to heaven. And behold, even before pronouncing the sentence of their banishment from the terrestrial paradise, God speaks to them the first words of forgiveness and hope.

Instead of being cursed and driven out for ever from the presence of their God, as were the rebel angels, they were to have a Redeemer; He it was Who should break the power won over them by the devil. And as their fall began by the prevarication of the woman, it was to be by the son of a woman that this redemption should be wrought: *Inimicitias ponam inter te et mulierem, et semen tuum et semen illius: ipsa conteret caput tuum.*[3]

---

1 "God, who at sundry times and in divers manners, spoke in times past to the fathers by the prophets...in these days, hath spoken to us by his Son," Hebr. i, 1–2.

2 II Cor. i, 3.

3 "I will put enmities between thee and the woman, and thy seed and her seed: she shall crush thy head," Gen. iii, 15.

This is what is called the "Protogospel," the first word of salvation. It is the first promise of redemption, the dawn of divine mercy to the sinful earth, the first ray of that light which was one day to vivify the world, the first manifestation of the mystery hidden in God from all eternity.

After this promise, all the religion of the human race, and, later, all the religion of the chosen people is concentrated around this "seed of the woman," this *semen mulieris* which is to deliver mankind.

Throughout the years as they pass by, and as the centuries advance, God makes His promise more precise; He repeats it with more solemnity. He assures the patriarchs, Abraham, Isaac and Jacob that it is from their race that the blessed seed shall come forth: *Et benedicentur in semine tuo omnes gentes terrae*[1]; to the dying Jacob, He shows that it is in the tribe of Juda that shall arise the One Who is to come, the desire of all peoples: *Donec veniat qui mittendus est, et ipse erit exspectatio gentium.*[2]

And now behold how the nations, forgetful of the primeval revelations, sink insensibly into error. God then chooses for Himself a people that shall be the guardian of His promises. To this people, throughout the centuries, God will recall His promises, renew them, render them clearer and more abundant: this will be the era of the prophets.

If you listen to the sacred oracles of the prophets of Israel, you will remark that the traits whereby God depicts the Person of the future Messias and specifies the character of His mission, are at times so opposed that it seems as if they could not be encountered in the same person. Sometimes the prophets attribute to the Redeemer prerogatives such as could only befit a God, sometimes, they predict for this Messias a sum of humiliations, contradictions, infirmities and sufferings with which the last of men could scarcely deserve to be overwhelmed.

You will constantly be coming across this striking contrast.

For example, there is David, the king dear to God's Heart; the Lord swore to confirm his race for ever: the Messias was to be of the royal family

---

1 "And in thy seed shall all the nations of the earth be blessed," Gen. xxii, 18; cf. Gal. iii, 16.

2 "Until he comes that is to be sent, and he shall be the expectation of nations," Ibid. xlix, 10.

of David. God reveals Him to David as "his son and his Lord"[1]: his son by reason of the humanity that He was one day to take from a Virgin of his family, his Lord, by reason of His divinity. David contemplates Him "in the brightness of the saints," begotten eternally before the rising of the day star; a supreme High Priest "according to the order of Melchisedech,"[2] anointed to reign over us because of His "truth and meekness and justice"[3]; in a word, the Son of God Himself to Whom all nations are to be given as an inheritance: *Dominus dixit ad me: Filius meus es tu, ego hodie genui te: postula a me et dabo tibi gentes haereditatem tuam.*[4] St. Paul says to the Hebrews that these are prerogatives wherein a God alone can glory.[5]

But David contemplates too the pierced Hands and Feet, the garments divided among the soldiers who cast lots upon His coat[6]; He beholds Him given gall and vinegar to drink.[7] Then again see the Divine attributes: He will not be touched by the corruption of the tomb, but, victorious over death, He will sit down at the right hand of God.[8]

This contrast is not less striking in Isaias, the great Seer; so precise and full of detail is he that he might be called the fifth Evangelist. One would say that he was relating accomplished facts rather than foretelling future events. The prophet, transported up to heaven, says of the Messias: "Who shall declare His generation": *Generationem ejus quis enarrabit?*[9] He gives Him names such as no man has ever borne: "His name shall be called, Wonderful, Counsellor, God the mighty, the Father of the world to come, the Prince of Peace."[10] Born of a Virgin, "His name shall be called *Emmanuel,*"[11] God with us. Isaias describes Him "come forth as brightness," and "lighted as a lamp"[12]; he sees Him opening the eyes of the blind and unstopping the ears of the deaf, loosing the tongue of the dumb and making the lame to walk[13]; he shows Him as "a Leader and a Master to the Gentiles"[14]; he sees the idols utterly destroyed before Him[15]; and he hears God promise by oath that before this Saviour "every knee shall be bowed" and every tongue shall confess His power.[16]

And yet this Redeemer, Whose glory the prophet thus exalts, is to be

---

1 Ps. cix, 1; cf. Matth. xxii, 41–45.

2 Ps. cix, 3–4.   3 Ibid. xliv, 5.   4 Ibid. ii, 7–8.   5 Hebr. i, 13.

6 Ps. xxi, 17–19.   7 Ibid. lxviii, 22.   8 Ibid. xv, 10.

9 Isa. liii, 8.   10 Ibid. ix, 6.   11 vii, 14.   12 lxii, 1.

13 xxxv, 5–6.   14 lv, 4.   15 ii, 14–18.   16 Isa. xlv, 24.

overwhelmed with such sufferings, and such humiliations are to crush Him that He will be looked upon as "the most abject of men...as it were a leper, and as one struck by God and afflicted;...led as a sheep to the slaughter...reputed with the wicked...because the Lord was pleased to bruise Him in infirmity."[1]

In most of the prophets you can see this opposition of traits with which they describe the greatness and the abasements, the power and the weakness, the sufferings and the glory of the Messias. You will see with what condescending wisdom God prepared the minds of His people to receive the revelation of the ineffable mystery of a God-Man, at once the supreme Lord Whom all nations adore, and the Victim for the sins of the world.

The economy of the Divine mercy is, as you know, wholly based upon faith; faith is the foundation and the root of all justification. Without this faith, even the bodily presence of Christ Jesus would be unable to produce the fulness of its effect in souls.

Now faith is communicated to us by the Holy Spirit's inward action which accompanies the statement of the divine truths made by prophets and preachers: *Fides ex auditu.*[2]

In so often recalling the ancient promises, in revealing, little by little through the mouths of the prophets, the traits of the Redeemer Who was to come, God willed to produce in the hearts of the just of the Old Covenant the requisite conditions whereby the coming of the Messias should be salutary for them. Besides the more the just of the Old Covenant were filled with faith and confidence in the promises announced by their prophets, the more they would burn with the desire to see them realized, and the more they would be ready to receive the abundance of graces that the Saviour was to bring to the world. It was thus that the Virgin Mary, Zachary and Elisabeth, Simeon, Anna, and the other faithful souls who lived at the time of Christ's coming, at once recognised Him and were inundated with His favours.

You see how God was pleased to prepare mankind for the coming of His Son upon earth. St. Peter could truly say to the Jews that they were

---

1 Ibid. liii, 3 seq.   2 "Faith cometh by hearing," Rom. x, 17.

"the children of the prophets."[1] St. Paul could write to the Hebrews that before God spoke to them in person, He "at sundry times, and in divers manners, spoke in times past to the fathers by the prophets": *Multifariam multisque modis.*[2]

The faithful Jews were, moreover, constantly in expectation of the Messias. Their faith discerned in the person of this Redeemer one sent by God, a King, a God Who was to put an end to their miseries, and deliver them from the burden of their sins. They have but one longing: "Send, O Lord, Him Who is to come." They have but one desire: to behold with their eyes the countenance of the Saviour of Israel. The promised Messias was the object towards which converged all the hopes, all the worship, all the religion of the Old Covenant. All the Old Testament is a prolonged Advent, the prayers of which are summed up in this prayer of Isaias: *Emitte Agnum, Domine, Dominatorem terrae.*[3] "Send forth, O Lord, the Lamb, the Ruler of the earth." "Drop down dew, ye heavens, from above, and let the clouds rain the just": *Rorate caeli desuper, et nubes pluant justum*; "Let the earth be opened, and bud forth a Saviour": *Aperiatur terra et germinet Salvatorem.*[4]

II

We have marvelled at the profound ways of Divine Wisdom in the preparations for the mystery of the coming of the God-Man. And yet this is not all.

While by a succession of marvels, Eternal Wisdom keeps intact, among the chosen people, the ancient promises, unceasingly confirmed and developed by prophecy, while even the successive captivities of the Jewish people, who at times became unfaithful, are made to serve to spread abroad the knowledge of these promises even among the nations of the Gentiles, Wisdom likewise directs the destinies of these nations.

You know how during this long period of several centuries God, Who holds the hearts of kings in His hand,[5] and Whose power equals His wisdom, establishes and destroys the most vast empires one after the other. To the empire of Ninive, reaching as far as Egypt, follows that of Babylon;

---

1 Act. iii, 25.   2 Hebr. i, 1.   3 Isa. xvi, 1.   4 Ibid. xlv, 8.
5 Cf. Prov. xxi, 1.

then, as Isaias had foretold, God "calls His servant Cyrus,"[1] king of the Persians, and places the sceptre of Nabuchodonosor within his hands; after Cyrus, He makes Alexander the master of the nations, until He gives the world's empire to Rome, an empire of which the unity and peace will serve the mysterious designs of the spread of the Gospel.

Now the "fulness of time"[2] has come: the world is flooded with sin and error; man at length realizes the weakness in which pride kept him; all peoples stretch out their arms towards this Liberator so often promised, so long awaited: *Et veniet desideratus cunctis gentibus.*[3]

When this fulness of time comes, God crowns all His preparations by the sending of St. John the Baptist, the last of the prophets, one whom He will render greater than Abraham, greater than Moses, greater than all, as He Himself declares: *Non surrexit inter natos mulierum major Joanne Baptista.*[4] It is Jesus Christ Who says this. Why is it?

Because God wills to make St. John the Baptist His herald above all others, the very Precursor of His beloved Son: *Propheta altissimi vocaberis....*[5] So as to enhance still further the glory of this Son Whom He is about to introduce into the world, after having so many times promised Him. God is pleased to reveal the dignity of the Precursor who is to bear witness that the Light and the Truth have at length appeared upon earth: *Ut testimonium perhiberet de lumine.*[6]

God wills him to be great because his mission is great, because he has been chosen to precede so closely the One Who is to come. In God's sight, the greatness of the saints is measured according to their nearness to His Son Jesus.

See how He exalts the Precursor in order to show yet once more, by the excellence of this last Prophet, what is the dignity of His Word. He chooses him from an especially saintly race; an angel announces his birth, gives the name that he is to bear and indicates the extent and greatness of his mission. God sanctifies him in his mother's womb; He works such

---

1 Isa. xlv, 1.   2 Gal. iv, 4.
3 "And the desired of all nations shall come," Agg. ii, 8.
4 "There hath not risen among them that are born of women a greater than John the Baptist," Matth. xi, 11; cf. Luc. vii, 28.
5 "Thou shalt be called the prophet of the Highest," Luc. i, 76.   6 Joan. i, 8.

miracles around his cradle that the fortunate witnesses of these marvels wonderingly ask each other: "What an one, think ye, shall this child be?"[1]

Later on, John's holiness appears so great that the Jews come to ask him if he is the looked-for Christ. But he, forestalled as he is with divine favours, protests that he is but "the voice of one crying in the wilderness, make straight the way of the Lord."[2]

The other prophets only saw the Messias afar off; he points Him out in person and in terms so clear that all sincere hearts understand them: "Behold the Lamb of God" behold the One Who is the object of all the desires of the human race, because He "taketh away the sins of the world": *Ecce Agnus Dei.*[3] You do not yet know Him, although He is in the midst of you: *Medius vestrum stetit quem vos nescitis*; He is greater than I, for He was before me; He is so great that I am not even worthy to loose the latchet of His shoe; so great, that "I saw the Spirit coming down, as a dove from heaven, and He remained upon Him...and I saw, and I gave testimony that this is the Son of God."[4] What more has he yet to say? "He that cometh from above, is above all. And what He hath seen and heard, that He testifieth;... He Whom God hath sent, speaketh the words of God; for God doth not give the Spirit by measure. The Father loveth the Son; and He hath given all things into His hand. He that believed in the Son, hath life everlasting; but He that believeth not the Son, shall not see life; but the wrath of God abideth on Him."[5]

These are the last words of the Precursor. By them he achieves his work of preparing souls to receive the Messias. Indeed, when the Incarnate Word, Who alone can speak the words from on high because He is ever *in sinu Patris,*[6] begins His public mission as the Saviour, John will disappear; he will no longer bear testimony to the Truth save with the shedding of his blood.

The Christ, Whom he announced, has come at last; He is that Light unto which John bore testimony, and all those who believe in that Light have life everlasting. It is to Him alone to Whom it must be said: "Lord, to Whom shall we go? Thou hast the words of eternal Life."[7]

---

1 Luc. i, 66.
4 Ibid. i, 26–27, 32 ad 34.
7 Ibid. vi, 69.

2 Joan. i, 23.
5 Ibid. iii, 31 seq.

3 Ibid. i, 29.
6 Ibid. i, 18.

III

We ourselves have the happiness of believing in this Light "which enlighteneth every man that cometh into this world."[1] We live, moreover, in the
blessed "fulness of time"; we are not deprived, like the Patriarchs, of seeing
the reign of the Messias. If we are not of those who looked upon Christ
in person and heard His words, those who beheld Him going about doing good everywhere, we have the signal happiness of belonging to those
nations of which David sang that they should be Christ's inheritance.

And yet the Holy Spirit, Who governs the Church and is the first author of our sanctification, wills that each year the Church should consecrate four weeks in recalling to memory the long duration of the divine
preparations, and that she should strive to place our souls in the interior
dispositions in which the faithful Jews lived whilst awaiting the coming
of the Messias.

You will perhaps immediately say: This preparation for Christ's coming,
these longings, these expectations, all that was excellent for those living
under the Old Covenant; but now that Christ has come, why this attitude
which does not seem to be in accordance with the truth?

The reason for it is manifold.

To begin with, God wills to be praised and blessed in all His works.

All, indeed, are marked with His infinite wisdom: *Omnia in sapientia
fecisti*[2]; all are admirable both in their preparation and their realisation.
This is above all true of those which have the glory of His Son for their
direct end, for it is the will of the Father that this Son should be for ever
exalted.[3] God wills that we should admire His works, that we should return
thanks to Him for having thus prepared, with so much wisdom and power,
the kingdom of His Son amongst us: we enter into the divine thoughts
when we recollect the prophecies and promises of the Old Covenant.

God wills also that in these preparations we should find confirmation
of our faith.

If God gave so many different and precise signs, such numerous and
clear prophecies, it was in order that we might recognise as His Son the

---

1 Ibid. i, 9.   2 Ps. ciii, 24.   3 Cf. Joan. xii, 23.

One Who has fulfilled them in His person.

See how in the Gospel Our Lord Himself invited His disciples to this contemplation. *Scrutamini Scripturas,* "Search the Scriptures,"[1] He said to them—"the Scriptures," which then consisted of the books of the Old Testament:—search them, you will find them full of My name; for "all things must need be fulfilled which are written...in the prophets, and in the psalms, concerning Me": *Necesse est impleri omnia quae scripta sunt in prophetis et psalmis de me.*[2] Again we hear Him on the day after His Resurrection explaining to the disciples of Emmaus, so as to strengthen their faith and dissipate their sadness, all that concerned Him throughout the Scriptures, "beginning at Moses and all the prophets": *Et incipiens a Moyse et omnibus prophetis, interpretabatur illis in omnibus scripturis quae de ipso erant.*[3]

When, therefore, we read the prophecies that the Church proposes to us during Advent, let us in the fulness of our faith, say like the first disciples of Jesus: "We have found Him of Whom...the prophets did write."[4] Let us repeat to Christ Jesus Himself: Thou art truly the One Who is to come; we believe it, and we adore Thee Who to save the world didst deign to become incarnate and to be born of a Virgin: *Tu ad liberandum suscepturus hominem non horruisti virginis uterum.*[5]

This profession of faith is extremely pleasing to God. Never let us weary of reiterating it. Our Lord will be able to say to us as to His Apostles: "The Father Himself loveth you, because you...have believed that I came forth from God."[6]

Finally, there is a third reason, one deeper and more intimate. Christ did not come only for the inhabitants of Judea, His contemporaries, but for us all, for all men of every nation and century. Do we not sing in the *Credo*: *Propter* NOS *et propter* NOSTRAM *salutem descendit de caelis*? The "fulness of time" is not yet ended; it will endure as long as there shall be souls to save.

But it is to the Church that Christ, since His Ascension, has left the mission of bringing Him forth in souls. "My little children," said St. Paul, the Apostle of Christ Jesus among nations, "of whom I am in labour

---

1 Joan. v, 39.   2 Luc. xxiv, 44.   3 Ibid. 27.
4 Joan. i, 45.   5 Hymn Te Deum.   6 Joan. xvi, 21.

again, until Christ be formed in you."¹ The Church, guided by the Holy
Spirit, Who is the Spirit of Jesus, labours at this work by making us contemplate every year the mystery of her Divine Bridegroom. For, as I said
at the beginning of these conferences, all Christ's mysteries are living
mysteries; they are not merely historical realities of which we recall the
remembrance, but the celebration of each mystery brings a proper grace,
a special virtue intended to make us share in the life and states of Christ
Whose members we are.

Now, at Christmas, the Church celebrates the Birthday of her Divine
Bridegroom: *tamquam sponsus procedens de thalamo suo*²; and she wills to
prepare us, by the weeks of Advent, for the grace of the coming of Christ
within us. It is an altogether inward, mysterious advent which is wrought
in faith, but brings forth much fruit.

Christ is already within us by the sanctifying grace which makes us
children of God. That is true, but the Church wills that this grace should
be renewed, that we should live a new life more exempt from sin and imperfection, more free from all attachment to ourselves and creatures: *Ut
nos Unigeniti tui nova per carnem nativitas liberet quos sub peccati jugo vetusta servitus tenet.*³ She wills above all to make us understand that Christ,
in exchange for the humanity which He takes from us, will make us partakers of His Divinity, and will take a more complete, more entire, more
perfect possession of us. This will be like the grace of a new divine birth
in us: *Ut tua gratia largiente, per haec sacrosancta commercia, in illius inveniamur forma, in quo tecum est nostra substantia.*⁴

It is this grace of a new birth that the Incarnate Word merited for us
by His Birth at Bethlehem.

However, we should remember that if Christ was born, and lived and
died for us all: *Pro omnibus mortuus est Christus,*⁵ the application of His
merits and the distribution of His graces are made according to the measure of the dispositions of each soul.

1 Gal. iv, 19.
2 "And he as a bridegroom coming out of his bridechamber," Ps. xviii, 6.
3 "That the new birth of thine Only-begotten Son in the flesh might set us free, who are
held by the old slavery under the yoke of sin," Collect for the Feast of Christmas.
4 "That by Thy generous grace, through this sacred interchange, we may be found in
likeness to Him, in whom our nature is united to Thee." Secret for the Midnight Mass.
5 II Cor. v, 15.

Consequently we shall only share in the abundant graces that Christ's Nativity should bring to us in proportion to our dispositions. The Church knows this perfectly, and therefore she neglects nothing that can produce in our souls that inward attitude required by the coming of Christ within us. Not only does the Church say by the mouth of the Precursor: "Prepare ye the way of the Lord," for "He is near," *prope est Dominus*[1]; but she herself, like a Bride attentive to the wishes of her Bridegroom, like a mother careful for her children's good, suggests to us and gives us the means of making this necessary preparation. She carries us back as it were under the Old Covenant so that we may appropriate to ourselves, although in an altogether supernatural sense, the thoughts and feelings of the faithful who longed for the coming of the Messias.

If we allow ourselves to be guided by her, our dispositions will be perfect, and the solemnity of the Birth of Jesus will produce within us all its fruits of grace, of light and life.

IV

What are these dispositions? They can be summed up in four.

Purity of heart. Who was the best disposed for the coming of the Word to earth? Without any doubt, it was the Blessed Virgin Mary. At the moment when the Word came into this world, He found Mary's heart perfectly prepared, and capable of receiving the Divine riches which He willed to heap upon her. What were the dispositions of her soul?

Assuredly she possessed all the most perfect dispositions; but there is one which shines with particular brilliancy: that is her virginal purity. Mary is a virgin. Her virginity is so precious to her that it is her first thought when the angel proposes to her the mystery of the divine maternity.

Not only is she a virgin, but her soul is stainless. The liturgy reveals to us that God's special design in granting to Mary the unique privilege of the Immaculate Conception was to prepare for His Word a dwelling place worthy of Him: *Deus qui per immaculatam Virginis conceptionem dignum Filio tuo* HABITACULUM PRAEPARASTI.[2] Mary was to be

---

1 Invitatory of Matins for the 3rd Sunday in Advent.
2 "O God, who by the Immaculate Conception of the Virgin didst prepare a worthy

the Mother of God; and this eminent dignity required not only that she should be a virgin, but that her purity should surpass that of the angels and be a reflection of the holy splendour wherein the Father begets His Son: *In splendoribus sanctorum.*[1] God is holy, thrice holy; the angels, the archangels, the seraphim hymn His infinite purity: *Sanctus, Sanctus, Sanctus.*[2] The bosom of God, of an infinite purity, is the dwelling-place of the Only-begotten Son of God. The Word is ever *in sinu Patris;* but, in becoming Incarnate, He also willed, in ineffable condescension, to be *in sinu Virginis Matris.* It was necessary that the tabernacle that Our Lady offered Him should recall, by its incomparable purity, the indefectible brightness of the light eternal where as God He ever dwells: *Christi sinus erat in Deo Patre divinitas, in Maria Matre virginitas.*[3]

Thus the first disposition that attracts Christ is a great purity. But as for ourselves, we are sinners. We cannot offer to the Word, to Christ Jesus, that immaculate purity which He so much loves. What is there that will take the place of it in us? It is *humility*.

God possesses in His besom the Son of His delight, but upon this bosom He also presses another son,—the prodigal son. Our Lord Himself tells us so. When, after having fallen so low, the prodigal returns to his father, he humbles himself to the dust, he confesses himself to be miserable and unworthy; and, at once, without a word or reproach, the father receives him into the bosom of his compassion: *Misericordia motus.*[4]

Do not let us forget that the Word, the Son, only wills what His Father wills. If He becomes Incarnate and appears upon earth, it is in order to seek sinners and bring them back to His Father: *Non veni vocare justos sed peccatores.*[5] This is so true that later Our Lord will often be found, to the great scandal of the Pharisees, in the company of sinners; He will allow Magdalen to kiss His Feet and bathe them with her tears.

We have not the Virgin Mary's purity, but let us at least ask for the humility of Magdalen, a contrite and penitent love. O Christ Jesus, I am not

---

dwelling place for Thy Son," Collect for the Feast of the Immaculate Conception.
1 Ps. cix, 3.   2 Isa. vi, 3.
3 "For the bosom of Christ was divinity in God the Father, virginity in His mother Mary," *Sermo* xii, in *Append. Operum S. Ambrosii.*
4 Luc. xv, 20.
5 "I am not come to call the just, but sinners," Matth. ix, 13; Marc. ii, 7; Luc. v, 32.

worthy that Thou shouldst come to me; my heart will not be for Thee a dwelling-place of purity, misery dwells there. But I acknowledge, I avow this misery; come and relieve me of it. O Thou Who art mercy itself; come and deliver me, O Thou Who art almighty: *Veni ad liberandum nos, Domine Deus virtutum!*

A like prayer, joined to the spirit of penance, draws Christ to us because the humility that abases itself in its nothingness thereby renders homage to the goodness and power of Jesus: *Et eum, qui venit ad me, non ejiciam foras.*[1]

The sight of our infirmity ought not, however, to discourage us; far from that. The more we feel our weakness, so much the more ought we to open our soul to *confidence,* because salvation comes only from Christ.

Pusillanimes, confortamini et nolite timere, ecce Deus noster veniet et salvabit nos.[2] "Ye faint-hearted, take courage and fear not: behold God, *our* God, will come and will save us." See what confidence the Jews had in the Messias. For them, the Messias was everything; in Him were summed up all the aspirations of Israel, all the wishes of the people, all the hopes of the race; to contemplate Him was all their ambition; to see His reign established would have fulfilled all their desires. And how confident and impatient the desires of the Jews became: "Come, O Lord and do not delay."[3] "Shew us Thy face, and we shall be saved."[4]

Oh, if we who possess Christ Jesus, true God as well as true Man, really understood what the Sacred Humanity of Jesus is, we should have an unshaken confidence in it; for in His Humanity are all the treasures of knowledge and of wisdom; in it the Divinity itself dwells. This God-Man, Who comes to us is the Emmanuel, He is "God with us," He is our Elder Brother. The Word has espoused our nature, He has taken upon Himself our infirmities so as to know by experience what suffering is. He comes to us to make us partakers of His divine life; all the graces for which we can hope He possesses in their fulness in order to grant them to us.

The promises that, by the voice of the prophets, God made to His people so as to arouse in them the desire of the Messias, are magnificent.

1 "And him that cometh to me, I will not cast out," Joan. vi, 37.
2 Communion for the 3rd Sunday of Advent, cf. Isa. xxxv, 4.
3 Alleluia for the 4th Sunday of Advent.   4 Ps. lxxix, 4.

But many of the Jews understood these promises in the material and gross sense of a temporal and political kingdom. The good things promised to the just who awaited the Saviour were but the figure of the supernatural riches which we find in Christ; we have the divine reality, that is to say the grace of Jesus. The liturgy for Advent constantly speaks to us of mercy, redemption, salvation, deliverance, light, abundance, joy, peace. "Behold the Saviour cometh; on the day of His Birth, the world shall be flooded with light"[1]; "exult then with joy, O Jerusalem, for the Saviour shall appear"[2]; "peace shall fill our earth when He shews Himself."[3] Christ brings with Him all the blessings that can be lavished upon a soul: *Cum illo omnia nobis donavit.*[4]

Let then our hearts yield themselves up to an absolute confidence in Him Who is to come. It is to render ourselves very pleasing to the Father to believe that His Son Jesus can do everything for the sanctification of our souls. Thereby we declare that Jesus is equal to Him, and that the Father "hath given all things into His hand."[5] Such confidence cannot be mistaken. In the Mass for the first Sunday in Advent, the Church thrice gives us the firm assurance of this. "None of them that wait on Thee shall be confounded": *Qui te exspectant non confundentur.*

This confidence will above all be expressed in the *ardent desire* to see Christ come to reign more fully within us. *Adveniat regnum tuum!* The liturgy gives us the formula of these desires. At the same time that she places the prophecies, especially those of Isaias, under our eyes, and causes us to read them again, the Church puts upon our lips the aspirations and the longings of the just men of old time. She wills to see us prepared for Christ's coming within our souls in the same way as God willed that the Jews should be disposed to receive His Son. "Come, O Lord, come and forgive the sins of Thy people."[6] "Shew us, O Lord, Thy mercy, and grant us Thy salvation."[7] "Come and deliver us, Lord, God Almighty! Raise up Thy power, and come."[8]

---

1 Antiphon for Lauds of the 1st Sunday in Advent.
2 Antiphon for Lauds for the 3rd Sunday in Advent.
3 Response for Matins for the 3rd Sunday in Advent.
4 Rom. viii, 32.   5 Joan. iii, 35.
6 Alleluia for the 4th Sunday of Advent.
7 Offertory for the 2nd Sunday of Advent.
8 Collect for the 4th Sunday of Advent.

The Church makes us constantly repeat these aspirations. Let us make them our own, let us appropriate them to ourselves with faith, and Christ Jesus will enrich us with His graces.

Doubtless, as you know, God is master of His gifts; He is sovereignly free, and none may hold Him to account for His preferences. But, in the ordinary ways of His Providence, He hears the supplications of the humble who bring their needs before Him: *Desiderium pauperum exaudivit Dominus.*[1] Christ gives Himself to us according to the measure of the desire that we have to receive Him, and the capacity of the soul is increased by the desires that it expresses: *Dilata os tuum, et implebo illud.*[2]

If then we want the celebration of Christ's Nativity to procure great glory for the Holy Trinity, and to be a consolation for the Heart of the Incarnate Word, a source of abundant graces for the Church and for ourselves, let us strive to purify our hearts, let us preserve a humility full of confidence, and above all let us enlarge our souls by the breadth and vehemence of our desires.

Let us ask our Lady to make us share in the holy aspirations that animated her during those blessed days that preceded the Birth of Jesus.

The Church has willed—and what is more just?—that the liturgy of Advent should be full of the thought of the Blessed Virgin; she continually makes us sing the divine fruitfulness of a Virgin, a wonderful fruitfulnes that throws nature into astonishment: *Tu quae genuisti, natura mirante, tuum sanctum genitorem, virgo prius ac posterius.*[3]

Mary's virginal bosom was an immaculate sanctuary whence arose the most pure incense of her adoration and homage.

There is something veritably ineffable about the inward life of the Virgin during these days. She lived in an intimate union with the Infant-God Whom she bore in her bosom. The soul of Jesus was, by the Beatific Vision, plunged in the Divine light; this light radiated upon His Mother. In the sight of the angels, Mary truly appeared as "a woman clothed with

---

1 "The Lord hath heard the desire of the poor," Ps. ix, 17.
2 "Open thy mouth wide, and I will fill it," Ps. lxxx, 11.
3 "You bore your holy Creator, to the wonderment of nature, virgin after as before," Antiphon *Alma Redemptoris Mater.*

the sun": *Mulier amicta sole,*[1] all irradiated with heavenly brightness, all shining with the light of her Son. Her feelings indeed reached the high level of her faith. She summed up in herself all the aspirations, all the impulses, all the longings of humanity awaiting the world's Saviour and God, at the same time going far beyond them and giving them a value that they had never hitherto attained. What holy intensity in her desires! What unshaken assurance in confidence! What fervour in her love!...

This humble Virgin is the Queen of Patriarchs; since she is of their holy lineage, and since the Child Whom she is about to bring into the world is the Son Who resumes in His person all the magnificence of the ancient promises.

She is, too, the Queen of Prophets, since she is to bring forth the Word by Whom all the prophets spoke, since her Son is to fulfil all prophecy and announce to all people the good news of redemption.[2]

Let us humbly ask her to make us enter into her dispositions. She will hear our prayer; we shall have the immense joy of seeing Christ born anew within our hearts by the communication of a more abundant grace, and we shall be enabled, like the Virgin, although in a lesser measure, to understand the truth of these words of St. John: "The Word was God...and the Word was made flesh, and dwelt among us, and we saw His glory... full of grace and truth.... And of His fulness we have all received, and grace for grace."[3]

---

1 Apoc. xii, 1.   2 Luc. iv, 19.   3 Joan. i, 14 ad 16.

O ADMIRABILE COMMERCIUM!

(Christmastide)

SUMMARY.—The mystery of the Incarnation is a wonderful exchange between divinity and humanity.—I. The Eternal Word asks of us a human nature in order to unite it to Himself by a personal union: *Creator... animatum corpus sumens.*—II. In becoming Incarnate, the Word brings us, in return, a share in His Divinity: *Largitus est nobis suam deitatem.*—III. This exchange appears still more wonderful when we consider the manner in which it is wrought. The Incarnation renders God visible so that we may hear and imitate Him.—IV. It renders God passible, capable of expiating our sins by His sufferings and of healing us by His humiliations.—V. We are to take our part in this exchange by faith: those who receive the Word-made-flesh by believing in Him have "power to be made the sons of God."

THE coming of the Son of God upon earth is so great an event that God willed to prepare the way for it during centuries. He made rites and sacrifices, figures and symbols, all converge towards Christ; He foretold Him, announced Him by the mouth of the prophets who succeeded one another from generation to generation.

And now it is the very Son of God Who comes to instruct us: *Multifariam multisque modis olim Deus loquens patribus...novissime locutus est nobis in Filio.*[1] For Christ is not only born for the Jews of Judea who lived in His time. It is for us all, for all mankind, that He came down from Heaven: *Propter nos et propter nostram salutem descendit de caelis.* He wills to distribute to every soul the grace that He merited by His Nativity.

---

[1] "God, who, at sundry times and in divers manners, spoke in times past to the fathers... In these days, hath spoken to us by his Son," Hebr. i, 1, 2.

This is why the Church, guided by the Holy Spirit, appropriates to herself, in order to place them upon our lips and with them to fill our hearts, the longings of the patriarchs, the aspirations of the just of ancient times, and the desires of the Chosen People. She wills to prepare us for Christ's coming, as if this Nativity was about to be renewed before our eyes.

See how when she commemorates the coming of her Divine Bridegroom upon earth, she displays the splendour of her solemnities, and makes her altars brilliant with lights to celebrate the Birth of the "Prince of Peace,"[1] the "Sun of Justice,"[2] Who rises in the midst of our darkness to enlighten "every man that cometh into this world."[3] She grants her priests the privilege, almost unique in the year, of thrice offering the Holy Sacrifice of the Mass.

These feasts are magnificent, they are likewise full of charm. The Church evokes the remembrance of the Angels singing in the sky the glory of the new-born Babe; of the Shepherds who come to adore at the manger; of the Magi who hasten from the East to offer Him their adorations and rich presents.

And yet, like every feast here below, this solemnity, even with the prolongation of its octave, is ephemeral: it passes by. Is it for the feast of a day, howsoever splendid it may be, that the Church requires such a long preparation from us? Certainly not! Why then? Because she knows that the contemplation of this mystery contains a special and choice grace for our souls.

I said at the beginning of these conferences that each one of Christ's mysteries constitutes not only a historical fact which takes place in time, but contains a grace proper to itself wherewith our souls are to be nourished so as to live thereby.

Now what is the intimate grace of the mystery of the Nativity? What is the grace for the reception of which the Church takes so much care to dispose us? What is the fruit that we ought to gather from the contemplation of the Christ Child?

The Church herself indicates this at the first Mass, that of midnight. After having offered the bread and wine which, in a few moments, are to be changed, by the consecration, into the Body and Blood of Jesus Christ,

---

1 Isa. ix, 6.   2 Malach. iv, 2.   3 Joan. c, 5, 9.

she sums up her desires in this prayer: "Grant, O Lord, that the oblation which in we offer to-day's festival may be acceptable unto Thee, and, by Thy grace, through this most sacred and holy intercourse, may we be found like unto Him in Whom is our substance united to Thee."[1]

We ask to be partakers of that divinity to which our humanity is united. It is like an exchange. God, in becoming incarnate, takes our human nature and gives us, in return, a participation in His Divine nature.

This thought, so concise in its form, is more explicitly expressed in the Secret of the second Mass: "Grant, O Lord, that our offerings may be conformed to the mysteries of this day's Nativity, that as He Who is born as man is also God made manifest, so this earthly substance (which He unites to Himself) may confer upon us that which is divine."[2]

To be made partakers of the Divinity to which our humanity was united in the Person of Christ, and to receive this Divine gift through this humanity itself,—such is the grace attached to the celebration of to-day's mystery.

Our offerings will be "conformed to the mysteries of this day's Nativity," according to the words of the above quoted Secret, if—by the contemplation of the Divine work at Bethlehem and the reception of the Eucharistic Sacrament,—we participate in the eternal life that Christ wills to communicate to us by His Humanity.

"O admirable exchange," we shall sing on the octave day, "the Creator of the human race, taking upon Himself a body and a soul, has vouchsafed to be born of a Virgin, and, appearing here below as man, has made us partakers of His Divinity": *O admirabile commercium!* CREATOR *generis humani,* ANIMATUM CORPUS SUMENS, *de virgine nasci dignatus est; et*

---

1 *Accepta tibi sit, Domine, quaesumus, hodiernae festivitatis oblatio: ut tua gratia largiente, per haec sacrosancta commercia, in illius inveniamur forma, in quo tecum est nostra substantia.* Secret of the Midnight Mass. The word *forma* is here taken in the sense of "nature," "condition," natura, as in the text of S. Paul: *Christus cum in forma Dei esset... exinanivit semetipsum formam servi accipiens et habitu inventus ut homo* (Christ, who being in the form of God...emptied himself, taking the form of a servant, in habit found as a man). Philipp. ii, 5–7.

2 *Munera nostra, quaesumus, Domine, nativitatis hodiernae mysteriis apta proveniant, ut sicut homo genitus idem refulsit et Deus, sic nobis haec terrena substantia conferat quod divinum est.* Secret of the Mass at Break of Day.

procedens homo sine semine, LARGITUS EST NOBIS SUAM DEITATEM.[1]

Let us, therefore, stay for a few moments to admire, with the Church, this exchange between the creature and the Creator between heaven and earth, an exchange upon which all the mystery of the Nativity is based. Let us consider what are the acts and the matter of it;—under what form it is wrought;—we will afterwards see what fruits are to be derived from it for us;—and to what it engages us.

I

Let us transport ourselves to the stable-cave at Bethlehem; let us behold the Child lying upon the straw. What is He in the sight of the profane, in the sight of an inhabitant of the little city who might happen to come there after the Birth of Jesus?

Only a new-born Babe to Whom a woman of Nazareth had given birth; only a son of Adam like unto us, for His parents have Him inscribed upon the register of enrolment; the details of His genealogy can be followed. There He lies upon the straw, a weak Babe Whose life is sustained by a little milk. Many Jews saw nothing more in Him than this. Later on you will hear His compatriots, astonished at His wisdom, ask themselves where He could have learnt it, for, in their eyes, He had never been anything but "the son of a carpenter": *Nonne hic est fabri filius?...*[2]

But to the eyes of faith, a life higher than the human life animates this Child: He possesses Divine life. What does faith, indeed, tell us on this subject? What revelation does it give us?

Faith tells us that this Child is God's own Son. He is the Word, the Second Person of the Adorable Trinity; He is the Son Who receives Divine life from His Father, by an ineffable communication: *Sicut Pater habet vitam in semetipso, sic dedit et Filio habere vitam in semetipso.*[3] He possesses the Divine nature, with all its infinite perfections. In the heavenly splendours, *in splendoribus sanctorum,*[4] God begets this Son by an eternal generation.

---

1 Antiphon of the Octave of Christmas.
2 Matth. xiii, 55; cf. Marc. vi, 3; Luc. iv, 22.
3 "For as the Father hath life in himself, so he hath given to the Son also to have life in himself," Joan. v, 26.   4 Ps. cix, 3.

It is to this Divine Sonship in the bosom of the Father that our adoration turns first of all; it is this Sonship that we extol in the midnight Mass. At day-break, the Holy Sacrifice will celebrate the Nativity of Christ according to the flesh, His birth, at Bethlehem, of the Virgin Mary; finally, the third Mass will be in honour of Christ's coming into our souls.

The Mass of the night, all enveloped with mystery, begins with these solemn words: *Dominus dixit ad me: Filius meus es tu, ego hodie genui te.*[1] This cry that escapes from the soul of Christ united to the Person of the Word, reveals to earth for the first time that which the heavens hear from all eternity: "The Lord hath said to Me: Thou art My Son: this day have I begotten Thee." "This day" is first of all the day of eternity, a day without dawn or decline.

The Heavenly Father now contemplates His Incarnate Son. The Word, although made man, nevertheless remains God. Become the Son of man, He is still the Son of God. The first glance that falls upon Christ, the first love wherewith He is surrounded, is the glance, the love of His Father. *Diliget me, Pater.*[2] What contemplation and what love! Christ is the Only-begotten Son of the Father; therein lies His essential glory. He is equal to and "consubstantial with the Father, God of God, Light of Light...by Whom all things were made," "and without Him was made nothing that was made." It is of this Son that these words were spoken: "Thou in the beginning, O Lord, didst found the earth, and the works of Thy hands are the heavens. They shall perish, but Thou shalt continue; and they shall all grow old as a garment; and as a vesture shalt Thou change them, and they shall be changed; but Thou art the selfsame, and Thy years shall not fail!"[3]

And this "Word was made Flesh": *Et verbum caro factum est.*

Let us adore this Word become Incarnate for us: *Christus natus est nobis, venite adoremus....*[4] A God takes our humanity: conceived by the mysterious operation of the Holy Ghost in Mary's womb, Christ is born of the most pure substance of the blood of the Virgin, and the life that He has from her makes Him like unto us! *Creator generis humani de virgine nasci dignatus est, et procedens homo sine semine.*[5]

---

1 Introit of the Mass of Midnight.   2 Joan. xv, 9.
3 Epistle for the Mass of Christmas Day.   4 Invitatory for Christmas Matins.
5 "The Creator of mankind deigned to be born of a virgin, and becoming man without man's seed."

This is what faith tells us: this Child is the Incarnate Word of God; He is the Creator of the human race become man. *Creator generis humani*; if He needs a little milk to nourish Him, it is by His hand that the birds of heaven are fed.

> *Parvoque lacte pastus est*
> *Per quem nec ales esurit.*[1]

Let us contemplate this Infant lying in the manger. His eyes are closed, He sleeps, He does not manifest outwardly what He is. In appearance, He is only like all other infants, and yet, being God, being the Eternal Word, He, at this moment, is judging the souls that appear before Him. "He lies upon straw, and as God, He sustains the universe and reigns in heaven": *Jacet in praesepio et in caelis regnat.*[2] This Child, just beginning to grow, *Puer crescebat...et proficiebat aetate,*[3] is the Eternal Whose divine nature knows no change: *Tu idem ipse es, et anni tui non deficient.*[4] He Who is born in time is likewise He Who is before all time; He Who manifests Himself to the shepherds of Bethlehem is He Who, out of nothing, created the nations that "are before Him as if they had no being at all"[5]:

> *Palamque fit pastoribus*
> *Pastor creator omnium.*[6]

To the eyes of faith there are two lives in this Babe; two lives indissolubly united in an ineffable manner, for the Human Nature belongs to the Word in such wise that there is but a single Person, that of the Word, Who sustains the Human Nature by His own Divine existence.

Undoubtedly, this human nature is perfect: *perfectus homo*[7]: nothing of that which belongs to its essence is lacking to Him. This Babe has a soul like to ours; He has faculties:—intelligence, will, imagination, sensibility—like ours. He is truly one of our own race Whose existence will be revealed, during thirty three years, as authentically human. Sin, alone,

---

1 Hymn of Christmas Lauds.
2 12th response at Matins on the Sunday of the Octave of Christmas.
3 Luc. ii, 40, 52.
4 "But thou art always the selfsame, and thy years shall not fail," Ps. ci, 28.
5 Isa. xl, 17.   6 Hymn of Christmas Lauds.
7 Creed attributed to S. Athanasius.

will be unknown to Him. *Debuit per omnia fratribus similari¹...absque peccato.*² Perfect in itself, this human nature will keep its own activity, its native splendour. Between these two lives of Christ—the Divine, which He ever possesses by His eternal birth in the bosom of the Father; the human which He has begun to possess by His Incarnation in the bosom of a Virgin—there is neither mingling nor confusion. The Word, in becoming man, remains what He was; that which He was not, He has taken from our race; but the divine in Him does not absorb the human, the human does not lessen the divine. The union is such, as I have often said, that there is however but a single Person—the Divine Person,—and that the human nature belongs to the Word, is the Word's own humanity: *Mirabile mysterium declaratur hodie: innovantur naturae, Deus homo factus est; id quod fuit permansit et quod non erat assumpsit, non commixtionem passus neque divisionem.*³

II

This then, if I may so express myself, is one of the acts of the contract. God takes our nature so as to unite it to Himself in a personal union.

What is the other act? What is God going to give us in return? Not that He owes us anything: *Bonorum meorum non eges.*⁴ But as He does all things with wisdom, He could not take upon Himself our nature without a motive worthy of Him.

What the Word Incarnate gives in return to humanity is an incomprehensible gift; it is a participation, real and intimate, in His Divine nature: *Largitus est nobis suam deitatem.* In exchange for the humanity which He takes, the Incarnate Word gives us a share in His Divinity; He makes us partakers of His Divine Nature. And thus is accomplished the most wonderful exchange which could be made.

Doubtless, as you know, this participation had already been offered

---

1 "It behoved him in all things to be made like unto his brethren," Hebr. ii, 17.
2 "...without sin," Ibid. iv, 15.
3 "A wondrous mystery is declared today: natures are renewed, God is made man; that which he was, he remains, and that which he was not, he has assumed, suffering neither mixture nor division," Antiphon of Lauds in the Octave of Christmas.
4 "Thou has no need of my goods," Ps. xv, 2.

and given, from the creation, to Adam, the first man. The gift of grace, with all its splendid train of privileges, made Adam like to God. But the sin of the first man, the head of the human race, destroyed and rendered this ineffable participation impossible on the part of the creature.

It is to restore this participation that the Word becomes Incarnate; it is to reopen to us the way to heaven that God is made man. For this Child, being God's own Son, has Divine life, like His Father, with His Father. In this Child "dwelleth all the fulness of the Godhead corporeally"[1]; in Him are laid up all the treasures of the divinity.[2] But He does not possess them for Himself alone. He infinitely desires to communicate to us the Divine life that He Himself is: *Ego sum vita.*[3] It is for this that He comes: *Ego veni* UT *vitam habeant.*[4] It is for us that a Child is born; it is to us that a Son is given: *Puer natus est* NOBIS *et Filius datus est nobis.*[5] In making us share in His condition of Son, He will make us children of God. "When the fulness of time was come, God sent His Son, made of a woman...that we might receive the adoption of sons."[6] What Christ is by nature, that is to say the Son of God, we are to be by grace; the Incarnate Word, the Son of God made man is to become the author of our divine generation: *Natus hodie Salvator mundi* DIVINAE NOBIS GENERA-TIONIS *est auctor.*[7] So that, although He be the Only-begotten Son, He will become the First-born of many brethren: UT *sit* IPSE PRIMOGEN-ITUS *in multis fratribus.*[8]

Such are the two acts of the wonderful "bargain" that God makes with us: He takes our nature in order to communicate to us His divinity; He takes a human life so as to make us partakers of His divine life: He is made man so as to make us gods: *Factus est Deus homo, ut homo fieret Deus.*[9] And His human Birth becomes the means of our birth to the divine life.

In us likewise there will be henceforth two lives. The one, natural, which we have by our birth according to the flesh, but which, in God's sight, is not only without merit but, before baptism, is stained in consequence of original sin; which makes us enemies of God, worthy of His

---

1 Col. ii, 9.   2 Cf. Ibid. 3.   3 Joan. xiv, 6.
4 Ibid. x, 10.   5 Introit of the Mass of the day.   6 Gal. iv, 4–5.
7 Postcommunion of the Mass of Christmas Day.   8 Rom. viii, 29.
9 Sermon attributed to S. Augustine, number cxxviii in the appendix to his works.

wrath; we are born *filii irae.*[1] The other life, supernatural, infinitely above the rights and exigencies of our nature. It is this life that God communicates to us by His grace, since the Incarnate Word merited it for us.

God begets us to this life by His Word and the infusion of His Spirit, in the baptismal font: *Genuit nos Verbo veritatis....*[2] *Per lavacrum regenerationis et renovationis Spiritus Sancti*[3]; it is a new life that is superadded to our natural life, surpassing and crowning it; *In Christo nova creatura.*[4] It makes us children of God, brothers and sisters of Jesus Christ, worthy of one day partaking of His beatitude and glory.

Of these two lives, in us as in Christ, it is the divine that ought to dominate, although in the Child Christ it is not as yet manifested, and in us it remains ever veiled under the outward appearance of our ordinary existence. It is the divine life of grace that ought to rule and govern, and make agreeable to our Lord, all our natural activity, thus deified in its root.

Oh! if the contemplation of the Birth of Jesus and participation in this mystery by the reception of the Bread of Life would bring us to free ourselves, once and for all, from everything that destroys and lessens the divine life within us; from sin, wherefrom Christ comes to deliver us: *Cujus Nativitas humanam repulit vetustatem*[5]; from all infidelity and all attachment to creatures; from the irregulated care for passing things: *Abnegantes saecularia desideria*[6]; from the trifling preoccupations of our vain self love!...

If we could thus be brought to give ourselves entirely to God, according to the promises of our baptism when we were born to the divine life; to yield ourselves up to the accomplishment of His will and good pleasure, as did the Incarnate Word in entering into this world: *Ecce venio...ut faciam Deus voluntatem tuam*[7]; to abound in those good works which make us pleasing to God: *Populum acceptabilem, sectatorem bonorum operum*![8]

---

1 Ephes. ii, 3.   2 Jac. i, 18.

3 "...by the laver of regeneration and renovation of the Holy Ghost," Tit. iii, 5. Epistle for the Mass of Day-break.

4 "In Christ a new creature," II Cor. v, 17; Gal. vi, 15.

5 "Whose birth revived mankind grown old," Postcommunion for the Mass of Day-break.

6 "Denying worldly desires," Tit. ii, 12. Epistle for the midnight Mass.

7 "I come...that I should do thy will, O God," Hebr. x, 7.

8 Tit. ii, 14. Epistle for the midnight Mass.

Then the divine life brought to us by Jesus would meet with no more obstacles, and would freely expand for the glory of our Heavenly Father; then "we who are bathed in the new light of the Incarnate Word should shew forth in our deeds what by faith shineth in our minds"[1]; then, "our offerings would befit the mysteries of this day's Nativity." *Munera nostra nativitatis hodiernae mysteriis apta proveniant.*[2]

III

What further renders this exchange "admirable" is the manner in which it is effected, the form wherein it is accomplished. How is it accomplished? How does this Child, Who is the Incarnate Word, make us partakers of His divine life? By His Humanity. The humanity that the Word takes from us is to serve Him as the instrument for communicating His divine life to us; and this for two reasons wherein eternal wisdom infinitely shines out; the humanity renders God visible; it renders God passible.

It renders Him *visible.*

The Church, using the words of St. Paul, celebrates with delight this "appearing" of God amongst us: *Apparuit gratia Dei Salvatoris nostri omnibus hominibus*[3]: "The grace of God our Saviour hath appeared to all men." *Apparuit benignitas et humanitas Salvatoris nostri Dei*[4]: "The goodness and kindness of God our Saviour hath appeared."

Lux fulgebit hodie super nos, quia natus est nobis Dominus[5]: "a light shall shine upon us this day: for our Lord is born to us"; *Verbum caro factum est et habitavit in nobis*: "The Word was made flesh, and dwelt among us."

The Incarnate Word brings about this marvel: men have seen God Himself abiding in the midst of them.

St. John loves to dwell upon this side of the mystery. "That which was from the beginning, which we have heard, which we have seen with our

---

1 *Da nobis quaesumus omnipotens Deus; ut qui nova incarnati Verbi tui luce perfundimur, hoc in nostro resplendeat opere, quod per fidem fulget in mente.* Collect for the Mass at Day-break.
2 Secret for the Mass at Day-break.
3 Tit. ii, 11. Epistle for the midnight Mass.
4 Tit. iii, 4. Epistle for the Mass at Day-break.
5 Introit of the Mass at Day-break.

eyes, which we have looked upon, and our hands have handled of the Word of life. For the life was manifested; and we have seen and do bear witness and declare unto you the Life Eternal which was with the Father, and hath appeared in us. That which we have seen and have heard, we declare unto you that...your joy may be full."[1]

What joy indeed, to see God manifesting Himself to us, not in the dazzling splendour of His omnipotence, nor in the unspeakable glory of His sovereignty, but under the veil of humble, poor, weak humanity, which we can see and touch!

We might have been afraid of the dreadful majesty of God: the Israelites fell on their faces to the ground, full of terror and fear, when God spoke to Moses upon Sinai, in the midst of lightnings. We are drawn by the charms of a God become a Babe. The Babe in the Crib seems to say to us: "You are afraid of God? You are wrong": *Qui videt me, videt et Patrem.*[2] Do not heed your imagination, do not form yourselves a God from the deductions of philosophy, nor ask of science to make My perfections known to you. The true Almighty God is the God that I am and reveal; the true God is I Who come to you in poverty, humility and infancy, but Who will one day give My life for you: I am "the brightness of [the Father's] glory, and the figure of His substance,"[3] His Only-begotten Son, God as He is; in Me you shall learn to know His perfections, His wisdom and His goodness, His love towards men and His mercy in regard to sinners: *Illuxit in cordibus nostris...in facie Christi Jesu.*[4] Come unto Me, for, God as I am, I have willed to be a man like you, and I do not reject those who draw near to Me with confidence: *Sicut homo genitus idem refulsit et Deus.*[5]

Why did God thus deign to render Himself visible?

First of all so as to instruct us: *Apparuit erudiens nos.* It is indeed God Who will henceforth speak to us by His own Son: *Locutus est nobis in Filio*[6]; we have but to listen to this beloved Son in order to know what God wills of us. The Heavenly Father Himself tells us so: *Hic est Filius meus*

---

1 I Joan. i, 1–4.
2 "He that seeth me seeth the Father also," Joan. xiv, 9.   3 Hebr. i, 3.
4 "He hath shined in our hearts...in the face of Christ Jesus," II Cor. iv, 6.
5 "He, though born a man, showed himself also God."   6 Hebr. i, 2.

dilectus: ipsum audite[1]; and Jesus delights in repeating to us that His doctrine is that of His Father: *Mea doctrina non est mea, sed ejus qui misit me.*[2]

Next the Word renders Himself visible to our sight so as to become the Example that we are to follow.

We have only to watch this Child grow, only to contemplate Him living in the midst of us, living, like us as man, in order to know how we ought to live in the sight of God, as children of God: for all that He does will be pleasing to His Father: *Quae placita sunt ei, facio semper.*[3]

Being the Truth Who has come to teach us, He will point out the way by His example; if we live in His light, if we follow this way, we shall have life: *Ego sum via, et veritas et vita.*[4] Thus, in knowing God manifested in the midst of us, we shall be drawn by Him to the love of invisible things: *Ut dum* VISIBILITER *Deum cognoscimus,* PER HUNC *in invisibilium amorem rapiamur.*[5]

IV

The humanity of Christ renders God visible, and above all—and it is in this that Divine Wisdom is shown to be "admirable"—it renders God passible.

Sin which destroyed the divine life within us demands a satisfaction, an expiation without which it would be impossible for divine life to be restored to us. Being a mere creature, man cannot give this satisfaction for an offence of infinite malice, and, on the other hand, the Divinity can neither suffer nor expiate. God cannot communicate His life to us unless sin be blotted out; by an immutable decree of Divine Wisdom, sin can only be blotted out if it be expiated in an adequate manner. How is this problem to be solved?

The Incarnation gives us the answer. Consider the Babe of Bethlehem. He is the Word made flesh. The humanity that the Word makes His own is passible; it is this humanity which will suffer, will expiate. These sufferings, these expiations will belong, however, to the Word, as this humanity itself does; they will take from the Divine Person an infinite

---

1 Matth. xvii, 5.
2 "My doctrine is not mine, but his that sent me," Joan. vii, 16.   3 Ibid. viii, 29.
4 "I am the way, and the truth, and the life," Ibid. xiv, 6.
5 Preface for Christmas.

value which will suffice to redeem the world, to destroy sin, to make grace superabound in souls like an impetuous and fructifying river: *Fluminus impetus laetificat civitatem Dei.*[1]

O admirable exchange! Do not let us stay to wonder by what other means God might have brought it about, but let us contemplate the way wherein He has done so. The word asks of us a human nature to find in it wherewith to suffer, to expiate, to merit, to heap graces upon us. It is through the flesh that man turns away from God: it is in becoming flesh that God delivers man:

> *Beatus auctor saeculi*
> *Servile corpus induit*
> *Ut carne carnem liberans*
> *Ne perderet quos condidit.*[2]

The flesh that the Word of God takes upon Himself, is to become the instrument of salvation for all flesh. *O admirabile commercium!*

Doubtless, as you know, it was necessary to await the immolation of Calvary for the expiation to be complete; but, as St. Paul teaches us, it was from the first moment of His Incarnation that Christ accepted to accomplish His Father's will and to offer Himself as Victim for the human race: *Ideo ingrediens mundum dicit: Hostiam et oblationem noluisti:* CORPUS *autem aptasti mihi....Et tune dixit: Ecce venio...ut faciam Deus voluntatem tuam.*[3] It is by this oblation that Christ begins to sanctify us: *In qua voluntate sanctificati sumus.*[4] It is from the Crib that He inaugurates this life of suffering such as He willed to live for our salvation, this life of which the term is at Golgotha, and that, in destroying sin, is to restore to us the friendship of His Father. The Crib is certainly only the first stage, but it radically contains all the others.

This is why, in the Christmas solemnities, the Church attributes our salvation to the temporal Birth itself of the Son of God. "Grant, we be-

---

1 "The stream of the river maketh the city of God joyful," Ps. xlv, 5.

2 "The blessed author of the age / put on a servant's body / so that freeing flesh by flesh / he might not lose that which he created." Hymn for Lauds at Christmas.

3 "Wherefore, when he cometh into the world he saith: Sacrifice and oblation thou wouldst not: but a body thou hast fitted to me....Then said I: Behold I come...that I should do thy will, O God," Hebr. x, 5, 7; cf. Ps. xxxix, 8.

4 Hebr. x, 10.

seech Thee, Almighty God, that the new Birth of Thine Only-begotten Son in the flesh may deliver us who are held captive by the old bondage under the yoke of sin."[1] This is why, from that moment, "deliverance, redemption, salvation, eternal life," will be spoken of constantly. It is by His Humanity that Christ, High Priest and Mediator, binds us to God; but it is at Bethlehem that He appears to us in this Humanity.

See, too, how from the moment of His Birth, He fulfils His mission. What is it that causes us to lose divine life?

It is *pride*. Because they believed that they would be like unto God, having the knowledge of good and evil, Adam and Eve lost, for themselves and for their race, the friendship of God. Christ, the new Adam, redeems us, brings us back to God, by the humility of His Incarnation. Although He was God, He annihilated Himself in taking the condition of the creature, in making Himself like unto men; He manifested Himself as man according to all appearances.[2] What a humiliation was that! Later, it is true, the Church will exalt to the highest heavens His dazzling glory as the conqueror over sin and death; but now, Christ knows only self-abasement and weakness. When our gaze rests upon this Little Child, Who is in no way distinguished from others, when we think that He is God, and that in Him are hidden all the treasures of wisdom and of knowledge, we feel our souls deeply moved, and our vain pride is confounded in the face of such abasement.

And what besides pride? Our *refusal to obey*. See what an example of wonderful obedience the Son of God gives. With the simplicity of little children, He yields Himself up into the hands of His parents; He allows Himself to be touched, taken up and carried about; and all His Childhood, all His Boyhood and Youth are summed up in the Gospel in those few words which tell how He was subject to Mary and Joseph: *Et erat subditus illis.*[3]

And next there is our covetousness "the concupiscence of the eyes,"[4] all that appears, glitters, fascinates and seduces; the essential inanity of the passing trifles that we prefer to God. The Word is made flesh; but He is born in poverty and abjection. *Propter nos egenus factus est cum esset*

---

1 *Concede quaesumus omnipotens Deus, ut non Unigeniti tui nova per carnem nativitus liberet, quos sub, peccati jugo vetusta servitus tenet.* Collect for the Mass of Christmas Day.
2 Philipp. ii, 6–7.   3 Cf. Luc. ii, 51.   4 I Joan. ii, 16.

dives.[1] "Being rich, He became poor." Although He is "the King of ages,"[2] although He is the One Who drew all creation out of nothing by a word, and has only to open His hand to fill "with blessing every living creature,"[3] He is not born in a palace; His Mother, finding no room in the inn, had to take refuge in a stable cave: the Son of God, Eternal Wisdom, willed to be born in destitution and laid upon straw.

If with faith and love we contemplate the Child Jesus in His Crib, we shall find in Him the Divine Example of many virtues; if we know how to lend the ear of our hearts to what He says to us, we shall learn many things; if we reflect upon the circumstances of His Birth, we shall see how the Humanity serves the Word as the instrument to instruct us, but likewise to raise us, to quicken us, to make us pleasing to His Father, to detach us from passing things, to lift us up even to Himself.

"Divinity is clad in our mortal flesh...and because God humbles Himself to live a human life, man is raised towards divine things": *Dum divinitas defectum nostrae carnes suscepit, humanum genus lumen, quod amiserat, recepit. Unde enim Deus humana patitur, inde homo ad divina sublevatur.*[4]

V

Thus from whatever side our faith contemplates this exchange, and whatever be the details of it that we examine, it appears admirable to us.

Is not this child-bearing of a virgin indeed admirable: *Natus ineffabiliter ex virgine?*[5] "A young Maiden has brought forth the King Whose name is Eternal: to the honour of virginity she unites the joys of motherhood; before her, the like was never seen, nor shall it ever be so again."[6] "Daughters of Jerusalem, why do you admire me? This mystery that you

---

1 II Cor. viii, 9.   2 I Tim. i, 17.   3 Ps. cxliv, 16.
4 "When divinity took up our weak flesh, the human race recovered the light which it had lost. For from God suffering as man, man is raised to the divine." S. Gregory, Homil. i, in Evangel.
5 Antiphon for the Octave of Christmas.
6 *Genuit puerpera Regem, cui nomen aeternum, et gaudia matris habens cum virginitatis honore, nec primam similem visa est, nec habere sequentem.* Antiphon for Lauds at Christmas.

behold in me is truly divine."[1]

Admirable is this indissoluble union, that is yet without confusion, of the divinity with the humanity in the one Person of the Word: *Mirabile mysterium: innovantur naturae.* Admirable is this exchange, by the contrasts of its realisation: God gives us a share in His divinity, but the humanity that He takes from us in order to communicate His divine life to us is a suffering humanity, "acquainted with infirmity," *homo sciens infirmitatem,*[2] that will undergo death and, by death, will restore life to us.

Admirable is this exchange in its source which is none other than God's infinite love for us. *Sic Deus dilexit mundum ut Filium suum Unigenitum daret.*[3] "God so loved the world as to give His Only-begotten Son." Let us, then, yield up our souls to joy and sing with the Church: *Parvulus natus est nobis et filius* DATUS *est* NOBIS.[4] And how is He given? "In the likeness of sinful flesh." This is why the love that thus gives Him to us in our passible humanity, in order to expiate sin, is a measureless love: *Propter* NIMIAM *caritatem suam, qua dilexit nos Deus, misit Filium suum in similitudinem carnis peccati.*[5]

Admirable, finally, in its fruits and effects. By this exchange, God again gives us His friendship, He restores to us the right of entering into possession of the eternal inheritance; He looks anew upon humanity with love and complacency.

Therefore, joy is one of the most marked characteristics of the celebration of this mystery. The Church constantly invites us to it, remembering the words of the angel to the shepherds: "Behold, I bring you tidings of great joy...for this day is born to you a Saviour."[6] It is the joy of deliverance, of the inheritance regained, of peace found once again, and, above all, of the vision of God Himself given to men: *Et vocabitur nomen ejus Emmanuel.*[7]

But this joy will only be assured if we remain firm in the grace that

---

1 *Filiae Jerusalem, quid me admiramini? Divinum at mysterium hoc quad cernitis.* Antiphon for the Feast of the *Expectatio Partus Virginis,* Dec. 18.
2 Isa. liii, 3.   3 Joan. iii, 16.
4 "A child is born to us, a son is given to us."
5 "Because God for his exceeding charity wherewith he loved us, sent his Son in the likeness of sinful flesh." Antiphon for the Octave of Christmas.
6 Luc. ii, 10–11.
7 "And his name shall be called Emmanuel," Isa. vii, 14; cf. Matth. i, 23.

comes to us from the Saviour and makes us His brethren. "O Christian," exclaims St. Leo, in a sermon that the Church reads during this holy night, "recognise thy dignity": *Agnosce, O Christiane, dignitatem tuam.* "And made a partaker of the divinity, take care not to fall back from so sublime a state."[1]

"If thou didst know the gift of God,"[2] said our Lord Himself. If thou didst know all that this Son is Who is given to thee! If, above all, we were to receive Him as we ought to receive Him! Let it not be said of us: *In propria venit, et sui eum non receperunt,*[3] "He came unto His own, and His own received Him not." By our creation, all of us are "His own"; we belong to God; but there are some who have not received Him upon this earth. How many Jews, how many pagans have rejected Christ, because He has appeared in the humility of passible flesh! Souls sunk in the darkness of pride and sensuality: *Lux in tenebris lucet, et tenebrae eam non comprehenderunt.*[4]

And how ought we to receive Him? By faith: *His qui credunt in nomine ejus.* It is to those who—believing in His Person, in His word, in His works,—have received this Child as God, that it has been given, in return, to become themselves children of God: *Ex Deo nati sunt.*

Such is, in fact, the fundamental disposition that we must have so that this "admirable exchange" may produce in us all its fruits. Faith alone teaches us how it is brought about; wherein it is realised; faith alone gives us a true knowledge of it and one worthy of God.

For there are many modes and degrees of knowledge.

"The ox knoweth his owner, and the ass his Master's Crib," wrote Isaias, in speaking of this mystery.[5] They saw the Child lying in the crib. But what could they see? As much as an animal could see: the form, the size, the colour, the movement,—an entirely rudimentary knowledge that does not pass the boundary line of sensation. Nothing more.

The passers-by, the curious, who approached the stable-cave saw the Child; but for them He was like all others. They did not go beyond this

---

1 *Sermo I de Nativitate.*   2 Joan. iv, 10.
3 Gospel for the Mass on Christmas Day.
4 "And the light shineth in darkness: and the darkness did not comprehend it." Joan. i, 5.
5 Isa. i, 3.

CHRIST IN HIS MYSTERIES

purely natural knowledge. Perhaps they were struck by the Child's love-
liness. Perhaps they pitied His destitution. But this feeling did not last
and was soon replaced by indifference.

There were the Shepherds, simple-hearted men, enlightened by a ray
from on high: *Claritas Dei circumfulsit illos.*[1] They certainly understood
more; they recognised in this Child the promised Messias, long awaited,
the *Expectatio gentium*[2]; they paid Him their homage, and their souls
were for a long time full of joy and peace.

The Angels likewise contemplated the New-born Babe, the Word made
Flesh. They saw in Him their God; this knowledge threw these pure spirits into awe and wonderment at such incomprehensible self-abasement:
for it was not to their nature that He willed to unite Himself: *Nusquam
angelos,* but to human nature, *sed semen Abrahae apprehendit.*[3]

What shall we say of the Blessed Virgin when she looked upon Jesus?
Into what depths of the mystery did her gaze penetrate—that gaze so
pure, so humble, so tender, so full of bliss? Who shall be able to express
with what lights the soul of Jesus inundated His Mother, and what perfect homage Mary rendered to her Son, to her God, to all the states and
all the mysteries whereof the Incarnation is the substance and the root.

There is finally—but this is beyond description—the gaze of the Father
contemplating His Son made flesh for mankind. The Heavenly Father
saw that which never man, nor angel, nor Mary herself could comprehend: the infinite perfections of the Divinity hidden in a Babe.... And
this contemplation was the source of unspeakable rapture: Thou art My
Son, My beloved Son, the Son of My dilection in Whom I have placed
all My delights....[4]

When we contemplate the Incarnate Word at Bethlehem, let us rise
above the things of sense so as to gaze upon Him with the eyes of faith
alone. Faith makes us share here below in the knowledge that the Divine
Persons have of One Another. There is no exaggeration in this. Sanctifying

---

1 "The brightness of God shone round about them," Luc. ii, 9.
2 "The expectation of the nations," Gen. xlix, 10.
3 "For nowhere doth he take hold of the angels: but of the seed of Abraham he taketh
hold," Hebr. ii, 16.
4 Marc. i, 11; Luc, iii, 22.

grace makes us indeed partakers of the divine nature. Now, the activity of the divine nature consists in the knowledge that the Divine Persons have the One of the Other, and the love that they have One for the Other. We participate therefore in this knowledge and in this love. And in the same way as sanctifying grace having its fruition in glory will give us the right of seeing God as He sees Himself, so, upon earth, in the shadows of faith, grace enables us to behold deep down into these mysteries through the eyes of God: *Lux tuae claritatis infulsit.*[1]

When our faith is intense and perfect, we do not stay to look only at the outside of the mystery, but we go deeply into it; we pass through the Humanity to penetrate as far as the Godhead which the Humanity at the same time hides and reveals; we behold divine mysteries in the divine light.

And ravished, astounded at such prodigious abasement, the soul, vivi-fied by this faith, falls prostrate in adoration and yields herself up entirely to procure the glory of a God Who, from love for His creature, thus veils the native splendour of His unfathomable perfections. She can never rest until she has given all, in return, to fill up her part in the exchange that He desires to contract with her, until she has brought herself wholly into subjection to this "King of Peace Who comes with so much magnificence"[2] to save, sanctify and, as it were, to deify her.

Let us then draw near to the Child God with great faith. We may wish to have been at Bethlehem to receive Him. Yet He is here giving Himself to us in Holy Communion with as much reality although our senses are less able to find Him. In the Tabernacle as in the Crib, it is the same God full of power, the same Saviour full of tender mercy.

If we will have it so, the admirable exchange still continues. For it is likewise through His Humanity that Christ infuses divine life into us at the Holy Table. It is in eating His Flesh and drinking His Blood, in uniting ourselves to His Humanity, that we draw at the very wellspring of everlasting life: *Qui manducat meam carnem, et bibit meum sanguinem, habet vitam aeternam...*[3]

Thus, each day, the union established between man and God in the Incarnation, is continued and made closer. In giving Himself in Commun-ion, Christ increases the life of grace in the generous and faithful soul,

---

1 "The light of your glory shone forth," Preface for Christmas.
2 Antiphon at Vespers on Christmas Day.   3 Joan. vi, 55.

making this life develop more freely and expand with more strength; He even bestows upon such a soul the pledge of that blessed immortality of which grace is the germ and whereby God will communicate Himself to us fully and unveiled: *Ut natus hodie Salvator mundi, sicut divinae nobis generationis est auctor, ita et immortalitatis sit ipse largitor.*[1]

This will be the consummation, magnificent and glorious, of the exchange inaugurated at Bethlehem in the poverty and humiliations of the Crib.

---

1 "That as the Saviour of the world born on this day is the author of our divine generation, so may he be the giver of immortality," Postcommunion of Christmas Day.

THE EPIPHANY

SUMMARY.—God, Eternal Light, is chiefly manifested by the Incarnation.—I. The manifestation to the Magi signifies the calling of the pagan nations to the light of the Gospel.—II. The Magi's faith, prompt and generous, is the model of what ours should be.—III. What the Magi did when the star disappeared.—IV. The greatness of their faith at Bethlehem; symbolism of the gifts offered by them to the Child-God; how we may imitate them.

WHENEVER a soul comes into a more intimate contact with God, she feels herself wrapt around with mystery: *Nubes et caligo in circuitu ejus.*[1] This mystery is the inevitable consequence of the infinite distance that separates the creature from the Creator. On all sides, the finite being is surpassed by Him Who, everlastingly, is the plenitude of Being.

This is why one of the most profound characters of the Divine Being is His incomprehensibility. The invisibility here below of the Divine Light is a truly wonderful thing.

"God is Light," says St. John; He is the Infinite Light, "and in Him there is no darkness": *Deus Lux est, et tenebrae in eo non sunt ullae.* St. John is careful to note that this truth constitutes one of the foundations of his Gospel: *Et haec est annuntiatio quam audivimus ab eo, et annuntiamus vobis.*[2] But this light, which bathes us all in its brightness, instead of manifesting God to the eyes of our souls, hides Him. It is with this light as with the sun: its very brilliancy prevents us from contemplating it: *Lucem*

---

1 "Clouds and darkness are round about him," Ps. xcvi, 2.
2 "And this is the declaration which we have heard from him and declare to you," I Joan. i, 5

inhabitat inaccessibilem.[1]

And yet this light is the life of the soul. You will have noticed that, in Holy Scripture, the ideas of life and light are frequently associated. When the psalmist wants to describe the eternal beatitude whereof God is the source, he says that in God is the principle of life: *Torrente voluptatis tuae potabis eos. Quoniam apud te est fons* VITAE; and he immediately adds: "And in Thy light we shall see light": *Et in lumine tuo* VIDEBIMUS LU-MEN.[2] It is in the same way that Our Lord declares Himself to be "the Light of the world." Again He says (and here is something more than a mere juxtaposition of words), "He that followeth Me walketh not in darkness, but shall have the light of life": *Habebit* LUMEN VITAE.[3] And this light of life proceeds from the Life by essence which is Light: *In ipso vita erat, et vita erat lux hominum.*[4] Our life in heaven will be to know the Eternal Light unveiled, and to rejoice in the splendour of this Light.

Already, here below, God gives a participation of this light by endowing the human soul with reason. *Signatum est super nos lumen vultus tui, Domine.*[5] Reason is a true light for man. All the natural activity of man, if he is to be worthy of himself, ought to be directed first of all by that light which shows him the good to be pursued; a light so powerful that it is even capable of revealing to man the existence of God and some of His perfections. St. Paul, writing to the faithful in Rome,[6] declares the pagans to be inexcusable for not having known God through contemplating the world, His handiwork. God's works contain a vestige, a reflection of His perfections, and thus, up to a certain point, declare the infinite light.

There is another deeper, more merciful manifestation that God has made of Himself: it is the Incarnation.

The divine light, too dazzling to be manifested in all its splendour to our feeble sight, is veiled beneath the sacred Humanity: *quod est velamen,* is the expression of St. Paul.[7] "The brightness of eternal light,"[8] light shin-

---

1 "Who inhabiteth light inaccessible," I Tim. vi, 16.
2 "Thou shalt make them drink of the torrent of thy pleasure. For with thee is the fountain of life," Ps. xxxv, 9–10.
3 Joan. viii, 12.   4 "In him was life: and the life was the light of men," Ibid. i, 4.
5 "The light of thy countenance, O Lord, is signed upon us," Ps. iv, 7.
6 Rom. i. 20.   7 Cf. Hebr. x, 20.   8 Sap. vii, 26.

ing forth from light, *lumen de lumine,* the Word had clad Himself in our flesh that through it we may contemplate the Divinity: *Nova mentis nostrae oculis lux tuae claritatis infulsit.*[1] Christ is God brought within our reach, showing Himself to us in a life authentically human; the veil of the Humanity prevents the infinite and dazzling splendour of the Divinity from blinding us.

But for every soul of good will, rays come forth from this Man revealing that He is likewise God. The soul enlightened by faith knows the splendour hidden behind the veil of this Holy of Holies. In the mortal Man that Jesus is, faith finds God Himself, and in finding God, she drinks at the source of light, salvation and immortal life: *Quia cum Unigenitus tuus in substantia nostrae mortalitatis apparuit, nova nos immortalitatis suae luce reparavit.*[2]

This manifestation of God to men is so extraordinary a mystery, a work so full of mercy; it constitutes one of the characters so essential to the Incarnation that, in the first centuries, the Church had no special feast in honour of the Saviour's Birth at Bethlehem. She celebrated the feast of the "Theophania," the feast of the "Divine manifestations" in the Person of the Incarnate Word:—the manifestation to the Magi,—the manifestation upon the banks of the Jordan at the Baptism of Jesus,—and the manifestation at the marriage feast of Cana where Christ wrought His first miracle. In passing from the Church of the East to that of the West, the feast has retained its name in Greek: *Epiphany,* the "manifestation"; but it has almost exclusively for its object the manifestation of the Saviour to the Gentile world, to the pagan nations, in the person of the Magi.

You well know the Gospel narrative of the coming of the Magi to Bethlehem, a narrative illustrated and popularised by tradition.[3] I will simply say a few words upon the general signification of the mystery; afterwards, whilst dwelling on certain details, I will point out some of the numerous

---

1 "The new reflection of your glory hath shone in our eyes," Preface for the Nativity.

2 "For when Thy Only-begotten Son was manifested in the substance of our mortality, with the new light of immortality, He restored us," Preface for the Epiphany.

3 Most authors place the coming of the Magi after the presentation of Jesus in the Temple; we here follow the order indicated by the Church which, in the liturgy, celebrates the Epiphany on January 6th and the Presentation on February 2nd.

lessons that it contains for our devotion.

I

The Fathers of the Church have seen in the call of the Magi to Christ's cradle the vocation of pagan nations to the Faith. This is the very foundation of the mystery, explicitly indicated by the Church in the collect wherein she sums up the desires of her children on this solemnity: *Deus qui hodierna die Unigenitum tuum* GENTIBUS *stella duce revelasti.*[1]

The Incarnate Word is first of all manifested to the Jews in the person of the shepherds. Why was this? Because the Jewish people were the Chosen People. From this people was to come forth the Messias, the Son of David. The magnificent promises to be realised in the establishing of the Messianic Kingdom had been made to this people; it was to them that God had entrusted the Scriptures and given the Law whereof each element prefigured the grace that was to be brought by Christ. It was then befitting that the Incarnate Word should first be manifested to the Jews. The shepherds, simple and upright men, represented the Chosen People at the Crib: *Evangelizo vobis gaudium magnum...quia natus est vobis hodie Salvator.*[2]

Later on, in His public life, Our Lord would again manifest Himself to the Jews, by the wisdom of His doctrine and the splendour of His miracles.

We shall even find that He restricts His teaching to the Jews alone. See, for example, when the woman of Canaan, from the pagan regions of Tyre and Sidon, asks Him to have mercy upon her. What does Christ answer to the disciples when they interpose in her favour? "I was not sent but to the sheep that are lost of the house of Israel."[3] It needed the ardent faith and profound humility of the poor pagan woman to wrest from Jesus, so to speak, the grace that she implored.

When, during His public life, Our Lord sent His Apostles to preach, like Himself, the good news, He likewise said to them: "Go ye not into

---

1 "O God, who on this day revealed Thine Only-begotten Son to the nations by the guidance of a star."
2 "I bring you good tidings of great joy....For this day is born to you a Saviour," Luc. ii, 10–11.
3 Matth. xv, 24.

the way of the Gentiles, and into the city of Samaritans enter ye not. But go ye rather to the lost sheep of the house of Israel."¹ Why this strange recommendation? Were the pagans excluded from the grace of redemption and salvation brought by Christ? No; but it entered into the divine economy to reserve the evangelization of the pagan nations to the Apostles, after the Jews should have definitely rejected the Son of God, by crucifying the Messias. When Our Lord dies upon the cross, the veil of the temple is rent in twain to show that the Ancient Covenant with the Hebrew people had ceased.

Many Jews indeed did not want to receive Christ. The pride of some, the sensuality of others, blinded their souls, and they would not receive Him as Son of God. It is of them that St. John speaks when he says: "The light shineth in darkness, and the darkness did not comprehend it."² Therefore Our Lord says to these incredulous Jews: "The Kingdom of God shall be taken from you, and shall be given to a nation yielding the fruit thereof."³

The pagan nations are called to become the inheritance promised by the Father to His Son Jesus: *Postula a me, et dabo tibi gentes haereditatem tuam.*⁴ Our Lord Himself says: "The good shepherd giveth His life for His sheep," adding immediately: "Other sheep I have, that are not of this fold": *Alia oves habeo, quae non sunt ex hoc ovili.* "Them also I must bring, and they shall hear my voice, and there shall be one fold and one shepherd."⁵

This is why, before ascending into heaven, He sends His Apostles to continue His work and mission of salvation, no longer among the lost sheep of Israel, but among all people. "Going therefore," He says to them, "teach ye all nations...preach the gospel to every creature....I am with you all days, even to the consummation of the world."⁶

The Word Incarnate did not, however, await His Ascension to shed abroad the grace of the Gospel upon the Gentile world. As soon as He appeared here below, He invited it to His cradle in the person of the Magi. He, Eternal Wisdom, would thus show us that He brought peace, *Pax hominibus bonae voluntatis,*⁷ not only to those who were nigh to Him—

1 Matth. x, 5–6.   2 Joan. i, 5, 11.   3 Matth. xxi, 43.   4 Ps. ii, 8.
5 Joan. x, 11, 16.   6 Matth. xxviii, 19–20; Marc. xvi, 15.
7 "Peace to men of good will," Luc. ii, 14,

the faithful Jews represented by the shepherds,—but also to those who "were afar off"—the Pagans represented by the Magi. Thus, as St. Paul says, of the two people He made but one: *Qui fecit utraque unum,* because He alone, by the union of His Humanity with His Divinity, is the perfect Mediator, and "by Him we have access both in one Spirit to the Father."[1]

The calling of the Magi and their sanctification signifies the vocation of the Gentiles to the faith and to salvation. God sends an angel to the shepherds, for the Chosen People were accustomed to the apparition of the celestial spirits; to the Magi, who studied the stars, He causes a marvellous star to appear. This star is the symbol of the inward illumination that enlightens souls in order to call them to God.

The soul of every grown-up person is in fact enlightened, once at least, like the Magi, by the star of the vocation to eternal salvation. To all the light is given. It is a dogma of our faith that God "will have all men to be saved": *Qui* OMNES *homines vult salvos fieri, et ad agnitionem veritatis venire.*[2]

On the day of judgment, all without exception will proclaim, with the conviction produced by evidence, the infinite justice of God and the perfect rectitude of His judgments: *Justus es, Domine, et rectum judicium tuum.*[3] Those whom God shall have told to depart from Him for ever will acknowledge that they are the workers of their own ruin.

Now this would not be true if the reprobate had not had the possibility of knowing and accepting the divine light of faith. It would be contrary not only to God's infinite goodness, but even to His justice, to condemn a soul on account of its invincible ignorance.

Doubtless, the star that calls men to the Christian faith is not the same for all; it shines in different ways, but its brightness is visible enough for hearts of good will to be able to recognise it and see in it the sign of the Divine call. In His providence full of wisdom, God incessantly varies His action, incomprehensible like Himself. He varies it according to the ever active promptings of His love and the ever holy exigencies of His justice. We ought herein to adore the unfathomable depths of God's ways and

---

1 Ephes. ii, 14, 17–18.
2 "Who will have all men to be saved and to come to the knowledge of the truth," I Tim. ii, 4.
3 Ps. cxviii, 137.

proclaim that they infinitely surpass our created views. Indeed "who hath known the mind of the Lord? Or who hath been His counsellor?" *O altitudo divitiarum sapientiae et scientiae Dei! Quam incomprehensibilia sunt judicia ejus et investigabiles viae ejus!*[1]

We have "seen the star" and have recognised as our God the Babe of Bethlehem; we have the happiness of belonging to the Church whereof the Magi were the first fruits.

In the office of the feast, the Liturgy celebrates this vocation of all humanity to faith and salvation in the person of the Magi as the nuptials of the Church with the Bridegroom. Hear with what gladness, in what magnificent symbolical terms, borrowed from the prophet Isaias, the liturgy proclaims[2] the splendour of this spiritual Jerusalem which is to receive into her maternal bosom the nations become the inheritance of her divine Bridegroom. "Arise, be enlightened, O Jerusalem, for thy light is come, and the glory of the Lord is risen upon thee. For behold, darkness shall cover the earth, and a mist the people; but the Lord shall arise upon thee, and His glory shall be seen upon thee. And the Gentiles shall walk in thy light, and kings in the brightness of thy rising. Lift up thy eyes round about, and see; all these gathered together, they are come to thee: thy sons shall come from afar, and daughters shall rise up at thy side. Then shalt thou see, and abound, and thy heart shall wonder and be enlarged, when the multitude of the sea shall be converted to thee, the strength of the Gentiles shall come to thee."[3]

Let us offer continual thanksgiving to God "Who hath delivered us from the power of darkness, and hath translated us into the kingdom of the Son of His love,"[4] that is to say into His Church.

The call to the faith is a signal benefit because it contains in germ the vocation to the eternal beatitude of the Divine vision. Never let us forget that this call was the dawn of all God's mercies towards us, and that for man all is summed up in fidelity to this vocation; faith is to bring us to the Beatific Vision.[5]

Not only ought we to thank God for this grace of the Christian faith, but we ought each day to render ourselves more worthy of it by safe-

---

1 Rom. xi, 33.   2 Epistle of the Mass.   3 Isa, lx, 15.
4 Col. i, 13.   5 Collect for the Feast.

guarding our faith against all the dangers that it encounters in our age of naturalism, scepticism, indifference, human respect, and by living a life of faith with constant fidelity.

Moreover, let us beseech God to grant this precious gift of the Christian faith to all the souls who yet "sit in darkness, and in the shadow of death"; let us beseech Our Lord that the star may shine upon them; that, through His tender mercy, He Himself will be the Sun to visit them from on high: *Per viscera misericordiae Dei nostri in quibus visitavit nos, Oriens ex alto.*[1]

This prayer is very pleasing to Our Lord; it is, in fact, to beseech Him that He may be known and exalted as the Saviour of all mankind and the King of kings.

It is likewise pleasing to the Father, for He desires nothing so much as the glorification of His Son. Let us then often repeat, during these holy days, the prayer that the Incarnate Word Himself has put upon our lips: O Heavenly Father, "Father of Lights," Thy Kingdom come, that kingdom whereof Thy Son Jesus is the head. *Adveniat regnum tuum!* May Thy Son be more and more known, loved, served, glorified, so that in His turn He may, by manifesting Thee the more to men, glorify Thee in the unity of the Holy Ghost: *Pater, clarifica Filium tuum ut Filius tuus clarificet te!*

II

If we now return to some of the details of the Gospel narrative, we shall see how rich in teaching is this mystery.

I have said that the Magi at Bethlehem represented the Gentiles in their vocation to the light of the Gospel. The way in which the Magi acted show us the qualities that our faith ought to have. What is at first apparent is the generous fidelity of this faith. Let us consider it. The star appeared to the Magi. Whatever be the country whence they originated—Persia, Chaldea, Arabia or India,—the Magi, according to tradition, belonged to a priestly caste and devoted themselves to the study of the stars. It is more than probable that they were not ignorant of the revela-

---

1 Luc. i, 78–79.

tion made to the Jews of a King Who would be their Deliverer and the Master of the world. The prophet Daniel, who had prophesied the time of his coming, had been in relation with some of the Magi; perhaps even, Balaam's prophecy that a star should "rise out of Jacob"[1] was not unknown to them. However that may be, behold now a wondrous star appears to them. Its extraordinary brightness attracting their gaze, awakens their attention at the same time that an inward grace of illumination enlightens their souls. This grace prepared them to recognize the prerogatives of the One Whose Birth the star announced; it inspired them to set out to seek Him in order to offer Him their homage.

The Magi's fidelity to the inspiration of grace is wonderful. Doubt takes no hold upon their minds; without staying to reason, they immediately begin to carry out their design. Neither the indifference nor the scepticism of those who surround them, nor the disappearance of the star, nor the difficulties inherent to an expedition of this kind, nor the length and dangers of the way stop them. They obey the divine call without delay or hesitation. "We have seen His star in the East and are come."[2]

In this the Magi are our models, whether it concerns the vocation to the faith, or whether it be a question of the call to perfection. There is indeed for every faithful soul a vocation to holiness: *Sancti estote quia ego sanctus sum.*[3] "Be holy because I am holy." The apostle St. Paul assures us that from all eternity there exists for us a divine decree full of love containing this call: *Elegit nos ante mundi constitutionem, ut essemus sancti et immaculati in conspectu ejus.*[4] And for those whom He calls to holiness God makes "all things work together unto good ": *Iis qui secundum propositum vocati sunt sancti.*[5] The manifestation of this vocation is for each of us his or her star. It takes different forms, according to God's designs, our character, the circumstances wherein we live, the events that befall us; but it shines in the soul of each one.

And what is the end and object of this call? For us as for the Magi, it is to lead us to Jesus. The Heavenly Father causes the star to shine in us; for,

---

1 Num. xxiv, 17.   2 Matth. ii, 2.   3 Lev, xi, 44.
4 "He chose us in him before the foundation of the world, that we should be holy and unspotted in his sight," Ephes. i, 4.
5 "To such as, according to his purpose, are called to be saints," Rom. viii, 28.

says Christ Himself, "no man can come to Me, except the Father, Who hath sent Me, draw him": *Nemo potest venire ad me, nisi Pater, qui misit me, traxerit eum.*[1]

If with fidelity we listen to the divine call, if we generously press onward with our gaze fixed upon the star, we shall come to Christ Who is the life of our souls. And whatever be our sins, our failings, our miseries, Jesus will welcome us with kindness. He has promised to do so: "All that the Father giveth Me shall come to Me; and him that cometh to Me, I will not cast out": *Omne, quod dat mihi Pater, ad me veniet: et eum qui venit ad me non ejiciam foras.*[2]

The Father drew Magdalen the sinner to the feet of Jesus. And see how Magdalen, at once following with a generous faith the divine ray of the star that shone in her soul, suddenly enters into the festal hall to manifest publicly to Christ her repentance and her love. Magdalen followed the star, and the star led Magdalen to the Saviour: "Thy sins are forgiven thee...thy faith hath made thee safe. Go in peace."[3] *Et eum qui venit ad me non ejiciam foras.*

The lives of the saints and the experience of souls show that there are often, in our supernatural life, decisive moments upon which depend all the value of our inner life, and sometimes our eternity itself.

Look at Saul upon the road to Damascus. He is the enemy and bitter persecutor of the Christians: *Spirans minarum,* "breathing out threatenings and slaughter," against those who bore that name. And then the voice of Jesus makes itself heard. It is for Saul the star, the divine call. He hears the call, and follows the star: "Lord, what wilt Thou have me to do?" What promptitude and what generosity! And from that moment, become a "vessel of election,"[4] he will live for Christ alone.

Look, on the other hand, at the young man full of good will, with upright and sincere heart, who approaches Jesus and asks what he must do to possess life everlasting. "Keep the commandments," answers our Divine Saviour. "Master, all these have I kept from my youth, what is yet wanting to me?" Then, says the Gospel, "Jesus, looking on him, loved him": *Jesus autem intuitus eum dilexit eum.* This look full of love was the

---

1 Joan. vi, 44.   2 Ibid., vi, 37.   3 Luc. vii, 48, 50.
4 Act. ix, 1, 6, 15.

ray of the star. And see how it is immediately manifested: "One thing is wanting unto thee: if thou wilt be perfect, go sell what thou hast, and give to the poor, and thou shalt have a treasure in heaven; and come follow me." But the youth does not follow the star. Sorrowful at this saying, "he went away sad; for he had great possessions." Some commentators see the prediction of the loss of this soul in the words that our Lord pronounced immediately afterwards: "How hardly shall they that have riches enter into the kingdom of God."[1]

Thus, whether it concerns the call to faith or holiness, we shall only find Christ and the life whereof He is the source on condition that we are attentive to grace and perseveringly faithful in seeking after divine union.

The Heavenly Father calls us to His Son by the inspiration of His grace. Like the Magi, as soon as the star shines in our hearts, we should instantly leave all: our sins, the occasions of sin, evil habits, infidelities, imperfections, attachment to creatures. Taking no account of criticism nor the opinion of men, nor the difficulties of the work to be done, we should set out at once to seek Jesus. He wills this whether we have lost Him by mortal sin, or whether, already possessing Him by sanctifying grace, He calls us to a closer and more intimate union with Himself.

Vidimus stellam: Lord, I have seen Thy star, and I come to Thee: what wilt Thou have me to do?

III

It happens at times that the star disappears from our sight. Whether the inspiration of grace bears with it an extraordinary character, as was the case with the Magi, or whether it be linked to the supernatural providence of each day, as is the most frequent case with us, the star sometimes ceases to be manifest. The soul then finds itself in spiritual darkness. What is to be done then?

Let us see what the Magi did under these circumstances. The star was shown to them only in the East, then it disappeared: *Vidimus stellam ejus in Oriente.* If it taught them concerning the Birth of the King of the Jews, it did not show the precise place where they might find Him. What were

---

1 Marc. x, 17–23; cf. Matth. xix, 16–23; Luc. xviii, 18–24.

they to do? The Magi directed their course towards Jerusalem, the capital of Judea, the metropolis of the Jewish religion. Where, better than in the holy city, could they learn what they sought to know?

In the same way, when our star disappears, when the divine inspiration leaves us in some incertainty, it is God's will that we should have recourse to the Church, to those who represent Him amongst us, in order to learn from them the path to be followed. This is the dispensation of Divine Providence. God loves that in our doubts and in the difficulties of our progress towards Christ, we should ask light and direction from those whom He has established as His representatives: *Qui vos audit, me audit.*[1]

Hear how Jesus replies to Saul's question: "Lord, what wilt Thou have me to do?" Does He make His will directly known? He might have done so since He revealed Himself as the Lord; but He instead sends Saul to His representative: "Go into the city, and there it shall be told thee"—by another—"what thou must do."[2]

In submitting the aspirations of our souls to the control of those who have the grace and mission to direct us in our seeking after divine union, we run no risk of going astray, whatever be the personal merits of those who guide us. At the time when the Magi arrived at Jerusalem, the assembly of those who had authority to interpret the Holy Scriptures was composed in great part of unworthy members; and yet God willed that it should be by their ministry and teaching that the Magi learnt officially where Christ was born. Indeed, God cannot permit a soul to be deceived when, with humility and confidence, she has recourse to the legitimate representatives of His sovereign authority.

On the contrary, the soul will again find light and peace. Like the Magi going out from Jerusalem, she will again see the star, radiant and splendid, and, also like them, full of gladness, she will go forward on her way: *Videntes autem stellam, gavisi sunt gaudio magno valde.*[3]

IV

Let us now follow the Magi to Bethlehem: it is there that we shall especially see the manifestation of the depth of their faith.

---

1 "He that heareth you heareth me," Luc. x, 16.
2 Act. ix, 7.   3 Matth. ii, 10.

The marvellous star leads them to the place where they were at last to find Him Whom they had so long sought. And what do they find? A palace, a royal cradle, a long train of attentive servants? No, but a poor dwelling. They seek a king, a God, and they see only a Babe on His Mother's knee; not a Babe transfigured by Divine rays as the Apostles were later to see the God-Man, but a little Child, a poor, weak little Child.

However, from this Little One so frail in appearance, invisibly went forth a divine power: *Virtus de illo exibat*. He, Who had made the star arise to lead the Magi to His cradle, now Himself enlightened them. He inwardly filled their minds with light and their hearts with love. And so it was that in this Child, they recognised their God.

The Gospel tells us nothing of their words, but it makes known to us the sublime act of their perfect faith: "And falling down they adored Him": *Et procidentes adoraverunt eum.*[1]

The Church would have us associate ourselves with this adoration of the Magi. When, during the Mass, she gives us these words of the Gospel narrative to read, she causes us to kneel down, to show that we, too, believe in the Divinity of the Babe of Bethlehem.

Let us adore Him with deep faith. God requires of us that, as long as we are here below, all the activity of our inner life should lead to union with Him by faith. Faith is the light which enables us to see God in the Virgin's Child, to hear God's voice in the words of the Incarnate Word, to follow the example of a God in the actions of Jesus, to appropriate to ourselves the infinite merits of a God in the sorrows and satisfactions of a Man suffering like ourselves.

Through the veil of a humble and passible Humanity, the soul enlightened by a living faith ever discovers God; where ever she encounters this Humanity—whether it be in the humiliations of Bethlehem, upon the roads of Judea, on the gibbet of Calvary, or under the Eucharistic species—the faithful soul falls in adoration because it is the Humanity of a God. At the feet of Jesus she listens to Him, in order to obey and follow Him until it shall please Him to reveal Himself in the beauty of His Infinite Majesty, in the holy splendours of the Beatific Vision: *Usque ad*

---

1 Ibid. ii, 11.

contemplandam speciem tuae celsitudinis perducamur.[1]

The attitude of adoration in the Magi translates in eloquent language the depth of their faith; the presents that they offer are likewise full of signification. The Fathers of the Church have laid stress on the symbolism of the gifts brought to Christ by the Magi. In ending this conference, let us stay to consider the depth of this symbolism: it will be a joy for our souls and food for our devotion.

As you know, the Gospel tells us that having found the Child with Mary His Mother, "opening their treasures, they offered Him gifts: gold, frankincense and myrrh."[2] It is evident that, in the intentions of the Magi, these gifts were meant to express the feelings of their hearts as well as to honour Him to Whom they were brought.

In examining the nature of these gifts which they had prepared before their departure, we see that divine illumination had already manifested to the Magi something of the eminent dignity of Him Whom they desired to contemplate and adore. The nature of these gifts likewise indicates the nature of the duties that the Magi would fulfil towards the King of the Jews. The symbolism of the gifts therefore refers both to the One to Whom they are offered and to those who present them.

Gold, the most precious of metals, is the symbol of royalty; it denotes, on the other hand, the love and fidelity that everyone owes to his prince.

Incense is universally acknowledged to be the symbol of divine worship; it is offered to God alone. In preparing this gift, the Magi showed that they had in view to proclaim the Divinity of Him Whose Birth was announced by the star, and to confess this Divinity by the supreme adoration that can be rendered to God alone.

Finally, they had been inspired to bring Him myrrh. What would they show by this myrrh which is used to dress wounds, and to embalm the dead? This gift signified that Christ was Man, a Man capable of suffering, Who would one day die. The myrrh also symbolised the spirit of penance and immolation which ought to characterise the life of the disciples of the Crucified.

---

1 "That we may be led even to contemplate the appearance of your Majesty," Collect for the Feast of the Epiphany.
2 Matth. ii, 11.

Thus grace inspired the Magi to bring presents to Him Whom they sought. It should be the same for us. "Let us who hear the story of the offering of the Magi," says St Ambrose, "learn how to open our treasures and present like offerings."[1] Each time that we draw near to Christ, let us, like the Magi, bring Him presents, but presents that are magnificent, that are, like theirs, worthy of Him to Whom we offer them.

You may perhaps say: we have neither gold, nor frankincense, nor myrrh. That is true; but we have what is better, we have much more precious treasures, the only ones, moreover, that Christ, our Saviour and our King, expects from us. Do we not offer gold to Christ when by a life full of love and fidelity to His commands, we proclaim that He is the King of our hearts? Do we not present frankincense when we believe in His Divinity, and confess it by our adoration and prayers? In uniting our humiliations, our sufferings, our sorrow and tears to His, do we not bring Him myrrh?

And if, of ourselves, we are destitute of these things, let us ask Our Lord to enrich us with the treasures that are pleasing to Him; He possesses them in order to give them to us.

This is what Christ Jesus Himself made known to St. Mechtilde, one feast of the Epiphany, after she had received Communion. "Behold," said He, "I give thee gold, that is to say My Divine love; frankincense, that is all My holiness and devotion; finally myrrh, which is the bitterness of My Passion. I give them to thee to such an extent that thou mayest offer them as gifts to Me, as if they were thine own property."[2]

Yes, this is an extremely consoling truth that we ought never to forget. The grace of divine adoption, which makes us brethren of Jesus and living members of His Mystical Body, gives us the right of appropriating to ourselves His treasures so that they may be accounted as our own by Himself and His Father. "You know the grace of Our Lord Jesus Christ," says St. Paul, "that being rich He became poor, for your sakes; that through His poverty you might be rich."[3]

Our Lord Himself supplies for what we lack; He is our riches, our thankoffering; He has in Himself, in an eminent degree, that which the gifts of the Magi signify; He perfectly realises in His Person their deep symbolism. Therefore let us offer Him to the Heavenly Father in thanks-

1 In Luc. ii, 44.   2 The Book of Special Grace. Part I, chapter viii.
3 II Cor. viii, 9.

giving for the inestimable gift of the Christian faith. God has given us His Son; according to Jesus' own words, the Infinite Being could not manifest His love for us in a more striking way: SIC *Deus dilexit mundum, ut Filium suum Unigenitum* DARET[1]; for, in giving Him to us, adds St. Paul, He has "given us all things": *Quomodo non etiam cum illo omnia nobis donavit.*[2]

But we owe, in return, signal acts of thanksgiving to God for this ineffable Gift. What can we give to God that is worthy of Him? His Son Jesus. In offering His Son to Him, we render to Him that which He gives us: *Offerimus praeclarae majestati tuae de tuis donis ac datis,*[3] and there is no gift that is more pleasing to Him.

The Church, knowing God's secret better than anyone, knows this so well! On this day, when her mystical nuptials with Christ begin, she offers to God no longer gold, frankincense, and myrrh, but the One Who is Himself represented by these gifts, immolated upon the altar and received into the hearts of His disciples: *Ecclesiae tuae, quaesumus, Domine, dona propitius intuere, quibus non jam aurum, thus et myrrha profertur, sed quod eisdem muneribus declaratur, immolatur et sumitur, Jesus Christus Filius tuus, Dominus noster.*[4]

Let us, then, with the priest, offer the Holy Sacrifice. Let us offer to the Eternal Father His Divine Son, after having received Him at the Holy Table; but let us also lovingly offer ourselves with Him, that in all things we may accomplish what His Divine will manifests to us: this is the most perfect gift we can present to God.

The Epiphany still continues; it is prolonged throughout the centuries. "We, too," says St. Leo,[5] "are to taste the joys of the Magi, for the mystery which is accomplished upon this day is not to remain confined to it. Through the munificence of God and the power of His goodness, we in our day enjoy the reality whereof the Magi had the first fruits."

The Epiphany is renewed, indeed, when God makes the light of the

---

1 "For God so loved the world, as to give his only begotten Son," Joan. iii, 16.
2 Rom. viii, 32.   3 Canon of the Mass.
4 "We beseech Thee, O Lord, to look graciously upon the offerings of Thy Church in which are no longer offered gold, frankincense, and myrrh, but He whom by these same gifts is signified, sacrificed and received, Jesus Christ, Thy Son, our Lord," Secret of the Mass for the Epiphany.
5 *Sermo xxxv, In Epiphaniae Solemnitate vi.*

Gospel shine in the sight of the pagans; each time that the truth is realized by those living in error it is a ray of the Magi's star that appears to them.

The Epiphany continues too in the faithful soul when her love becomes more fervent and steadfast. Fidelity to the inspirations of grace—it is Our Lord Himself Who tells us so,—becomes the source of a more ardent and brighter illumination: *Qui diligit me...manifestabo ei meipsum.*[1] Happy the soul that lives by faith and love! Christ Jesus manifests Himself ever more and more within her; He makes her enter into an ever deeper and closer comprehension of His mysteries.

Holy Scripture compares the life of the just man to a path which "as a shining light, goeth forwards and increaseth even to perfect day,"[2] to that day whereon every veil will fall away, all shadows flee, when the eternal splendours of the divinity will appear in the light of glory. In the heavenly city, says St. John, in his mysterious book of the Apocalypse where he describes the magnificence of the Jerusalem which is on high, there is no need of the sun, for the Lamb, that is to say Christ, is Himself the Light which enlightens and gladdens the souls of all the elect.[3]

That will be the heavenly Epiphany.

"O God, Who upon this day by the leading of a star, didst reveal Thine Only-begotten Son to the Gentiles; mercifully grant, that we who already know Thee by faith, may be brought to the contemplation of the beauty of Thy majesty": *Deus, qui hodierna die Unigenitum tuum gentibus stella duce revelasti: concede propitius, ut qui jam te ex fide cognovimus, usque ad contemplandam speciem tuae celsitudinis perducamur.*

---

1 "He that loveth me...I will manifest myself to him," Joan. xiv, 21.
2 Prov. iv, 18.   3 Apoc. xxi, 23; xxii, 5.

THE BLESSED VIRGIN MARY, THE MYSTERIES OF THE CHILDHOOD AND HIDDEN LIFE OF CHRIST

(Time after the Epiphany)

SUMMARY.—The Divine Word takes a Human Nature in order to unite Himself to it personally.—I. How, in the mystery of the Annunciation to the Virgin, the exchange between the Divinity and Humanity is concluded; the Divine Maternity.—II. Mary's Purification and the Presentation of Jesus in the Temple.—III. Jesus lost at the age of twelve.—IV. The Hidden Life at Nazareth.—V. Inward dispositions of the Blessed Virgin during the years of the Hidden Life.

The mystery of the Incarnation can be summed up as an exchange, in every point admirable, between the Divinity and our humanity. In return for the human nature that He takes, the Eternal Word makes us partakers of His Divine life.

It is indeed to be remembered that it is we who give a human nature to the Word. God could have created, so as to unite it to His Son, a humanity fully established in the perfection of its organism, as was Adam on the day of his creation. Christ would have been truly man because nothing that constitutes the essence of man would have been lacking to Him; but in not joining Himself directly to us by a human birth, He would not have been, properly speaking, of our race.

God did not will to act thus. What was the design of Infinite Wisdom?

That the Word should take from us the humanity to which He was to be united. Christ would thereby be truly "the Son of man"; He would be a member of our race: *Factum ex muliere*[1]...*ex semine David.*[2] When at Christmas we celebrate Christ's Nativity, we go back through the centuries in order to read the list of His ancestors, His human genealogy. The successive generations pass before us till we see Him born of David's race, of the Virgin Mary: *De qua natus est Jesus qui vocatur Christus.*[3]

As you know, God is by His nature infinitely generous; it is of the essence of goodness to diffuse itself: *Bonum est diffusivum sui.* Infinite Goodness is urged in an infinite manner to give itself. God is this boundless Goodness; revelation teaches us that there are between the Divine Persons, from the Father to the Son, and from the Father and the Son to the Holy Spirit, infinite communications wherein God finds the full satisfaction of this natural tendency of His Being to give itself.

But beyond this natural communication of Infinite Goodness, there is another, arising from God's *free* love towards the creature. The fulness of Being and of Good that is God has overflowed beyond, through love. And how has this come to pass? God has chosen in the first place to give Himself in an altogether special manner to a creature by uniting it in a personal manner with His Word. This gift of God to a creature is unique: it makes of this creature chosen by the Holy Trinity the very Son of God, *Filius meus es tu: ego hodie genui te.*[4] It is Christ, it is the Word united personally and in an indissoluble manner to a human nature, like to ours in all things, excepting sin.

From us He asks this human nature. It is as if the Eternal Father were saying to us: Give Me your nature for My Son, and I, in return, will give to this nature, and, through it, to every man of good will, a participation in My Divinity.

For God thus communicates Himself to Christ only in order to give Himself, through Christ, to us all; God's plan is that Christ should receive the Divinity in its fulness and that we should draw, in our turn, from this

---

1 "Made of a woman," Gal. iv, 4.   2 "Of the seed of David," Rom. i, 3.
3 "Of whom was born Jesus, who is called Christ," Matth. i, 16.
4 "You are my son, this day have I begotten thee," Ps. ii, 7.

fulness: *De plenitudine ejus nos omnes accepimus.*[1]

Such is this communication of God's goodness to the world: *Sic Deus dilexit mundum, ut Filium suum Unigenitum daret.*[2] This is the wonderful order that rules the exchange between God and humanity.

But who is it, out of all others, that God will ask to be a mother to this humanity to which He wills to unite Himself so closely, in order to make of it the instrument of His graces to the world?

We have already named her whom all generations declare blessed: the human genealogy of Jesus ends with Mary, the Virgin of Nazareth. From her, and through her from us, the Word asked a human nature, and Mary gave it to Him; this is why we shall henceforward see her inseparable from Jesus and from His mysteries. Wherever Jesus is found, we shall see her: He is her Son as much as He is the Son of God.

However, if Jesus everywhere remains the Son of Mary, it is above all in the mysteries of His Childhood and Hidden Life that He is revealed under this aspect; if Mary everywhere occupies a unique place, it is in these mysteries that her position as His Mother is most actively manifested outwardly and her divine Maternity shines forth most brightly. This incomparable dignity is the source of all the other privileges of the Virgin.

Those who do not know the Blessed Virgin, those who do not truly love the Mother of Jesus, run the risk of not profitably understanding the mysteries of Christ's Humanity. Christ is the Son of man as well as the Son of God; these two characters are essential to Him. If He is the Son of God by an eternal ineffable generation, He became Son of man by being born of Mary in time.

Let us then contemplate this Virgin at the side of her Son; in return she will obtain for us the power of entering more deeply into the comprehension of these mysteries to which she is so closely united.

I

In order that the exchange which God willed to contract with humanity should be possible, it was necessary that humanity should consent to it.

1 "And of his fulness we all have received," Joan. i, 16.
2 "For God so loved the world, as to give his only begotten Son," Joan. iii, 16.

Let us transport ourselves to Nazareth. The fulness of times has come. God decreed, says St. Paul, to send His Son into the world in causing Him to be born of a woman. The Angel Gabriel, God's messenger, brings to the young Maiden the heavenly proposals. A sublime dialogue takes place whereon hangs the deliverance of the human race. The Angel first salutes the Maiden declaring her, in the name of God, "full of grace": *Ave gratia plena*. Indeed, not only is she sinless, no stain has tarnished her soul,— the Church has defined that she, alone among all creatures, has not been touched by original sin;—but moreover, because He predestined her to be the Mother of His Son, the Eternal Father has lavished His gifts upon her. She is full of grace, not, doubtless, as Christ is to be, *plenum gratiae*, for He is so by right and with the Divine plenitude itself; Mary receives all in participation, but in a measure which cannot be estimated, and in correlation with her eminent dignity as Mother of God. "Behold," says the Angel, "thou shalt bring forth a Son, and thou shalt call His name Jesus....He shall be called the Son of the Most High, and He shall reign in the house of Israel for ever." "How shall this be done," asks Mary, "because I know not man?" For she wishes to keep her virginity. "The Holy Spirit shall come upon thee, and the power of the Most High shall overshadow thee. And therefore also the Holy which shall be born of thee shall be called the Son of God." "Behold the handmaid of the Lord; be it done to me according to thy word": *Ecce ancilla Domini, fiat mihi secundum Verbum tuum.*[1]

In this solemn moment, the exchange is concluded. When Mary pronounces her *fiat,* all humanity says to God by her mouth: "Yes, O God, I consent, so be it." And immediately the Word is made Flesh: *Et Verbum caro factum est.* At this instant, the Word becomes incarnate by the operation of the Holy Spirit; the Blessed Virgin becomes the Ark of the New Covenant between God and man.

When the Church sings, in the *Credo,* the words that recall this mystery: *Et incarnatus est de Spiritu Sancto ex Maria virgine, et homo factus est,*[2] she obliges her ministers to bend the knee in token of adoration. Let us too adore this Divine Word made man for us in the womb of a Virgin; let us adore Him with so much the more love the more He humbles

---

1 Luc. i, 28, 31–35, 38.
2 "And became incarnate by the Holy Spirit of the Virgin Mary: and was made man."

Himself in taking, as St. Paul says, "the form of a servant": *Formam servi accipiens.*[1] Let us adore Him, in union with Mary, who, enlightened with light from above, bows down before her Creator become her Son; let us adore Him with the Angels marvelling at this infinite condescension towards humanity.

Let us next salute Our Lady, and thank her for having given Jesus to us. It is to her consent that we owe Him: *Per quam meruimus auctorem vitae.*[2] Let us add our congratulations. Consider how the Holy Spirit by the mouth of Elizabeth, *Et repleta est Spiritu Sancto Elisabeth,* saluted her on the morrow of the Incarnation. "Blessed art thou among women, and blessed is the fruit of thy womb!...And blessed art thou that hast believed, because those things shall be accomplished that were spoken to thee by the Lord"[3]: Blessed, for this faith in God's word made the Virgin the Mother of Christ. What simple creature has ever received like praises from the infinite Being?

Mary refers to the Lord the glory of the marvels wrought in her. She sings within her heart a canticle full of love and gratitude. With her cousin Elisabeth, she lets the innermost feelings of her heart overflow; she sings the Magnificat which, throughout the centuries, her children will repeat after her in praise of God for having chosen her out of all women: "My soul doth magnify the Lord, because He hath regarded the humility of His handmaid...because He that is mighty, hath done great things to me," *Magnificat anima mea Dominum: quia fecit mihi magna qui potens est.*[4]

Mary was at Bethlehem, for the enrolment ordered by Caesar, when, says St. Luke, "her days were accomplished, that she should be delivered. And she brought forth her firstborn Son, and wrapped Him in swaddling clothes, and laid Him in a manger; because there was no room for them in the inn."[5] Who is this Child? He is Mary's Son, since he has just been born of her: *Primogenitum suum.*

But she saw in this Child, a child like other children, the Very Son of God. Mary's soul was full of immense faith, which went far beyond the

---

1 Philipp. ii, 7.
2 "Through whom we have deserved [to receive] the author of life," Collect for the office of the Circumcision.
3 Luc. i, 41–42, 45.   4 Ibid. i, 46, 49.   5 Ibid, ii, 6–7.

faith of all the just of the Old Testament; and therefore in her Son she saw her God.

This faith translated itself outwardly in an act of adoration. As soon as she looked upon Jesus, the Maiden-Mother adored Him with an intensity we cannot conceive.

To this intense faith, this deep adoration, were added the transports of an incommensurable love, a love both human and supernatural.

God is love, and so that we may have some idea of this love, He gives a share of it to mothers. The heart of a mother with her unwearying tenderness, the constancy of her solicitude, the inexhaustible delicacy of her affection is a truly divine creation, although God has placed in her only a spark of His love for us. Yet, however imperfectly a mother's heart reflects the divine love towards us, God gives us our mothers to take His place in some manner with us. He places them at our side, from our cradles, to guide us, guard us, especially in our earliest years when we have so much need of tenderness.

Hence imagine with what predilection the Holy Trinity fashioned the heart of the Blessed Virgin chosen to be the Mother of the Incarnate Word. God delighted in pouring forth love in her heart, in forming it expressly to love a God-Man.

In Mary's heart were perfectly harmonised the adoration of a creature towards her God, and the love of a mother for her only Son.

The supernatural love of Our Lady is not less wonderful. As you know, a soul's love for God is measured by its degree of grace. What is it that, in us, hinders the development of grace and love? Our sins, our deliberate faults, our voluntary infidelities, our attachment to creatures. Each deliberate fault narrows the heart, and strengthens egotism. But Our Lady's soul is of perfect purity; unstained by sin, untouched by any shadow of a fault, she is full of grace: *Gratia plena*. Far from encountering in her any obstacle to the unfolding of grace, the Holy Spirit ever found her heart wonderfully docile to His inspirations, and therefore full of love.

What must have been the joy of the soul of Jesus to feel Himself loved to such an extent by His Mother! After the incomprehensible joy arising for Him from the Beatific Vision and from the look of infinite complacency wherewith the Heavenly Father contemplated Him, nothing can have rejoiced Him so much as the love of His Mother. He found in it a more abundant compensation for the indifference of those who would not receive Him. He found in the heart of this young Virgin a fire of undying love that He Himself further enkindled by His divine glances and the inward grace of His Spirit.

Jesus gave Himself to Mary in such an ineffable manner, and Mary corresponded so fully that after the union of the Divine Persons in the Trinity, and the hypostatic union of the Incarnation, we cannot conceive one greater nor deeper.

Let us draw near to Mary with a humble but entire confidence. If her Son is the Saviour of the world, she enters too deeply into His mission not to share the love that He bears to sinners. "O Mother of our Redeemer," let us sing to her with the Church, "thou didst bear thy Creator whilst remaining a Virgin, succour this fallen race which thy Son came to save in taking from us a human nature": *Alma Redemptoris mater...succurre cadenti surgere qui curat populo*; "Have pity upon the sinners whom thy Son came to redeem"; *Peccatorum miserere*. For, O Mary, it was to redeem us that He vouchsafed to descend from the eternal splendours into thy virginal bosom.

II

Mary understands this prayer, for she is closely associated with Jesus in the work of our redemption.

Eight days after the Birth of her Son, she has Him circumcised according to the Jewish Law; she then gives Him the name told her by the Angel, the name of Jesus, which denotes His mission of salvation and His work of redemption.

When Jesus is forty days old, the Blessed Virgin associates herself yet more directly and deeply with the work of our salvation by presenting Him in the Temple. She is the first to offer to the Eternal Father His Divine Son. After the oblation that Jesus, the supreme High Priest, made of Himself from the moment of His Incarnation and that He consummated on Calvary, Mary's offering is the most perfect. It goes beyond all the sacerdotal acts of men, because Mary is the Mother of Christ, while men are but His ministers.

Let us contemplate Mary in this solemn act of the Presentation of her Son in the Temple of Jerusalem.

All the magnificent and circumstantial ceremonial of the Old Covenant converged towards Christ; in the New Covenant, the obscure symbols were to find their perfect reality.

You know that every Jewish mother has to present herself in the Temple a few weeks after the birth of her child, in order to be purified from the legal stain thereby contracted in consequence of original sin. Moreover, if it was her firstborn and a son, she must present him to the Lord to be consecrated to Him as to the sovereign Master of every creature: *Omne masculinum adaperiens vulvam sanctum Domino vocabitur.*[1] However, he could be "redeemed" by a more or less considerable offering—a lamb or a pair of turtledoves according as the parents could afford.

Certainly this prescription obliged neither Mary nor Jesus. Jesus was the supreme Law-giver of all the Jewish ritual; His Birth had been miraculous and virginal; there was nothing about it but what was pure: *Quod nascetur ex te* SANCTUM, *vocabitur Filius Dei.*[2] It was therefore unnecessary to consecrate Him to the Lord as He was the very Son of God. Neither was it requisite that she who had conceived Him by the Holy Spirit and remained a virgin should be purified.

But Mary, guided by the Holy Spirit, was in perfect conformity of soul with the soul of her Son. Jesus had said to His Father on coming into this world: "Behold I come...that I should do Thy will, O God": *Ecce venio.*[3] And the Blessed Virgin's words were "Behold the handmaid of the Lord; be it done to me according to thy word": *Ecce ancilla Domini, fiat mihi secundum verbum tuum.*

Therefore she willed to accomplish this ceremony, showing thereby the depth of her submission. With Joseph, her husband, she brought her Firstborn, *Primogenitum suum.* He who was to remain her only Son, was to become "the Firstborn amongst many brethren" who, by grace, were

---

1 "Every male opening the womb shall be called holy to the Lord," Luc, ii, 23; cf. Exod. xiii, 2.
2 "The Holy which shall be born of thee shall be called the Son of God," Luc. i, 35.
3 Hebr. x, 5–7.

to be like unto Him: *Primogenitus in multis fratribus.*[1]

When we meditate upon this mystery, we are forced to say: "Verily Thou art a hidden God," O Saviour of the world! *Deus absconditus, Deus Israel Salvator.*[2] Upon this day, Christ enters for the first time into the Temple, and it is into *His* temple that He enters. This wonderful temple, the admiration of the nations and the pride of Israel, wherein were performed all the religious rites and sacrifices of which God Himself had regulated the details, this temple belongs to Him; for this Child carried in the arms of a young Maiden is the King of kings and the Sovereign Lord: *Veniet ad templum* SUUM *Dominator.*[3]

And how does He come? In the splendour of His majesty? As the One to Whom all these offerings alone are due? No, He comes thither absolutely hidden.

Listen to what the Gospel relates. There must have been a hustling crowd at the approach of the sacred building—merchants, levites, priests, doctors of the Law. A little group passes unnoticed through this crowd. They are poor people for they do not bring a lamb, the offering of the rich; they bring only two pigeons, the offering of the poor. No one heeds them, for they have no following of servants; the great, the haughty among the Jews have not so much as a glance for them, and it is needful that the Holy Spirit should enlighten the old man Simeon and Anna the prophetess in order that they should recognise the Messias. He Who is the Saviour promised to the world, the Light to be revealed to all nations, *Salutare tuum quod parasti ante faciem omnium populorum,*[4] comes into His temple as a hidden God: *Vere Deus absconditus.*

Nothing, moreover, outwardly betrays the feelings of the holy soul of Jesus. The Light of His Divinity remains hidden, veiled; but He renews, here in the Temple, the self-oblation He had made at the moment of His Incarnation. He offers Himself to God to belong to Him by every right: *Sanctum Domino vocabitur.* It was like the offertory of the Sacrifice that was to be consummated on Calvary.

This act was extremely pleasing to the Father. To outward appearance, there was nothing particular in this simple action that all Jewish moth-

---

1 Rom. viii, 29. 2 Isa. xlv, 15.
3 "The Lord shall come to his temple," Malach. iii, 1. 4 Luc. ii, 30–31.

ers performed. But on this day God receives infinitely more glory in the temple than He had ever received by all the sacrifices and holocausts of the Old Law, for on this day it is His Son Jesus Who is offered and Who Himself offers infinite homage of adoration, thanksgiving, expiation and supplication. The Heavenly Father receives with incommensurable joy this sacred offering, this Gift worthy of Himself, and all the heavenly court fix their ravished gaze upon this unique oblation. There is now no more need of holocausts and sacrifices of animals. The only Victim worthy of God had just been offered to Him.

And it is by the hands of Our Lady, Our Lady full of grace, that this offering is presented. Mary's faith was perfect. Filled with the light of the Holy Spirit, her soul understood the value of the offering that she was making to God at this moment; by His inspirations, the Holy Spirit put her soul in harmony with the inward dispositions of the Heart of her Divine Son.

In the same way as she had given her consent in the name of the whole human race when the Angel announced to her the mystery of the Incarnation, so upon this day, Mary offered her Son Jesus in the name of the human race. She knew that her Son is "the glorious King of the new Light... begotten before the day-star...the Lord of life and death." And so she presents Him to God in order to obtain for us all the graces of salvation that Jesus, according to the Angel's promise, is to bring to the world: *Ipsa enim portat Regem gloriae novi luminis; subsistit Virgo adducens manibus Filium ante lucifernum genitum.*[1]

Do not forget besides that the One she thus offers is her own Son, Whom she bore in her virginal and fruitful womb. What priest, what saint ever presented the Eucharistic oblation to God in such close union with the Divine Victim as was the Virgin at this moment? Not only was she united to Jesus by faith and love, as we ourselves can be, although in an infinitely lesser degree, but the bond that united her to Christ Jesus was unique. This is why Mary, from the day on which she presents Jesus as the first fruits of the future sacrifice, has such a great part in the work

---

1 "For she carries the King of glorious new light; she remains a Virgin, bring with her hands a Son, begotten before the morning star," Antiphon *Adorna* at the Blessing of the Candles on the Feast of the Purification.

of our redemption.

And see how, also from this instant, Christ Jesus associates His Blessed Mother with His state of Victim.

The old man, Simeon, guided by and filled with the Holy Spirit, is led thither: *Et Spiritus Sanctus erat in eo...et venit in Spiritu in templum.* He recognizes the Saviour of the world in this Child, He takes Him in his arms and sings his joy in having at length seen with his eyes the promised Messias. After having exalted "the Light of the revelation of the Gentiles," he says, as he restores Him to His Mother: "Behold this Child is set for the fall, and for the resurrection of many in Israel, and for a sign which shall be contradicted; and thy own soul a sword shall pierce."[1] It was the foreshadowing of the Sacrifice of Calvary.

The Gospel tells us nothing of how Our Lady received this prediction which she could never forget. St. Luke reveals to us later that Mary "kept all these words in her heart" *Mater ejus conservabat omnia verba haec in corde suo.*[2] Could not this be already said of Simeon's unexpected announcement? Yes, she kept the memory of these words, so terrible in their mystery; now and henceforward they pierced her soul. But Mary, whose pure heart was in full accord with the Heart of her Son, already accepted to be thus closely associated with His Sacrifice.

We shall one day see her consummate, like Jesus, her oblation upon the mount of Golgotha; we shall see her standing, *Stabat mater ejus,*[3] to offer again her Son, the fruit of her womb, for our salvation, as she had offered Him thirty-three years before in the Temple of Jerusalem.

Let us thank Our Lady for having presented her Divine Son for us; let us render fervent acts of thanksgiving to Jesus Himself for offering Himself to His Father for our salvation.

At Holy Mass, Christ offers Himself anew; let us present Him to His Father; let us unite ourselves to Him, like Him, in perfect submission to the will of His heavenly Father; let us unite our faith to the intense faith of our Lady. It is by this true faith and faithful love, *Te veraciter agnoscamus et fideliter diligamus,*[4] that our offerings will deserve to be pleasing to God: *Oculis tuae majestatis digna sint munera.*[5]

---

1 Luc. ii, 25, 27, 32–35.   2 Ibid. ii. 51.   3 Cf. Joan. xix, 25.
4 Collect for the Blessing of Candles.
5 Cf. Secret of the Mass for the Feast of the Purification.

III

Whilst awaiting the fulfilment of Simeon's prophecy, Mary was to have even then her share of sacrifice.

She must soon flee into Egypt, into an unknown land, to snatch her Son from the wrath of the tyrant Herod; she stays there until the Angel, after the king's death, bids Joseph retrace the road to Palestine. The Holy Family now takes up its abode at Nazareth. It is there that the life of Jesus is to be spent until the age of thirty, so much so that He will be called "Jesus of Nazareth."

The Gospel has preserved for us only one episode of this period of Christ's life: Christ lost in the Temple.

You know the circumstances that had taken the Holy Family to Jerusalem. The Child Jesus was twelve years old. It was the age when young Israelites began to be subject to the precepts of the Mosaic Law, notably that of going to the Temple three times a year, at the feasts of the Pasch, of Pentecost and of Tabernacles. Our Divine Saviour who had willed, by His Circumcision, to bear the yoke of the Law, went then with Mary and His foster-father to the Holy City. It was doubtless the first time that He made this pilgrimage.

When this Boy entered into the Temple, none suspected that He was the God Who was there adored. Jesus was there mingling with the crowd of Israelites, taking part in the ceremonies of the worship and in the chanting of the psalms. He understood, as none other ever will, the significance of the sacred rites and the symbolism of this liturgy whereof God Himself had laid down the details. Jesus, seeing prefigured all that was to be accomplished in His Person, offered perfect praise to His Father in the name of all humanity. In this praise, God received a homage infinitely worthy of Him.

"And having fulfilled the days," says the Evangelist, "the Child Jesus remained in Jerusalem, and His parents knew it not."[1] At the time of the Pasch the throng of Jews was very considerable, and, in returning, the caravans cannot have been easy to form, so it was not until late in the day that it could be recognized how they were composed. Moreover, ac-

---

1 Luc ii. 43.

cording to the custom, the young people might join, as it pleased them, such or such a group of their caravan. Mary believed that Jesus was with Joseph. She journeyed then in peace, singing the sacred hymns; above all she thought of Jesus, hoping soon to see Him again.

But what was her sorrowful surprise when, upon rejoining the group where Joseph was, she did not find the Child. Where was Jesus? Neither she nor Joseph could tell.

When God wills to lead a soul to the heights of perfection and contemplation, He makes her pass through great trials. Our Lord has said that when a branch united to Him, Who is the Vine, bears fruit, His Father purges it: *Purgabit eum.* And why? "That it may bring forth more fruit": *Ut fructum plus afferat.*[1] Spiritual darkness falls upon the soul. She feels forsaken by God Who thus tries her in order to make her worthy of a closer and higher union with Himself.

The Virgin Mary had certainly no need of such trials. What branch was ever more fruitful, since she herself gave the Divine Fruit to the world? But when she lost Jesus, she knew those sharp sufferings which were to increase her capacity of love and the extent of her merits. We can scarcely measure the greatness of this affliction. In order to comprehend it, we should have to comprehend all that Jesus was for His Mother.

Mary knew Jesus too well to think that He had left them without some purpose. When would He return? Would she ever see Him again? She had not lived several years with Jesus at Nazareth without being aware that there was in Him an ineffable mystery. And this was for her at that moment a source of unequalled anguish.

The Child must now be sought. What days were those! God permitted that our Lady should be in darkness during those anxious hours. She did not understand why Jesus had not forewarned her. Her sorrow was immense in being thus deprived of Him Whom she loved at once as her Son and her God.

Mary and Joseph returned to Jerusalem with troubled hearts. The Gospel tells us that they everywhere sought Jesus among their kinsfolk and acquaintance[2]; but none of them had seen Him. Finally, you know

---

1 Joan. xv, 2.   2 Luc. ii, 44.

how after three days they found Him in the Temple, sitting in the midst of the doctors of the Law.

The Doctors of Israel assembled in one of the halls of the Temple to explain the Holy Scriptures. Anyone might come and join himself to the group of disciples and listeners. This is what Jesus did. He came into the midst of them, not to teach,—the hour when He would present Himself to all as the one and only Lord Who had come to reveal the secrets from on high, had not yet struck;—He came there, like other young Israelites, among the doctors "hearing them, and asking them questions," as the Gospel tells us.[1]

And what was the object of the Child Jesus in thus questioning the doctors of the Law? He wished, doubtless, to enlighten them, to lead them, by His questions and His replies, by the quotations that He made from the Scriptures, to speak of the coming of the Messias; to direct their search towards this point, so that their attention should be awakened as to the circumstances of the appearing of the promised Saviour. This is, apparently, what the Eternal Father willed of His Son, the mission that He gave Him to accomplish, and for which He caused Him to interrupt, for a short space of time, His hidden and silent life. And the doctors of Israel "were astonished at His wisdom and His answers": *Stupebant...prudentia et responsis ejus.*[2]

Mary and Joseph, overjoyed at finding Jesus, drew near to Him, and His Mother said: "Son, why hast Thou done so to us?" It is not a reproach,—the humble Virgin-Mother was too wise to dare to blame Him Whom she knew to be God;—but it is the cry of a heart betraying its maternal feelings. "Behold Thy father and I have sought Thee sorrowing," *dolentes.* And what is Christ's answer? "How is it that you sought me? Did you not know, that I must be about My Father's business?"[3]

These are the first words fallen from the lips of the Incarnate Word that have been gathered up by the Gospel. They epitomise the whole Person and work of Jesus; they tell of His Divine Sonship and indicate His supernatural mission. All Christ's existence will be but a striking and

---

1 Luc. ii. 46.   2 Ibid. ii, 47.   3 Ibid. ii, 48–49.

magnificent commentary on these words.

They contain, too, precious teaching for our souls.

As "Son of man," *Filius hominis,* Christ was bound to observe the natural law, and the Mosaic Law commanded children to show respect, love and submission to their parents. And who did so better than Jesus? He will say later that He was not come to destroy the Law, but to fulfil it.[1] In whose heart could there be a deeper fund of human tenderness?

As "Son of God," *Filius Dei,* He had duties towards His Heavenly Father that were higher than human duties, and at times seemed to be in opposition to the latter. His Father had given Him to understand that He was to stay that day in Jerusalem.

By the words that He uttered on this occasion, Christ gives us to understand that when God requires us to accomplish His will, we must not allow ourselves to be stayed by any human consideration; it is on these occasions that we must say: I must give myself up wholly to the interests of my Heavenly Father.

St. Luke, who had doubtless gathered the humble avowal from Our Lady herself, tells us that "they understood not the word that He spoke unto them."[2] She well knew that her Divine Son could only act in a perfect manner; but why had He not forewarned her? She did not realize what relation there was between this manner of acting and His Father's interests, nor how it entered into the plan of salvation which His Heavenly Father had given Him.

But if she did not perceive all the meaning of the present conduct of Jesus, she knew that He was the Son of God: Therefore she submitted silently to the Divine will which had just required such a sacrifice from her love. She "kept all these words in her heart": *Conservabat omnia verba haec in corde suo.* Her heart was the tabernacle where she adored the mystery of her Son's words whilst awaiting the full light that was to be given her.

IV

The Gospel tells us that after having been found in the Temple, Jesus went down to Nazareth with His Mother and St. Joseph and that He there

---

1 Matth. v, 17.   2 Cf. Luc. ii, 50.

remained until the age of thirty years. And the sacred scribe sums up all this long period in these simple words. *Et erat subditus illis*[1]: "and He... was subject to them."

Thus out of a life of thirty-three years, He Who is Eternal Wisdom chose to pass thirty of these years in silence and obscurity, submission and labour.

Herein lies a mystery and teaching of which many souls, even pious souls, do not grasp all the meaning.

He Who is infinite and eternal, one day after centuries of waiting, humbles Himself to take a human form: *Semetipsum exinanivit, formam servi accipiens...et habitu inventus ut homo.*[2] Although He is born of a spotless Virgin, the Incarnation constitutes an incommensurable abasement for Him: *Non horruisti virginis uterum.*[3] And why does He descend into these abysses? To save the world, in bringing to it the Divine Light.

Now,—excepting those rays granted to a few privileged souls: the shepherds, the Magi, Simeon and Anna,—this Light is hidden; it remains voluntarily, during thirty years, "under a bushel," *sub modio,* to be at last manifested only for the duration of scarcely three years.

Is not this mysterious; is it not even disconcerting for our reason? If we had known the mission of Jesus, should we not have asked Him, as many of His kinsfolk did later, to manifest Himself to the world: *Manifesta teipsum mundo.*[4]

But God's thoughts are not our thoughts, and His ways are higher than our ways. He Who comes to redeem the world wills to save it first of all by a life hidden from the eyes of the world.

Truly, my Saviour, You are a hidden God: *Deus absconditus, Israel Salvator.* Doubtless, O Jesus, You grow "in wisdom age, and grace with God and men."[5] Your soul possesses the fulness of grace from the first moment of Your entrance into this world, and all the treasures of knowledge and wisdom, but this wisdom and this grace are only manifested little by little. You remain a hidden God in the eyes of men. Your Divinity is veiled beneath the outward appearance of a workman. O Eternal Wisdom Who, to draw us out of the abyss into which Adam's proud disobedience had

---

1 Ibid. ii, 51.   2 Philipp. ii, 7.
3 "You did not abhor the womb of the virgin," Hymn *Te Deum.*
4 Joan. vii. 4   5 Luc. ii, 52.

plunged us chose to live in a humble workshop and therein to obey creatures, I adore and bless You!

In the sight of His contemporaries, the life of Jesus Christ at Nazareth then appeared like the ordinary existence of a simple artizan. We see
how true this is. Later, when Christ reveals Himself in His public life, the
Jews of His country are so astonished at His wisdom and His words, at
the sublimity of His doctrine and the greatness of His works, that they
ask each other: "How came this man by this wisdom and miracles? Is
not this the carpenter's son? Is not His Mother called Mary?...Whence
therefore hath He all these things?" *Unde huic sapientia haec et virtutes?*
Nonne hic est fabri filius? Nonne mater ejus dicitur Maria? Unde ergo huic
omnia ista?[1] Christ was a stumbling block for them.

This mystery of the hidden life contains teachings which our faith
ought eagerly to gather up.

First of all there is nothing great in the sight of God except that which
is done for His glory, through the grace of Christ. We are only acceptable
to God according to the measure in which we are like unto His Son Jesus.

Christ's Divine Sonship gives infinite value to His least actions; Christ
Jesus is not less adorable nor less pleasing to His Father when He wields
the chisel or plane than when He dies upon the Cross to save humanity.
In us, sanctifying grace, which makes us God's adoptive children, deifies
all our activity in its root and renders us worthy, like Jesus, although by
a different title, of His Father's complacency.

The most precious talents, the most sublime thoughts, the most generous and splendid actions are without merit for eternal life if not vivified
by sanctifying grace. The passing world may admire and applaud them;
eternal life neither accepts them nor holds them of account. "What doth
it profit a man," said Jesus, the infallible Truth, "if he gain the whole world,
and suffer the loss of his own soul?"[2]

What does it serve a man to conquer the world by the force of arms,
by the charm of eloquence or the authority of knowledge, if, not having
God's grace, he be shut out from the kingdom that has no end?

See, on the other hand, that poor workman who painfully gains his

---

1 Matth. xiii, 54–56; cf. Marc. vi, 2–3.   2 Matth. xvi, 26.

livelihood, this humble servant ignored by the world, this beggar disdained by all: no one heeds them. If Christ's grace animates them, these souls delight the angels, they are continual objects of love for the Infinite Being; they bear within them, by grace, the very features of Christ.

Sanctifying grace is the first source of our true greatness. It confers upon our life, however commonplace it may seem, its true nobility and imperishable splendour.

Oh! if you knew the gift of God!...

But this gift is hidden.

The Kingdom of God is built up in silence; it is, before all things, interior, and hidden in the depths of the soul: *Vita vestra est abscondita cum Christo in Deo.*[1] Undoubtedly grace possesses a virtue which nearly always overflows in works of charity, but the principle of its power is entirely within. It is in the depths of the heart that the true intensity of the Christian life lies, it is there that God dwells, adored and served by faith, recollection, humility, obedience, simplicity, labour and love.

Our outward activity has no stability nor supernatural fruitfulness save in so far as it is linked to this interior life. We shall truly only bear fruit outwardly according to the measure of the supernatural intensity of our inner life.[2]

What can we do greater here below than promote Christ's reign within souls. What work is worth so much as that? It is the whole work of Jesus and of the Church.

We shall, however, succeed in it by no other means than those employed by our Divine Head. Let us be throughly convinced that we shall do more work for the good of the Church, the salvation of souls, the glory of our Heavenly Father, in seeking first of all to remain united to God by a life of love and faith of which He is alone the object, than by a devouring and feverish activity which leaves us no leisure to find God

---

1 "Your life is hid with Christ in God," Col. iii, 3.

2 This truth has been remarkably demonstrated and set forth in a work which we strongly recommend to our readers: The True Apostolate by Dom J. B. Chautard, Abbot of Sept-Fons, translated from the French by Rev. F. Girardey, C. SS. R. The work is especially addressed to priests and religious, but it is not less useful to all lay-people who are occupied in works of zeal.

again in solitude, recollection, prayer and self-detachment.

Nothing favours this intense union of the soul with God like the hidden life. And this is why souls living the inner life, and enlightened from on high, love to contemplate the life of Jesus at Nazareth. They find in it a special charm and, moreover, abundant graces of holiness.

V

It is especially through the Blessed Virgin Mary that we shall obtain a share in the graces that Christ merited for us by His hidden life at Nazareth. Those years must have been for the Mother of God a wellspring of priceless graces. We are dazzled by the very thought of them, and intuitions scarcely to be expressed in words are awakened within us when we reflect upon what those thirty years must have been for Mary and how every movement, word and action of Jesus were for her as so many revelations.

Doubtless there must have been much that was incomprehensible even for the Blessed Virgin. No one could live in continual contact, as she did, with the Infinite, without at times feeling and touching mystery. But yet what abundant light for her soul, what a continual increase of love this ineffable intercourse with a God, working under her eyes, must have wrought in her immaculate heart!

Mary lived with Jesus in a union surpassing all that can be said of it. They were truly one; the mind, heart, soul, in a word the whole existence of the Virgin-Mother was in absolute accord with the mind, heart, soul and life of her Son. Her life was, as it were, a pure and perfect vibration, tranquil and full of love, of the very life of Jesus.

What was the source of this union and of this love in Mary? It was her faith. The Blessed Virgin's faith is one of her most characteristic virtues.

How wondrous and how full of confidence is her faith in the word of the Angel! The heavenly messenger announces to her an unheard of mystery which astonishes and overthrows nature: the conception of a God in a virginal womb. And Mary says: *Fiat mihi secundum verbum tuum.*[1] It is because she gives the full assent of her mind to the Word of

---

1 "Be it done to me according to thy word," Luc. i, 38.

the Angel that she merits to become the Mother of the Incarnate Word: *Prius concepti mente quam corpore.*[1]

Mary's faith in the Divinity of Jesus is never shaken. She ever sees in her Son the Infinite God.

And yet to what trials is not this faith subjected! Her Son is God. The Angel tells her that Jesus will sit in the throne of David, that He will save the world, and of His kingdom there shall be no end. And Simeon predicts to her that Jesus will be a sign of contradiction, a cause of ruin as well as of salvation. Then Mary has to flee into Egypt to snatch her Son from Herod's tyrannical fury; until He is thirty years old, her son, Who is God and comes to redeem the human race, lives, in a poor workshop, a life of labour, submission and obscurity. Later on, she will see her Son pursued by the hatred of the Pharisees, she will see Him forsaken by His disciples, in the hands of His enemies, she will see Him hanging upon the Cross, mocked and despised, she will hear Him cry out from the depths of anguish:" My God, my God, why hast Thou forsaken Me"—but her faith will remain unshaken. It is even then, at the foot of the Cross, that it shines in all its splendour. Mary ever recognises her Son as her God, and therefore the Church proclaims her "the Faithful Virgin" supereminently: *Virgo fidelis.*

And this faith is the source of all Mary's love for her Son; it is through this faith that she remains ever united to Jesus. Let us ask her to obtain for us a firm and practical faith that has its culmination in love and in the accomplishment of the Divine will: "Behold the handmaid of the Lord, be it done to me according to Thy word." These words sum up all Mary's existence. May they likewise sum up ours!

This intense faith which was a source of love for the Mother of God was also a principle of joy. The Holy Spirit Himself teaches us this, by the mouth of Elizabeth, when He declares that the Virgin is blessed because of her faith: *Beata credidisti.*[2]

It will be the same for us. St. Luke relates that once after Jesus had

---

1 "She conceived the Word first with her mind then with her body," S. Augustine in, *De Virgin.,* c. 3; *Sermo ccxv,* n. 4; S. Leo, *Sermo I de Nativitate Domini,* c. 1; S. Bernard, *Sermo I de Vigilia Nativit.*

2 Luc. i, 45.

been speaking to the multitude, a woman lifting up her voice, cried out: "Blessed is the womb that bore Thee, and the paps that gave Thee suck": *Beatus venter qui te portavit, et ubera quae suxisti.* And Christ answered: "Yes rather, blessed are they who hear the word of God and keep it."[1] Jesus in nowise contradicted the acclamation of the Jewish woman; was it not He Who inundated His Mother's heart with incomparable joys? He only wishes to show us where the principle of joy is to be found for us as for her. The privilege of the Divine maternity is unique. From all eternity God chose Mary for the wondrous mission of being the Mother of His Son. That is the root of all Mary's greatness.

The Blessed Virgin merited the joys of Divine Motherhood by her faith and love, and Jesus wishes to teach us that we may share, certainly not in the glory of having given birth to Christ, but in the joy of bringing Him forth in souls. And how are we to obtain this joy? By hearing and keeping the word of God. We hear it by faith, we keep it by doing with love what it ordains.

Such is for us, as for Mary, the source of the soul's true joy and the way of happiness. If, after having inclined our heart to the teaching of Jesus, we obey His will and remain united to Him, we shall become as dear to Him—it is He again Who declares it,—as if we were for Him, a mother, brother, sister: *Quicumque enim fecerit voluntatem Patris mei, qui in caelis est, ipse meus frater, et soror, et mater est.*[2]

What closer union than this could we desire?

---

1 Ibid. xi, 27.   2 Matth. xii, 50; cf. Luc. viii, 21; Marc. iii, 35.

THE BAPTISM AND THE
TEMPTATION OF JESUS

(Lent)

SUMMARY.—I. In coming to St. John to receive the baptism of penance, Christ Jesus accomplishes an act of profound humility.—II. Christ is glorified on coming forth from the waters of the Jordan; how this testimony of the Eternal Father at the outset of the Public Life characterises one of the aspects of Christ's redeeming mission.—III. Directly after His baptism, Jesus is led by the Spirit into the desert to encounter the assaults of the devil: reasons for this mystery.—IV. The Gospel narrative of the Temptation.—V. The grace that Christ has merited for us by this mystery:—to triumph over temptation by remaining united to the Incarnate Word. The promises of spiritual invulnerability set forth in the Psalm *Qui habitat in adjutorio Altissimi.*[1] —VI. Faith is, preeminently, the weapon of resistance.

IN THE different mysteries of Christ Jesus upon earth, Eternal Wisdom has ordered events in such a way that the humiliations of the Incarnate Word are always accompanied by a revelation of His Divinity. Christ thus appears to us in the truth of His Divine nature as likewise in the reality of His human condition.

The far-reaching reason of this heavenly dispensation is both to help and exercise our faith, the foundation of all spiritual life. The astonishing abasements into which love plunges Christ give faith its merit; the manifestation of His Divine prerogatives gives faith its support.

The mysteries of the Birth and Childhood of Jesus are marked by these

---

1 "He that dwelleth in the aid of the most High," Ps. xl, 1.

contrasts of shadow and light which make our faith "reasonable," while leaving it free; the Public Life will be full of them to the point that the Jews will dispute bitterly among themselves about the personality of Christ; to some He will only appear as the son of an artizan of Nazareth, while for others He can be none other than the One sent by the Most High, and announced by all the prophets, to enlighten and save the world.

We shall find this supernatural dispensation again in the events wherewith Christ, after the thirty years of His Hidden Life, enters upon His Public Life: namely, His Baptism by John in the waters of the Jordan, and His Temptation in the desert.

Let us contemplate Jesus in these two mysteries so closely linked together. We shall see in them how wonderful are the decrees of Infinite Wisdom, and how far Christ, our Model, has gone before us in the way wherein we must follow Him in order to be like Him.

I

You know that God had appointed John, the son of Zachary and Elizabeth, as the Forerunner charged to announce to the Jews the coming of the Incarnate Word.

After a life given up to austerity and when in about his thirtieth year, John, urged by divine inspiration, had begun his teaching upon the banks of the Jordan. All his teaching was summed up in these words: "Do penance; for the kingdom of heaven is at hand."[1] To these urgent exhortations he joined baptism in the river, thereby to show his hearers the necessity of purifying their souls in order to render them less unworthy of the Saviour's coming. This baptism was only conferred on those who acknowledged themselves to be sinners and confessed their faults.

Now, one day when the Precursor administered "baptism for the remission of sins,"[2] Christ Jesus, Whose hour had come to leave the obscurity of the Hidden Life and manifest the Divine secrets to the world, mingled with the multitude of sinners and came with them to receive from John the purifying ablution.

---

1 Matth. iii, 2.   2 Marc. i, 4; Luc. iii, 2,

When we ponder on this thought that He Who thus proclaims Himself a sinner and voluntarily presents Himself to receive the baptism of penance, is the Second Person of the Holy Trinity, before Whom the Angels veil their faces, singing, "Holy, holy, holy,"[1] we are confounded at such a prodigious abasement.

The Apostle tells us that Christ is "holy, innocent, undefiled, separated from sinners,"[2] and here Jesus Himself comes asking baptism for the remission of sins! What is this mystery?

It is that in all His states, the Word Incarnate fills a double office: that of the Son of God, in virtue of His Eternal generation, and that of the head of a fallen race whose nature He has taken, and this race He has come to redeem.

As Son of God, He can claim to sit on the right hand of His Father and enjoy the glory and splendour of heaven.

But as Head of fallen humanity, having taken flesh, guilty in the rest of the human race, although wholly pure in Him, *In similitudinem carnis peccati,*[3] He can enter Heaven at the head of this mystical body only after having passed through the humiliations of His life and the sufferings of His Passion: *Nonne haec oportuit pati Christum, et ita intrare in gloriam suam?*[4]

Possessing the Divine nature, says St. Paul, Christ thought it not robbery to declare Himself equal to God in perfection[5]; but for us, for our salvation, He descended into the depths of humiliation; and, on this account, the Father exalted Him, giving Him the name of Jesus which signifies our redemption; in exalting His Son, the Father has raised us up together with Him to the heights of heaven: *Consedere fecit [nos] in caelestibus.*[6] It is truly to prepare the way before us that Christ enters into heaven: *Ubi praecursor pro nobis introivit Jesus.*[7]

However He will enter there only after having, by His Blood, paid off all our debt to Divine Justice: *Per proprium sanguinem introivit...in sancta,*

---

1 Isa, vi, 3.   2 Hebr. vii, 26.   3 Rom. vii, 3.
4 "Ought not Christ to have suffered these things and so, to enter into his glory?" Luc. xxiv, 26.
5 Cf. Philipp. ii, 6.   6 Ephes. ii, 6.
7 "Where the forerunner Jesus is entered for us," Hebr. vi, 20.

aeterna redemptione inventa.[1]

It is true that Christ comes to deliver us from the tyrannical slavery of the devil into whose power humanity had fallen in consequence of sin: *Qui facit peccatum, servus est peccati*[2]; He comes to save us from the eternal punishment that Satan, as the minister of Divine justice, had power to inflict upon us: *Ne forte tradat te judici, et judex tradat te ministro.*[3]

Now, the Incarnate Word, the God-Man, will only bring this redemption into effect by voluntarily substituting Himself for us sinners, making Himself answerable for our sin, to the point, as St. Paul says, that God accounted Him, as it were, a living sin: *Eum qui non noverat peccatum, pro nobis peccatum fecit.*[4]

If He takes our iniquities upon Himself, He will also take upon Himself our chastisement. He is to undergo an incommensurable sum of abasements and humiliations.

Such is the eternal decree.

We now understand why, at the beginning of His public life, when about to manifest His redeeming mission, Jesus submits to an act of profound humility—to a rite whereby He is numbered among sinners.

See, in fact, how when John, enlightened from on high, recognises in Him the Son of God, of Whom he had said: "The same is He Who shall come after me....Who is preferred before me, the latchet of Whose shoe I am not worthy to lose,"[5] he refuses with all his might to confer upon Christ the baptism of penance, "I ought to be baptized by Thee, and comest Thou to me?" *Joannes autem prohibebat eum.* But Christ replies: "Suffer it to be so now. For so it becometh us to fulfil all justice."[6]

What is this justice? It is the humiliation of the adorable Humanity of Jesus, which, in rendering supreme homage to Infinite Holiness, constitutes the full payment of all our debts towards Divine Justice. Jesus, just and innocent, takes the place of all our sinful race, *Justus pro injustis*[7]; and, by His immolation, He becomes "the Lamb of God Who takes away the

---

1 "By his own blood, he entered, having obtained eternal redemption," Ibid. ix, 12.
2 "Whosoever committeth sin is the servant of sin," Joan. viii, 34.
3 "Lest perhaps he deliver thee to the judge, and the judge deliver thee to the officer," Matth. v, 25.
4 "Him, who knew no sin, he hath made sin for us," II Cor. v, 21.
5 Joan. i. 27; cf. Matth. iii, 11; Marc. i, 7; Luc. iii, 16.
6 Matth. iii, 14–15.   7 "The just for the unjust," I Petr. iii, 18.

sins of the world,"[1] the "propitiation for our sins and...for those of the whole world."[2] It is thus that He fulfils all justice.

As we meditate on the deep meaning of these words of Jesus, let us humble ourselves with Him, let us acknowledge that we are sinners, and above all, let us renew the renunciation of sin made at our baptism.

The Precursor announced this baptism, which was far to surpass his own, since it was to be instituted by Christ in person: "I indeed baptize you in water unto penance, but He that shall come after me, is mightier than I....He shall baptize you in the Holy Ghost and fire."[3] The Baptism of Jesus is outwardly a baptism of water, like that of John; but at the same time that it is conferred, the Divine virtue of the Holy Spirit, Who is a spiritual fire, inwardly purifies and transforms the soul: *Per lavacrum regenerationis, et renovationis Spiritus sancti.*[4]

Let us, then, often renew our renunciation of sin. You know that the "character" given in Baptism remains indelibly on the soul; and when we repeat the promises made at the hour of our initiation, a new virtue springs from baptismal grace to strengthen our power of resistance against all that leads to sin:—the suggestions of the devil, and the seductions of the world and of the senses. It is thus that we can safeguard the life of grace within us.

By this, we likewise show our deep sense of gratitude to Christ Jesus for having taken upon Himself our iniquities so as to deliver us from them. "Who loved me," said St. Paul on recalling this mystery of infinite charity—"Who loved me, and delivered Himself for me!"[5] May I live for Him, for His glory, and no longer for myself, no longer to satisfy my covetousness, my self-love, my pride, my ambition. *Ut qui vivunt, jam non sibi vivant, sed ei, qui pro ipsis mortuus est!*[6]

I I

"And Jesus being baptized, forthwith came out of the water; and lo, the heavens were opened to Him: and He saw the Spirit of God descending

---

1 Joan. i, 29.　　2 I Joan. ii, 2.　　3 Matth. iii, 11; Marc. i, 8; Luc. iii, 16.

4 "By the laver of regeneration and renovation of the Holy Ghost," Tit. iii, 5.

5 Gal. ii, 20.

6 "That they who live may not now live to themselves, but unto him who died for them," II Cor. v, 15.

as a dove, and coming upon Him. And behold a voice from heaven, saying: This is My beloved Son, in Whom I am well pleased."[1]

This mysterious scene is but another special application of the divine law which I pointed out at the beginning of this conference: whenever Christ undergoes humiliation, for us, He must be glorified.

Jesus stoops so low as to mingle with the multitude of sinners, and forthwith the heavens are opened to magnify Him;—He asks for the baptism of penance, of reconciliation, and behold, the Spirit of Love testifies that He abides in Jesus with the plenitude of His gifts of grace;—He acknowledges Himself worthy of the strokes of divine justice, and behold, the Father declares that He takes all His delight in Him: *Humiliavit semetipsum...propter quod et Deus exaltavit illum.*[2]

This glorification of Christ concerns not only His Person; it has a very wide application upon which I want to lay stress.

It is at this moment that the mission of Jesus, as One sent by God, is declared authentic. The Father's testimony accredits, so to speak, His Son before the world, and hence this testimony relates to one of the characters of Christ's work as regards ourselves.

The mission of Jesus has a twofold aspect: it bears at the same time the character of redemption and of sanctification. It is to redeem souls, and, this done, to infuse life into them. That is the whole work of the Saviour. These two elements are inseparable, but distinct.

We find the germ of them in the circumstances which marked Christ's Baptism, the prelude to His public life.

We have just seen how, in coming to receive the baptism of penance, the Incarnate Word bears testimony to His office as Redeemer; His work is to be achieved by the gift of Divine life which He confers upon us in virtue of the merits of His Passion and Death: *Unigenitum misit Deus in mundum ut vivamus per eum,*[3] God gave us His Son "that whosoever believeth in Him...may have life everlasting": *Ut omnis qui credit in ipsum,*

---

1 Matth. iii, 16–17; Marc. i, 10–11; Luc. iii, 21–22.
2 "He humbled himself...for which cause God also hath exalted him," Philipp. ii, 8–9.
3 "God hath sent his only begotten Son into the world, that we may live by him," I Joan. iv, 9.

NON PEREAT,—*sed* HABEAT VITAM *aeternam.*[1]

The source of eternal life is, in us, a light.

In heaven, it is the light of the Beatific Vision. In that light, we shall live by the very life of God: *Quoniam apud te est fons vitae: et in lumine tuo videbimus lumen.*[2]

Here below, the source of our supernatural life is likewise a light, the light of faith. Faith is a participation in the knowledge that God has of Himself. This participation is communicated to the soul by the Incarnate Word; it becomes for us a light which guides us in all our ways, and therefore it must quicken all our supernatural activity: *Justus meus ex fide vivit.*[3]

Now, the foundation of this faith is the testimony which God renders to His Son Jesus: "This is My beloved Son in Whom I am well pleased."

Christ is solemnly presented to the world as One sent by the Father. All that He says will be the echo of that eternal truth which He ever contemplates in the bosom of the Father: *Unigenitus Filius, qui est in sinu Patris, ipse enarravit.*[4] His doctrine will not be His own, but that of the Father Who sends Him[5]; all that He hears, He will repeat; and thus, at the last day, Jesus will be able to say to His Father: "I have glorified Thee on the earth; I have finished the work which Thou gavest Me to do."[6]

The teaching of the Incarnate Word has not produced in every soul the light which should be for them the principle of salvation and life. He is "the Light of the world" undoubtedly, but we must follow Him if we would not walk in darkness and if we would arrive at the eternal light which is the source of our life in heaven: *Qui sequitur me, non ambulat in tenebris, sed habebit lumen vitae*[7]; God only accepts those who accept His Son.

To hear with profit the word of Christ, we must be drawn by the Father: *Omne, quod dat mihi Pater, ad me veniet*[8]; those whom the Father does not draw, do not hear the voice of the Word: *Vos non auditis, quia ex Deo non estis.*[9] And who are those whom the Father draws? Those who

---

1 Joan. iii, 15.

2 "For with thee is the fountain of life; and in thy light we shall see light," Ps. xxxv. 10.

3 "My just man liveth by faith," Hebr. x, 38.

4 "The only begotten Son who is in the Bosom of the Father, he hath declared him," Joan. i, 18.

5 Cf. Ibid. vii, 16.   6 Ibid. xvii, 4.   7 Ibid. viii, 12.

8 "All that the Father giveth to me shall come to me," Ibid. vi, 37.

9 Ibid. viii, 47.

acknowledge Jesus to be God's own Son: OMNIS *qui credit quoniam Jesus est Christus, ex Deo natus est.*[1]

This is why the public testimony given by the Father to Jesus after His Baptism constitutes both the point of departure of all the public life of Jesus, the Incarnate Word, Light of the world,—and the very basis of all Christian faith as well as of our sanctification.

Therefore, this mystery of the baptism of Jesus, which marks the beginning of His public life, contains, as it were, the summary of His whole mission here below.

By the humiliation which He willed to undergo in receiving this rite of penance "for the remission of sins,"—presage of His baptism of blood upon the Cross,—"Christ fulfils all justice." He renders to His Father's infinite perfections, outraged by sin, the supreme homage of the humiliations whereby He effects our redemption.

In return, the heavens are opened; the Eternal Father authentically introduces His Son to the world; the glorious splendour that this Divine testimony reveals, announces the mission of the enlightening of souls which the Word-made-Flesh is about to inaugurate; the Holy Spirit rests upon Him to show the plenitude of gifts that adorn His blessed soul and, at the same time, to symbolize the unction of grace that Christ is to communicate to the world.

Baptism, with faith in Jesus Christ, has become for us the Sacrament of Divine adoption and Christian initiation.

It is in the Name of the Holy Trinity that it is conferred upon us, the Trinity that was revealed to us upon the banks of the Jordan.

Sanctified by contact with the Humanity of Jesus, and united to "the Word of truth,"[2] the water has the virtue of washing away the sins of those who detest their faults and declare their faith in the Divinity of Christ; it is the "baptism," not only of water "for the remission of sins," but of the Spirit Who alone can "renew the face of the earth."[3] From being "children of wrath"[4] as we were, it makes us children of God, so that we are henceforward with Jesus, although in a lesser measure, the objects of the Heavenly Father's delight.

---

1 "Whosoever believeth that Jesus is the Christ, is born of God," I Joan. v, 1.

2 Jac. i, 15.   3 Cf. Ps. ciii, 30.   4 Ephes. ii, 3.

St. Paul says that we have by baptism put off the old man (descended from Adam) with the works of death, and have put on the new man created in justice and truth (the soul regenerated by the Word and the Holy Spirit) who is renewed unceasingly "according to the image of Him that created him."[1]

In the same way as baptism constituted for Christ the summary of all His mission, at once redeeming and sanctifying,—so baptism contains for us in germ the whole development of the Christian life with its twofold aspect of "death to sin" and of "life unto God."[2]

So true is it, according to the Apostle's words, that "as many...as have been baptized in Christ, have put on Christ"[3]; so true is it that we make only one with Jesus in all His mysteries.

O happy state of faithful Christians! O foolish blindness of those who forget their baptismal promises! O terrifying destiny of those who tread them underfoot!...

"For" said the Precursor to the Jews, "now the axe is laid to the root of the trees. Every tree therefore that doth not yield good fruit, shall be cut down and cast into the fire...." He says again: "There shall come one mightier than I...Whose fan is in His hand, and He will purge His floor, and will gather the wheat into His barn; but the chaff He will burn with unquenchable-fire..."[4] The Father loveth the Son, and He hath given all things into His hand. He that believeth in the Son (with a practical faith) hath life everlasting; but He that believeth not the Son, shall not see life: but the wrath of God abideth on Him."[5]

III

Scarcely was Jesus baptised, the Gospel tells us, than He was led by the Spirit into the desert. The sacred writers use different expressions to signify the action of the Holy Spirit. According to St. Mark, Jesus was "driven."[6] What does this term signify if not the vehemence of the Holy Spirit's action over the soul of Christ? And to what end was He thus driven into the desert? *Ut tentaretur a diabolo*: "to be tempted by the devil," That is

---

1 Cf. Col. iii, 9–10; Ephes. iv, 24.   2 Cf. Rom. vi, 11.
3 Cf. Gal. iii, 27.   4 Matth. iii, 10–12; Luc. iii, 9, 16–17.
 5 Joan. iii, 35–36.   6 Marc. i, 12.

the testimony of the Gospel itself.

Is not this an extraordinary thing? The Father has just proclaimed that Jesus is His beloved Son, the object of His complacency; the Spirit of Love rests upon Him and behold "immediately": statim, this Spirit drives Him into the desert there to be exposed to the suggestions of the devil. What a mystery! What, then, can such an extraordinary episode signify in the life of Christ? Why does it thus occur at the opening of His Public Life?

In order to understand the depth of this mystery, and before commenting on the Gospel account of it, we must first of all recall the place that temptation holds in our spiritual life.

The Divine perfections exact that every rational, free creature should be subjected to trial before being admitted to enjoy future beatitude. It is needful that, standing in God's sight, this creature should be placed in the face of trial and should freely renounce all satisfaction of self in order to acknowledge God's sovereignty and to obey His law. God's sanctity and justice demand this homage.

This choice, glorious for the Infinite Being, is for us the foundation of that merit which the Lord rewards with heavenly beatitude. The Council of Trent has declared that it is God Who saves us, but in such a way that salvation shall be at the same time a gift of His mercy and the reward of our merits.[1] Eternal life will be our recompense because, having had to choose, we resisted temptation in order to cleave to God; undergoing trial, we remained faithful to the Divine Will. Gold is tried in the furnace; constancy in the midst of temptation reveals a soul worthy of God.

Such is the noble condition of every free creature.

The angels were the first to be submitted to trial. Although we do not know exactly in what this trial consisted, we do know that it was of a na-

---

1 *Ideo bene operantibus usque in finem et in Deo sperantibus proponenda est vita aeterna et tamquam gratia filiis Dei per Jesum Christum misericorditer promissa, ut tamquam merces ex ipsius Dei promissione bonis ipsorum operibus et meritis fideliter reddenda... [Domini] tanta est erga homines bonitas ut eorum velit esse merita quae sunt ipsius dona.* (Eternal life is placed before those hoping in God and performing good works until the end, both as grace mercifully promised to the sons of God through Jesus Christ, and as a reward according to the promise of God Himself to be rendered faithfully to their good works and merits...Such is the goodness of the Lord towards men that He wishes their merits to be those things which are His gifts.) Sess. vi, cap. 16.

ture corresponding to the condition of angelic beings.

Remember that the angels are exclusively spiritual beings. Their acts are not, like ours, measured by time. Moreover, these acts possess a power, a range and a depth such as no human act can attain.[1] Being pure spirits, the angels do not reason; with us, the extreme mobility of our imagination, this sensitive faculty joined to the corporal organism, presents to our choice a number of particular enjoyments of which the variety retards the action of our intelligence and will; we pass from one enjoyment to another and perhaps we afterwards return to the one which we had at first decided to reject. It is not the same for the angel; having an altogether spiritual nature, he knows no hesitation; in him, the acts of intelligence and will bear a character of plenitude, of fixity and irrevocableness conferring upon these acts an incomparable strength.[2]

No human existence, however prolonged it might be, could attain, by all its operations put together, the power, amplitude or intensity of the single act by which the angels had to fix their choice in the midst of trial.

This is why the fidelity of the good angels was so pleasing to God; this is also why the sin of revolt of the rebellious spirits possessed a gravity which we cannot measure and of which we are incapable. Their depth of knowledge which permitted them to act in full light imbued this single sin with such malice that Divine justice had to punish it by an immediate sentence of eternal damnation.

For us, the acceptation of trial and resistance to temptation go on through our whole life here below. Daily we have to struggle against corrupting seductions, and to be patient in the contradictions willed or permitted by Providence: *Militia est vita hominis super terram.*[3]

But this gives us each day, too, a magnificent occasion of steadfast fidelity to God. A soul who, from the hour when she first takes consciousness of her actions until the moment of being separated from the body, should never have given way to a deliberate fault; who, placed between God and temptation capable of turning her away from Him, should always have freely chosen the Divine will, that soul would give immense glory to God. Why is this? Because in each of her acts, she would have proclaimed that

---

1　We are speaking evidently of the order of nature.
2　S. Thom. *De Veritate,* 9, xxiv, a. 10 and 11.
3　"The life of man upon earth is a warfare," Job. vii, 1.

God alone is her Lord. Happy this soul "that could have transgressed, and hath not transgressed; and could do evil things, and hath not done them!"[1] For the Lord will reward her magnificently: "Well done, good and faithful servant...enter thou into the joy of thy Lord...!"[2]

The first man was subjected to trial. He faltered, he fell away, he preferred the creature and his own satisfaction to God. He drew all his race into his rebellion, his fall and his chastisement.

That is why it was necessary that the second Adam, Who represented all the predestined, should act in a directly contrary manner. In His adorable wisdom, God the Father willed that Christ Jesus, our Head and our Model, should be placed in the face of temptation, and, by His free choice, come forth victorious in order to teach us to do the same. This is one of the reasons of this mystery.

There is a deeper reason, a reason that intimately links this mystery with that of baptism.

What, in fact, did Jesus say to the Precursor when the latter refused to fulfil his ministry of penance towards Christ? "Suffer it to be so now. For so it becometh us to fulfil all justice."[3] This justice, as we have seen, consisted in Jesus undergoing the sum of expiation decreed by His Father for the redemption of the human race: *Dare animam suam redemptionem pro multis.*[4] From the time of Adam's sin, the human race was the slave of Satan, and it is from the hands of the Prince of darkness that Christ Jesus is to save it. "For this purpose, the Son of God appeared, that He might destroy the works of the devil": *In hoc apparuit Filius Dei, ut dissolvat opera diaboli.*[5] This is why, as soon as He has received baptism by which He is marked as "the Lamb of God Who taketh away the sin of the world,"[6] and snatches all the flock from the power of the devil, the Word-made-Flesh enters into the lists with "the prince of this world"[7]; this is why the Holy Spirit immediately drives Him into the desert, as the scape-goat was formerly driven out laden with all the sins of the people: *Ut tentaretur a diabolo.*

---

1 Eccl. xxxi, 10.   2 Matth. xxv, 21.   3 Ibid. iii, 15.
4 "To give His life as a redemption for many," Ibid. xx, 28; Marc. x, 45.
5 I Joan. iii, 8.   6 Joan. i, 29.   7 Ibid. xiv, 30.

IV

Let us contemplate our Divine Captain in combat with the prince of the rebellious spirits.

We know that Jesus remained forty days and forty nights in the desert in the midst of the beasts, in complete solitude and in fasting; this is the Gospel's own testimony: *Nihil manducavit in diebus illis....*[1] *Eratque cum bestiis.*[2]

To well understand *this* mystery of the temptation of Jesus, let us recall what I have so often said: namely, that Christ is like to us in all things, *Debuit per omnia fratribus similari.*[3] Now imagine to what a state of weakness a man would be reduced who allowed himself no nourishment for forty days. Our Lord did not will to work a miracle to prevent in Himself the effects of this fast; therefore the Gospel relates that after this time, Jesus was hungry: *Postea esuriit.*[4] And assuredly after so prolonged a lapse of time, He must have been in a state of extreme exhaustion. We are about to see how the devil took occasion of this to tempt Him.

However, although sharing in our infirmities and weakness, Christ's Sacred Humanity cannot know sin: *Absque peccato*[5]; the soul of Christ is not subject to any ignorance, nor error, nor moral weakness.

Is there need to add that neither does He experience any of those disordered movements which in us are the results of original sin or of habits of sin? If, for us, Jesus has suffered hunger and languor, in Himself He remains the Saint of saints. What is the consequence of this doctrine? That the temptation that Christ can undergo does not touch His soul and remains wholly exterior; He can be tempted only by "principalities and powers...the rulers of the world of this darkness...the spirits of wickedness."[6]

Amongst these spirits, we may suppose that the one who tempted Christ was endowed with special power; but however marvellous his intelligence, he did not know who Christ was. No creature can see God except in the Beatific Vision. The devil is deprived of that.

In the same way, he had not the key to the mystery of the union of the Divinity with the Humanity in Jesus. He certainly suspected something; he did not forget the curse that had weighed upon him since God put an

---

1 Luc. iv, 2. 2 Marc. i, 13. 3 Hebr. ii, 17.
4 Matth. iv, 2. 5 Heb. iv, 15. 6 Ephes. vi, 12.

eternal enmity between him and the woman who was to crush his head, that is to say to destroy his power over souls; he could not be ignorant of the prodigies that had been wrought since the Birth of Jesus. The account of the temptation clearly shows this. But his knowledge was uncertain. He wanted, in tempting Christ, to know, without any manner of doubt, if it were possible to triumph over Him, for at all events he held Him to be an extraordinary being.

Therefore, as the Gospel tells us, the tempter approaches Jesus: *Et accedens tentator.* And seeing Him in a state of exhaustion, he seeks to make Him fall into a sin of gluttony. Not a sin of great gluttony by presenting Christ with savoury food—the devil had too high an opinion of the One Whom he attacked to believe that he would succumb to a suggestion of that kind—but he represents to Jesus, faint with hunger, that if He be the Son of God He has the power of working a miracle to satisfy this hunger. Thereby he tries to urge Christ to advance the hour of His Father by performing a prodigy of which the end was altogether personal. "If Thou be the Son of God, command that these stones"—pointing out the stones lying at the feet of Jesus—"be made bread." And what does Jesus answer? Does He make known that He is the Son of God? No. Does He perform the miracle suggested by the devil? No. He contents Himself with replying in the words of Scripture: "Not in bread alone doth man live, but in every word that proceedeth from the mouth of God...."[1] Later, during His public life; when one day His Apostles will bring Him food, saying: "Master, eat," *Rabbi, manduca,* Christ will give a like reply: "I have meat to eat, which you know not.... My meat is do to the will of Him that sent Me."[2] This is what He gives the devil to understand. He will wait to satisfy His hunger until the Father comes to His aid; He will not forestall the moment fixed by the Father in which to show forth His power; when the Father speaks He will hear His voice.

Seeing himself repulsed, the devil understands that he has before him, if not the Son of God, at least a being of great holiness. Thus he sets about employing a more dangerous weapon. He knows human nature wonderfully; he knows that those who have attained a high degree of perfection

---

1 Matth. iv, 3–4; Luc. iv, 3–4.   2 Joan. iv, 31–32, 34.

and of union with God, are above the reach of the gross appetites of the senses, but can be seduced by more subtle suggestions of pride and presumption; they can believe themselves to be better than others, and think that, even if they voluntarily expose themselves to danger, God owes them a quite special protection, on account of their fidelity. The devil, therefore, tries to tempt Christ in this way. Making use of his spiritual power, he transports Jesus upon the pinnacle of the temple and says to Him: "If Thou be the Son of God, cast Thyself down, for it is written: That He hath given His angels charge over thee, and in their hands they shall bear thee up, lest perhaps thou dash thy foot against a stone."[1] If Jesus be the Son of God, what a wonderful sign of His messianic mission, what an evident proof of God being with Him, if He were to appear from on high and thus descend in the midst of the multitude thronging the temple court! And to render his suggestion more seductive, the devil in his turn employs the divine word to support it. But Jesus replies, in a sovereign manner, with another sacred text: "It is written again: Thou shalt not tempt the Lord thy Lord."[2] This time again, the devil is defeated: the Word of God triumphs over his snares.

The spirit of darkness endeavours to vanquish Christ in a last assault. Taking Him upon a high mountain, he shows Him all the kingdoms of the world, he displays before His eyes all their riches, splendour and glory. What a temptation for the ambition of one believing himself to be the Messias! But a price has to be paid for this. This is only another stratagem of the evil spirit to learn at last who this Man may be who resists him so powerfully. "All this I will give thee, if falling down thou wilt adore me." You know the response of Jesus, and with what vigour He repulses the sacrilegious suggestion of the Evil One: "Begone, Satan, for it is written, the Lord thy God shalt thou adore, and Him only shalt thou serve."[3]

The prince of darkness now knows himself to be entirely unmasked; there is nothing left for him but to withdraw. However the Gospel says that the devil departed from Jesus only for a time: *Usque ad tempus.*[4] By this, the sacred writer indicates that, during the public life, the devil will make other attempts; by his instruments, if not in person, he will pursue Our Lord without intermission; during the Passion especially, he will,

---

1 Matth. iv, 5–6; Luc. iv, 9–11. 2 Matth. iv, 7; Luc. iv, 12.
3 Matth. iv, 8–10; Luc. iv, 5–8. 4 Luc. iv, 13.

through the hands of the Pharisees, be bent upon the ruin of Jesus: *Haec est hora vestra, et potestas tenebrarum.*[1] Satan will urge them, and they will urge the multitude to demand that Jesus be crucified: *Tolle, tolle, crucifige eum.*[2] But the Saviour's death upon the Cross was to be precisely the decisive stroke whereby to overthrow the devil's empire. So greatly does the Wisdom of God shine forth in all His works! *Qui salutem humani generis in ligno crucis constituisti...et qui in ligno vincebat in ligno quoque vinceretur.*[3]

The Gospel adds that "then the devil left Him; and behold angels came and ministered to Him."[4] This was the outward manifestation of the exaltation given by the Father to His Son, in reward for having stooped so low as to undergo in our name the attacks of the devil. The faithful angels appeared, and served Jesus with that bread which He awaited to be given Him at the hour appointed by His Father's providence.

Such is the Gospel narrative of the Temptation of Jesus.

If the Christ, the Incarnate Word, the Son of God, willed to enter into combat with the evil spirit, shall we be astonished if the members of His Mystical Body must follow the same path? So many, even pious people, believe that temptation is a sign of reprobation. But most often it is the contrary! Having become disciples of Jesus through baptism, we cannot be above our Divine Master.[5] QUIA *acceptus eras Deo,* NECESSE FUIT *ut tentatio probaret te*[6]: "Because thou wast acceptable to God, it was necessary that temptation should prove thee." It is God Himself Who tells us so.

Yes, the devil can tempt us, and tempt us strongly, and tempt us just when we think that we are the most secure from his shafts:—at the hours of prayer, after Holy Communion; yes, even at those blessed moments, he can whisper thoughts against faith, against hope, he can urge us to a spirit of independence and of revolt against the rights of God, he can raise up all evil passions in us. He can,—and he will not fail to do so.

Once more, do not let us be surprised; never let us forget that Christ, our Model in all things, was tempted before us, and not only tempted, but

---

1 "This is your hour and the power of darkness," Ibid. xxii, 53.   2 Joan. xix, 15.
3 "Who didst establish the salvation of mankind on the wood of the Cross...and he who conquered by a tree would also be conquered by a tree," Preface of the Cross.
4 Matth. iv, 11; Marc. i, 13.
5 Cf. Matth. x, 24; Luc. vi, 40; Joan. xiii, 16; xv, 20.   6 Tob. xii, 13.

touched by the spirit of darkness; He permitted the devil to lay a hand upon His most holy Humanity.

Above all, do not let us forget that it was not only as the Son of God that Jesus overcame the devil, but likewise as Head of the Church; in Him and by Him, we have triumphed and we triumph still over the suggestions of the rebel spirit.[1]

This is in fact the grace that the Saviour won for us by this mystery; herein is to be found the source of our confidence in trials and temptations; and it only remains for us to see how unshaken this confidence ought to be, and how, by our faith in Christ, we shall ever find the secret of victory.

V

The grace that the Incarnate Word merited for us in undergoing temptation is the grace of strength to defeat the devil in our turn, to come forth victorious from the conflict through which we must necessarily pass before we are admitted to enjoy divine life in the blessedness of Heaven. Christ Jesus has merited that those who are united to Him shall share,—and share according to the measure of their union with Him,—in this impeccability.

We here approach the very centre of the mystery.

We see in the Gospel that Christ was impeccable, inaccessible to the evil of sin, to the least imperfection. But what is the source of this moral invulnerability?

It is the fundamental truth that He is the very Son of God; as the Second Person of the Trinity, He is infinite Holiness, and cannot succumb to evil.

However, if we examine the Humanity of Jesus in itself, we see that it is a humanity created like unto our own; union with the Divinity did not take away from it those weaknesses which are compatible with the state of Son of God. Christ suffers hunger, thirst. He is overcome with fatigue; sleep weighs down His eyelids; fear, sadness, weariness take real possession of His soul;—and yet there is not the shadow of an imperfection in Him. If then the Humanity of Jesus, *as such,* enjoys impeccability, it is because it

---

1 *Justum quippe erat ut sic tentationes nostras suis tentationibus vinceret.* (He certainly was just in that he overcame our temptations by his own temptations.) S. Gregory, Homil. xvi in Evangel.

is strengthened in holiness in a marvellous way. Now, what is the means that God uses in order to render the blessed soul of Jesus inaccessible to moral evil, to sin, so as to establish it in impeccability?

It is to place Him under the protection of the Most High, *in adjutorio Altissimi*[1]; or according to the more significant rendering of the original text, "in the secret sanctuary of the Divinity": *In sanctuario secreto divinitatis.* And what is this sanctuary? It is the Beatific Vision.

As you know, the Beatific Vision is the blessed contemplation of God such as He is in Himself. They to whom this grace is granted can nevermore separate themselves from God, because they see that God is the Sovereign Good, and that no particular good, however vast it be, can be compared to Him. Hence sin, which consists in turning away from the law of God, from His will, or, what comes to the same thing, in turning away from God Himself, to attach oneself to some good as seen in self or in the creature,—is rendered radically impossible. In this blessed state wherein the intellect contemplates the very Truth, there is no room for any ignorance, nor illusion, nor error; and the will, cleaving to the absolute Good that contains the plenitude of all good, knows neither hesitation, nor falling away, nor defection of any kind. The soul that reaches this summit is, in theological language, perfectly "confirmed in grace."

This confirmation in grace is a consequence of predestination; it allows of different degrees measured by the perfection and extent of this predestination.

The Humanity of Jesus was predestinated to be united to the Eternal Word; that is why the soul of Christ, from the first instant of its existence, possessed, as the privilege resulting from this union, as the "connatural" attribute, the Beatific Vision; it was confirmed in grace in the highest degree, that is to say in *essential* and *absolute* impeccability. This is why we hear Our Lord, the Head of all the predestined, offer this challenge to the Jews: "Which of you shall convince me of sin?"[2] Likewise we hear Him say to His Apostles at the Last Supper: "I will not now speak many things with you. For the prince of this world cometh, and in Me he hath not anything."[3] Even as Man, Christ Jesus is the Saint of saints: *Tu solus*

---

1 Ps. xc, 1.   2 Joan. viii, 46.   3 Ibid. xiv, 30.

sanctus, Jesu Christe![1]

In heaven, the blessed have reached the perfect age of Christ[2]; they have attained the measure of the divine gift: *Secundum mensuram donationis Christi*[3]; they enjoy the beatific vision in the fulness of the grace bestowed upon them; they participate in a perfect manner, each according to his degree, in the Divine Sonship of Jesus: that is why they remain, like Him, fixed for ever *in sanctuario secreto divinitatis*: that is eternal impeccability.

Here below, it is not given to us to abide perfectly in this "sanctuary of the Divinity." But what is it that takes the place of the Beatific Vision for us upon earth? It is faith. Through faith we have God ever present: *Per fidem enim ambulamus.*[4] This faith in the light of which we walk, is the source of our union with Jesus and the root of our perfection: *Ambula coram me, et esto perfectus.*[5] In the measure whereby, through faith, we live in the contemplation of God, and remain united to Jesus Christ, in this same measure, we become invulnerable to temptation.

Already, upon earth, souls are to be met with who are so united to Jesus, so full of faith, that they are even now confirmed in grace. For example the Blessed Virgin was predestined to perfect exemption from sin, even from original sin; that is a unique privilege: *Tota pulchra es, Maria, et macula originalis non est in te.*[6] St. John the Precursor was sanctified from his mother's womb, and the Fathers of the Church tell us that he was confirmed in divine grace. It was the same with the Apostles, after they had received the gift of the Spirit on the day of Pentecost.

God offers to all a share in this confirmation in grace; and this share is measured, as I have said, by our life of faith. A soul who, through faith, lives habitually in the contemplation of God, draws continually from this fountain of life: *Quoniam apud te est fons vitae*[7]; she shares in Christ's union with His Father: *Ego in eis, et tu in me;* and hence also in the love that the Father bears towards His Son Jesus: *Ut dilectio qua dilexisti me in ipsis sit, et ego in ipsis.*[8]

---

1 "Thou only are holy, Jesus Christ!" Gloria of the Mass.   2 Ephes. iv, 13.
3 Ibid. 7.   4 "For we walk by faith," II Cor. v, 7.
5 "Walk before me, and be perfect," Gen. xvii, 1.
6 "Thou art all fair, Mary, and the original stain is not in thee," Antiphon for the Feast of the Immaculate Conception.
7 Ps. xxxv, 10.
8 "I in them, and thou in me," "That the love wherewith thou hast loved me may be in

This is why God takes such delight in such a soul; He protects her; He renders her, little by little, invulnerable. All her enemies may attack her; a thousand shall fall at her side, and ten thousand at her right hand and they shall not come nigh her; she will tread the devils underfoot; all the universe may rise up and be let loose against her, she will say to God: "Thou art my Protector and my Refuge," and God will deliver her from all snares and dangers: *Quoniam in me sperabit, liberabo eum.*[1]

Our Mother the Church, who is full of solicitude for her children, knows to what perils they are ever exposed; she knows, on the other hand, what powerful graces of life are given to us through the mysteries of the Incarnate Word, and through our union with Him, and so she recalls to us each year, at the beginning of Lent, the mystery of the Temptation of Jesus. She wills that during forty days, we should live like Him in the spirit of penance, retreat, solitude and prayer.

In order to help us to pass this time well, and to arouse within us the sentiments which should animate us, she gives us the account of Christ's fasting, temptation and triumph at the opening of these forty holy days.

At the same time she places upon our lips the whole 90th psalm, which begins with the words which I have just been explaining: "He that dwelleth in the sanctuary of the divinity shall abide under the protection of the God of heaven." It is pre-eminently the psalm of confidence in the midst of struggle, trial and temptation.

The magnificent promises contained in it apply first of all to Christ Jesus, and next to all the members of His mystical body according to the measure of their life of grace and of faith.

This is the reason why the Church is not content with making us read it in its entirety on the first Sunday of Lent; but she extracts from it, for her canonical office, verses which she makes us recite each day of this long period, so as to place constantly before our eyes the loving care of our Heavenly Father: "He hath given His angels charge over thee; to keep thee in all thy ways: *Angelis suis [Deus] mandavit de te: ut custodiant te in omnibus viis tuis*; "He hath delivered me from the snare of the hunter; and from the sharp word": *Ipse liberavit me de laqueo venantium et a*

---

them, and I in them," Joan. xvii, 23, 26.
1 Ps. xc, 2, 7, 14.

verbo aspero; "He will overshadow thee with His shoulders; and under His wings thou shalt trust": *Scapulis suis obumbrabit tibi et sub pennis ejus sperabis*; "His truth shall compass thee with a shield; thou shalt not be afraid of the terror of the night": *Scuto circumdabit te veritas ejus; non timebis a timore nocturno.*[1]

What confidence arises within us at the daily recalling of such promises! What assurance they give us for walking in the path of salvation: *Ecce nunc dies salutis,*[2] however surrounded this path may be with pitfalls, however full it may be of enemies! God is with us; and "If God be for us," says St. Paul, "who is against us?"[3] For, he adds, God will not suffer us to be tempted or tried above our strength; but He will protect us, and with His protection, He will grant us to rise above trial, to surmount temptation, and to prove to Him our fidelity, the source of merit and of glory: *Cum tentatione proventum.*[4]

VI

We see what invincibility the soul has that dwells in the sanctuary of the Divinity.

But never let us forget that we only attain to it through faith in Jesus Christ, our Head and our Model.

Indeed the psalmist says that, to protect us against the shafts of the enemy, God will encompass us with His truth as with a shield: *Scuto circumdabit te* VERITAS EJUS. This is likewise the thought of St. Paul, when he mentions in detail the weapons with which the Christian ought to be armed for the spiritual conflict: IN OMNIBUS *sumentes scutum* FIDEI, *in quo possitis* OMNIA *tela nequissimi ignea extinguere.*[5] "In all things taking the shield of faith, wherewith you may be able to extinguish all the fiery darts of the most wicked one." St. Peter speaks in the same manner: "Your adversary the devil, as a roaring lion, goeth about seeking whom he may devour; whom resist ye, strong in faith": *Cui resistite* FORTES IN FIDE.[6]

You will have remarked that in order to repulse the devil, Christ Jesus each time has recourse to the Divine Word. The same tactics will lead us to victory.

---

1 Ps. xc, 5, 11.   2 "Behold, now is the day of salvation," II Cor. vi, 2.
3 Rom. viii, 31.   4 I Cor. x, 13.   5 Ephes. vi, 16.   6 I Petr. v, 9.

When, therefore, the devil tempt us, for example, against the faith, let us recall to mind the testimony of the Eternal Father proclaiming that Jesus is His beloved Son: let us remember that those only are born of God who believe in Jesus, the Son of God.[1] When the devil prompts us to want of confidence, let us repeat those words of Christ: "Come to me, all you that labour, and I will refresh you...."[2] "Him that cometh to Me, I will not cast out": *Et eum, qui venit ad me, non ejiciam foras.*[3] If he seeks to overwhelm us with the remembrance of our faults and sins, let us answer him with the words of the Saviour: "I am not come to call the just, but sinners."[4] If he suggests thoughts of pride or ambition: "Whosoever shall exalt himself shall be humbled"[5]; if he excites us to revenge: "Blessed are the meek"[6]; if he causes deceitful joys to glitter before our eyes: "Blessed are the clean of heart."[7]

On every occasion, let us arm ourselves with the Word of God: it is a shield against which all the shafts of the enemy will be broken and brought to nought.

Faith is the chief of weapons. "I hold it for certain," wrote St. Teresa, "that God will never allow the devil to deceive a person who, mistrustful of herself in every thing, is so firm in the faith that she should be ready to suffer a thousand deaths for the smallest revealed truth."[8]

At the hour of trial, at the moment of temptation, it is faith that recalls to us God's sovereign right to the obedience of His creature, His infinite holiness, the adorable exigencies of His justice, the indescribable sufferings with which Jesus expiated sin, the gratuity of grace, the necessity of prayer, the eternity of pain with which God punishes the sinner who dies unrepentant, the endless beatitude with which He magnificently rewards the fidelity of a few years. All these truths are repeated to us by faith; and however redoubtable the darts of the enemy may be, however violent his suggestions, however prolonged the combat, a soul that has living faith finds in her faith and in her union with Christ, which is born of faith, the power of resistance, the very principle of her stability in good, the true secret of victory.

---

1 I Joan. v, 1.   2 Matth. xi, 28.   3 Joan. vi, 37.
4 Matth. ix, 13; Marc. ii, 17; Luc. v, 32.
5 Matth. xxiii, 12; Luc. xiv, 11; xviii, 14.
6 Matth. v, 4.   7 Ibid. 8.   8 Life by Herself, ch. 25.

Blessed is the soul,—God Himself tells us so—blessed is the soul that endures temptation without exposing herself to it; who, relying upon the Divine promises, passes through fire, with the eye of faith intent upon Christ's words and example; that soul will triumph even here below, and will later receive the reward of her generosity and love: BEATUS *vir qui suffert tentationem: quoniam cum probatus fuerit, accipiet coronam vitae quam repromisit Deus diligentibus se.*[1]

For, says St. Paul, Christ does not forsake His disciples in the conflict; being a compassionate High-priest Who has suffered temptation, He knows what trial is, and is able to uphold us in the midst of the combat.[2] He succours us with His grace, He helps us with His prayer. He repeats for us the petition that He made to His Father at the moment when He was about to undergo the last assaults of hell from which He was to come forth victorious: "I pray not that Thou shouldst take them out of the world, but that Thou shouldst keep them from evil...."[3]

And the Father will "keep us from evil"; He will send His good Angels to approach us invisibly and minister to us, because we believe in His Son Jesus; because we will not turn away from Him; because, mistrustful of ourselves, we, by our prayers, place all our hope in Him alone; because He sees us and loves us in His Son, *Quia tui sunt.*[4]

This is besides the magnificent promise that He Himself made to us through the mouth of the sacred writer in that beautiful 90th psalm which I wish to quote once more in ending this conference: "Because he hoped in Me," saith the Lord, "I will deliver him; I will protect him because He hath known My name; he shall call to Me, and I will hear him; I am with him in tribulation, I will deliver him and I will glorify him; I will fill him with length of days, and I will shew him (so that he may rejoice in it for ever) My salvation" which I alone can give him: *Clamabit ad me, et ego exaudiam eum; cum ipso sum in tribulatione; eripiam eum et glorificabo eum; longitudine dierum replebo eum, et ostendam illi salutare meum.*[5]

---

1 "Blessed is the man that endureth temptation: for, when he hath been proved, he shall receive the crown of life which God hath promised to them that love him," Jac. i, 12.
2 Hebr. ii, 18; v. 2.   3 Joan. xvii, 15.   4 "Because they are thine," Ibid. 9.
5 Ps. xc, 14–16.

SOME ASPECTS OF THE PUBLIC LIFE OF JESUS

(Lent)

SUMMARY.—Variety of the aspects of the Public Life of Jesus.—I. The testimonies which Christ bears to His Divinity.—II. How these testimonies are likewise the foundation of our faith in Jesus Christ.—III. The human actions of the Incarnate Word declare the Divine perfections; the human kindness in Christ reveals the eternal love.—IV. Christ's mercy towards sinners: the Prodigal Son, the Samaritan Woman, Magdalen, the Woman taken in adultery.—V. The Saviour's mercy is the first source of our confidence; how this confidence is strengthened by penitence.—VI. Severity of Jesus towards the hypocritical pride of the Pharisees.

THE Apostle St. John says at the end of his Gospel: "There are also many other things which Jesus did; which, if they were written every one, the world itself, I think, would not be able to contain the books that should be written."[1]

This thought is brought home to us in a special manner as we are about to contemplate Our Lord's public life. If we would comment in detail upon each of His words, consider and explain each of His actions, a whole lifetime would not suffice.

We will at least take some characteristic points from this period of the Saviour's life.

First of all we will see how Christ Jesus declares and establishes the divinity of His mission and person;—we will next contemplate with what

---

1 Joan. xxi, 25.

unwearying condescension towards misery under every form, He reveals to the world the depths and riches of Infinite Goodness;—this revelation will be the more striking if we consider it in contrast with Our Saviour's attitude towards the pride of the Pharisees.

These are, out of a thousand others, three aspects of the public life of Jesus from which, dwelling upon them, we may draw graces of light and principles of life.

I

At the Baptism of Jesus, which marks the beginning of His public life, we hear the Father testifying that Christ is His beloved Son in Whom He is well pleased.[1]

The teaching of Jesus during the three years of His exterior ministry towards souls is but the unceasing commentary on this testimony. We shall see Christ manifest Himself in His actions and words, not as the adoptive Son of God, as one chosen to fulfil a special mission towards His people, as were the simple prophets,—but as the very Son of God, Son by nature, possessing in consequence the Divine prerogatives, the absolute rights of the Sovereign Being, and requiring from us faith in the divinity of His work and of His Person.

When we read the Gospel, we see that Christ speaks and acts not only as man, like unto us, but also as God, high above all creatures.

We see that He speaks of Himself as greater than Jonas, than Solomon, than Moses[2]; if, as Man, born of Mary, He is the Son of David, He is also the Lord, seated at the right hand of God,[3] sharing in His eternal power and infinite glory.

Thus He declares Himself to be the Supreme Lawgiver, by the same title as God. As God gave the Law to Moses, so Christ establishes the code of the Gospel: "You have heard that it was said to them of old...but I say to you...."[4] This is the formula that is repeated throughout the Sermon on the Mount. He shows Himself to be the sovereign Master of the Law to such a degree that He derogates from it by His own authority when He

---

1 Matth. iii, 17; Marc, i, 11; Luc. iii, 22.   2 Matth. xii, 41–42; Luc. xi, 31–32.
3 Cf. Ps. cix, 1.   4 Matth. v, 22, 28, 32, 34, 39, 44.

so pleases, with an entire independence, as being He Who instituted it.

This power is boundless. Jesus forgives sins, a privilege which God alone enjoys, because it is God alone Whom sin offends. "Be of good heart, son, thy sins are forgiven thee," He says to the man sick of the palsy who is brought to Him. The Pharisees, scandalized at hearing a man speak thus, murmur among themselves: "Who can forgive sins, but God only." But Jesus reads the secret thoughts of their hearts; and to prove, to those who contest it, that He possesses this divine power, not by delegation but as being personally entitled to it, He immediately works a miracle: "That you may know that the Son of man hath power on earth to forgive sins, (then said He to the man sick of the palsy), Arise, take up thy bed, and go into thy house."[1]

This is a characteristic example: Christ Jesus works His miracles by His own authority. Except before the raising of Lazarus, when He asks His Father that the miracle He is about to perform may enlighten those who are to witness it, He never prays before manifesting His power, as did the prophets; but with a word, a gesture, a single act of the will, He heals the maimed, makes the paralyzed walk, multiplies the loaves, calms the furious waves, casts out devils, raises the dead.

In fine, His power is so great that He will come upon the clouds to judge every creature; all power has been given to Him by His Father in heaven and in earth[2]; like His Father, He promises eternal life to those who follow Him.[3]

These words and actions show us that Jesus is equal to God, participating in the supreme power of the Divinity, in God's essential prerogatives and infinite dignity.

We have still more explicit testimonies.

You know the episode wherein Peter confesses his faith in his Master's divinity, saying: "Thou art Christ, the Son of the living God." "Blessed art thou, Simon Bar-Jona: because flesh and blood hath not revealed it to thee, but My Father Who is in heaven." And in order to mark the greatness of this act of faith, the Saviour promises that He will make Peter the

---

1 Matth. ix, 2–4, 6; Marc. ii, 5–7, 9; Luc. v, 22–22, 24.
2 Cf. Matth. xxviii, 18.   3 Ibid. xix, 28–29.

foundation of His Church.[1]

At the hour of His Passion, standing before His judges, Our Lord proclaims His Divinity yet more authoritatively. In his position of president of the great counsel, Caiphas says to the Saviour: "I adjure Thee by the Living God, that Thou tell us if Thou be the Christ the Son of God." "Thou hast said it," answers Jesus; "hereafter you shall see the Son of man sitting on the right hand of the power of God, and coming in the clouds of heaven." You know that "to sit at the right hand of God" was regarded by the Jews as a divine prerogative, and that to arrogate this prerogative to oneself constituted a blasphemy punishable by death. This is why Caiphas has scarcely heard the reply of Jesus than he rends his garments in sign of protestation, and cries out: "He has blasphemed; what further need have we of witnesses?" And all the others reply: "He is guilty of death."[2] And rather than retract, Christ accepts His condemnation.

It is above all in St. John's Gospel that we find upon the lips of Jesus testimonies[3] to a union existing between Himself and His Father such as can only be explained by the Divine nature that He indivisibly possesses with the Father and Their common Spirit.

You will notice that, except when He teaches His disciples how to pray, Christ Jesus never says: "Our Father"; always, when speaking of His relations with God, He says: "the Father, My Father"; and in speaking to His disciples: "your Father." Our Lord is careful to denote the essential difference that exists, in this matter, between Himself and other men: He is the Son of God by nature, they are so only by adoption.

He has, therefore, personal relations of a unique character with the Father, which can only result from His Divine origin.

One day He says in the presence of His disciples: "I confess to Thee, O Father, Lord of heaven and earth, because Thou hast hid these things from the wise and prudent, and hast revealed them to little ones. Yea, Father; for so hath it seemed good in Thy sight. All things are delivered to Me by My Father. And no one knoweth the Son but the Father; neither doth anyone know the Father, but the Son, and he to whom it shall please

---

1 Ibid. xvi, 17–18.   2   Matth. xxvi, 63–66; Marc. xiv, 63–64.
3 Many of these testimonies are read at the Masses of Lent, especially after Passion Sunday.

the Father to reveal Him."[1] By these words, the Word Incarnate shows us clearly that between Himself and His Father there is a perfect equality of knowledge incomprehensible for us. This Son Who is Jesus is so great and His Sonship so ineffable that only the Father, Who is God, can know Him; the Father is of such majesty, His Fatherhood is so sublime a mystery, that the Son alone can know what the Father is. This knowledge so far surpasses all created science that no man can participate therein unless it be revealed to him.

Thus Our Lord testifies to His Divine union with the Father,—a union which is not limited to the knowledge which He has of the Father, but extends to all the works wrought by Christ as Man.

See how, on the Sabbath day, Jesus heals the paralytic man, telling him to take up his bed and walk. Immediately the Jews, quite scandalized, reproach the Saviour with not observing the Sabbath day. And what does Our Lord answer? In order to show that He is, by the same right as His Father, the supreme Master of the Law, He replies to the Pharisees: "My Father worketh until now; and I work." His hearers so thoroughly understand that, by these words, He claims to be God that they seek to put Him to death; "because He did not only break the Sabbath, but also said, that God was His Father, making Himself equal to God." Far from contradicting them, Our Lord confirms their interpretation: "Amen, amen, I say unto you, the Son cannot do anything of Himself, but what He seeth the Father doing; for what things soever He doth, these the Son also doth in like manner. For the Father loveth the Son, and sheweth Him all things which He Himself doth...."[2] Read, in the Gospel, the sequel and development of these words, you will see with what authority Christ Jesus proclaims Himself in all things equal to the Father, God with Him and like to Him.

The whole discourse after the Last Supper, and all the sacerdotal prayer of Jesus at that solemn moment, are full of these affirmations showing that He is the very Son of God, having the same Divine nature, possessing the same sovereign rights, enjoying the same eternal glory: *Ego et Pater unum sumus.*[3]

---

1 Matth. xi, 25–27.   2 Joan. v, 16–20.
3 "I and the Father are one," Joan. x, 30.

II

If now we seek to know why Christ thus attests His Divinity, we shall see that it is in order to lay the foundation of our faith.

St. Paul exhorts us to "consider the Apostle and High Priest of our confession, Jesus": *Considerate apostolum et pontificem confessionis nostrae Jesum.*[1] "Apostle" means one who is sent to fulfil a mission, and St. Paul says that Christ is the Apostle of our faith. How is this?

The Incarnate Word is, according to the expression of the Church, *Magni Consilii Angelus,*[2] "the Angel of great counsel" who dwells in the splendours of the divinity. And wherefore is He sent? To reveal to the world "the mystery which hath been hidden from eternity in God," the mystery of the salvation of the world by a God-Man. Such is the funda-mental truth to which Christ is to give testimony: *Ego in hoc natus sum et ad hoc veni in mundum* UT *testimonium perhibeam veritati.*[3]

The great mission of Jesus, above all during His public life, is then to manifest His Divinity to the world: *Ipse enarravit.*[4] All His teaching, all His conduct, all His miracles, tend to inculcate this truth in the minds of His hearers. See, for example, how at the tomb of Lazarus, before He raises His friend to life, Christ, lifting up His eyes to heaven, says: "Father, I give Thee thanks that Thou hast heard Me. And I know that Thou hearest Me always; but because of the people who stand about have I said it, that they may believe that Thou has sent Me": *Ut credant quia tu me misisti.*[5]

Doubtless, Our Lord only inculcates this truth gradually in consid-eration of the Jews's monotheistic notions; but with admirable wisdom, He makes all converge towards this manifestation of His Divine Sonship. At the end of His life, when upright minds are sufficiently prepared, He does not hesitate to confess His Divinity before His judges, at the peril of His life. Jesus is the King of martyrs, of all those who, by the shedding of their blood, have professed their faith in His Divinity.

In His prayer at the Last Supper, He renders account, as it were, to His Father of His mission, and He sums up all in these words: "I have

---

1 Hebr. iii, 1. 2 Introit to the third Mass on Christmas Day.
3 "For this was I born, and for this came I into the world; that I should give testimony to the truth," Joan. xviii, 37.
4 Ibid. i, 18. 5 Ibid. xi, 41–42.

finished the work which Thou gavest Me to do." And what is the result of His work? That His disciples have accepted His testimony. "They have known in very deed that I came out from Thee: and they have believed that Thou didst send Me."[1]

Thus this faith in His Son's Divinity is, according to the very words of Jesus, the work that God especially demands of us: *Hoc est opus Dei, ut credatis in eum quem misit ille.*[2]

It is this faith that brings healing to many sick with divers diseases: *Secundum fidem vestram fiat vobis*[3]; to Magdalen it brings the forgiveness of her sins: *Fides tua te salvam fecit, vade in pace.*[4] It is this faith whereby Peter merits to be established as the indestructible foundation of the Church; it is this faith which makes the Apostles pleasing to the Father, and the objects of His love: *Pater amat vos, quia vos me amastis, et credidistis.*[5]

Again it is this faith that gives us "power to be made the sons of God": *His qui credunt in nomine ejus*[6]; which makes the divine fountains of the grace of the Holy Spirit spring in our hearts: *Qui credit in me, flumina de ventre ejus fluent aquae vivae*[7]; which scatters death's shadows: *Veni ut omnis qui credit in Me in tenebris non maneat*[8]; which brings us divine life, "for God so loved the world, as to give His Only-begotten Son; that whosoever believeth in Him may not perish, but may have life everlasting": *Ut omnis qui credit in ipsum non pereat, sed habeat vitam aeternam.*[9]

It is for lack of this faith that the enemies of Jesus will perish: "If I had not come, and spoken to them, they would not have sin; but now they

---

1 *Pater, opus consummavi, quod dedisti mihi ut faciam...et ipsi acceperunt et cognoverunt vere quia a te exivi, et crediderunt quia tu me misisti* (Father, I have finished the work which thou gavest me to do...and they have received them and have known in very deed that I came out from thee, and they have believed that thou didst send me). Joan. xvii, 4, 8.

2 Joan. vi, 29.

3 "According to your faith, be it done unto you," Matth. ix, 29; cf. Marc. v, 34; x, 52; Luc. xvii, 19.

4 "Thy faith hath made thee safe. Go in peace," Luc. vii, 50.

5 "The Father loveth you, because you have loved me and have believed," Joan. xvi, 27.

6 "To them that believe in his name," Ibid., i, 12.

7 "He that believeth in me, out of his belly shall flow rivers of living water," Ibid. vii, 38.

8 "I am come, that whosoever believeth in me may not remain in darkness," Ibid. xii, 46.

9 Ibid. iii, 16.

have no excuse for their sin."[1] And it is why "he that doth not believe is already judged: because he believeth not in the name of the Only-begotten Son of God": *Qui autem non credit, jam judicatus est, quia non credit in nomine Unigeniti Filii Dei.*[2]

This faith in Jesus Christ, the eternal Son of God, is then the basis of all our spiritual life, the deep root of all justification, the essential condition of all progress, the assured means of attaining the summit of all sanctity.

Let us cast ourselves down at the feet of Jesus, and say to Him: O Christ Jesus, Incarnate Word, Who camest down from heaven to reveal to us the secrets that Thou, the Only-begotten Son of God, dost ever contemplate in the bosom of the Father, I believe and I confess that Thou art God, like the Father, equal to Him; I believe in Thee; I believe in Thy works; I believe in Thy Person; I believe that Thou art come forth from God, that Thou art one with the Father; that he that seeth Thee, seeth the Father; I believe that Thou art the Resurrection and the Life. I believe this and, believing it, I adore Thee and consecrate to Thy service, all my being, all my activity, all my life. I believe in Thee, O Christ Jesus, but increase my faith: *Credo, Domine, sed adjuva incredulitatem meam!*

III

If Christ reveals to the world the dogma of His eternal filiation, it is by means of His Humanity that He manifests to us the perfections of His Divine nature. Although He be the true Son of God, He loves to call Himself "the Son of man." He gives Himself this title even on the most solemn occasions when He claims with most authority the prerogatives of the Divine Being.

Indeed each time that we come in contact with Him, we are in presence of this sublime mystery; the union of two natures—Divine and Human—in one and the same Person,—without mingling or confusion of natures. This is the initial mystery that we ought ever to have before our eyes when we contemplate Our Lord. Each of His mysteries places in relief either the oneness of His adorable Person, the truth of His Divine nature, or the reality of His human nature.

---

1 Joan. xv, 22.   2 Ibid. iii, 18.

One of the principal and most touching aspects of the economy of the Incarnation is the manifestation of the Divine perfections made to men through the Human Nature. God's attributes, His eternal perfections are incomprehensible to us here below, they surpass our understanding. But, in becoming man, the Incarnate Word reveals to the most simple minds the inaccessible perfections of His Divinity, by the words which fall from His human lips and by the actions performed by His human nature. We are charmed and drawn to Him as He enables us to grasp these divine perfections by His visible actions: *Ut dum visibiliter Deum cognoscimus, per hunc in invisibilium amorem rapiamur.*[1]

It is above all during the public life of Jesus that this economy full of wisdom and mercy is declared and carried into effect.

Of all the Divine perfections, love is certainly the one that the Incarnate Word is most pleased to reveal to us.

The human heart needs a tangible love in order to realize something of infinite love, deeper far as it is than this tangible love and surpassing our understanding. Nothing, indeed, so much attracts our poor hearts as to contemplate Jesus Christ, true God as well as true Man, translating the eternal goodness into human deeds. When we see Him lavishly scattering around Him inexhaustible treasures of compassion and mercy, we are able to conceive something of the infinity of that ocean of Divine kindness whence the Sacred Heart draws these treasures for us.

Let us dwell on some traits; we shall see with what condescension, at times surprising, Our Saviour stoops towards human misery under every form, sin included. And never forget that, even when He stoops towards us, He remains the very Son of God, God Himself, the Almighty Being, Infinite Wisdom, Who, ordering all things in truth, does nothing save what is sovereignly perfect. This undoubtedly gives to the words of kindness that He utters, to the deeds of mercy that He performs, an inestimable value that infinitely enhances them, and especially wins our hearts by manifesting to us the profound charms of the Heart of our Christ, of our God.

You know the first miracle of the public life of Jesus: the water changed

---

1   "That the recognition of God made visible might draw us to love what is invisible," Preface for the Feast of the Nativity.

into wine at the marriage feast of Cana, at the prayer of His Mother.[1] For our human hearts, what an unexpected revelation of the Divine tenderness and delicacy! Some austere ascetics may be scandalized to see a miracle asked or wrought in order to hide the temporal need of a poor household during a wedding banquet. And yet it is this that the Blessed Virgin does not hesitate to ask, it is this that Christ vouchsafes to work. Jesus allows Himself to be touched by the embarrassment in which these poor people were about to find themselves; so as to spare them, He works a great prodigy. And what His Heart herein reveals to us of human goodness and humble condescension is but the outward manifestation of divine goodness whence the other has its source.

A short time afterwards, in the synagogue of Nazareth, Jesus quoting from Isaias, appropriates to Himself these words unveiling the plan of His work of love: "The Spirit of the Lord is upon me. Wherefore He hath anointed me to preach the Gospel to the poor, He hath sent me to heal the contrite of heart, to preach deliverance to the captives, and sight to the blind, to set at liberty them that are bruised, to preach the acceptable year of the Lord, and the day of reward."

"This day," Jesus adds, "is fulfilled this scripture in your ears."[2]

And indeed Jesus reveals Himself to all as a King full of meekness and kindness.[3] I should need to quote every page of the Gospel if I would show you how misery, weakness, infirmity and suffering have the gift of touching Him, and in so irresistible a manner that He can refuse them nothing. St. Luke is careful to note how He is "moved with compassion": *Misericordia motus.*[4] The blind and the lame, the deaf and dumb, those with the palsy, lepers come to Him; the Gospel says that He "healed all": *Sanabat omnes.*[5]

He welcomes them all, too, with unwearying gentleness. He allows Himself to be pressed on all sides, continually, even "after sunset"[6]; one day He "could not so much as eat bread"[7]; another time, on the shore of the Lake of Tiberias, He is obliged to enter into a ship so as to be more at liberty to distribute the divine word.[8] Elsewhere the multitude throng into the house where He is, so that in order to enable a paralytic man ly-

---

1 Joan. ii, 11   2 Luc. iv, 18–19, 21; cf. Isa. lxi, 1.   3 Matth. xxi, 5.
4 Luc. vii, 13.   5 Luc. vi, 19.   6 Marc. i, 32–33.   7 Ibid. iii, 20.
8 Ibid. iv, 1–2.

ing upon his bed to come near to Him, there is no other resource save to let down the sick man through an opening made in the roof.[1]

The Apostles themselves were often impatient. The Divine Master took occasion of this to show them His gentleness. One day they want to send away the children that are brought to Him. "Suffer the little children to come unto Me," Jesus says, "and forbid them not, for of such is the kingdom of God." And He stays to lay His hands upon them and bless them.[2] Another time, the disciples, being angry because He had not been received in a city of Samaria, urge Him to allow them to "command fire to come down from heaven" to consume the inhabitants: *Domine, vis dicimus ut ignis descendat de caelo?* And Jesus immediately rebukes them: *Et conversus increpavit illos:* "You know not of what spirit you are. The Son of man came not to destroy souls, but to save."[3]

This is so true that Jesus works miracles even to raise the dead to life. Behold how at Naim He meets a poor widow following the mortal remains of her only son. Jesus sees her, He sees her tears; His Heart, deeply touched, cannot bear this sorrow. "O woman, weep not!" *Noli flere.* And at once He commands death to give up its prey: "Young man, I say to Thee, arise." The young man sits up, and Jesus restores him to his mother.[4]

All these manifestations of the mercy and goodness of Jesus, which reveal to us the sensibility of His human Heart, touch the deepest fibres of our being; they reveal, under a form which we are able to grasp, the infinite love of our God. When we see Christ weeping at the tomb of Lazarus, and hear the Jews, who witnessed this sight, say to one another: "Behold how He loved him,"[5] our hearts comprehend this silent language of the human tears of Jesus, and we penetrate into the sanctuary of eternal love that they unveil: *Qui videt me, videt et Patrem.*[6]

We see too how everything that Christ does condemns our selfishness, our harshness, our dryness of heart, our impulses of anger and revenge, our resentment towards our neighbour!... We too often forget those words of Our Saviour: "As long as you did it to one of these My least brethren,

---

1 Ibid. ii, 4.   2 Marc. x, 13–14, 16.   3 Luc. ix, 54–56
4 Ibid. vii, 11–15.   5 Joan. xi, 36.
6 "He that seeth me seeth the Father also," Joan. xiv, 9.

you did it to Me."[1]

O Jesus, Who hast said: "Learn of Me because I am meek and humble of Heart," make our hearts like to Thine. Following Thy example, may we be merciful so that we may "obtain mercy" for ourselves, but above all so that by imitating Thee, we may become like to our Father in Heaven.

IV

The deepest form of misery is sin. If there is a trait particularly striking in the conduct of the Incarnate Word during His public life, it is the strange preference that He manifests for His ministry towards sinners.

The sacred writers tell us that "as He was sitting at meat...behold many publicans[2] and sinners came, and sat down with Jesus and His disciples": *Ecce* MULTI *publicani et peccatores venientes discumbebant cum Jesu et discipulis ejus.*[3] Jesus was even called "the friend of publicans and sinners": *Publicanorum et peccatorum amicus.*[4] And when the Pharisees showed that they were scandalized, far from denying the fact, Jesus confirmed it, in giving the reason that lay at the root of it: "They that are well have no need of a physician, but they that are sick. For I came not to call the just but sinners."[5]

In the eternal plan, Jesus is our Elder Brother: *Praedestinavit [nos Deus] conformes fieri imaginis Filii sui, ut sit primogenitus in multis fratribus.*[6] He has taken our nature, sinful in the race, but pure in His Person, *In similitudinem carnis peccati.*[7] He knows that the great mass of mankind fall into sin and need forgiveness; that souls, the slaves of sin, sitting "in the darkness and in the shadow of death," do not understand the direct revelation of divine things; they can only be drawn to the Father by the condescension of the Sacred Humanity. This is why a great part of His

---

1 Matth. xxv, 40.
2 Tax-collectors in the pay of the Roman masters of Judea; recruited from the lowest class, they were regarded as contemptible on account of their exactions; they were ranked among thieves.
3 Matth. ix, 10; cf. Marc. ii, 15; Luc. v, 29.   4 Matth. xi, 19; Luc. vii, 34.
5 Ibid. ix, 12–13; Marc. ii, 17; Luc. v, 31–32.
6 "God also predestinated us to be made conformable to the image of his Son; that he might be the Firstborn amongst many brethren," Rom. viii, 29.
7 Ibid. 3.

teaching and doctrine, and countless acts of benignity and forgiveness towards sinners, tend to make these poor souls understand something of the depths of Divine mercy.

In one of His most beautiful parables,[1] that of the Prodigal Son, Jesus discloses to us an authentic portrait of His Heavenly Father.

This parable has, however, for its immediate end, as the Gospel clearly indicates, to explain His own condescension towards sinners. St. Luke tells us indeed that "the Pharisees and the Scribes murmured, saying: This man receiveth sinners, and eateth with them." Thereupon, in order to justify what He did "He spoke to them this parable."[2]

He shows first of all the extraordinary goodness of the father, who forgets all the ingratitude, all the baseness of the prodigal, remembering only that his son "was dead and is come to life again; he was lost, and is found."[3]

Christ Jesus might have made this parable consist only in showing forth the mercy of the father towards the prodigal. So wide is this mercy that we cannot conceive of a greater; we are so touched by it, so full of wonder, that it holds all our attention and most often we lose sight of the lesson that Jesus wishes to give to the murmurers, to those who blasphemed His behaviour towards sinners.

For He goes on to represent the odious attitude of the elder son who refuses to take part in the common joy and to sit down at the feast prepared for his brother.

He wishes to make the Pharisee understand not only how hard was their proud behaviour, and how contemptible was the scandal that they took, but likewise to teach them that He, our Elder Brother, far from avoiding contact with His repentant brethren, the publicans and sinners, sought them out and took part in their feasts. For "there shall be joy in heaven upon one sinner that doth penance, more than upon ninety-nine who need not penance."[4]

Of itself alone, the parable of the Prodigal Son forms a magnificent revelation of divine mercy. But it pleased Our Saviour to illustrate this teaching and lay stress upon this doctrine by deeds of mercy that deep-

---

1 The Church reads to us this parable on the Saturday after the 2nd Sunday in Lent.
2 Luc. xv, 1–3, 11.   3 Ibid. 32.   4 Luc. xv, 7.

ly charm and move us. You know the conversation between Jesus and the Samaritan woman.[1] It was quite at the beginning of Christ's public life. Our Lord was going from Jerusalem into Galilee. Having to journey a long distance, He set out early in the morning. Towards the hour of noon, He arrived near Sichar a city of Samaria. The holy Gospel tells us that Jesus was "wearied with His journey." He was tired, as we ourselves should have been after having travelled a considerable distance: *Fatigatus ex itinere.* And He sat down on the side of the well of Jacob that was there: *Sedebat sic supra fontem.*

All the actions of the Incarnate Word are wonderfully beautiful in their simplicity. If I may thus express it, Jesus, God as He is, is very human in the full and noble sense of the word: *Perfectus Deus, perfectus homo.*[2] We recognise in Him truly one of our own.

He is sitting then on the well-side, whilst His disciples go to seek food in the neighbouring town. But what has Jesus come to do there? Is it only to take a little rest? to await the return of His disciples? No, He has come above all to seek a wandering sheep, to save a soul.

Jesus Christ came down from heaven to redeem souls: *Dedit redemptionem semetipsum pro omnibus.*[3] During thirty years He had to repress the ardour of this zeal for souls which burnt within Him. Doubtless He laboured, He suffered, He prayed for them; but He did not go out to them. Now the hour had come wherein it was the will of His Father that in order to gain souls He should undertake the preaching of the truth and the revelation of His mission. Our Lord came to Sichar to save one predestined from all eternity.

And who was this soul? Certainly, in this locality, there were many to be met with far less corrupted than the sinner whom He willed to save; and yet it is this one whom He now awaits. He knows all the sin, all the shame of this poor woman, and it is she, in preference to all others, to whom He is about to manifest Himself.

The sinful woman then arrives, bearing her pitcher wherewith to draw water from the well. Christ at once speaks to her. And what does He say to her? Does He begin to reproach her with her evil conduct, and speak

---

1 Joan. iv, 5–29. This episode is read on the Friday after the 3rd Sunday in Lent.
2 "Perfect God, perfect man," Creed attributed to S. Athanasius.
3 I Tim. ii, 6; cf. Matth. xx, 28; Marc. x, 45.

to her of the chastisements that she deserves? In nowise. A Pharisee would have spoken in that way, but Jesus acts altogether differently. He takes occasion of their surroundings to draw her into converse: *Da mihi bibere,* "Give Me to drink."

The woman looks at Him in astonishment. She has just recognised that He who speaks to her is a Jew, and the Jews despised the Samaritans who hated the inhabitants of Judea. Between the Jews and Samaritans there was no communication: *Non coutuntur.* "How dost Thou, being a Jew, ask of me to drink," she says to Our Lord. And He, seeking to excite in her a holy curiosity, answers: "If thou didst know the gift of God": *Si scires donum Dei!* "If thou didst know...Who He is that saith to thee, Give Me to drink, thou perhaps wouldst have asked of Him, and He would have given thee living water."

This poor creature, sunk in the life of sense, grasps nothing of spiritual things. She is more and more astonished; she asks herself how her interlocutor could give her water, having no means of drawing any, and what water could be better than that of this well whereat the patriarch Jacob came to drink, he and his sons and his cattle. "Art Thou greater than our father Jacob?" she asks of Christ. Jesus insists upon His reply: "Whosoever...shall drink of the water that I will give him, shall not thirst for ever." It "shall become in him a fountain of water, springing up into life everlasting." "Sir, give me this water," says the woman.

The Saviour then makes her understand that He knows the evil life that she is leading. This sinner, whom grace begins to enlighten, sees that she is in presence of One Who sees to the depth of the heart: *Propheta es tu.* And immediately her soul, touched by grace, ascends towards the light. She says to Him: "Our fathers adored on this mountain: and You say that at Jerusalem is the place where men must adore." As we know, this was a perpetual subject of dispute between the Jews and Samaritans.

Jesus Christ beholds arising in this soul, in the midst of its corruption, a glimmer of good will, enough for Him to grant a still greater grace; for as soon as He see uprightness and sincerity in the search after truth, He brings light, He rejoices to reward this desire of good and of justice.

Thus He is about to make a double revelation to this soul. He teaches her that "the hour cometh and now is when the true adorers shall adore the Father in spirit and in truth. For the Father also seeketh such to adore

Him": *Pater tales quaerit qui adorent eum.* He manifests Himself to her as the Messias: *Ego sum qui, loquor tecum,*[1] a revelation that He had not yet made to anyone, not even to His disciples.

Is it not remarkable that these two great revelations were made first of all to a poor creature, who had no other title to be the object of such a privilege except her need of salvation and a glimmer of goodwill?...

This woman returns justified. She had received grace and faith. She "left her water-pot" and went into the city to preach the Messias Whom she had met. Her first act is to make known "the gift of God," communicated to her with such liberality.

Meanwhile, the disciples return with the food. They offer some to their Master: *Rabbi, manduca.* What does Jesus answer? "I have meat to eat, which you know not. My meat is to do the will of Him that sent Me": *Meus cibus est ut faciam voluntatem ejus qui misit me.*[2] And what is the will of the Father? He wills that every soul should come to the truth that leads to salvation.[3]

It is for this end that Jesus spends Himself. The Father's will is that Jesus should bring to Him the souls that the Father desires to save, that He should show them the way, and reveal to them the truth that leads them to life: *Omne quod dat mihi Pater, ad me veniet, et eum qui venit ad me non ejiciam foras.*[4] That is the whole work of Jesus.

There was nothing in the sinful woman of Sichar to distinguish her from others, unless it was the depth of her misery; but she was drawn to Christ by the Father. Then the Saviour receives her, enlightens, sanctifies, transforms her, and makes her His apostle: *Et eum qui veniet ad me non ejiciam foras.* For "this is the will of the Father Who sent Me, that of all that He hath given Me, I should lose nothing; but should raise it up again" to grace here below, whilst awaiting "the last day," when I will raise it up again in glory.

The woman of Samaria is one of the first to be raised up to grace by Jesus. Magdalen is another, but how much more glorious!

---

1 "I am he, who am speaking with thee," Joan. iv, 26.
2 Joan. iv, 31–32, 34.   3 I Tim. ii, 4.
4 "All that the Father giveth to me shall come to me: and him that cometh to me, I will not cast out," Joan. vi, 37.

Erat in civitate peccatrix: "And behold a woman that was in the city, a sinner." Thus the Gospel begins her story with the attestation of her evil life. For Magdalen's profession was to give herself up to sin, as the profession of a soldier is to bear arms and that of a politician to direct the destinies of the state. Her sinful life was notorious. Seven devils, symbol of the abyss into which she had fallen, made of her soul their abode.

One day, Christ is invited to the house of Simon the Pharisee. Scarcely has He taken His place at table than the woman, "who was a sinner," bearing an alabaster box of ointment comes suddenly into the festal hall. Coming near to Jesus, "she began to wash His feet with tears, and wiped them with the hairs of her head, and kissed His feet, and anointed them with the ointment."

As soon as she has entered, the Pharisee, utterly scandalized, says within himself: "This man, if He were a prophet, would know surely who and what manner of woman this is that toucheth him, that she is a sinner": *Quae et qualis est mulier, quae tangit eum, quia peccatrix est!* "Answering," (notice the word *respondens,* the Pharisee had said nothing aloud, but Christ *answers* his inmost thought), Jesus proposes to him the question that you know. Of two insolvent debtors, whose debts the creditor remits, which will love him most? "I suppose that he to whom he forgave most," Simon replies. "Thou hast judged rightly," answers Jesus. Then turning towards Magdalen: "Dost thou see this woman?" this woman who is indeed a sinner; whom thou despisest in thy heart, "she hath loved much" as she hath even now testified: therefore "many sins are forgiven her": *Remittuntur ei peccata multa, quoniam dilexit multum.*[1]

Magdalen the sinner has become the triumph of the grace of Jesus, one of the most magnificent trophies of His Precious Blood.

This compassion of the Incarnate Word towards sinners is so wide that He sometimes seems to forget the rights of His justice and holiness. The enemies of Jesus know this so well that they go so far as to lay snares for Him on this ground.

And lo, they bring to Christ a woman taken in adultery.[2] It is impossible to deny the crime or to diminish its gravity; the Gospel tells us that the

---

1 Luc. vii, 37–47.
2 We read this episode on the Saturday after the 3rd Sunday in Lent.

guilty woman has been taken in the very act; the law of Moses ordained that she should be stoned. The Pharisees, knowing the compassion of Jesus, count upon His absolving this woman; that would be to place Himself in opposition with their lawgiver: *Tu ergo, quid dicis?*

But if Jesus is goodness itself, He is likewise eternal wisdom. At first He answers nothing to the perverse injunction of the accusers. They insist. Then Our Lord says to them: "He that is without sin among you, let him first cast a stone at her." Such a response puts His enemies out of countenance. They have no other resource save to withdraw one after the other.

Jesus is left alone with the guilty woman. Great misery and great mercy are in presence of one another. And behold mercy stoops to misery: "Woman, where are they that accused thee? Hath no man condemned thee?" "No man, Lord." "Neither will I condemn thee. Go, and now sin no more."[1]

The goodness of Jesus appeared so excessive to certain Christians of the early Church that this episode is suppressed in several manuscripts of the first centuries; but it is quite authentic, and its insertion in the Gospel was willed by the Holy Spirit.

All these examples of the kindness of the Heart of Jesus are but the manifestations of a higher love: the infinite love of the Heavenly Father towards poor sinners. Never let us forget that we are to see in what Jesus does as Man, a revelation of what He does as God, with the Father and Their common Spirit. Jesus receives sinners and forgives them: it is God Himself, Who, under a human form, stoops towards them, and welcomes them into the bosom of His eternal loving kindness.

V

The revelation of the Divine mercy made through Christ Jesus is the first source of our confidence.

To all of us come moments of grace when, in the divine light, we perceive the abyss of our sins, of our miseries and nothingness. We say to Christ, like St. Peter: "Depart from me, for I am a sinful man, O Lord."[2]

---

1 Joan. viii, 3–11.   2 Luc. v, 8.

Could it be possible for You to bind Yourself in a close union with a soul touched by sin? Seek rather privileged souls that are noble and pure. As for me, I am too unworthy to remain so near to You.

But let us remember what Christ Himself said: "I am not come to call the just, but sinners." And indeed did He not call Matthew the publican to the rank of an apostle? And whom did He place at the head of His Church that He willed to be without "spot or wrinkle, or any such thing; but that it should be holy, and without blemish," and for the sanctification whereof He came to give all His precious Blood?[1] Whom did He chose? Was it John the Baptist, sanctified from his mother's womb, confirmed in grace and of such eminent perfection that he was taken for Christ Himself? No. Was it John the Evangelist, the virgin disciple, he whom Christ loved with a special love, who alone remained faithful to Him even to the foot of the Cross? Again no. Whom then did He choose? Knowingly, deliberately, Our Lord chose a man who was to forsake Him. Is it not remarkable?

Christ, being God, knew beforehand all that was to happen. When He promised Peter that He would build upon him His Church, He knew that Peter, wonderful as was the spontaneity of his faith, would deny Him. Despite all the miracles wrought under his eyes by the Saviour, despite the glory with which he beheld Christ's Humanity resplendent on Thabor, Peter on the very day of his first communion and his ordination, swore saying: "I know not the Man!..."[2] And it was he whom Jesus chose in preference to all others. Why was this?

Because His Church would be composed of sinners. Except the most pure Virgin Mary, we are all sinners; we have all need of the divine mercy; and therefore Christ willed that the visible head of His kingdom should be a sinner whose fault would be related in Holy Scripture with every detail showing its cowardice and ingratitude.

See again Mary Magdalen. We read in the Gospel that women followed Jesus in His apostolic journeys in order to minister to His needs and those of His disciples. Among all these women of unwearying devotedness, whom did He single out? Madgalen. He willed that the sacred scribe should hide nothing of the fact of her sinful life; but He willed too that

---

1 Ephes. v, 25–27.   2 Matth. xxvi, 72, 74.

we should read how He accepted the presence of Magdalen at the foot of the Cross, by the side of His Mother, the Virgin of virgins[1]; and how it was to her, before all others, that He first appeared after His Resurrection.[2]

Yet once more, why so much condescension? *In laudem gloriae gratiae suae*[3]: to exalt the triumphant glory of His grace in the sight of all. Such is indeed the greatness of divine forgiveness that it raised to the highest holiness a sinner who had fallen so low: *Abyssus abyssum invocat.*[4] An author of the first centuries says: Christ "found a fallen woman and made her [by the depth of her repentance] purer than a virgin": *Invenit meretricem, et virgine castiorem reddidit.*[5]

God wills that "no man may glory" in his own righteousness,[6] but that all should magnify the power of His grace and the wideness of His mercy: *Quoniam in aeternum misericordia ejus.*[7]

Our miseries, our failings, our sins, we know them well enough; but what we do not know,—souls of little faith!—is the value of the Blood of Jesus and the power of His grace.

Our confidence has its source in God's infinite mercy towards us, and increases in proportion to our sorrow for sin.

The extreme condescension of Jesus towards sinners cannot serve as a motive for remaining in sin or falling into sin again after having been set free from it. "Shall we continue in sin" says St. Paul, "that grace may abound? God forbid. For we that are dead to sin, how shall we live any longer therein?"[8]

You will have noticed that in forgiving the woman taken in adultery, Jesus gives her a grave warning: "Sin no more." He says the same to the paralytic man, adding the reason: "Behold thou art made whole; sin no more, lest some worse thing happen to thee."[9] It is indeed as Jesus Himself has said: When the evil spirit has been cast out of a soul, he returns to besiege it with "other spirits more wicked than himself," and if he again

---

1 Joan. xix, 25.   2 Marc, xvi, 9.   3 Ephes. i, 6.
4 "Deep calleth on deep," Ps. xli, 8.
5 This text is found among the sermons attributed to S. John Chrysostom.
6 Ephes. ii, 9.   7 "For his mercy endureth forever," Ps. cxxxv.
8 Rom. vi, 1–2.   9 Joan. v, 14.

makes himself master, the last state of that soul is worse than the first.[1]

Repentance is the requisite condition for receiving and safeguarding within us divine forgiveness. Look at Peter: he sinned, sinned grievously, but the Gospel relates that he "wept bitterly" for his sin: *Flevit amare*[2]; afterwards he was to efface his threefold denial by a threefold protestation of love, "Yea, Lord, Thou knowest that I love Thee!"[3] Again look at Magdalen, for she is, as well as one of the most magnificent trophies of Christ's grace, the splendid symbol of penitent love. St. Paul says that the hair of a woman "is a glory to her; for her hair is given to her for a covering."[4] And this adornment which had served Magdalen to allure and ruin souls she now uses to wipe the Saviour's feet. In thus humbling herself publicly in the sight of the guests who knew her, and this by the movement of her contrite love, she attracts and holds treasures of mercy: *Remittuntur ei peccata multa quoniam dilexit multum.*[5]

However numerous be the falls of a soul, we ought never to despair of it. "How often shall my brother offend against me, and I forgive him?" Peter asked Our Lord. "Seventy times seven times," Jesus replied, meaning by this that there should be no limit to our forgiveness.[6]

Here below, this inexhaustible measure towards repentance is that of God Himself.

To complete what I have just said of the goodness and condescension of Christ Jesus toward us, I will add another trait which further reveals His tenderness, namely His affection for Lazarus and his two sisters.

In all the public life of the Incarnate Word, there is perhaps nothing to be met with that brings us nearer to Him and brings Him nearer to us than this intimate picture of His relations with His friends in the little town. If our faith tells us that He is the Son of God, God Himself, the way in which He vouchsafes His friendship reveals to us, so it seems to me, His quality as "Son of Man."

The sacred writers have only sketched the outline of the picture of this holy affection, but they have done so sufficiently to give us a glimpse

---

1 Matth. xii, 45; Luc. xi, 26.　　2 Ibid. xxii, 62.　　3 Joan. xxi, 15–17.
4 I Cor. xi, 15.
5 "Many sins are forgiven her, because she hath loved much," Luc. vii, 47.
6 Matth. xviii, 21–22.

of what was infinitely delightful about it. St. John tells us that "Jesus loved Martha, and her sister Mary, and Lazarus": *Diligebat autem Jesus Martham, et sororem ejus Mariam, et Lazarum.*[1] They were His friends and the friends of His Apostles. Speaking of Lazarus to the apostles, He calls him "our friend": *Lazarus amicus noster.*[2] The Gospel adds that "Mary was she that anointed the Lord with ointment, and wiped His feet with her hair."[3]

Their house in Bethania was the home which Christ, the Incarnate Word, had chosen here below as His place of repose, and the scene of that holy friendship whereof He Himself, the Son of God, has deigned to give us the example. There is nothing sweeter for our human hearts than the picture of this home that the Holy Spirit discloses to us in the tenth chapter of the Gospel of St. Luke. Jesus is truly the honoured, but very intimate, friend of this household. He must have been a very familiar friend for one day Martha, who was busily serving Him, dares to complain to Him of her sister Mary who was sitting quietly at the feet of Jesus and listening enraptured to the Saviour's words. "Lord, hast Thou no care that my sister hath left me alone to serve? Speak to her therefore, that she help me": *Domine, non est tibi curae quod soror mea reliquit me solam ministrare? Die ergo illi ut me adjuvet.* And, far from resenting a like familiarity, which included Him as it were in the reproach made by Martha to her sister, Christ Jesus intervenes and settles the question in favour of her who symbolizes prayer and union with God: "Martha, Martha, thou art careful, and art troubled about many things. But one thing is necessary. Mary hath chosen the better part, which shall not be taken away from her."[4]

When, in a spirit of faith, we assist at this delightful scene, we feel in our hearts that Jesus is truly one of us: *Debuit per omnia fratribus similari*[5]; we feel that in His Person is wonderfully verified the revelation made to the world by Eternal Wisdom: "My delights were to be with the children of men."[6] We realize at the same time that "neither is there any other nation so great, that hath gods so nigh them, as our God is present to our petitions."[7]

---

1 Joan. xi, 5.   2 Joan. xi, 11.   3 Ibid. 2.   4 Luc. x, 40–42.
5 Hebr. ii, 17.   6 Prov. viii, 31.   7 Deut, iv, 7.

Christ Jesus is truly the "Emmanuel,"[1] God living amongst us, with us.

VI

The life of Jesus is a manifestation of the perfection of God, of the liberality of His supreme goodness and unfathomable mercy. It is in the Incarnate Word that God discloses to us His inmost character: *Illuxit in cordibus nostris...in facie Christi Jesu.*[2] Christ is "the [visible] image of the invisible God"[3]; His words and deeds are the authentic revelation of the Infinite Being.

Now, our contemplation of the character of Jesus and our idea of God would be incomplete, if, in meditating upon Christ's attitude of unwearying condescension towards every form of misery, sin included, we neglected to examine also His conduct towards that form of human malice which is most opposed to the divine nobility and goodness and is resumed in one word: pharisaism.

You know who the Pharisees were. After the return from the Babylonian captivity some zealous Jews had done everything possible to neutralize the foreign influence, perilous for the orthodoxy of Israel; above all, they had striven to replace in honour the precepts of the Law of Moses and to guard their purity.

This zeal which was worthy of all praise and manifested a high ideal, unhappily degenerated little by little into fierce fanaticism and in an attachment beyond all measure to the letter of the Law. A class of Jews was formed, called the Pharisees, that is to say the "Separated", separated from all foreign contact and from all intercourse with those who did not observe their "traditions."[4]

Interpreting the Law with a rare refinement of casuistry, the Pharisees added thereto a great number of oral prescriptions that most often ren-

---

1 Matth. i, 23.
2 "He hath shined in our hearts...in the face of Christ Jesus," II Cor. iv, 6.
3 Col. i, 15.
4 To the Pharisees must be joined the Scribes, affiliated to that sect; they were principally concerned with the text of the Law, its interpretation and its observance. Sharing in the errors of the Pharisees, they are included in the maledictions which the Saviour heaped upon them.

dered it impracticable, and, in many cases, childish and ridiculous. Two points of which the details were subjects of endless discussion, especially attracted their attention. These were the observance of the repose of the Sabbath day, and the legal purifications. More than once in the Gospel, we shall see the Pharisees take Our Saviour to task upon these points.

They had fallen into the narrowest formalism. Without troubling about the inward purity of the soul, they clung to the outward, material and trifling observance of the letter of the Law. That was all their religion and perfection. From this resulted a profound moral obliteration. They neglected the great precepts of the natural law only to dwell upon absurd details, based upon their personal interpretations. Thus, under pretext of not violating the repose of the Sabbath, they taught that none might care for the sick nor give alms to the poor upon that day; and we see them reproaching the disciples of Jesus for not having observed the Sabbath because they had rubbed in their hands the ears of corn that they had gathered to eat.[1]

This excessive formalism led of necessity to pride. Being themselves the authors of many precepts, they believed themselves to be equally the authors of their own sanctity. They were the "separated," the pure, untouched by anything unclean. Hence what had they wherewith to reproach themselves! Were they not perfectly "correct" in every way? Therefore they had the utmost esteem for themselves. Their overweening pride urged them "to love salutations in the market-place, and the first chairs in the synagogues, and the chief rooms at feasts."[2]

This pride was displayed even in the sanctuary. You know the parable in which Christ strikingly depicts this odious ostentation.[3] Our Divine Saviour places before us the humility of the Publican who dare not so much as lift up his eyes towards heaven on account of his sins, and the self-sufficiency of the Pharisee who, standing, gave thanks to God that he was above the rest of men because of his exact observance of the Law. The Pharisee, as it were, claimed from God the entire approbation of his conduct.[4] What rendered many of the Pharisees contemptible was that

---

1   Matth. xii, 1–2; Marc. ii, 23–24; Luc. v, 1–2.
2   Luc. xx, 46.   3   Luc. xviii, 9–14.
4   In another series of conferences, Christ the Ideal of the Monk, chapter xi, Humility, we have commented in detail upon this parable which throws a strong light upon the

this pride was coupled with profound hypocrisy. In consequence of the multitude of ordinances that they laid down, and that Our Lord Himself declared "intolerable,"[1] many among them only attained a name for the kind of sanctity of which they boasted by the clever dissimulation of their sins and backslidings, and by making the text of the Law subject to disloyal interpretations. In this way they could infringe the Law, whilst saving appearances in the eyes of the common people who admired them.

For their authority and influence were considerable. They were regarded as the interpreters and guardians of the Law of Moses. Whilst making a show of profound respect for all the outward practice of their observance, they imposed upon the multitude by whom they were considered as saints.

Thus they took offence at anything that could lessen this ascendency. They began to oppose Our Lord from the outset of His public life. Besides the fact that Christ did not attach His teaching to their school, the doctrine that He preached and the way in which He required them to act up to it were the antipodes of their opinions and their conduct. The Saviour's extraordinary condescension towards publicans and sinners, rejected by them as unclean, His independence in regard to the Law of the Sabbath—for He said He was the Lord of the Sabbath[2]—the miracles whereby He drew the people to Him could not fail to disquiet them.

Sinking deeper and deeper into their blindness, despite the warnings of Jesus Himself, they lay snares for Him. They ask of Him "a sign from heaven"[3] as a proof of His mission; they bring to Him a woman taken in adultery to put Him in opposition with the Law of Moses[4]; they insidiously ask Him if tribute must be paid to Caesar.[5] Throughout the Gospel we see them full of hatred against Jesus, striving to destroy His authority with the multitude, to turn His disciples away from Him and to deceive the people in order to hinder Him from fulfilling His mission of salvation.

More than once Our Saviour had warned His disciples to beware of their hypocrisy[6]; but at the end of His public ministry, He willed, as the Good Shepherd, Who was about to give His life for His sheep, to com-

---

character that our relations with God ought to bear.
1 Matth. xxiii, 4; Luc. xi, 46.   2 Matth. xii, 8; Marc. ii, 28; Luc. vi, 5.
3 Matth. xvi, 1.   4 Joan. viii, 3–6.
5 Matth. xxii, 15–17; Marc. xii, 13–14; Luc, xx, 20–22.
6 Matth. xvi, 11–12; Luc. xii, 1.

pletely unmask those wolves who showed themselves under the guise of sanctity so as to deceive simple souls and lead them to their ruin.

In His Sermon on the Mount, Christ had astonished His Jewish audience by the revelation of a doctrine that ran counter to their inveterate instincts and worldly prejudices. He had declared before them all that the blessed of His Kingdom are the poor of spirit, the meek, those that mourn, those that hunger after justice; He had declared that it is the merciful, the clean of heart, the peacemakers who are the true children of His Heavenly Father, and that the greatest of the beatitudes is to be an object of persecution for His sake.[1]

This doctrine which forms the Gospel's "great charter" of the poor, the little, the humble, is the antithesis of that which the Pharisees preached by works and example.

This is why we hear Our Saviour pronounce against them a series of eight maledictions which form the counterpart of the eight beatitudes.

Read them in their entirety in the Gospel where they fill a whole page[2]; you will see with what indignation Christ, the Infallible Truth and Life of souls, warns the multitude, and His disciples in particular, against a teaching and conduct that turned souls away from the Kingdom of God, concealed cupidity and false zeal, distorted the truth and precepts of the Law, established a wholly exterior religion, merely surface purity, under which corruption and persecuting hatred were hidden.

"Woe to you scribes and Pharisees, hypocrites; because you shut the kingdom of heaven against men, for you yourselves do not enter in; and those that are going in, you suffer not to enter.[3]

"Woe to you scribes and Pharisees, hypocrites; because you devour the houses of widows, praying long prayers. For this you shall receive the greater Judgment...

"Woe to you scribes and Pharisees, hypocrites; because you tithe mint, and anise, and cummin, and have left the weightier things of the Law; judgment, and mercy, and faith. These things you ought to have done, and not to leave those undone. Blind guides, who strain out a gnat, and

---

1 Matth. v, 3–11.   2 Matth. xxiii, 13–33.
3 By obstructing the path to heaven by the multitude of their intolerable ordinances, and above all by turning souls away from Christ.

swallow a camel.[1]

"Woe to you scribes and Pharisees, hypocrites; because you make clean the outside of the cup and of the dish, but within you are full of rapine and uncleanness.[2]

"You serpents, generation of vipers, how will you flee from the judgment of hell?"

What a contrast between these terrible denunciations, these vehement invectives and Our Lord's attitude towards the greatest sinners, the Samaritan woman, Magdalen, the woman taken in adultery, whom He forgives without a word of reproach; towards malefactors, such as the good thief, to whom He promises Paradise![3]

Whence comes this difference? It is because every form of weakness, of misery, when humbly acknowledged and avowed, draws forth the compassion of His Heart and the mercy of His Father: *Quomodo miseretur pater filiorum, misertus est Dominus timentibus se; quoniam ipse cognovit figmentum nostrum*[4]; whilst pride, especially intellectual pride, like to the sin of the demons, excites the indignation of the Lord: *Deus superbis resistit.*[5]

Now the pharisaical spirit is the epitome of all that is odious and hypocritical in pride. These "proud in the conceit of their heart," rich in their own estimation, are "sent empty away" for ever, from the presence of God: *Divites dimisit inanes.*[6]

It is to be remarked that pharisaism takes many forms.

Our Lord did not reproach the Pharisees only on account of their hypocritical pride which hid corruption under a cloak of perfection: "Whited sepulchres, which outwardly appear to men beautiful, but within are full

---

1 The Law forbade the eating of any unclean animal; the Pharisees, exaggerating this precept, drank nothing that had not been scrupulously filtered, but, on the other hand, they neglected the other precepts of the Law.

2 The Pharisees avoided with ridiculous care the least purely legal stain, but were not careful to avoid sin, which stains the soul.

3 Luc. xxiii, 43.

4 "As a father hath compassion on his children, so hath the Lord compassion on them that fear him; for he knoweth our frame," Ps. cii, 13–14.

5 Jac. iv, 6; I Petr. v, 5.   6 Luc. i, 53.

of dead men's bones, and of all filthiness."[1] He reproached them, moreover, for having substituted a formalism of human origin for the eternal law of God.

The Pharisees were scandalized to see Christ healing the sick upon a Sabbath day; they took offence because the apostles did not submit before sitting down to table to all the childish series of legal ablutions which they had invented and wherein they made all the purity of man to consist. Placing all sanctity in the minute observance of traditions and practices issued from their own brain, they neglected even the gravest precepts of the divine law. Thus, according to them, a man could, by pronouncing a single word, consecrate all his goods or money to the service of the Temple, and thereby render them inviolable, so that the devout Pharisees could not dispose of them even to pay his debts or to provide for the needs of his parents in their necessity. This was, according to our Saviour's own words, to "have made void the commandment of God" by their tradition.[2]

This narrow formalism, all of human invention, which perverted and diminished religion, and this false conscience were so repugnant to the nobility of heart and the sincerity of Jesus that He unmasked and condemned them unsparingly. What judgment did He in fact pass upon this casuistry? "I tell you, that unless your justice abound more than that of the scribes and Pharisees, you shall not enter into the kingdom of heaven."[3]

What a revelation of the intimate character of God! What a manifestation of His manner of judging and appreciating men! What a precious light do these bitter reproaches addressed to the Pharisees throw upon the notion of true perfection!

In the Sermon upon the Mount, Christ points out the height of true holiness; in His condemnation of the Pharisees, He discloses the abysses of the false piety of which the Pharisee is the faithful type.

The devil has no more fatal snare nor one more to be dreaded than that of making some from of pharisaism pass for the holiness required by the Gospel. In this way the prince of darkness even attacks souls seeking after perfection; he darkens the eyes of their souls by the appearance of an altogether formal virtue substituted for the truth of the Gospel. Far from making progress in such a path, one remains barren before God.

---

1 Matth. xxiii, 27.   2 Ibid. xv, 1–9; Marc. vii, 1–13.   3 Matth. v, 20.

"Every plant which My heavenly Father hath not planted, shall be rooted up."[1] This is the inexorable sentence of Jesus against the race of Pharisees.

We see how important it is in this matter to distrust our own judgment, our own lights; how important it is not to base our holiness upon such or such a practice of devotion, however excellent, which we choose for ourselves, nor upon such or such an observance of our religious rule. Such an observance may be suspended by a higher law, as is, for example, the law of charity towards our neighbour. Holiness for us must be based before and above all upon the fulfilment of the divine law: the natural law, the precepts of the decalogue, the commandments of the Church, and the duties of our state. A piety that does not respect this hierarchy of duties ought to be held suspect: all ascetism that is not governed by the precepts and doctrine of the Gospel cannot come from the Holy Spirit Who inspired the Gospel. "Whosoever are led by the Spirit of God," says St. Paul, "they are the sons of God."[2]

The tenderness of Jesus is so wide that at the very hour when He is heaping terrible maledictions upon the Pharisees and forewarning them of divine anger, the Gospel shows Him to us deeply moved. The thought of the chastisement that was to fall upon the Holy City for having, in listening to these "blind leaders of the blind,"[3] rejected the Messias, forces accents of anguish from His Sacred Heart.

"Jerusalem, Jerusalem, thou that killest the prophets, and stonest them that are sent unto thee, how often would I have gathered together thy children, as the hen doth gather her children under her wings, and thou wouldst not !" And in allusion to the Temple, into which He is not again to enter, for it is the eve of His Passion, He adds: "Behold, your house shall be left to you desolate. For I say unto you, you shall not see Me henceforth till you say: Blessed is He that cometh in the name of the Lord?"[4]

As long as we are here below, God in His eternal kindness never ceases to call us: *Quoties volui!*... But let us not be of those who by the continual squandering of grace and the habit of deliberate sin, even though slight,

---

1 Matth. xv, 13.
2 Rom. viii, 14. The development of these ideas are to be found in the conference, The Truth in Charity of our work *Christ, the Life of the Soul.*
3 Matth. xv, 14.   4 Matth. xxiii, 37–39.

harden their hearts to the point of no longer comprehending: *Et nolu-isti.* Let us take care not to drive away the Holy Spirit from the temple of our soul by wilful and obstinate resistance: God would leave us to our blindness: *Ecce relinquetur domus vestra deserta.*[1] Mercy is never lacking to a soul; it is the soul that closing itself against mercy, provokes justice.

Let us strive rather to remain faithful, with a fidelity that is not bounded by the letter, but that has its source in love, and is supported by confidence in a Saviour full of kindness. Then, whatsoever be our weaknesses, our miseries, our shortcomings, and the faults that escape us, the day will arise when we shall for ever bless the One Who appeared upon earth under a human form. He came to heal our diseases, to redeem us from the abyss of sin; it is again He Who will crown us for ever with the gifts of His mercy and love: *Benedic anima mea Domino...qui sanat omnes in-firmitates tuas,—qui redimit de interitu vitam tuam,—qui coronat te in misericordia et miserationibus.*[2]

---

1 "Behold your house shall be left to you desolate," Luc. xiii, 35.
2 "Bless the Lord, O my soul...who health all thy diseases. Who redeemeth thy life from destruction: who crowneth thee with mercy and compassion," Ps. cii, 1, 3–4.

ON THE HEIGHTS OF THABOR

(Second Sunday in Lent)

SUMMARY.—I. The Gospel narrative of the Transfiguration.—II. Signification of this mystery for the Apostles who witness it: Christ wishes, by the manifestation of His Divinity, to forearm them against the "scandal" of His Passion.—III. Threefold grace that this mystery contains for us: it strengthens our faith; it marks our supernatural adoption in a special way; it makes us worthy of one day participating in Christ's eternal glory.—IV. Means of coming to the glorious state presaged by the Transfiguration, namely to listen to Jesus, the Father's beloved Son: *Ipsum audite.*

THE life of Christ Jesus upon earth has, even in its details, such an extensive bearing that we are unable to exhaust all its depths. A single utterance of the Incarnate Word, of Him Who is ever *In sinu Patris,*[1] is so great a revelation that it might suffice, like a fountain of living and health-giving water, to make all our spiritual life bear fruit. We see this in the lives of the saints: one word of His has often been enough to convert a soul wholly to God. His words come from heaven: hence their fruitfulness.

It is the same with Christ's least actions. They are for us examples, rays of light, sources of grace.

In the preceding conference, I strove to point out some of the aspects of His public life sufficiently to afford a glimpse of that which is ineffably divine and also inexpressibly human in this period of three years. I have had, to my great regret, to pass over in silence many of the scenes

---

1 "In the Bosom of the Father," Joan. i, 18.

recounted by the sacred writers. There is, however, one page, a page so unique and complete in itself, one mystery so full of grandeur and at the same time so profitable for our souls that we must consecrate a whole conference to it. This is the Transfiguration.[1]

Nothing ought to be dearer to us than the dogma of the Divinity of Jesus: first of all because nothing is more pleasing to Him; secondly, because this dogma is at once the foundation, the centre and the crown of all our inner life. Now the Transfiguration is one of those episodes whence the splendour of the Divinity especially shines out before our eyes.

Let us then contemplate it with faith, but likewise with love. The more ardent this faith is, the greater will be the love wherewith we shall approach Jesus in this mystery, and the richer and deeper will be our capacity of being inwardly filled with His light and flooded by His grace.

Christ Jesus, Eternal Word, Divine Master, You are the splendour of the Father and the brightness of His substance; You Yourself have said: "If anyone love Me, I will manifest Myself to him," grant that we may love You fervently so that we may receive from You an intenser light upon Your Divinity; for, as You again told us, the secret of our life, of everlasting life, is to know that our Heavenly Father is the one true God, and that You are His Christ, sent here below to be our King and the High Priest of our salvation. Enlighten the eyes of our souls with a ray of those divine splendours that shone on Thabor, so that our faith in Your divinity, our hope in Your merits, and our love for Your adorable Person may be thereby strengthened and increased.

I

Let us first follow the Gospel narration; we will afterwards endeavour to penetrate its meaning.

It is the last year of the public life of Jesus. Until now Our Lord has only made very rare allusions to His future Passion; but, says St. Matthew:

---

[1] The Church makes us read the Gospel narrative of the Transfiguration twice: on the second Sunday in Lent, so as to encourage us to do penance by the distant perspective of the glory that Christ promises to us in His Transfiguration; and again on August 6th, on the Feast she celebrates in honour of the manifestation of the Divine splendour of Jesus on Mount Thabor.

"From that time Jesus began to shew to His disciples that He must go to Jerusalem, and suffer many things from the ancients and scribes and chief priests, and be put to death, and the third day rise again." And He adds: "There are some of them that stand here that shall not taste death till they see the Son of man coming in His kingdom."[1]

Soon after this prediction, our Divine Saviour takes with Him some of His disciples. These are the three apostles of predilection: Peter upon whom a few days before He had promised to found His Church[2]; James who was to be the first martyr of the apostolic college; John, the disciple of love. Christ Jesus had already chosen them to be the witnesses of the raising of the daughter of Jairus; now He leads them upon a high mountain to be the witnesses of a still greater manifestation of His Divinity. Tradition sees in this "high mountain" Mount Thabor. Isolated, it rises at some leagues to the east of Nazareth. It is covered with a rich vegetation; from its summit, the view extends in every direction.

It is here, upon this height, far distant from the sounds of earth, *Seorsum*,[3] that Jesus goes with His disciples. And, according to His custom, He enters into prayer; it is St. Luke who gives this detail: *Et facta est, dum oraret, species vultus ejus altera,*[4] and whilst He prays, He is transfigured. His countenance shines like the sun, His raiment becomes white as snow; He is surrounded with a divine atmosphere.

When Jesus begins to pray, His disciples fall asleep; but presently the dazzling light awakes them, they behold Him resplendent, and at His side are Moses and Elias, talking with Him. And Peter is filled with such joy at the sight of the Master's glory that beside Himself, not knowing what he says, he cries out: *Bonum est nos hic esse.*[5] "Master, it is good for us to be here." O Lord, it is good to be here with Thee; it is good that this should be the end of the conflict with the Pharisees, and the snares laid by them, the end of weariness and journeyings, and humiliations. Let us stay here; we will make three tents: one for Thee, one for Moses, one for Elias, and, as for us, we will dwell with Thee.

The Apostles believe themselves to be as it were in heaven, so resplendent is the glory of Jesus, so greatly does the sight of Him satisfy their hearts.

While Peter is thus speaking, a bright cloud overshadows them, and a

---

1 Matth. xvi, 21, 28. 2 Ibid. 18. 3 Ibid. xvii, 1; Marc. ix, 1.
4 Luc. ix, 29. 5 Matth. xvii, 24; Marc. ix, 4–5; Luc. ix, 33.

voice comes out of this cloud, saying: "This is My beloved Son, in Whom I am well pleased: hear ye Him." Immediately, filled with awe and reverence, the apostles throw themselves down in adoration before God.

But Jesus touches them and says to them: "Arise, and fear not." They, lifting up their eyes, see "no one but only Jesus": *Neminem viderunt nisi solum Jesum.*[1] They see Jesus, as they had seen Him a few moments before, when they ascended the mountain with Him; they see the same Jesus Whom they were accustomed to see; Jesus, the Son of the carpenter of Nazareth; Jesus Who before long is to die upon a cross.

II

Such is the mystery as it is described in the Holy Gospel. Let us now see what is its meaning.

For everything in the life of Jesus, the Incarnate Word, is full of signification. Christ, if I may thus express myself, is the great Sacrament of the New Law. What is a sacrament? In the wide sense of the word, it is the outward sign of an inward grace. It may then be said that Christ is the great Sacrament of all the graces that God has given to humanity. As the Apostle St. John tells us, Christ appeared in the midst of us as "the Only-begotten of the Father, full of grace and truth"; and he immediately adds: "and of His fulness we all have received."[2] Christ Jesus gives us all graces as the God-Man, because He has merited them for us, and because the Eternal Father constituted Him the one High Priest, and supreme Mediator; He gives us these graces in each one of His mysteries.

I have said that each of Our Lord's mysteries ought to be for us an object of contemplation; His mysteries ought also to be, as it were, sacraments producing within us, according to the measure of our faith and love, their own special grace.

And this is true of each of the states of Jesus, of each of His actions. For if Christ is always the Son of God, if in all that He says and does He first of all glorifies His Father, neither does He ever separate us from the thought of Him. To each of His mysteries, He attaches a grace which is to help us to reproduce within ourselves His divine features in order to

---

1 Matth. xvii, 5–8; cf. Marc. ix, 6–7; Luc. ix, 34–36.
2 Joan. i, 14, 16.

make us like unto Him.

This is why Christ Jesus desires that we should know His mysteries, and search deeply into them, with reverence certainly, but likewise with confidence; and that, above all, as members of His Mystical Body, we should live supernaturally by means of the inward grace that He attached to them when He lived them for us.

This is what the great St. Leo in speaking of the Transfiguration tells us: "The Gospel narrative which we have just heard with our bodily ears and which has touched the inward hearing of our minds, invites us to seek out the meaning of this great mystery."[1] It is a precious grace to be able to penetrate into the mysteries of Jesus, because "this is eternal life" *Haec est vita aeterna.*[2] Our Saviour Himself said to His disciples that He gave this grace of spiritual understanding only to those who followed Him: *Vobis datum est nosse mysterium regni Dei, caeteris in parabolis.*[3]

This grace is so important for our souls that the Church, under the guidance of the Holy Spirit, makes it the very object of her petition in the Postcommunion of the Feast: "Grant, we beseech Thee, Almighty God, that with purified minds, we may apprehend the most holy mystery of the Transfiguration of Thy Son, which we now celebrate with a solemn office...." *Ut sacrosancta Filii tui transfigurationis mysteria quae solemni celebramus officio, purificatae mentis intelligentia consequamur.*[4]

Let us, therefore, consider the meaning of this mystery.

First of all for the Apostles, since it was before three of them that the mystery was manifested.

Why was Christ transfigured in their sight?

---

1 *Evangelica lectio, dilectissimi, quae per aures corporis interiorem mentium nostrorum pulsavit auditum, ad magni sacramenti nos intelligentiam vocat. Sermo li Sabbato ante secundam dominicam Quadrages.* A section of this beautiful sermon forms the lesson of the second nocturn of Matins of the Feast.

2 Joan. xvii, 3.

3 "To you it is given to know the mystery of the kingdom of God; but to the rest in parables," Luc. viii, 10; cf. Matth. xiii, 11; Marc. iv, 11.

4 To say it in passing, it is noteworthy that this demand forms also the object of the Postcommunion of the Epiphany, that other "manifestation" of the Divinity of Jesus; the same idea is emphasized in the Postcommunion of the Mass of the Ascension.

St. Leo tells us this, too, very clearly: "The principal end of this transfiguration was to remove the scandal of the Cross from the hearts of the disciples; the humiliations of a Passion freely chosen would no longer trouble their faith after the splendour of the hidden majesty of the Son of God had been revealed."[1]

The Apostles, who lived in close intercourse with the Divine Master and yet remained imbued with the prejudices of their race touching the destinies of a glorious Messias, would not admit that the Christ could suffer. Look at St. Peter, the prince of the Apostolic College. A short time before, he had proclaimed, in the presence and in the name of all, the Divinity of Jesus. "Thou art the Christ, the Son of the Living God."[2] Both the love that he bore to Our Lord, and the earthly conceptions of His Kingdom to which he yet clung, made him reject the idea of his Master's death. Therefore, when Christ Jesus, a few days before His transfiguration, had spoken openly to His disciples of His approaching Passion, Peter was disturbed. Taking Jesus aside, he had protested: "Lord, be it far from Thee, this shall not be unto Thee." But our Divine Saviour at once rebuked His apostle: "Go behind Me, Satan, (that is to say adversary), thou art a scandal unto Me, because thou savourest not the things that are of God, but the things that are of men."[3]

Our Lord foresaw then that His apostles would be scandalized by His abasements, that His Cross would be for them an occasion of falling away. These three apostles whom He chose to be present at His transfiguration, He would likewise take, in preference to the others, to be soon afterwards the witnesses of His weakness, His anguish and distress in the Garden of Olives. He wishes to arm them in advance against the shock which His state of humiliation would then cause to their faith. He wishes to strengthen this faith by His Transfiguration. How will He do this?

To begin with, by the mystery itself.

During His mortal life, Christ Jesus appeared to be a man like other men: *Habitu inventus ut homo,* says St. Paul.[4] This is so true that many of those who saw Him took Him for an ordinary man; even those near-

---

1 *In qua transfiguratione illud quidem principaliter agebatur, ut de cordibus discipulorum crucis scandalum tolleretur; nec conturbaret eorum fidem voluntariae humilitas passionis, quibus revelata esset absconditae excellentiae dignitatis.* Ibid.

2 Matth. xvi, 16. 3 Matth. xvi, 22–23. 4 Philipp. ii, 7.

est to Him, *Sui,* that is to say those whom the sacred writer, according to the expression of the time, calls the *fratres Domini,*[1] His cousins, on hearing His doctrine which seemed to them so extraordinary, accused Him of madness[2]; those who had known Him in Joseph's workshop were astonished and asked one another whence came this wisdom: *Nonne hic est fabri filius?*[3]

Doubtless, there was in Jesus a divine inward virtue which was manifested by miracles: *Virtus de illo exibat et sanabat omnes.*[4] An aroma of divinity, as it were, went forth from Him and drew the multitude after Him; we read in the Gospel that it sometimes happened that the Jews, although gross and earthly, remained three days without food in order to follow Him.[5]

But, outwardly, the Divinity was veiled under the infirmity of mortal flesh. Jesus was subject to the varied and ordinary conditions of weak and passible human life: subject to hunger, thirst, weariness, sleep, conflict, flight. That was Christ's ordinary life, the humble existence whereof the apostles were the daily witnesses.

And now, upon the Mount, they behold Christ transfigured: the Divinity shines out, all powerful, through the veil of His Humanity. The countenance of Jesus shines like the sun; His garments become shining white, "as no fuller upon earth can make white," says St. Mark.[6] The apostles understand by this marvel that this Jesus is truly God; the majesty of His Divinity overpowers them; the eternal glory of their Master is fully revealed to them.

And lo, Moses and Elias also appear beside Jesus, speaking with Him and adoring Him.

You know that for the apostles, as for all faithful Jews, Moses and the Prophets summed up everything; Moses was their Lawgiver, the Prophets are here represented by Elias, one of the greatest amongst them. The Law and the Prophets came, in these personages, to attest that Christ is truly the Messias, prefigured and predicted. The Pharisees may henceforth make their attacks upon Jesus, some of His disciples may leave Him; the presence of Moses and Elias proves to Peter and his companions that Je-

1 Cf. Joan. vii, 3.　　2 Marc. iii, 21.
3 "Is not this the carpenter's son?" Matth. xiii, 55.
4 Luc, vi, 19.　　5 Matth. xv, 32.　　6 Marc. ix, 2.

sus respects the Law, and is in accord with the Prophets; He is truly the One sent by God.

Finally, to reach the climax of all these testimonies, to complete the evidence of this manifestation of the Divinity of Jesus, the voice of the Eternal Father is heard. God the Father declares that Jesus is His Son, God like Himself. All this combines to consolidate the faith of the apostles in Him Whom Peter had confessed as the Christ, the Son of the Living God.

III

The disciples of Jesus did not perhaps at this moment penetrate into all the greatness of this scene nor all the depths of the mystery of which they were privileged witnesses. It was enough for them to be forearmed against the scandal of the Cross; this is why Christ forbade them to speak then of this vision.[1]

Later, after the Resurrection, when on the day of Pentecost the Holy Spirit had confirmed them in their dignity as apostles, they then revealed, by the voice of Peter, the splendours they had contemplated. Peter, the visible head of the Church, he who had received from the Incarnate Word the mission of confirming his brethren in the faith,[2] announces how the majesty of Jesus had been revealed to him, and "Jesus received from God the Father, honour and glory...when we were with Him in the Holy Mount."[3] Peter, the supreme pastor, recalls this vision in order to exhort the faithful, and us with them, not to waver in the faith.

For it was likewise for us that the Transfiguration took place. The disciples chosen to witness it, says St. Leo, represent the whole Church; it is to her, as well as to the Apostles, that the Father speaks in declaring the Divinity of His Son Jesus and in bidding us hear Him.[4]

The Church, in the collect for the Feast, perfectly sums up the precious

---

1 Matth. xvii, 9; Marc. ix, 8.   2 Luc. xxii, 32.
3 II Petr. i, 16–18. Epistle of the Feast.
4 *Haec, dilectissimi, non ad illorum tantum utilitatem dicta sunt, qui ea propriis auribus audierunt, sed in illis tribus apostolis universa Ecclesia didicit quidquid eorum et aspectus vidit et auditus accepit* (These words, dearly beloved, were not said only for the benefit of those who heard them with their own ears, but through those three apostles, the whole Church learned of them and seeing beheld and hearing received). i, c.

teachings of this mystery. For us, as for the Apostles, the Transfiguration "confirms our faith": *Fidei sacramenta patrum testimonio roborasti;* secondly, "our adoption of children of God is herein shewn forth in a wonderful manner": *Et adoptionem filiorum perfectam, voce delapsa in nube lucida, mirabiliter praesignasti;*—finally, the Church beseeches "that we may one day be made coheirs with the King of glory and share in His triumph": *Ut ipsius Regis gloriae nos coheredes efficias, et ejusdem gloriae tribuas esse consortes.*

The Transfiguration confirms our faith.

What in fact is faith? It is a mysterious participation in the knowledge that God has of Himself. God knows Himself as Father, Son and Holy Spirit. The Father in knowing Himself begets from all eternity a Son like unto and equal to Himself. *Hic est Filius meus dilectus in quo mihi bene complacui.*[1] These words are the greatest revelation that God has made to the world, they are like the very echo of the life of the Father. The Father, inasmuch as He is Father, lives to beget His Son; this begetting which has neither beginning nor end constitutes the very property of the Father. In eternity, we shall see with wonder, admiration and love, this procession of the Son begotten in the bosom of the Father. This procession is eternal: *Filius meus es tu, ego hodie genui te.*[2] This "to-day," this *hodie*, is the now of eternity.

When He tells us that Jesus is His beloved Son, the Father reveals to us His life; and when we believe in this revelation, we participate in the knowledge of God Himself. The Father knows the Son in endless glory; as for us, we know Him in the shadows of faith whilst awaiting the light of eternity. The Father declares that the Babe of Bethlehem, the Youth of Nazareth, the Preacher of Judea, the Victim of Calvary is His Son, His well-beloved Son; our faith is to believe this.

It is an excellent thing in the spiritual life to have this testimony of the Father ever present, as it were, before the eyes of the heart. Nothing upholds our faith so powerfully. When we read the Gospel, or a *Life* of our Lord, when we celebrate His mysteries, when we visit Him in the Blessed Sacrament, when we prepare ourselves to receive Him in our hearts in

---

1 "This is my beloved Son in whom I am well pleased."
2 "Thou art my son, this day have I begotten thee," Ps. ii, 7.

Holy Communion, or when we adore Him after having received Him, in our whole life, in fine, let us try to have these words habitually before us: "This is My beloved Son in Whom I am well pleased."

And let us then say: Yea, Father, I believe these words, I will repeat them after Thee: this Jesus Who is within me through faith, through Communion, is Thy Son; and because Thou has said it, I believe it; and because I believe it, I adore Thy Son, so as to render Him my homage; and by Him, in Him, so likewise to render to Thee, O Heavenly Father, in union with Thy Spirit, all honour and all glory.

Such a prayer is extremely pleasing to our Father in Heaven; and when it is true, pure, frequent, it makes us the object of the Father's love; God includes us in the delight that He takes in His own Son Jesus. Our Lord Himself tells us so: "The Father Himself loveth you, because you have... believed that I came out from God,"[1] that I am His Son. And what happiness for a soul to be the object of the love of the Father, of this Father from Whom comes down "every perfect gift"[2] to rejoice the heart!

It is likewise very pleasing to Jesus. He has it at heart that we should confess His Divinity, that we should have in it a living, strong and deep faith, secure against every attack. "Blessed is he that shall not be scandalized in Me,"[3] says Jesus; who—despite the abasements of My Incarnation, the obscure labours of My Hidden Life, the humiliations of My Passion, the attacks and blasphemies of which I am unceasingly the object, the conflicts that My disciples and the Church must sustain here below,— remains firm in His faith in Me, and is not ashamed of Me.

Look at the Apostles during the Passion of Jesus: their faith was weak; they took to flight. St. John alone followed His Divine Master as far as Calvary. And we know that after the Resurrection, when Magdalen and the other holy women came to say on behalf of Christ Himself that they had seen Him risen, the apostles did not believe them; "these words seemed to them as idle tales."

Look again at the two disciples on the way to Emmaus; it was necessary that Our Lord should join them and, opening to them the meaning of the Scripture, show them that "all things must needs be fulfilled, which are written in the Law of Moses, and in the Prophets, and in the Psalms,"[4]

---

1 Joan. xvi, 27.   2 Jac. i, 17.   3 Matth. xi, 6; Luc. vii, 23.
4 Luc. xxiv, 44.

before He entered into His glory.

Let us, then, believe firmly in the Divinity of Jesus; never let us tamper with this faith; let us, in order to sustain it, recall the testimony of the Eternal Father on the day of the Transfiguration; our faith will find therein one of its best supports.

The collect for the Feast says secondly that our adoption of children of God was wonderfully foreshewn by the Divine Voice that came from the bright cloud.

The Eternal Father makes known to us that Jesus is His Son; Jesus is also "the Firstborn amongst many brethren."[1] Having taken a human nature, He makes us partakers, by His grace, of His Divine Sonship. If He is God's own Son by nature, we are so by grace. Jesus is one of ourselves by His Incarnation; He makes us like to Him in bestowing upon us a participation in His Divinity, so that we make with Him only one mystical body. That is the Divine adoption: *Ut filii Dei nominemur et simus.*[2]

In declaring that Jesus is His Son, the Father declares that those who, by grace, are partakers of His divinity, are equally, although by another title, His children. It is through Jesus, the Incarnate Word, that this adoption is given to us: *Genuit nos verbo veritatis.*[3] And in adopting us as His children, the Father gives us the right of one day sharing His divine and glorious life. That is the "perfect adoption," *Adoptio perfecta.*

On God's part, it is perfect, for the seal of infinite wisdom is set upon all His works: *Domine, omnia in sapientia fecisti.*[4] See indeed what incomparable riches God heaps upon His adopted children:—sanctifying grace, the infused virtues, the gifts of the Holy Spirit, the actual graces granted to us daily: all that constitutes the supernatural domain for us here below. And to assure us of all these riches, there is the Incarnation of His Son, the infinite merits of Jesus applied to us in the Sacraments, the Church with all the privileges which the title of Bride of Christ confers upon her. Yes, this adoption, on God's part, is perfect.

But on our part? Here below it cannot be perfect. It ever goes on developing from the day when it was given to us in baptism; it is a germ which

---

1 Rom. viii, 29.
2 "That we should be called and should be the sons of God," I Joan. iii, 1.
3 Jac. i, 18.   4 Ps. ciii, 24.

has to grow, an outline which has to be filled in, a dawn which must reach its full noontide. We shall attain perfection when, after we have been perseveringly faithful, our adoption comes to its fruition in glory: *Si filii et heredes, heredes quidem Dei, coheredes autem Christi.*[1]

This is why the Church ends the collect for this Feast by asking that we may come to perfect adoption which is only consummated in the glory of Heaven: *Concede propitius...ut ipsius Regis gloriae nos coheredes efficias et ejusdem gloriae tribuas esse consortes.*[2]

In the Transfiguration we see, in fact, the revelation of our future greatness. This glory which surrounds Jesus is to become our portion because He gives to us, His members, the right of participating in the inheritance that He possesses as the very Son of God.

This is the thought of St. Leo: "In this mystery of the Transfiguration, God's Providence has laid a solid foundation for the hope of the Church; so that the whole body of Christ may know what a transformation will be granted to it, and that the members may be assured that they will be sharers in the glory which shone forth in their Head."[3]

Here below, by grace, we are God's children; but "it hath not yet appeared what we shall be" one day in consequence of this adoption: *Nunc filii sumus; et nondum apparuit quid erimus*[4]; that day will come when the lightnings having enlightened the world, and the voice of judgment having made the earth to shake and tremble to its foundations,[5] the just, according to the words of Jesus Himself, shall "shine as the sun in the kingdom of their Father": *Tunc justi fulgebunt sicut sol in regno Patris eorum.*[6] Their bodies will be glorious like unto Christ's Body upon Thabor; it is the same glory which shines upon the Humanity of the Incarnate Word

---

1 "If sons, heirs also; heirs indeed of God and joint heirs with Christ," Rom. viii, 17.
2 "Mercifully grant...that we be made coheirs of the King of glory Himself and be sharers in the same glory."
3 *Sed non minore providentia spes sanctae Ecclesiae fundabatur, ut totum corpus Christi agnosceret quali esset commutatione donandum, ut ejus sibi honoris consortium membra permitterunt qui in capite praefulsisset.* i, c.
4 I Joan. iii, 2.
5 *Illuxerunt coruscationes tuae orbi terrae, commota est et contremuit terra* (Introit of the Feast).
6 Matth. xiii, 43.

that will transfigure our bodies. St. Paul expressly tells us so: *Reformabit corpus humilitatis nostrae, configuratum corpori claritatis suae.*[1]

Doubtless, we ought not to believe that Christ, upon the holy Mount, had all the glory wherewith His Humanity is now resplendent in Heaven; it was only a reflection of that glory and yet it was so dazzling that the disciples were ravished.

Whence then came this wonderful radiance? From the Divinity. It was an overflowing of the Divinity upon the holy Humanity, an irradiation from the furnace of eternal life which was ordinarily hidden in Christ, and now at this hour caused His sacred body to shine with marvellous splendour. This was not a borrowed light, coming from without, but rather a reflection of that incommensurable majesty which Christ contained within Himself. For love of us, Jesus, during His earthly life, habitually hid the divine life under the veil of mortal flesh. He prevented it from overflowing in a continuous light which would have blinded our feeble eyes; but at the Transfiguration, the Word gave full liberty to His eternal glory; He allowed it to throw its splendour upon the humanity which He had taken.

This shows us that our holiness is no other thing than our resemblance to Christ Jesus, not a holiness of which we ourselves can be the first source, but a flowing forth in us of the Divine life.

Through the grace of Christ, this holiness began to "dawn" in us at the time of our baptism which inaugurated our transformation into the image of Jesus. Indeed, here below, holiness is but an inward transfiguration modelled upon Christ: *Praedestinavit nos [Deus] conformes fieri imaginis Filii sui.*[2] By our fidelity to the Holy Spirit's action, this image grows, little by little, is developed and perfected until we reach eternal life. Then the transformation will appear in the sight of the angels and the elect. This will be the supreme ratification of "the perfect adoption," which will cause an inexhaustible spring of joy to well up within us.

---

1 "He will reform the body of our lowness, made like to the body of his glory," Philipp. iii, 21.
2 "God predestinated us to be made conformable to the image of his Son," Rom. viii, 29.

IV

Such is the glorious state which awaits us, because it is the glorious state of Jesus, our Head, Whose members we are—the wonderful state whereof the Transfiguration upon Thabor gives us a glimpse and proposes to our faith as an object of hope.

But, you may say, what are we to do in order to attain to it? What path must be followed so as to arrive at this blessed glory of which we contemplate a ray in the Transfiguration of our Divine Saviour?

There is but one path, and it is the Father Who shows it to us. The Father, Who adopts us, Who calls us to the heavenly inheritance that we may be partakers of His beatitude, and share one unending day in the plenitude of life, the Father Himself points out the way to us, and it is in this same mystery that He points it out: "This is My beloved Son in Whom I am well pleased."

It is true that we already heard these words at the Baptism of Jesus; but at the Transfiguration, the Father adds something new which contains all the secret of our life: *Ipsum audite,* "Hear ye Him." It is as if, in order to make us attain to Him, God referred us to Jesus. And such is, indeed, the economy of the Divine designs.

Being God's Son, Who lives for ever in the bosom of the Father, Jesus, the Word Incarnate, makes known to us the Divine secrets: *Ipse enarravit.*[1] He is the Light that enlightens every man coming into this world; where that light shines, there is no darkness; to hear Him is truly to hear the Father Who calls us, because the doctrine of Jesus is not His own doctrine, but the doctrine of Him Who sent Him[2]; all that which He teaches us, His Father has bidden Him reveal to us: *Omnia quaecumque audivi a Patre meo, nota feci vobis.*[3] He is henceforward the only way that leads to the Father, *Nemo venit ad Patrem, nisi per me.*[4] In former times, God had spoken by Moses and the Prophets; now, He speaks to us only by His Son: *Multifariam multisque modis olim Deus loquens patribus in prophetis, novissime, diebus istis, locutus est nobis in Filio.*[5]

And see how in order to made us understand this more clearly, Moses and Elias disappear when the voice of the Father tells us to hear His Son:

---

1 Joan. i, 18.   2 Cf. Joan. vii, 16.   3 Ibid. xv, 15.
4 Ibid. xiv, 6.   5 Hebr. i, 1–2.

Et dum fieret vox (Patris), inventus est Jesus solus.[1] Christ alone is henceforth the one Mediator; He alone fulfils the prophecies and sums up the Law. He substitutes realities for figures and predictions; He replaces the Old Law of servitude by the New Law of adoption and love. To be the child of the Eternal Father, to attain the perfect and glorious adoption, we have but to listen to Jesus: *Oves meae vocem meam audiunt.*[2]

And when does He speak to us? He speaks to us in the Gospel; He speaks to us by the voice of the Church; by that of events and trials; by the inspiration of His Spirit.

But in order to listen well, silence is needful; it is needful that we should often, like Jesus at the Transfiguration, go apart into a solitary place, *Seorsum.* Certainly Jesus is to be found everywhere, even in the turmoil of great cities, but He is only heard well in a peaceful soul surrounded by an atmosphere of silence; He is only well understood in a soul that prays: *Dum oraret.* It is then above all that He reveals Himself to the soul, drawing her to Him and transfiguring her in Him. At the hour of prayer, let us think that the Father is showing us His Son: *Hic est Filius meus dilectus.* Then, let us adore Him with deep reverence, living faith and ardent love. And then too, we shall hear Him; He alone has the words of eternal life: *Domine, ad quem ibimus? Verba vitae aeternae habes.*[3]

Let us listen to Him by faith, by this acceptation of all that He says to us. Yea, Lord, I believe it because Thou dost say it; Thou art ever *in sinu Patris*: Thou seest the Divine secrets in the splendour of eternal light; we believe what Thou dost reveal to us. Faith is for us that lamp spoken of by the Apostle who witnessed Thy Transfiguration[4]: that light that shines in the darkness in order to guide us: *Lucerna lucens in caliginoso loco.*

It is in this light surrounded by darkness that we walk; and, despite this very darkness, we must walk valiantly. To hear Jesus is not only to listen to Him with the ears of the body, He is to be heard too with the ears of the heart. Our faith must be practical, and put into action by works worthy of a true disciple of Jesus, conformed to the spirit of His Gospel. This is what St. Paul calls "to please God," *placere Deo,*[5] a term that the Church

---

1 Luc. ix, 36.   2 "My sheep hear my voice," Joan. x, 27.
3 Joan. vi, 69.   4 II Petr. i, 16–18. Epistle for the Feast.
5 I Thess. iv. Epistle for the second Sunday in Lent.

herself repeats[1] when she asks for us that we may be worthy children of our Heavenly Father.

And this, despite temptations, trials, sufferings. Do not let us listen to the voice of the Evil One: his suggestions are those of a prince of darkness; do not let us be led away by the prejudices of the world: its maxims are deceptive; let us take care not to be seduced by the solicitations of the senses: to satisfy them only brings trouble upon the soul.

It is Jesus alone Whom it behoves us to hear and follow. Let us yield ourselves to Him by faith, confidence, love, humility and obedience. If the soul is closed to earth's clamours, to the tumult of the passions and senses, the Incarnate Word will Himself become Master of it, little by little. He will make us understand that true joys, the deepest joys, are those that are found in His service. The soul that has the happiness of being admitted, like the privileged Apostles, into the Divine Master's intimacy, will sometimes feel constrained to cry out with St. Peter: *Domine bonum est nos hic esse,* "Lord, it is good for us to be here."

Doubtless, Jesus does not always lead us to Thabor, there where "it is good to be"; He does not always give us sensible consolations; if He does give them, we ought not to reject them, for they come from Him; we must accept them humbly, but without seeking them for themselves and without being attached to them. St. Leo remarks that our Lord answered nothing when St. Peter proposed to build tabernacles thereby to make a permanent abode in this place of beatitude; not, continues St. Leo, that this was wrong but because it was not the hour. As long as we are here below, it is much more often to Calvary that Jesus leads us, that is to say through contradictions, trials and temptations.[2]

---

1 *Tibi etiam placitis moribus dignantes deservire concedes* (Grant that we may worthily serve thee by conduct pleasing to Thee). Postcommunion for the second Sunday in Lent.

2 *Huic suggestioni Dominus non respondit, significans non quidem improbum, sed inordinatum esse quod cuperet; eum salvari mundus nisi Christi morte non posset, et exemplo Domini in hoc vocaretur credentium fides, ut licet non oporteret de beatitudinis promissionibus dubitari, intelligeremus tamen inter tentationes hujus vitae prius nobis tolerantiam postulandam esse quam gloriam; quia tempora patiendi non potesi felicitas praevenire regnandi* (The Lord did not respond to this suggestion, not meaning that it was wrong, but that which he desired was disordered; the world could not be saved except by the death of Christ, and the faith of believers called except by the example of the Lord, so that although there was no need to doubt the promises of happiness, we should understand

What did Jesus speak of when He was upon the mountain with Moses and Elias? Of His Divine prerogatives, of His glory which transported His disciples? No; He spoke of His approaching Passion, of the excess of His sufferings which filled Moses and Elias with wonderment as much as did the excess of His love. It is by the Cross that Christ leads us to life, and, because He knows that we are weak in time of trial, He willed to show us by His Transfiguration what glory we are called to share with Him, if we remain faithful: *Coheredes autem Christi, si tamen compatimur, ut et conglorificemur.*[1] Here below, it is not the time for repose, but the time for toil, effort, struggle and patience.

Let us remain faithful to Jesus in spite of everything. We have heard that He is the Son of God, equal to God; His words do not pass away: He is the Eternal Word. Now, He affirms that he that follows Him shall have the "light of life": *Habebit lumen vitae.*[2] Happy the soul that listens to Him, and Him only, and listens always, without doubting His word, without being shaken by the blasphemies of His enemies, without being overcome by temptation or cast down by trial![3] We know not, says St. Paul, what a weight of glory is laid up for us in return for the least suffering borne in union with Christ Jesus.[4] "God is faithful"[5]; and in all the vicissitudes through which a soul passes, God infallibly leads her to this transformation which makes her like unto His Son.

Thus our transfiguration into Jesus is inwardly brought about, little by little, until the day comes when the soul will appear radiant in that company of the elect who bear the mark of the Lamb, those whom the

---

however, that among the temptations of this life, endurance will be demanded of us first then glory; because the times of suffering cannot prevent the happiness of ruling). i, c.

1 "Joint heirs with Christ: yet so, if we suffer with him, that we may be also glorified with him," Rom. viii, 17.

2 Joan. viii. 12.

3 *Nec ideo quisquam aut pati pro justitia timeat, aut de promissorum retributione diffidat quia per laborem ad requiem, et per mortem transitur ad vitam: cum omnem humilitatis nostrae infirmitatem ille susceperit, in quo si in confessione et in dilectione ipsius permaneamus, et quod vicit vincimus, et quod promisit accipimus* (Therefore no one should either fear to suffer for justice, or distrust about the recompense of promises, because through labors he passed to rest, and through death to life: since he received all the weakness of our humility, then, should we remain in confession of him and in his love, in him we both conquer what he conquered, and receive that which he promised). i, c.

4 Cf. II Cor. iv, 17.   5 I Cor. i, 9; x, 13; II Thess. iii, 3.

Lamb transfigures because they are His own.

Our Lord Himself has promised this to us. "The world shall rejoice,"[1] He said before leaving us, but here below you shall be in sorrow and trial as I was before entering into My glory: *Oportuit pati Christum et ita intrare in gloriam suam.*[2] That is necessary, it is the way of My providence; but remain steadfast. "Have confidence," *confidite.*[3] "I am with you all days, even to the consummation of the world."[4] Now your faith receives Me each day in the mystery of My self-abasement, but I will come one day in the full revelation of My glory. And you, My faithful disciples, shall share this glory, for you are one with Me. Did I not ask this of My Father when about to pay the price of it by My Sacrifice? "Father, I will that where I am, they also whom Thou hast given Me may be with Me; that they may see My glory which Thou hast given Me, because Thou hast loved Me before the creation of the world": *Pater,* VOLO *ut ubi sum ego, et illi sint* MECUM, *ut videant claritatem meam quam dedisti mihi.*[5] As for you whom I have called My friends, to whom I have confided the secrets of My Divine life, as My Father ordained; you who have believed, and have not left Me, you shall enter into My joy, and live by Me. Full life, perfect joy, because it will be My own life and My personal joy that I will give you, My life and My joy as Son of God, *Ut gaudium* MEUM *in vobis sit, et gaudium vestrum* IMPLEATUR.[6]

1 Joan. xvi, 20. 2 Luc. xxiv, 26. 3 Joan. xvi, 33.
4 Matth. xxviii, 20. 5 Joan. xvii, 24. 6 Ibid. xv, 11,

CHRIST LOVED THE CHURCH AND DELIVERED HIMSELF UP FOR IT, THAT HE MIGHT SANCTIFY IT

(Passiontide)

SUMMARY.—I. Love is the motive power which urges Christ to undergo the sufferings of the Passion.—II. Christ delivers Himself up wholly to sorrow and death.—III. How, by His immolation, Christ sanctifies the Church.—IV. Necessity for us of communicating in the sufferings of Jesus; different ways of sharing in them:—to contemplate, with faith, Christ in His Passion; to assist at the Holy Sacrifice of the Mass which reproduces the oblation of Calvary; to unite our sufferings with His. The strength that Christ has merited for us to carry our cross with Him.—V. The Passion does not terminate the cycle of the mysteries of Jesus; by His sufferings Christ merits to enter into eternal glory. This law is likewise ours: if we share in the sufferings of Jesus on the Cross, we shall share too in His glorious life: *Ego dispono vobu regnum.*[1]

I N NARRATING the account of the Transfiguration, St. Luke brings up this detail that Moses and Elias spoke with Jesus of His death.[2]

Thus, at the moment when Christ raises, for His chosen disciples, a corner of the veil that hides the splendours of His Divinity from the multitude, He speaks of His Passion and Death. This may seem strange, and yet it is not so in reality, for the Passion marks the culminating point

---

1 "I dispose to you a kingdom," Luc. xxii, 29.   2 Ibid. ix, 31,

of the work that Christ came to do here below. It is the hour wherein Jesus consummates the sacrifice that is to give infinite glory to His Father, to redeem humanity, and reopen to mankind the fountains of everlasting life. Moreover Our Lord Who, from the first moment of His Incarnation, delivered Himself up wholly to His Father's good-pleasure, ardently desired to see arrive what He called "His hour."[1] *Baptismo habeo baptizari, et quomodo coarctor usquedum perficiatur!*[2] I have a baptism whereby to be baptized—a baptism of blood—and how am I straitened until it be accomplished!" Jesus longed for the hour to come when He might be plunged in suffering and undergo death in order to give life to us.

Certainly, He will not advance this hour. Jesus is fully submissive to His Father's Will. St. John more than once notes that the Jews try to take Jesus by surprise and put Him to death; Our Lord ever escapes them, even by miracle, "because His hour was not yet come": *Nondum venerat hora ejus.*[3]

But when it does come, Jesus delivers Himself up with the greatest ardour, although He knows in advance all the sufferings that He is to bear in body and soul: *Desiderio desideravi hoc Pascha manducare vobiscum antequam patiar.*[4] "With desire I have desired to eat *this* Pasch with you, before I suffer." It has at last come, that hour so long awaited.

Let us contemplate Jesus at this hour. The mystery of His Passion is ineffable, even to the smallest details, as, moreover, everything is in the life of the God-Man. Here especially we are on the threshold of a sanctuary where we can only enter with living faith and deepest reverence.

A text of the Epistle of St. Paul to the Ephesians resumes the essential points that we have to consider in this mystery. "Christ," he says, "loved the Church, and delivered Himself up for it...that He might present it to Himself a glorious Church, not having spot or wrinkle, or any such thing; but that it should be holy and without blemish."[5]

The mystery of the Passion itself is indicated by these words: Jesus "delivered Himself up": *Seipsum tradidit.* And what urged Him to deliver Himself up? Love is the deep meaning of the mystery: *Dilexit Ecclesiam.*

---

1 Joan. xiii, 1.   2 Luc. xii, 50.   3 Joan. vii, 30; viii, 20.
4 Luc. xxii, 15.
5 *Christus dilexit Ecclesiam, et seipsum, tradidit pro ea, ut illam sanctificaret, ut exhiberet ipse sibi gloriosam Ecclesiam, non habentem maculam, aut rugam, aut aliquid hujusmodi, sed ut sit sancta et immaculata.* Ephes. v, 25–27.

And the fruit of this oblation of His entire self, through love, is the sanctification of the Church: *Ut illam sanctificaret...ut sit sancta et immaculata.*

Each of these truths revealed by the Apostle contains many treasures and fruits of life for our souls. Let us contemplate them for some moments; we shall afterwards see how we ought to share in the Passion of Jesus so as to draw from this treasury and gather these fruits.

I

St. Paul tells us that Christ "loved the Church."

The Church here means the kingdom of those who, as the Apostle likewise says,[1] are to form the Mystical Body of Jesus. Christ loved the Church, and because He loved it, He gave Himself up for it. Love ordained the Passion.

Doubtless, first and above all, it was out of love of His Father that Jesus willed to undergo the death of the Cross. He says so Himself explicitly: *Ut cognoscat mundus quia diligo Patrem, sic facio,*[2] "That the world may know, that I love the Father," I do His will which is to deliver Myself up to death.

Behold Christ during His agony. During three hours, weariness, sadness, sorrow and anguish sweep over His soul like a torrent, and take possession of it to such a point that the blood escapes from His sacred veins. What an abyss of sorrow there is in this agony! And what does Jesus say to His Father? "Father, if Thou wilt, remove this chalice from me." Is it, then, that Christ no longer accepts His Father's Will? Certainly He does accept it. But this prayer is the cry of the sensitive part of poor human nature crushed by weariness and suffering. At this moment, Christ is above all *Vir sciens infirmitatem*:[3] a Man of Sorrows. Our Lord feels the terrible burden of agony weigh upon His shoulders; He would have us know this, and therefore He thus prays.

Hear, what He immediately adds: "But yet not My will, but Thine be done." This is love's triumph. Because He loves His Father, He places the will of His Father above all things, and He accepts to suffer everything. It is to be remarked that the Father, if He had so decreed in His eternal designs, could have lessened Our Lord's sufferings and changed the circum-

---

1 I Cor. xii, 27; Ephes. i, 23; iv, 12; v, 23.   2 Joan. xiv, 31.   3 Isa. liii, 3.

stances of His death. He did not so will. In His justice, He exacted that, in order to save the world, Christ should yield Himself to every sorrow. Did this will diminish the love of Jesus? Certainly not; He does not say: My Father might have arranged things otherwise. No, He fully accepts all that His Father wills: *Non mea voluntas, sed tua fiat.*[1]

Henceforward He will go to the very end in His sacrifice. Soon after His agony, at the moment of His arrest, when St. Peter wishes to defend Him and with his sword strikes one of those who come to seize his Master, what does the Saviour at once say to him? "Put up the sword into the scabbard. The chalice which My Father hath given Me, shall I not drink it?" *Calicem quem dedit mihi Pater, non bibam illum?*[2]

Hence it is, before all, love for His Father that urges Christ to accept the sufferings of the Passion. But the love that He bears towards us likewise urges Him.

At the Last Supper, when the hour for achieving His oblation draws near, what does He say to His apostles gathered around Him? "Greater love than this no man hath, that a man lay down his life for his friends," *Majorem hac dilectionem nemo habet, ut animam suam ponat quis pro amicis suis.*[3] And this love which surpasses all love, Jesus is about to show forth to us, for, says St. Paul, "Christ dies for all."[4] He died for us when we were His enemies[5]: What greater mark of love could He give us? None.

Thus the Apostle does not cease to declare that Christ delivered Himself up and gave Himself for us, because He loved us.[6] And in what measure did He "deliver" and "give" Himself? Even unto death: *Semetipsum tradidit.*

What infinitely enhances this love is the sovereign liberty wherewith Christ offered Himself: *Oblatus est quia ipse voluit.*[7] These words tell us how spontaneously Jesus accepted His Passion. Did He not one day say, when speaking of the Good Shepherd Who gives His life for His sheep: "Therefore doth the Father love Me, because I lay down My life, that I may take it again [upon My Resurrection day]. No man taketh it away from

---

1 "Not my will, but thine be done," Luc. xxii, 42. 2 Joan. xviii, 11.
3 Ibid. xv, 13. 4 II Cor. v, 15. 5 Rom. v, 10.
6 Gal. ii, 20; Ephes. v, 2.
7 "He was offered because it was his own will," Isa. liii, 7.

Me: but I lay it down of Myself and I have power to lay it down; and I have power to take it up again."[1]

And see how these words have come to pass. At the moment of His arrest, He asks those who would lay their hands upon Him, "Whom seek ye?" "Jesus of Nazareth." "I am He." "And at this answer they fall backward upon the ground."[2] If He asked His Father, His Father would have sent "more than twelve legions of angels"[3] to deliver Him. Jesus adds: "I sat daily with you, teaching in the temple, and you laid not hands on Me."[4] It might have been the same now, but He does not will to have it so, for this is "His hour." See Him before Pilate; He acknowledges that the power of the Roman governor to condemn Him to death comes only from His Father: *Non haberes potestatem adversum me ullam, nisi tibi datum esset desuper.*[5] If He so willed, He might deliver Himself from Pilate's hands, but because it is His Father's will, He submits Himself to an unjust judge: *Tradebat judicanti se injuste.*[6]

This freedom with which Jesus gives His life is entire. And this is one of the most admirable perfections of His sacrifice, one of the aspects that touch our human hearts most deeply. "God so loved the world, as to give His Only-begotten Son."[7] Christ loved His brethren to this point that He spontaneously and entirely gave Himself up to save them.

I I

All is perfect in the sacrifice of Jesus:—the love that inspires it, and the liberty with which He accomplishes it. Perfect, too, in the gift offered: Christ offers Himself: *Semetipsum tradidit.*

Christ offered the whole of Himself; His soul and body were bruised and broken by suffering; there is no suffering that Jesus has not known. If we read the Gospel attentively, we see that the sufferings of Jesus were ordered in such a way that no member of His Sacred Body was spared; there was no fibre of His Heart but was torn by the ingratitude of the

---

1 Joan. x, 17–18.   2 Ibid. xviii, 4–6.   3 Matth. xxvi, 53.
4 Ibid. xxvi, 55; Marc. xiv, 49; Luc. xxii, 53.
5 "Thou shouldst not have any power against me, unless it were given thee from above," Joan. xix, 11.
6 I Pet ii, 23.   7 Joan. iii, 16.

multitude, by being forsaken by His own disciples, and by the sorrows of His Mother. He underwent all the outrages and humiliations wherewith a man can be oppressed. He fulfilled to the letter the prophecy of Isaias: "Many have been astonished at Thee, so shall His visage be inglorious among men....There was no sightliness that we should be desirous of Him...and we have thought Him as it were a leper, and as one struck by God and afflicted...."[1]

I spoke just now of the Agony in the Garden of Olives. Christ, Who exaggerates nothing, reveals to His Apostles that His innocent soul is now oppressed with sadness so poignant and bitter that it is enough to cause His death: *Tristis est anima mea usque ad mortem.*[2] What an abyss! A God, Infinite Power and Beatitude, is overcome by sadness, fear and heaviness: *Coepit pavere, et taedere*[3] *et moestus esse!*[4] The Word Incarnate knew all the sufferings that were to fall upon Him throughout the long hours of His Passion. This vision awoke in His sensitive nature all the repulsion that a simple creature would thereby have experienced; in the Divinity to which it was united, His soul saw clearly all the sins of mankind, all the outrages committed against God's holiness and infinite love.

He had taken upon Himself all these iniquities; He was, as it were, clad with them, He felt all the wrath of divine justice weigh upon Him: *Ego sum vermis, et non homo: opprobrium hominum et abjectio plebis.*[5] He foresaw that for many men His Blood would be shed in vain, and this sight brought the grief of His blessed soul to its climax. But, as we have seen, Christ accepted all. He now arises, and goes forth from the garden to meet His enemies.

It is here that this series of humiliations and sufferings, which we can scarcely attempt to describe, begins for Our Lord.

Betrayed by the kiss of one of His apostles, bound by the soldiery as a malefactor, He is led before the high priest. There He holds His peace in the midst of the false accusations brought against Him: *Ille autem tacebat.*[6]

He only speaks in order to declare that He is the Son of God: *Tu dixisti,*

---

1 Isa. lii, 14: liii, 2–4.   2 Matth. xxvi, 38; Marc. xiv, 34.   3 Marc. xiv, 33.
4 Matth. xxvi, 37.
5 "But I am a worm, and no man: the reproach of men, and the outcast of the people," Ps. xxi, 7.
6 Marc. xiv, 61; cf. Matth. xxvi, 63.

ego sum.[1] This profession is the most solemn that has ever been made to the Divinity of Christ: Jesus, King of Martyrs, dies for having confessed His Divinity, and all the martyrs were to give their lives for the same cause.

Peter, the chief of the apostles, had followed his Divine Master afar off; he had promised never to forsake Him. Poor Peter! We know how he thrice denied Jesus. For Our Lord, this was doubtless one of the deepest pains of that terrible night.

The soldiers set a guard round Jesus and load Him with insults and cruel treatment. Not being able to bear His gentle gaze, they blindfold Him in derision; they insolently strike Him; they dare to defile with their filthy spittle that Adorable Face whereof the contemplation ravishes the angels.

The Gospel next shows us how Jesus, from break of day, is dragged from tribunal to tribunal; how He is treated by Herod as a fool, He, Eternal Wisdom, and scourged by order of Pilate; the executioners pitilessly strike their innocent Victim Whose body is soon but one wound. And yet this cruel scourging does not suffice for these men who do not deserve the name of men; they press a crown of thorns upon the head of Jesus and make Him the butt of their mockeries.

The cowardly Roman governor imagines that the Jews' hatred will be satisfied in seeing Christ in such a pitiable state; he presents Him to the crowd: *Ecce homo.*[2] "Behold the Man…!" Let us at this moment behold Our Divine Master plunged in this abyss of sufferings and ignominies, and let us think that the Father, He too, presents Him to us and says to us: Behold My Son, the splendour of My glory—but "for the wickedness of My people have I struck Him" *Propter scelus populi mei percussi eum....*[3]

Jesus hears the clamour of the furious populace who prefer a brigand before Him and, in return for all His benefits, demand His death: *Crucifige, crucifige eum.*[4]

The sentence of death is then pronounced, and Christ, taking His heavy cross upon His lacerated shoulders, sets out on the way to Calvary. What sorrows are yet reserved for Him! The sight of His Mother whom He so tenderly loves, she whose immense affliction He understands as none other can; the being stripped of His garments, the piercing of His Hands and Feet; the burning thirst. Then the malignant sarcasms of His

---

1 "Thou hast said it, I am," Matth. xxvi, 64; Marc. xiv, 62.
2 Joan, xix, 5.   3 Isa. liii, 8.   4 Joan. xix, 6, 15.

most mortal foes. "Vah! thou that destroyest the temple of God, save thy own self," and we will believe thee.... "He saved others; Himself he cannot save."[1] Finally, the abandonment by His Father Whose holy will He has ever done: "My God, My God, why hast Thou forsaken Me!"[2]

He has truly drunk the chalice to the dregs, He has fulfilled to the last iota, that is to say, to the least detail, all that was foretold of Him. Thus, when all is accomplished, when He has exhausted to the depths every sorrow and every humiliation, He can utter His *Consummatum est*. Yes, all is consummated: He has now only to give up His soul to His Father: *Et inclinato capite, tradidit spiritum.*[3]

When the Church, during Holy Week, reads us the account of the Passion, she interrupts herself at this place, in order to adore in silence.

Like her, let us fall down in adoration before the Crucified Who has just breathed forth His last sigh; He is truly the Son of God: *Deus verus de Deo vero.*[4] Let us take part, on Good Friday, in the solemn adoration of the Cross, which, in the spirit of the Church, is intended to repair the numberless outrages heaped upon the Divine Victim by His enemies upon Golgotha. During this touching ceremony, the Church places some moving reproaches upon the lips of the innocent Saviour. These literally apply to the deicide people; we can take them in an altogether spiritual sense: they will give birth in our souls to intense feelings of compunction: "O My people, what have I done to thee? or in what have I afflicted thee? Answer Me. What ought I to have done for thee that I have not done? I planted thee as My most beautiful vineyard, and thou art become to Me exceedingly bitter; for, in My thirst, thou hast given Me vinegar to drink, and with a spear hast thou pierced the side of thy Saviour....For thy sake, I scourged Egypt with its firstborn; and thou hast scourged Me....I led thee out of Egypt, drowning Pharao in the Red Sea; and thou didst deliver Me up to the chief priests....I opened a passage for thee in the midst of the sea, and thou didst open My side with a lance....I went before thee as a pillar of fire, and thou didst lead Me to the judgment-hall of Pilate....I fed

1 Matth. xxvii, 40–42; Marc. xv, 29–32; Luc. xxiii, 35.
2 Matth. xxvii, 46; Marc. xv, 34.
3 "And bowing his head, he gave up the ghost," Joan. xix, 30.
4 Creed of the Mass.

thee with manna in the desert and thou didst strike Me with blows and scourges....I gave to thee a royal sceptre and thou didst give to My head a crown of thorns....I lifted thee up with great power, and thou didst hang Me on the gibbet of the Cross!"

Let our hearts be touched by these plaints of a God suffering for men; let us unite ourselves to this loving obedience which led Him to the immolation of the Cross: *Factus obediens usque ad mortem, mortem autem crucis.*[1] Let us say to Him: O Divine Saviour, Who suffered so much for love of us, we promise to do all that we can in order to sin no more; grant us by Your grace, O adorable Master, to die to all that is sin, attachment to sin and to the creature, and to live no longer save for You.

For, says St. Paul, the love that Christ showed us in dying for us "presseth us...that they also who live, may not now live to themselves, but unto Him Who died for them": *Ut et qui vivunt, jam non sibi vivant, sed ei qui pro ipsis mortuus est.*[2]

III

Christ's sacrifice, begun at the moment of the Incarnation, is now achieved. From the pierced side of Jesus flow the streams of living water which are to purify and sanctify the Church: *Ut sanctificaret Ecclesiam.... Ut sit sancta et immaculata.*[3] This is the perfect immolation. "For by one oblation He hath perfected for ever them that are sanctified": *Una enim oblatione, consummavit in sempiternum sanctificatos.*[4]

How has Christ Jesus, by His oblation, sanctified the Church?

As we know, our sanctification essentially consists in a participation in the Divine nature through sanctifying grace. This grace makes us children of God, His friends, just in His sight, heirs of His glory.

We were, by sin, deprived of grace, enemies of God, shut out from the beatitude of heaven.

By His sacrifice, Christ destroyed sin, and restored grace to us. According to the expression of St. Paul, Christ in letting Himself be nailed to the Cross, blotted out "the handwriting of the decree [of condemnation and

---

1 Philipp. ii, 8. 2 II Cor. v, 14–15. 3 Ephes. v, 26–27.
4 Hebr. x. 14.

of death] that was against us"[1] and reconciled us for ever to His Father.[2]

Never let us forget that Christ represented the whole of humanity. He united Himself to a sinful race, although sin did not touch personally: *Absque peccato*[3]; but He bore "the iniquity of us all": *Posuit in eo iniquitatem omnium nostrum.*[4] Through love, Christ made Himself surety for our sins, and we, through grace, have solidarity in His satisfactions.

Moreover, Christ merited for His Church all the graces whereof she has need in order to form that society which He wills to be "holy and without blemish."

The value of these merits is indeed infinite. How is this? Because although His sufferings, extensive and deep as they were, were not unlimited, yet He, Who through them merited for us, is a God. He suffered only in His human nature, but these sufferings and the merit they create belong to a God, therefore their value is without limit.

Christ Jesus, then, merited for us every grace and every light: His death opened again for us the gates of life, and translated us from darkness into light[5]; it is the cause of our salvation and sanctification: *Et consummatus, factus est omnibus obtemperantibus sibi, causa salutis aeternae.*[6]

The Sacraments, which are the channels whereby grace and divine life reach our souls, are of value only through the Sacrifice of Jesus. If we are to-day in a state of grace, to what do we owe it? To our Baptism. And what merited for us the fruits of our Baptism? The death of Christ Jesus. In the same way, in the Sacrament of Penance, we are washed in the Saviour's Blood. The virtue of the Sacraments is derived from the Cross; they have efficacy only in continuity with Christ's Sacred Passion.

Chief and Head of the Church, Christ merited for her the grace that makes her beautiful and glorious. The zeal of the Apostles, the strength of Martyrs, the constancy of Confessors, the purity of Virgins are nourished by the Blood of Jesus. All the favours, all the gifts that gladden souls, even to the unique privileges bestowed upon the Blessed Virgin Mary, were bought by His Precious Blood. And as the price paid is infinite, there is

---

1 Col. ii, 14.   2 Rom. v, 10.   3 Hebr. iv, 15.   4 Isa. liii, 6.
5 Cf. Col. i, 12–13.
6 "And being consummated, he became, to all that obey him, the cause of eternal salvation," Hebr. v, 9.

no grace for which we may not hope, beseeching it from our High Priest and Mediator.

So that in Jesus we have everything; nothing that we need for our sanctification is lacking to us. *Et copiosa apud eum redemptio.*[1] His sacrifice, offered for all, has given Him the right of communicating to us all that He has merited.

Oh! if we understood that in Him we have everything! That His infinite merits are ours! If we had absolute confidence in these merits! During His mortal life, Jesus said to the Jews, and now repeats to us: *Ego si exaltatus fuero a terra, omnia traham ad meipsum.*[2] When once I have been lifted up on the Cross, My power will be such that I shall be able to lift up to Myself all those who have faith in Me. Those who, of old, in the desert, looked at the brazen serpent lifted up by Moses, were healed of the wounds with which they had been stricken on account of their sins[3]; thus all those who look upon Me with faith and love merit to be drawn to Me. I, Who am God, consented, through love of you, to he hung upon the Cross as one who was cursed[4]; in return for this humiliation, I have the power of drawing you to Myself, of purifying you, of adorning you with My grace, of lifting you up as high as heaven where I now am. I came down from heaven; I have ascended thither, after having offered My sacrifice; I have power to make you enter there with Me, for in this I am your Forerunner. I have power to unite you to Myself, in so close a manner that "no man shall pluck...out of My hand that which the Father hath given Me," and that I have redeemed by My precious Blood. *Et ego vitam aeternam do eis; et non peribunt in aeternum, et non rapiet eas quisquam de manu mea.*[5]

"And I, if I be lifted up from the earth, will draw all things to Myself." Let us think on this infallible promise of our Supreme High-priest when we gaze on the crucifix: it is the source of most absolute confidence. If Christ died for us while we were His enemies,[6] what graces of forgiveness, of sanctification can He refuse us, now that we detest sin, and strive to

---

1 "And with him plentiful redemption," Ps. cxxix, 7.   2 Joan. xii, 32.
3 Num. xxi, 9.   4 Deut. xxi, 23; Gal. iii, 13.
5 "And I give them life everlasting: and they shall not perish for ever. And no man shall pluck them out of my hand," Joan. x, 28.
6 Rom. v, 10,

detach ourselves from the creature and from ourselves, so as to please Him alone?

O Father, draw me to the Son!... O Christ Jesus, Son of God, draw me entirely to Thee....

IV

The Death of Jesus is the source of our confidence. But in order that it may be fully efficacious, we ourselves must share in His Passion. Upon the Cross, Christ Jesus represented us all; but although He suffered for all, He applies the fruits of His immolation to us only if we associate ourselves with His Sacrifice.

How are we to share in the Passion of Jesus?

In several ways.

The first is to contemplate Christ Jesus, with faith and love, along the Sorrowful Way.

Each year, during Holy Week, the Church lives over again with Jesus, day by day, hour by hour, all the phases of the mystery of blood of her Divine Bridegroom. She places her children before the spectacle of those sufferings which saved humanity. Formerly, servile works were forbidden during those holy days. All law cases were suspended as well as all business. The thought of a God-Man, redeeming the world by His sorrows, occupied every mind, moved every heart. Now, many souls, saved by Christ's Blood, pass these days in indifference. Let us be so much the more faithful to contemplate, in union with the Church, the various episodes of this sacred mystery. We shall find therein a source of priceless graces.

The Passion of Jesus holds such a large place in His life, it is so much His work, He attaches such a price to it that He has willed that the remembrance of it should be recalled amongst us, not only once a year, during the solemnities of Holy Week, but every day. He has instituted a sacrifice whereby the memory and the fruits of His oblation on Calvary should be perpetuated: this is the Sacrifice of the Mass: *Hoc facite in meam commemorationem.*[1]

---

1 "Do this for a commemoration of me," Luc. xxii, 19; I Cor. xi, 24.

To assist at this Holy Sacrifice, or to offer it with Christ, constitutes an intimate and very efficacious participation in the Passion of Jesus.

Indeed, upon the altar the same Sacrifice as that of Calvary is reproduced; it is the same High Priest, Jesus Christ, Who offers Himself to His Father by the hands of the priest; it is the same Victim; the only difference is the manner in which He is offered. We sometimes say: Oh! if I could have been at Golgotha with the Blessed Virgin, St. John and Magdalen! But faith brings us face to face with Jesus immolated upon the altar; He there renews His Sacrifice, in a mystical manner, in order to give us a share in His merits and satisfactions. We do not see Him with our bodily eyes; but faith tells us that He is there, for the same ends for which He offered Himself upon the Cross. If we have a living faith, it will make us cast ourselves down at the feet of Jesus, Who immolates Himself: it will unite us to Him in His love for His Father and for mankind and in His hatred of sin: it will make us say with Him: Father, behold I come to do Thy will: *Ecce venio, ut faciam, Deus, voluntatem tuam.*[1]

We shall enter especially into these sentiments if, after offering ourselves with Jesus, we unite ourselves to Him by Sacramental Communion. Christ then gives Himself to us, as the One Who comes to expiate and destroy sin within us. Upon the Cross, He caused us to die with Him to sin: "With Christ, I am nailed to the Cross,"[2] says St. Paul. In those supreme moments, Christ did not separate us from Himself; He enabled us to destroy within ourselves the reign of evil, the cause of His death, so that we might make part of the holy fellowship of the elect: *Sine ruga, sine macula.*[3]

Finally, we may further associate ourselves with this mystery by bearing, for love of Christ, the sufferings and adversities which, in the designs of His providence, He permits us to undergo.

When Jesus was ascending the road to Calvary, bowed down under His heavy Cross, He fell beneath the weight. We see Him humbled, weak, prostrate upon the ground. He Whom Scripture calls "the strength of God," *Virtus Dei,*[4] is incapable of carrying His Cross. It is a homage that His Humanity renders to the power of God. If He so willed, Jesus could,

---

1 Hebr. x, 7; cf. Ps. xxxix, 8–9. 2 Gal. ii, 19.
3 "Without spot, without wrinkle." 4 Cf. I Cor. i, 24.

despite His weakness, bear His Cross as far as Calvary: but, at this moment, the Divinity wills, for our salvation, that the Humanity should feel its weakness, in order that it should merit for us the strength to bear our sufferings.

God gives us, too, a cross to carry, and each one thinks that his own is the heaviest. We ought to accept the one given to us without reasoning, without saying: "God might have changed such or such a circumstance in my life." Our Lord tells us: "If any man will come after Me, let him... take up *his* cross and follow Me."[1]

In this generous acceptation of *our* cross, we shall find union with Christ. For in bearing our cross, we truly bear our share in that of Jesus. Consider what is related in the Gospel. The Jews, seeing how faint and weary their Victim was becoming, and fearing that He would not arrive as far as Calvary, stop Simon the Cyrenean upon the way, and force him to come to the Saviour's aid.[2] As I have just said, Christ could, had He so willed, derive the necessary strength from His Divinity, but He consented to be helped. He wishes to show us thereby that each of us ought to help Him to bear His Cross. Our Lord says to us: "Accept this share of My sufferings which, in My Divine foreknowledge, on the day of My Passion, I reserved for you."

How shall we refuse to accept, from Christ's hands, this sorrow, this trial, this contradiction, this adversity? To drink some drops from the chalice which He Himself offers to us and from which He drank the first? Let us then say: "Yes, Divine Master, I accept this share, with all my heart, because it comes from You." Let us take it, as Christ took His Cross, out of love for Him and in union with Him. We shall sometimes feel ready to sink beneath the burden. St. Paul confesses that certain hours of his life were so full of weariness and disappointment that he was "weary even of life": *Ut taederet nos etiam vivere.*[3] But, like the great Apostle, let us look upon Him Who loved us so much as to deliver Himself up for us; let us unite ourselves to Christ with yet more love at those hours when the body is tortured, or the soul is crushed, or the mind is in darkness, or the deep action of the Spirit in His purifying operations is making itself felt. Then the virtue and unction of His Cross will be communicated to

---

1 Matth. xvi, 24; Marc. viii, 34; Luc. ix, 23.   2 Matth. xxvii, 32; Marc. xv, 21.
3 II Cor. i, 8.

us, and we shall find peace in it as well as strength, and that innermost joy which knows how to smile in the midst of suffering: *Superabundo gaudio in omni tribulatione nostra.*[1]

These are the graces which Our Lord has merited for us. Indeed when He went up Mount Calvary, helped by the Cyrenean, Christ Jesus, the God-Man, thought of all those who, in the course of the centuries, would help Him to carry His Cross in accepting their own; He merited for them, at that moment, inexhaustible graces of strength, resignation and self-surrender which would cause them to say like Him: "Father, not My will, but Thine be done."[2]

There is here an essential truth upon which we ought to meditate.

The Word Incarnate, Head of the Church, took His share, the greater share, of sorrows; but He chose to leave to His Church, which is His mystical Body, a share of suffering. St. Paul demonstrates this by a profound and strange saying. "I...fill up those things that are wanting of the sufferings of Christ, in my flesh, for His body, which is the Church."[3] Is there then something wanting to the sufferings of Christ? Certainly not. They were superabundant, immense; and their merit is infinite: *Et copiosa apud eum redemptio.*[4] There is nothing wanting to the sufferings whereby Christ saved us. Then why does St. Paul speak of "filling up" what is wanting? St. Augustine gives us the answer: The whole Christ, he says, is formed by the Church united to its Head, which is Christ; the Head has suffered all that He had to suffer; it remains for the members, if they wish to be worthy of the Head, to bear, in their turn, their share of sorrow: *Impletae erant omnes passiones, sed in capite: restabant adhuc Christi passiones in corpore; vos autem estis corpus Christi et membra.*[5]

We have then, as Christ's members, to join in His sufferings; Christ has reserved for us a share in His Passion; but in doing so, He has placed by the side of the cross, the strength necessary to carry it. For, says St. Paul,

1 "I exceedingly abound with joy in all our tribulation," Ibid. vii, 4.
2 Luc. xxii, 42. 3 Col. i, 24.
4 "And with him plentiful redemption," Ps. cxxix, 7.
5 "The sufferings were fulfilled, but in the head; there were yet remaining the sufferings of Christ in His body; and we are the body and members of Christ," S. Augustine, *Enarrat.* in Ps. lxxxvi, 5.

Christ having experienced suffering has become for us a High Priest full of compassion.[1]

V

There is yet more: we, having obtained the grace to bear our cross with Him, Christ Jesus likewise grants us to share His glory, after we have been associated with His sufferings: *Si tamen compatimur, ut et conglorificemur.*[2] For us as for Him, this glory will be measured by our "passion." The glory of Jesus is infinite, because in His Passion, He, being God, reached the lowest depths of suffering and humiliation. And it is by reason of His deep self-abasement that God has given Him such glory: *Propter quod et Deus exaltavit illum.*[3]

Indeed the Passion of Jesus, important as it was in His life, necessary as it is to our salvation and our sanctification, does not terminate the cycle of His mysteries.

We notice in reading the Gospel, that when Our Lord speaks of His Passion to the Apostles, He always adds that "the third day He will rise again": *Et tertia die resurget.*[4] These two mysteries are likewise linked together in the thought of St. Paul, whether he speaks of Christ alone, or whether he alludes to His Mystical Body.[5] Now, the Resurrection is for Jesus the dawn of His glorious life.

This is why the Church, when she solemnly commemorates the sufferings of her Bridegroom, mingles her accents of compassion with those of triumph. The liturgical ornaments of black or purple, the stripping of the altars, the "lamentations" borrowed from Jeremias, the silence of the bells, attest the bitter desolation that oppresses the heart of the Bride during these anniversary days of the great drama. And yet she breaks forth into accents of triumph and glory:

> *Pange, lingua gloriosi*
> *Lauream certaminis...*

"Exalt, O my tongue, the laurels of a glorious combat! Upon the tro-

---

1 Cf. Hebr. ii, 17–18; iv, 15; v, 2,
2 "Yet so, if we suffer with him, that we may be also glorified," Rom. viii, 17.
3 Philipp. ii, 9.   4 Matth. xvi, 21; xvii, 22; xx, 19.   5 Rom. iv, 25; v, 1–2.

phies of the Cross, proclaim the great triumph; Christ, the Redeemer of the world, comes forth as Victor from the combat in delivering Himself up to death." *Vexilla Regis prodeunt:* "The standard of the King advances, the mystery of the Cross shines forth....Thou art beautiful and glorious, tree decked with royal purple....Happy art thou to have borne the World's Ransom, suspended in thy arms...." Christ is Conqueror through the Cross: *Regnavit a ligno Deus.* The Cross represents the humiliations of Christ; but since the day when Jesus was fastened to it, the Cross occupied the place of honour in our churches. The instrument of our salvation has become for Christ the price of His glory: *Nonne haec oportuit pati Christum, et ita intrare in gloriam suam?*[1] It is the same for us. Suffering is not the last word in the Christian life. After having shared in the Passion of the Saviour, we shall also share in His glory.

Upon the very eve of His death, Jesus said to His disciples: *Vos estis qui permansistis mecum in tentationibus meis:* "You are they who have continued with Me in My temptation," and He immediately adds: "and I dispose to you, as My Father hath disposed to Me, a kingdom": *Et ego dispono vobis sicut disposuit mihi Pater meus regnum.*[2] This divine promise likewise concerns us. If we "continue" with Jesus in His "temptations," if we often contemplate His sufferings with faith and love, Christ will come, when our last hour strikes, to take us with Him that we may enter into the kingdom of His Father.

The day will come, sooner than we think, when death will be near. We shall lie motionless upon our bed; those who will then surround us will look upon us, silent in their powerlessness to help us; we shall no longer have any vital contact with the outer world. The soul will be alone with Christ. We shall then know what it is to have continued with Him in His temptations; we shall hear Him say to us, in this supreme and decisive agony, which is now our own: "You did not forsake Me in My agony, you accompanied Me when I went to Calvary to die for you. Behold Me now; I am near you to help you, to take you with Me. Fear not, have confidence,

---

1 "Ought not Christ to have suffered these things and so, to enter into his glory?" Luc. xxiv, 26.
2 Ibid. xxii, 28–29.

it is I!" *Ego sum, nolite timere!* [1] We shall then be able to repeat the words of the Psalmist with all assurance: *Et si ambulavero in medio umbrae mortis, non timebo mala; quoniam tu mecum es* [2]: O Lord, now that the shadows of death already surround me, I am not afraid "for Thou art with me."

---

1 Luc. xxiv, 36; Joan. vi, 20.
2 "For though I should walk in the midst of the shadow of death, I will fear no evils, for thou art with me," Ps. xxii, 4.

IN THE FOOTSTEPS OF JESUS
FROM THE PRETORIUM
TO CALVARY

SUMMARY.—I. Why the contemplation of the sorrows of the Word Incarnate is extremely fruitful for souls; no detail is negligible in the Passion of Christ, the Son of God, the object of His Father's complacency. Jesus especially manifests His virtues in the course of His Passion. Ever living, He produces within us the perfection that we contemplate in His immolation.—II. Meditations upon the "Stations" of the Way of the Cross.

THE Passion constitutes the "Holy of Holies" among the mysteries of Jesus. It is the crowning point of His public life, the summit of His mission here below, the work to which all the others converge or from which they draw their value.

Each year, during Holy Week, the Church commemorates in detail, the various phases of the Passion; each day, in the Sacrifice of the Mass, she renews the remembrance and the reality of it in order to apply its fruits to us.

To this central action of the liturgy is attached a practice of piety which, without belonging to the public official worship organised by the Bride of Christ, has become, on account of the abundance of graces whereof it is the source, very dear to faithful souls. This is the devotion to the Passion of Jesus under the well-known form of the "Way of the Cross."

The immediate preparation that the Saviour made before His oblation as High Priest upon Calvary was to bear His Cross from the Pretorium to Calvary, overwhelmed by sufferings, despised and insulted.

The Blessed Virgin Mary and the first Christians evidently more than once retraced this path, shedding tears of compassion at the places sanctified by the sufferings of the God-Man.

We know with what glowing fervour the faithful of the West undertook in the Middle Ages the long and painful pilgrimage to the Holy Places, there to venerate the Saviour's blood-stained footsteps; their piety was nourished at an unfailing source of priceless graces. Returned to their own country they had it at heart to preserve the remembrance of the days passed in prayer at Jerusalem. From this it befell that, especially from the fifteenth century, the sanctuaries and "stations" of the holy city were almost everywhere reproduced. The piety of the faithful thus found a means of satisfying itself by a spiritual pilgrimage renewed at will. Later on, at a comparatively recent period, the Church enriched this practice with the same indulgences gained by those who make the "stations" at Jerusalem.

I

This contemplation of the sufferings of Jesus is very fruitful. After the Sacraments and liturgical worship, there is no practice more useful for our souls than the Way of the Cross made with devotion. Its supernatural efficacy is beyond compare. What is the reason of this?

First of all because the Passion of Jesus is His essential work; nearly all the details of it were foretold. There is no other mystery of Jesus whereof the circumstances were announced with so much care by the Psalmist and prophets. And when we read, in the Gospel, the account of the Passion we are struck to see how attentive Christ Jesus is to "fulfil" what had been announced concerning Him. If He permits the presence of the traitor at the Last Supper, it is "that the Scripture may be fulfilled"[1]; He tells the Jews who had come to lay hands upon Him that He delivers Himself up to them "that the Scriptures...might be fulfilled": *Ut adimplerentur Scripturae.*[2] St. John relates how Our Saviour upon the Cross calls to mind that the Psalmist had predicted of Him: "In My thirst they gave Me vinegar to drink."[3] Then in order that this prophecy might be accomplished, Jesus cried: "I thirst": *Postea, sciens Jesus quia omnia consummata sunt,* UT *consummaretur Scriptura, dixit, Sitio.*[4] Nothing, in this, is little or negligible,

---

1 Joan. xiii, 18.   2 Matth. xxvi, 56.   3 Ps. lxviii, 22.
4 Joan. xix, 28.

because all these details mark the actions of a God-Man.

With all these actions of Jesus the Father is well pleased. He contemplates His Son with love, not only on Thabor when Christ is in the splendour of His glory; but likewise when Pilate shows Him to the multitude, crowned with thorns, and become the outcast of humanity; in the ignominies of His Passion as well as in the splendours of the Transfiguration: *Hic est Filius meus dilectus in quo mihi bene complacui.*[1]

During the Passion, Jesus honours and glorifies His Father in an infinite measure, not only because He is the Son of God, but also because He yields Himself up to all that His Father's justice and love demand of Him. If He could say, in the course of His public life, that He always did the things that pleased His Father: *Quae placita sunt ei facio semper,*[2] it is especially true of those hours when, in order to acknowledge the rights of divine majesty outraged by sin, and to save the world, He delivered Himself up to death, and to the death of the Cross: *Ut cognoscat mundus quia diligo Patrem.*[3] The Father loves Him with a boundless love because He gives His life for His sheep, and because by His sufferings, by His satisfactions, He merits for us all the graces that win back for us the friendship of His Father: *propterea me diligit Pater, quia ego pono animam meam.*[4]

Moreover, we should love to meditate upon the Passion because it is also therein that Christ's virtues shine forth with such brilliancy. He possesses every virtue within His soul, but the occasions of manifesting them especially arise in His Passion. His immense love for His Father, His charity for mankind, hatred of sin, forgiveness of injuries, patience, meekness, fortitude, obedience to lawful authority, compassion, all these virtues shine out in a heroic manner in these days of sorrow.

When we contemplate Jesus in His Passion, we see the Exemplar of our life, the Model,—admirable and accessible at the same time,—of those virtues of compunction, abnegation, patience, resignation, abandonment to God's will, charity, meekness, which, we ought to practise so as to become like unto our Divine Head: *Si quis vult post me venire,*

---

1 "This is my beloved Son, in whom I am well pleased," Matth. xvii, 5.
2 Joan. viii, 29.
3 "That the world may know that I love the Father," Ibid. xiv, 31.
4 "Therefore doth the Father love me: because I lay down my life," Ibid. x, 17.

abneget semetipsum, et tollat crucem suam et sequatur me.[1]

There is a third aspect which we too often forget, an aspect which is, however, of extreme importance. When we contemplate the sufferings of Jesus, He grants us, according to the measure of our faith, grace to practise the virtues which He revealed during those holy hours. How is this?

When Christ dwelt upon earth, an all-powerful virtue went out from His Divine Person, healing bodily infirmities, enlightening the mind, and quickening the soul: *Virtus de illo exibat, et sanabat omnes.*[2]

Something analogous comes to pass when we place ourselves in contact with Jesus by faith. To those who lovingly followed Him along the road to Golgotha or were present at His immolation, Christ surely granted special graces. This virtue which then went out from Him still does so; and when, in a spirit of faith, in order to compassionate His sufferings, and to imitate Him, we follow Him from the Pretorium to Calvary and take our stand at the foot of the Cross, He gives us the same graces, He makes us partakers of the same favours. Never let us forget that Christ Jesus is not a dead and inert model; but, ever living, He supernaturally produces in those who draw near to Him in the right dispositions, the perfection that they contemplate in His Person.

At each "station," Our Divine Saviour presents Himself to us in this triple character: as the Mediator Who saves us by His merits, the perfect Model of sublime virtues, and the efficacious Cause Who can, through His Divine Omnipotence, produce in our souls the virtues of which He gives us the example.

It may be said that these characters are to be found in all the mysteries of Jesus Christ. This is true, but with how much more plenitude in the Passion!

This is why if, every day, during a few moments, interrupting your work, laying aside your preoccupations, and closing your heart to all outward things, you accompany the God-Man along the road to Calvary, with faith, humility and love, with the true desire of imitating the virtues He

---

1 "If any man will come after me, let him deny himself, and take up his cross, and follow me," Matth. xvi, 24; cf. Marc. viii, 34; Luc. ix, 23; xiv, 27.
2 "For virtue went out from him and healed all," Luc. vi, 19.

manifests in His Passion, be assured that your souls will receive choice graces which will transform them little by little into the likeness of Jesus and of Jesus Crucified. And is it not in this likeness that St. Paul sums up all holiness?

It suffices, in order to gather the precious fruits of this practice, as well as to gain the numerous indulgences with which the Church has enriched it, to visit the fourteen stations without notable interruption, to stay a while at each of them and there to meditate upon the Saviour's Passion. No formula of prayer is prescribed, no form of meditation is imposed, not even that of the subject suggested by the "station." Full liberty is left to the attraction of each one and to the inspiration of the Holy Spirit.

II

Let us now make together the Way of the Cross; the considerations here presented at each station have no other end than to help us in our meditation. We can each take what we will, varying these considerations and affections, according to our aptitudes and the needs of our souls.

Before beginning, let us recall St. Paul's recommendation: "Let this mind be in you, which was also in Christ Jesus.... He humbled Himself, becoming obedient unto death, even to the death of the Cross."[1] The more we enter into those dispositions that filled the Heart of Jesus as He passed along the Sorrowful Way,—love towards His Father, charity towards men, hatred of sin, dispositions of humility and obedience,—the more our souls will receive graces and lights, because the Father will behold in us a more perfect image of His Divine Son.

My Jesus, You followed this path for love of me in bearing your Cross. I wish to follow it with You and like You; pour into my heart the sentiments which overflowed from Yours in those holy hours. Offer to Your Father for me the Precious Blood that You then shed for my salvation and sanctification.

---

1 Philipp. ii, 5, 8.

I. JESUS IS CONDEMNED TO DEATH BY PILATE

"And Jesus stood before the governor": *Stetit ante praesidem.*[1] He stands, because, being, the second Adam, He is the Head of all the race which He is about to redeem by His immolation. The first Adam has merited death by his sin: *Stipendia enim peccati mors.*[2] Jesus, innocent, but laden with the sins of the world is to expiate them by His Sacrifice of blood. The chief priests, the pharisees, His own nation, surround Him with furious clamours.[3] Through these clamours our sins cry out and tumultuously demand the death of the Just: *Tolle, tolle, crucifige eum!*[4] The cowardly Roman governor delivers the Victim up to His enemies that they may hang Him upon the Cross: *Tradidit eis illum ut crucifigeretur.*[5]

Let us contemplate Jesus at this moment. If He stands because He is our Head; if, as St. Paul says, He gives testimony[6] to the truth of His doctrine, to the Divinity of His Person and of His mission, He yet humbles Himself in interior self-abasement before the sentence pronounced by Pilate in whom He acknowledges an authentic power: *Non haberes potestatem adversum me ullam, nisi tibi datum esset desuper.*[7] In this earthly power, unworthy but legitimate, Jesus beholds the majesty of His Father. Therefore He rather delivers Himself up than He is delivered: *Tradebat judicanti se injuste.*[8] He humbles Himself in obeying even unto death; for us He voluntarily accepts the sentence of condemnation, in order to restore life to us: *Oblatus est quia ipse voluit.*[9] "As by the disobedience of one man, many were made sinners, so also by the obedience of one, many shall be made just."[10]

We ought to unite ourselves to Jesus in His obedience, to accept all that our Heavenly Father lays upon us, through whomsoever it may be, even a Herod or a Pilate, from the moment that their authority becomes legitimate. Let us also, even now, accept death in expiation for our sins, with all the circumstances wherewith it shall please Providence to surround

---

1 Matth. xxvii, 11.   2 Rom. vi, 23.   3 Ps. xxi, 13.
4 "Away with him: Away with him: Crucify him," Joan. xix, 15
5 Ibid. 16.   6 I Tim. vi, 13.
7 "Though shouldst not have any power against me, unless it were given thee from above," Joan. xix, 11.
8 "He delivered himself to him that judged him unjustly," I Petr. ii, 23.
9 "He was offered because it was his own will," Isa. liii, 7.   10 Rom. v, 19.

it; let us accept it as a homage rendered to Divine justice and holiness outraged by our iniquities; united with the death of Jesus it will become "precious in the sight of the Lord."[1]

My Divine Master, I unite myself to Your Sacred Heart in Its perfect submission and entire abandonment to the Father's Will. May the virtue of Your grace produce in my soul that spirit of submission which will yield me unreservedly and without murmuring to the Divine good pleasure and to all that it shall please You to send me at the hour when I must leave this world.

II. JESUS IS LADEN WITH HIS CROSS

"Then therefore [Pilate] delivered Him to them to be crucified. And they took Jesus, and led Him forth...bearing His own Cross": *Bajulans sibi crucem.*[2]

Jesus had made an act of obedience; He had delivered Himself up to the will of the Father, and now the Father shows Him what obedience imposes upon Him; it is the Cross. He accepts it as coming from the Father's hands, with all that it brings with it of distress and ignominy. At that instant, Jesus accepted the increase of suffering that this heavy burden, laid upon His bruised shoulders, brought to Him, and the indescribable sufferings wherewith His sacred members were to be afflicted at the moment of the crucifixion. He accepted the bitter sarcasms, the malignant blasphemies, with which His worst enemies, apparently triumphant, were about to heap upon Him as soon as they should see Him hung upon the infamous gibbet; He accepted the three hours' agony, the being forsaken by His Father....We shall never sound the depths of the abyss of afflictions to which our Divine Saviour consented in receiving His Cross. At this moment, too, Christ Jesus Who represented us all, and was going to die for us, accepted the cross for all His members, for each one of us: *Vere languores nostros ipse tulit, et dolores nostros ipse portavit.*[3] He then united to His own sufferings all the sufferings of His mystical body, causing them to find in this union their value and price.

Let us, therefore, accept our cross in union with Him, like Him, so that

---

1 Ps. cxv, 5.   2 Joan. xix, 16–17.
3 "Surely he hath borne our infirmities and carried our sorrows," Isa. liii, 4.

we may be worthy disciples of this Divine Head; let us accept it without reasoning, without repining. Although the Cross that the Father laid upon Jesus was of such weight, was His love, His confidence towards His Father diminished thereby? Quite the contrary. "The chalice which My Father hath given Me, shall I not drink it?" *Calicem quem dedit mihi Pater, non bibam illum?*[1] Let it be the same with us. "If any man will come after Me let him...take up his cross and follow Me." Do not let us be of those whom St. Paul calls "enemies of the cross of Christ."[2] Rather let us take up our cross, the one that God lays upon us. In the generous acceptation of this cross, we shall find peace. Nothing brings such peace to the soul that is in suffering as this utter self-surrender to God's good pleasure.

My Jesus, I accept all the crosses, all the contradictions, all the adversities that the Father has destined for me. May the unction of Your grace give me strength to bear these crosses with the submission of which You gave us the example in receiving Yours for us. May I never seek my glory save in the sharing of Your sufferings![3]

III. JESUS FALLS THE FIRST TIME UNDER THE CROSS

He shall be "a man of sorrows, and acquainted with infirmity": *Vir dolorum, sciens infirmitatem.*[4] This prophecy of Isaias is fulfilled to the letter. Jesus, exhausted by His sufferings of soul and body, sinks under the weight of His Cross; He, the Omnipotent, falls from weakness. This weakness of Jesus is a homage to His Divine power. By it He expiates our sins, He repairs the revolt of our pride, and raises up a fallen world, powerless to save itself: *Deus qui in Filii tui humilitate jacentem mundum erexisti....*[5] Moreover, at that moment, He merited for us the grace to humble ourselves for our sins, to acknowledge our falls and sincerely confess them; He merited for us the grace of fortitude to sustain our weakness.

With Christ, prostrate before His Father, let us detest the risings of our vanity and ambition; let us acknowledge the extent of our frailty. As God casts down the proud, so the humble avowal of our infirmity draws down His mercy: *Quomodo miseretur pater filiorum...quoniam ipse cogno-*

---

1 Joan. xviii, 11.   2 Philipp. iii, 18.   3 Gal. vi, 14.   4 Isa. liii, 3.
5 Collect for the 2nd Sunday after Easter.

vit figmentum nostrum.[1] Let us then cry to God for mercy, in the moments when we feel that we are weak in face of the cross, of temptation, of the accomplishment of the Divine will: *Miserere mei, quoniam infirmus sum.*[2] It is when we thus humbly declare our infirmity that grace, which alone can save us, triumphs within us: *Virtus in infirmitate perficitur.*[3]

O Christ Jesus, prostrate beneath Your Cross, I adore You. "Power of God,"[4] You show Yourself overwhelmed with weakness so as to teach us humility and confound our pride. O High Priest, full of holiness, Who passed through our trials in order to be like unto us and to compassionate our infirmities,[5] do not leave me to myself, for I am but frailty. May Your power dwell in me, so that I fall not into evil: *Ut inhabitet in me virtus Christi.*[6]

IV. JESUS MEETS HIS HOLY MOTHER

The day has come for the Blessed Virgin whereon Simeon's prophecy is to be fulfilled in her: "Thy own soul a sword shall pierce."[7] In the same way that she was united to Jesus when offering Him, in years gone by, in the Temple, so now in this hour when Jesus is about to consummate His sacrifice, she is to enter, more than ever, into His dispositions and share in His sufferings. She sets out towards Calvary where she knows that her Son is to be crucified. Upon the way she meets Him. What immense sorrow to see Him in this terrible state! Her gaze meets His, and the abyss of the sufferings of Jesus calls upon the abyss of His Mother's compassion. What is there that she would not do for Him!

This meeting was at once a source of sorrow and of joy for Jesus. Of sorrow, in seeing the deep desolation wherein His suffering state plunged His Mother's soul; of joy, in the thought that His sufferings were to pay the price for all the privileges she had already received and for those yet to be lavished upon her.

This is why He scarcely lingers. Christ had the most tender Heart that

---

1 "As a father hath compassion on his children...for he knoweth our frame," Ps. cii, 13–14.

2 "Have mercy on me, O Lord, for I am weak," Ibid. vi, 3.

3 "Power is made perfect in infirmity," II Cor. xii, 9.

4 I Cor. i, 24.   5 Hebr. iv, 15.   6 II Cor. xii, 9.   7 Luc. ii, 35.

ever beat. He shed tears at the tomb of Lazarus, He wept over the evils that were to fall upon Jerusalem. Never did son love his mother as He did; when He met her so desolate upon the road to Calvary, every fibre of His Heart must have been torn. And yet, He passes on, He continues His way towards the place of His execution, because it is His Father's will. Mary is one with Him in all that He feels, she knows that all things must be accomplished for our salvation; she takes her share in the sufferings of Jesus in following Him as far as Golgotha where she will become co-redemptress.

Nothing that is human should hold us back in our path towards God; no natural love should trammel our love for Christ; we must pass onwards so as to remain united to Him.

Let us ask the Blessed Virgin to associate us with her in the contemplation of the sufferings of Jesus, and to make us share in the compassion that she shows towards Him, that we may gain therefrom the hatred of sin which required such an expiation. It has at times pleased God to manifest sensibly the fruit produced by the contemplation of the Passion, by imprinting on the bodies of some saints, such as St. Francis of Assisi, the stigmata of the Wounds of Jesus. We ought not to wish for these outward marks; but we ought to ask that the image of the suffering Christ may be imprinted upon our hearts. Let us implore this precious grace from the Blessed Virgin: *Sancta mater istud agas, crucifixi fige plagas cordi meo valide.*[1]

O Mother, behold your Son; by the love that we bear towards Him, obtain for us that the remembrance of His sufferings may everywhere follow us; it is in His name that we ask this of you; to refuse it to us would be to refuse it to Himself, since we are His members. O Christ Jesus, behold Your Mother, for her sake, grant that we may compassionate Your sorrows so that we may become like unto You.

V. SIMON THE CYRENEAN HELPS JESUS
TO CARRY HIS CROSS

"And going out they found a man of Cyrene, named Simon, him they

---

1 "Holy Mother, may you do this, fix the wounds of the Crucified deep in my heart," Stabat Mater.

forced to take up His Cross."[1]

Jesus is exhausted. Although He be the Almighty, He wills that His Sacred Humanity, laden with all the sins of the world, shall feel the weight of justice and expiation. But He wants us to help Him carry His Cross. Simon represents us all, and Christ asks all of us to share in His sufferings; we are His disciples only upon this condition: "If any man will come after Me, let him...take up his cross, and follow Me." The Father has decreed that a share of sorrow shall be left to His Son's mystical body, that a portion of expiation shall be borne by His members: *Adimplebo ea quae desunt passionum Christi in carne mea pro corpore ejus, quod est Ecclesia.*[2] Jesus wills it likewise and it was in order to signify this Divine decree that He accepted the help of the Cyrenean.

But at the same time, He merited for us the grace of fortitude wherewith to sustain trials generously. In His Cross He has placed the unction that makes ours tolerable; for in carrying our cross, it is truly His own which we accept. He unites our sufferings to His sorrow, and He confers upon them, by this union, an inestimable value, the source of great merits. Our Lord said to St. Mechtilde: "As My Divinity drew to itself the sufferings of My Humanity, and made them its own (it is the dowry of the bride), thus will I transport thy pains into My Divinity; I will unite them to My Passion, and will make thee to share in that glory which My Father bestowed upon My Sacred Humanity in return for all its sufferings."[3]

This it is that St. Paul gives us to understand in His Epistle to the Hebrews in order to encourage us to bear all things for the love of Christ: "Let us run by patience to the fight proposed to us; looking on Jesus, the author and finisher of faith. Who having joy set before Him, endured the cross despising the shame, and now sitteth on the right hand of the throne of God. Think diligently upon Him Who endured such opposition from sinners against Himself; that you be not wearied, fainting in your minds."[4]

My Jesus, I accept from Your hand the particles that You detach for me from Your Cross. I accept all the disappointments, contradictions, sufferings and sorrows that You permit or that it pleases You to send me. I

---

1 Matth. xxvii, 32; Marc. xv, 21.
2 "I will fill up those things that are wanting of the sufferings of Christ, in my flesh, for his body, which is the church," Col. i, 24.
3 The Book of Special Grace. 2nd part, chapter xxxvi.   4 Hebr. xii, 1–3.

accept them as my share of expiation. Unite the little that I do to Your unspeakable sufferings, for it is from them that mine will draw all their merit.

VI. A WOMAN WIPES THE FACE OF JESUS

Tradition relates that a woman, touched with compassion, drew near to Jesus, and offered Him a linen cloth to wipe His adorable Face.

Isaias had foretold of the suffering Jesus: "There is no beauty in Him, nor comeliness, and we have seen Him, and there was no sightliness, that we should be desirous of Him": *Non est species ei, neque decor, nec reputavimus eum.*[1] The Gospel tells us that during those terrible hours after his apprehension the soldiers had dealt Him insolent blows, that they had spat in His face; the crowning with thorns had caused the blood to trickle down upon His sacred countenance. Christ Jesus willed to suffer all this in order to expiate our sins; He willed that we should be healed by the bruises that His Divine Face received for us: *Livore ejus sanati sumus.*[2]

Being our Elder Brother, He has restored to us, by substituting Himself for us in His Passion, the grace that makes us the children of His Father. We must be like unto Him, since such is the very form of our predestination: *Conformes fieri imaginis Filii sui.*[3] How can this be? All disfigured as He is by our sins, Christ in His Passion remains the beloved Son, the object of all His Father's delight. We are like to Him in this, if we keep within us the principle of our divine similitude, namely, sanctifying grace. Again we are like to Him in practising the virtues that He manifests during His Passion, in sharing the love that He bears towards His Father and towards souls, His patience, fortitude, meekness and gentleness.

O Heavenly Father, in return for the bruises that Thy Son Jesus willed to suffer for us, glorify Him, exalt Him, give unto Him that splendour which He merited when His adorable countenance was disfigured for our salvation.

VII. JESUS FALLS THE SECOND TIME.

Let us consider our Divine Saviour again sinking under the weight of the

---

1 Isa. liii, 1–2.   2 Ibid. liii, 5.   3 Rom. viii, 29.

Cross. God has laid all the sins of the world upon His shoulders: *Posuit Dominus in eo iniquitatem omnium nostrum.*[1] They are our sins that crush Him. He beholds them all in their multitude and in their every detail. He accepts them as His own to the extent that He no longer appears, according to St. Paul's own words, anything but a living sin: *Pro nobis peccatum fecit.*[2] As the Eternal Word, Jesus is All-powerful; but He chooses to feel all the weakness of a burdened humanity: this wholly voluntary weakness honours the justice of His Heavenly Father, and merits strength for us.

Never let us forget our infirmities; never let us give way to pride. However great may be the progress that we believe we have made, we always remain too weak of ourselves to carry our cross after Jesus: *Sine me nihil potestis facere.*[3] The divine virtue that goes out from Him alone becomes our strength: *Omnia possum in eo qui me confortat*[4]; but it is only given to us if we often ask for it.

O Jesus, become weak for love of me, crushed under the weight of my sins, give me the strength that is in You, so that You alone may be glorified by my works!

VIII. JESUS SPEAKS TO THE WOMEN OF JERUSALEM.

"And there followed Him a great multitude of people, and of women, who bewailed and lamented Him. But Jesus, turning to them, said: Daughters of Jerusalem, weep not over Me; but weep for yourselves and for your children. For behold the days shall come, wherein they will say: Blessed are the barren....Then shall they begin to say to the mountains: Fall upon us....For if in the green wood they do these things, what shall be done in the dry?"[5]

Jesus knows the ineffable exigencies of His Father's justice and holiness. He reminds the daughters of Jerusalem that this justice and this holiness are adorable perfections of the Divine Being. Jesus Himself is "a high priest, holy, innocent, undefiled, separated from sinners."[6] He does but substitute Himself for them; and yet see with what rigour Divine Justice strikes Him. If this justice requires of Him so extensive an expiation, what

---

1 Isa. liii, 6.   2 II Cor. v, 21.
3 "Without me you can do nothing," Joan. xv, 5.
4 "I can do all things in him who strengtheneth me," Philipp. iv, 13.
5 Luc. xxiii, 27–31.   6 Hebr. vii, 26.

will be the rigour of the stripes dealt to the guilty who obstinately refuse to unite their share of expiation to the sufferings of Christ? *Horrendum est incidere in manus Dei viventis.*[1] Upon that day, the confusion of human pride will be so great, so terrible will be the chastisement of those who wanted to do without God that these unhappy ones, outcast from God for ever, will gnash their teeth in despair; they will call upon the hills to cover them, as if the hills could hide them from the fiery darts of a justice of which they will clearly see the entire equity....

Let us implore mercy from Jesus for the dreadful day when He will come, no longer as a Victim bowed down under the weight of our sins, but as the Supreme Judge to Whom the Father has given all power.[2]

O my Jesus, grant me mercy! O Jesus, True Vine, grant that I may remain united to You by grace and good works, so that I may bear fruit worthy of You. Grant that I may not become, through my sins, a dead branch, good for nothing but to be gathered up and cast into the fire.[3]

IX. JESUS FALLS FOR THE THIRD TIME.

"The Lord was pleased to bruise Him in infirmity," said Isaias, speaking of Christ during His Passion: *Dominus voluit conterere eum in infirmitate.*[4] Jesus is crushed beneath the weight of justice. We shall never be able, even in heaven, to measure what it was for Jesus to be subject to the darts of Divine justice. No creature has borne the weight of it in all its fulness, not even the damned have done so. But the Sacred Humanity of Jesus, united to this Divine Justice by immediate contact, has undergone all its power and all its rigour. This is why, as a Victim Who has delivered Himself out of love to all its action, He falls prostrate, crushed and broken beneath its weight.

O my Jesus, teach me to detest sin which obliges justice to require of You such expiation. Grant that I may unite all my sufferings to Yours, so that by them my sins may be blotted out and I may make satisfaction even here below.

---

1 "It is a fearful thing to fall into the hands of the living God," Ibid. x, 31.
2 Cf. Matth. xxviii, 18.   3 Cf. Joan. xv, 6.   4 Isa. liii, 10.

X. JESUS IS STRIPPED OF HIS GARMENTS.

"They parted My garments amongst them; and upon My vesture they cast lots."[1] This is the prophecy of the Psalmist. Jesus is stripped of everything and placed in the nakedness of utter poverty; He does not even dispose of His garments; for, as soon as He is raised upon the Cross, the soldiers will divide them among themselves and will cast lots for His coat. Jesus, moved by the Holy Spirit: *Per Spiritum sanctum semetipsum obtulit Deo*,[2] yields Himself to His executioners as the Victim for our sins.

Nothing is so glorious to God or so useful to our souls as to unite the offering of ourselves, absolutely and without condition, to the offering which Jesus made at the moment when He gave Himself up to the executioners to be stripped of His raiment and fastened to the Cross, "that through His poverty, [we] might be rich."[3] This offering of ourselves is a true sacrifice; this immolation to the Divine good pleasure is the basis of all spiritual life. But in order that it may gain all its worth, we must unite it to that of Jesus, for it is by this oblation that He has sanctified us all: *In qua voluntate sanctificati sumus.*[4]

O my Jesus, accept the offering that I make to You of all my being; join it to that which You made to Your Heavenly Father at the moment of reaching Calvary; strip me of all attachment to created things and to myself!

XI. JESUS IS NAILED TO THE CROSS.

"They crucified Him, and with Him two others, one on each side, and Jesus in the midst."[5] Jesus delivers Himself up to His executioners "dumb as a lamb before his shearer." The torture of the nails being driven into the Hands and Feet is inexpressible. Still less could anyone describe all that the Sacred Heart of Jesus endured in the midst of these torments? Jesus must doubtless have repeated the words He had said on entering into this world: Father, Thou wouldst no more holocausts of animals; they are insufficient to acknowledge Thy sanctity..."but a body Thou hast fitted to

---

1 Ps. xxi, 19.   2 Hebr. ix, 14.   3 II Cor. viii, 9.   4 Hebr. x, 10.
5 Joan. xix, 18.

Me": *Corpus autem aptasti mihi.* "Behold I come."[1]

Jesus unceasingly gazes into the face of His Father, and, with incommensurable love, He yields up His body to repair the insults offered to the Eternal Majesty: *Factus obediens usque ad mortem.* And what manner of death does He undergo? The death of the Cross: *Mortem autem crucis.*[2] Why is this? Because it is written: "Cursed is everyone that hangeth on a tree."[3] He willed to be "reputed with the wicked,"[4] in order to declare the sovereign rights of the Divine Sanctity.

He delivers Himself likewise for us. Jesus, being God, saw us all at that moment; He offered Himself to redeem us because it is to Him, High Priest and Mediator, that the Father has given us: *Quia tui sunt.*[5] What a revelation of the love of Jesus for us! *Majorem hac dilectionem nemo habet, ut animam suam ponat quis pro amicis suis.*[6] He could not have done more: *in finem dilexit.*[7] And this love is likewise the love of the Father and the Holy Spirit, for these Three are but One....

O Jesus Who "in obeying the will of the Father, and through the co-operation of the Holy Ghost did by Your death give life to the world; deliver me, by Your most sacred Body and Blood, from all my iniquities and from all evils; make me ever adhere to Your commandments and never suffer me to be separated from You."[8]

XII. JESUS DIES UPON THE CROSS.

"And Jesus crying with a loud voice said: Father, into Thy hands I commend My spirit. And saying this, He gave up the ghost."[9] After three hours of indescribable sufferings, Jesus dies. The only oblation worthy of God, the one sacrifice that redeems the world, and sanctifies souls is consummated: *Una enim oblatione consummavit in sempiternum sanctificatos.*[10]

Christ Jesus had promised that when He should be lifted up from the earth, He would draw all things to Himself: *Et ego si exaltatus fuero*

---

1 Hebr. x, 5–7; Cf. Ps. xxxix, 8. 2 Philipp. ii, 8.
3 Deut. xxi, 23; Gal. ii, 13. 4 Isa. liii, 12; Marc. xv, 28; Luc. xxii, 37.
5 Joan. xvii, 9.
6 "Greater love than this no man hath, that a man lay down his life for his friends," Ibid. xv, 13.
7 Ibid. xiii, 1. 8 Ordinary of the Mass. 9 Luc. xxiii, 46.
10 "For by one oblation he hath perfected for ever them that are sanctified," Hebr. x, 14.

a terra, omnia traham ad meipsum.[1] We belong to Him by a double title: as creatures drawn out of nothing by Him, for Him;—as souls redeemed by His Precious Blood: *Redemisti nos, Domine, in sanguine tuo.*[2] A single drop of the Blood of Jesus, the God-Man, would have sufficed to save us, for everything in Him is of infinite value; but besides many other reasons, it was to manifest to us the extent of His love that He shed His Blood to the last drop when His Sacred Heart was pierced. And it was for all of us that He shed it. Each one can repeat in all truth the burning words of St. Paul: He "loved me, and delivered Himself for me."[3]

Let us implore Him to draw us to His Sacred Heart by the virtue of His death upon the Cross; to grant that we may die to our self-love and our self-will, the sources of so many infidelities and sins, and that we may live for Him Who died for us. Since it is to His death that we owe the life of our souls, is it not just that we should live only for Him? *Ut et qui vivunt, jam non sibi vivant, sed ei qui pro ipsis mortuus est.*[4]

O Father, glorify Thy Son hanging upon the gibbet. Since He humbled Himself even to the death of the Cross, exalt Him; may the name that Thou hast given Him be glorified, may every knee bow before Him, and every tongue confess that Thy Son Jesus lives henceforward in Thy eternal glory!

XIII. THE BODY OF JESUS IS TAKEN DOWN FROM THE CROSS AND GIVEN TO HIS MOTHER.

The mangled Body of Jesus is restored to Mary. We cannot imagine the grief of the Blessed Virgin at this moment. Never did mother love her child as Mary loved Jesus; the Holy Spirit had fashioned within her a mother's heart to love a God-Man. Never did human heart beat with more tenderness for the Word Incarnate than did the heart of Mary; for she was full of grace, and her love met with no obstacle to its expansion.

Then she owed all to Jesus; her Immaculate Conception, the privileges that make of her a unique creature had been given to her in prevision of the death of her Son. What unutterable sorrow was hers when she re-

---

1 Joan. xii, 32. 2 Apoc. v, 9. 3 Gal. ii, 20.
4 "That they also who live may not now live to themselves, but unto him who died for them and rose again," II Cor. v, 15.

ceived the bloodstained Body of Jesus into her arms!

Let us throw ourselves down at her feet and ask her forgiveness for the sins that were the cause of so many sufferings. "O Mother, fount of love, make me understand the strength of your love, so that I may share your grief; make my heart glow with love for Christ, my God, so that I may think only of pleasing Him."[1]

XIV. JESUS IS LAID IN THE SEPULCHRE.

Joseph of Arimathea having taken the body of Jesus down from the Cross, "wrapped Him in fine linen, and laid Him in a sepulchre that was hewed in stone, wherein never yet any man had been laid."[2]

St. Paul says that Christ was "in all things to be made like unto His brethren"[3]; even in His burial, Jesus is one of us. They bound the body of Jesus, says St. John, "in linen cloths, with the spices, as the manner of the Jews is to bury."[4] But the body of Jesus, united to the Word, was not "to suffer corruption." He was to remain scarcely three days in the tomb; by His own power, Jesus was to come forth victorious over death, resplendent with life and glory, and death was no more to "have dominion over Him."[5]

The Apostle St. Paul tells us again that "we are buried together with Him by baptism" so that we may die to sin: *Consepulti enim sumus cum illo per baptismum in mortem.*[6] The waters of baptism are like a sepulchre, where we have left sin behind, and whence we come forth, animated by a new life, the life of grace. The sacramental virtue of our baptism for ever endures. In uniting ourselves by faith and love to Christ laid in the tomb, we renew this grace of dying to sin in order to live only for God.[7]

Lord Jesus, may I bury in Your tomb all my sins, all my failings, all my infidelities; by the virtue of Your Death and Burial, give me grace to renounce more and more all that separates me from You; to renounce Satan, the world's maxims, my self-love. By the virtue of Your Resurrection grant that, like You, I may no longer live save for the glory of Your Father!

1 *Stabat Mater.*   2 Luc. xxiii, 53.   3 Hebr. ii, 17.
4 Joan. xix, 40.   5 Rom. vi, 9.   6 Ibid. 4.   7 Cf. Rom. vi, 11.

SI CONSURREXISTIS
CUM CHRISTO

(Paschal time)

SUMMARY.—The Church calls the Resurrection of Jesus "holy." Double element constituting holiness.—I. The Risen Christ is exempt from all human infirmity.—II. Glorious plenitude of "life unto God" in the triumphant Christ.—III. Baptism inaugurates the Paschal grace in us. Doctrine of St. Paul. How the Christian, by avoidance of sin and detachment from creatures, must, during his whole life, imitate the spiritual liberty of the glorious Christ.—IV. How we should belong fully to God: *Viventes Deo;* the realisation of this in the soul.—V. How this twofold Paschal grace is strengthened within us by the contemplation of the mystery of the Resurrection and by Eucharistic Communion.—VI. The resurrection of the body completes the manifestation of the greatness of this glorious mystery. The joy that union with the Risen Christ gives rise to in our souls: the Easter *Alleluia.*

THE whole of the mystery of Christ during the days of His Passion can be summed up in those words of St. Paul: *Humiliavit semetipsum, factus obediens usque ad mortem:* "He humbled Himself, becoming obedient unto death." [1] We have seen Christ's self-abasement; He touched the lowest depths of humiliation; He chose the death of one accursed, as it was written: *Maledictus omnis qui pendet in ligno.* [2]

But these abysses of ignominies and suffering into which Our Saviour

---

1 Philipp. ii, 8.
2 "For he is accursed of God that hangeth on a tree," Deut. xxi, 23; Gal. iii, 13.

willed to descend were likewise abysses of love; and this love has merited for us the mercy of His Father, and all graces of salvation and sanctification.

If the word "humiliation" sums up the mystery of the Passion, there is another word of St. Paul which recapitulates the mystery of Christ in His Resurrection: *Vivit Deo*[1]: "He liveth unto God." *Vivit*: there is henceforth in Him only perfect and glorious life without infirmity or perspective of death: *Jam non moritur, mors illi ultra non dominabitur*[2]; life wholly for God, more than ever consecrated to His Father and to His glory.

In her litanies, the Church applies certain qualifying titles to some of the mysteries of Jesus. She says of His Resurrection that it is "holy": *Per sanctam resurrectionem tuam*. What does that mean? Are not all the mysteries of Jesus holy? Certainly they are. He Himself is the Saint of saints: *Tu solus sanctus*, we sing at Mass in the *Gloria*. And all His mysteries are holy. His birth is holy: *Quod nascetur ex te sanctum*[3]; all His life is holy; He does "always the things that please" His Father[4]; and none can convince Him of sin.[5] His Passion is holy; true it is that He dies for the sins of men, but yet the Victim is sinless, He is the spotless Lamb. The High Priest Who immolates Himself is "holy, innocent, undefiled, separated from sinners."[6]

Why is the Resurrection, in preference to all the other mysteries of Jesus, called "holy" by the Church?

Because it is in this mystery that Christ particularly fulfils the conditions of holiness; because this mystery principally places in relief the elements that formally constitute human holiness whereof the model and source are found in Christ; because if, by all His life, He is the Way,[7] and the Light,[8] if He gives the example of every virtue compatible with His Divinity,—in His Resurrection, Christ is above all the Example of holiness.

What, then, are the elements that constitute holiness? Holiness can be resumed for us into two elements: separation from all sin, detachment from every creature; and the belonging totally and steadfastly to God.

Now, in Christ's Resurrection, these two characters are found in a degree not manifested before His coming forth from the tomb. Although

---

1 Rom. vi, 10.
2 "He dieth now no more. Death shall no more have dominion over him," Ibid. 9.
3 Luc. i, 35.   4 Joan. viii, 29.   5 Cf. Joan. viii, 46.
6 Hebr. vii, 26.   7 Joan. xiv, 6.   8 Ibid. viii, 12.

the Word Incarnate had been, during His entire existence, the "Holy One" like to none other, it is with effulgent brightness that He especially reveals Himself to us under this aspect in His Resurrection and it is therefore that the Church sings: *Per sanctam resurrectionem tuam.*

Let us contemplate this mystery of Jesus coming forth living and glorious from the sepulchre; we shall see how the Resurrection is the mystery of the triumph of life over death, of the heavenly over the earthly, of the divine over the human, and that it eminently realises the ideal of all holiness.

I

What was Christ Jesus before His Resurrection?

He was God and Man. The Eternal Word had espoused a nature belonging to a sinful race; without any doubt, this Humanity has not contracted sin, but it has been subject to such corporal infirmities as are compatible with the Divinity, infirmities which, in us, are often the consequences of sin; *Vere languores nostros ipse tulit, et dolores nostros ipse portavit.*[1]

See Our Lord during His mortal life. In the manger, He is a feeble little Infant, Who needs His Mother's milk to sustain His life; later, He feels real fatigue: *Fatigatus ex itinere sedebat:*[2] sleep, real and unfeigned sleep, closes His eyelids, the apostles have to awaken Him when the ship in which He sleeps is tossed about by the tempest[3]; He knows hunger: *Esuriit*[4]; He knows thirst: *Sitio*[5]; He knows suffering. He also feels interior desolation; in the Garden of Olives, fear, weariness, anguish and sadness sweep over His soul: *Coepit pavere et taedere...et moestus esse; tristis est anima mea usque ad mortem.*[6] Finally He endures death: *Emisit spiritum.*[7]

It is thus He shares our weakness, our infirmities, our sorrows; sin alone, and all that is the source or moral consequence of sin, is unknown

---

1 "Surely he hath borne our infirmities and carried our sorrows," Isa. liii, 4.

2 "Being wearied with his journey, he sat," Joan. iv, 6.

3 Matth. viii, 24–25; Marc. iv, 35; Luc. vii, 23–24.

4 Matth. iv, 2; Luc. iv, 2.   5 Joan. xix, 28.

6 "He began to grow sorrowful and to be sad....My soul is sorrowful even unto death," Matth. xxvi, 37–38; Marc. xiv, 33–34.

7 Joan. xix, 28.

to Him: *Debuit per omnia fratribus similari, absque peccato.*[1]

But after the Resurrection, all these infirmities have disappeared. There is in Him no longer any weariness, nor any need of sleep, neither has He any infirmity whatsoever. Our Lord no longer experiences anything of the kind: it is a total separation from all that is weakness. Is His body no longer real? Certainly it is. It is truly the Body which He received from the Virgin Mary, the Body which suffered death upon the Cross.

See how Christ Himself shows this. On the evening of His Resurrection, He appears to the Apostles. "But they being troubled and frightened, supposed that they saw a spirit. And He said to them: Why are you troubled, and why do thoughts arise in your hearts? See My hands and feet, that it is I Myself; handle and see: for a spirit hath not flesh and bones as you see Me to have. And when He had said this, He shewed them His hands and feet."[2] Thomas was then absent. "We have seen the Lord," the other Apostles say to him on his return. Thomas will not believe; he remains incredulous. "Except I shall see in His hands the print of the nails, and put my finger into His side, I will not believe." Eight days later, Jesus again appears to them; and after having wished them peace, He says to Thomas: "Put in thy finger hither, and see My hands; and bring hither thy hand, and put it into My side; and be not faithless but believing."[3]

Thus, Jesus Himself proves to His Apostles the reality of His Risen Body; but it is a body henceforward exempt from earthly infirmities; this body is agile; matter forms no barrier to it; Jesus rises from the sepulchre hewn out of the rock and whereof the entrance is closed by a heavy stone; He appears in the midst of His disciples: *Januis clausis,*[4] the doors of the place where they were gathered together being shut. If He takes food with His disciples, it is not because He hungers, but because He wills, by this merciful condescension, to confirm the reality of His Resurrection.

This Risen Body is henceforth immortal. Christ "died once": *Quod enim mortuus est, mortuus est semel;*[5] but, says St. Paul, "Christ rising again from the dead, dieth now no more, death shall no more have dominion over Him": *Mors illi ultra non dominabitur:* the body of the Risen Jesus is no longer subject to death nor to the conditions of time: it is free from all servitude, from all infirmities; it is impassible, spiritual, living in a sov-

---

1 Hebr. ii, 17; iv, 15.   2 Luc. xxiv, 37–40.   3 Joan. xx, 24–27.
4 Ibid. xx, 26.   5 Rom. vi, 10.

ereign independence.

Herein is represented in Christ the first element of holiness: separation from all that is dead, from all that is earthly, from all that is creature: freedom from all weakness, all infirmity, all suffering. On the day of His Resurrection, Christ Jesus left in the tomb the linen cloths, which are the symbol of our infirmities, of our weaknesses, of our imperfections; He comes forth triumphant from the sepulchre; His liberty is entire, He is animated with intense, perfect life with which all the fibres of His being vibrate. In Him, all that is mortal is absorbed by Life.

II

Doubtless, we shall see the Risen Christ still touching earth. Out of love for His disciples, and condescension for the weakness of their faith, He vouchsafes to appear to them, to converse with them, to share their repasts; but His life is before all things heavenly: *Vivit Deo.*

We know scarcely anything of this heavenly life of Jesus after He had risen from the tomb; but can we doubt that it was wonderful?

He had proved to His Father how much He loved Him by giving His life for men; now, all the price is paid, all is expiated; satisfied justice demands from Him no more expiation; friendship is restored between men and God; the work of redemption is accomplished. But the worship rendered by Jesus towards His Father continues, more living, more entire, than ever. The Gospel tells us nothing of this constant homage of adoration, of love, of thanksgiving, that Christ then rendered to His Father; but St. Paul sums up all in saying: *Vivit Deo,* He "liveth unto God."

This is the second element of holiness: the adhering, the belonging, the consecration to God. We shall only know in heaven with what plenitude Jesus lived for His Father during those blessed days; it was certainly with a perfection that ravished the angels. Now that His Sacred Humanity is set free from all the necessities, from all the infirmities of our earthly condition, it yields itself more than ever before to the glory of the Father. The life of the Risen Christ becomes an infinite source of glory for His Father; there is no longer any weakness in Him; all is light, strength, beauty, life; all in Him sings an uninterrupted canticle of praise.

If man gathers up into his being all the kingdoms of creation in order therein to sum up the song of praise of every creature, what shall we say of the unceasing canticle that the Humanity of the glorious Christ, the supreme High Priest, triumphant over death, sings to the Trinity? This canticle, the perfect expression of the Divine life that henceforward envelops and penetrates with all its power and splendour the human nature of Jesus, is ineffable....

III

Such is the life of the Risen Christ. It is the model of ours, and Christ has merited for us the grace of living for God as He did, the grace of being associated with His risen life. True, it was not by His Resurrection that Christ actually merited this grace. All that He acquired for us was won by His sacrifice which was inaugurated at His Incarnation and consummated by His death upon the Cross. In drawing His last breath, Christ reached the term of His mortal existence: He can hence no longer merit.

But His merits remain to us after His glorious coming forth from the tomb. See how Christ Jesus has willed to keep the marks of His Wounds: He shows them to His Father in all their beauty, as titles to the communication of His grace: *Semper vivens ad interpellandum pro nobis.*[1]

It is from our baptism that we share in this grace of the Resurrection. St. Paul affirms this: "We are buried together with Him by baptism unto death; that as Christ is risen from the dead by the power of the Father, so we also may walk in newness of life."[2]

The holy water into which we are plunged at baptism is, according to the Apostle, the figure of the sepulchre; upon coming forth from it, the soul is purified from all sin, from all stain, set free from all spiritual death, and clad with grace, the principle of divine life: in the same way as upon coming forth from the tomb, Christ freed Himself from all infirmity so as to live henceforth a perfect life. This is why, in the early Church, baptism was administered only on the Paschal night, and at Pentecost which closes the Paschal season. We shall understand scarcely anything of the liturgy of Easter week, if we do not keep before our eyes the thought of baptism which was then solemnly conferred upon the catechumens.[3]

---

1 "Always living to make intercession for us," Hebr. vii, 25.   2 Rom. vi, 4.
3 See in *Christ, the Life of the Soul,* the conference: Baptism, the Sacrament of Adoption

We are therefore risen with Christ, by Christ, for He infinitely longs to communicate to us His glorious life. And what is necessary in order to respond to this divine longing and become like unto the Risen Jesus? It is that we should live in the spirit of our baptism. That, renouncing all that sin has vitiated in our lives, we should die more and more to "the old man"[1]; that all in us should be dominated and governed by grace. All holiness for us lies in this: to keep away from all sin, all occasion of sin, to be detached from creatures and all that is earthly, so as to live in God, unto God, with the greatest plenitude and steadfastness possible.

This work, begun at baptism, continues during our whole earthly existence. Christ, it is true, dies but once; He has given us thereby to die like Him to all that is sin. But we must "die" daily, for we have remaining in us the roots of sin, and the old enemy labours unceasingly to make them spring up. To destroy these roots in us, to keep ourselves from all infidelity, from loving any creature for itself, to remove from our actions not only every culpable motive but even every motive that is merely natural; to keep our hearts free, with a spiritual freedom, from all that is created and earthly: such is the first element of our holiness which Christ shows us realised in Him by this supreme and admirable independence wherein His Risen Humanity lives.

This is indeed one of the most marked aspects of the Paschal grace. St. Paul puts it in bold relief. "Purge out the old leaven that you may be a new paste," he says. For since Christ our Paschal Lamb, has been immolated for you, you have become unleavened bread. Therefore let us share in the feast, "not with the old leaven, nor with the leaven of malice and wickedness, but with the unleavened bread of sincerity and truth."[2]

This pressing exhortation of the Apostle forms the Epistle for the Mass on Easter Sunday. It must appear obscure to more than one Christian of our days, and yet it is this passage that the Church has chosen out of all others to sum up what our conduct ought to be when we celebrate the mystery of the Resurrection. Why this choice?

Because it so distinctly, although at the same time so profoundly, denotes the fruit that the soul should gather from this mystery. What, then, do these words signify?

and Initiation: death and life.
1 Rom. vi, 6.   2 I Cor. v, 7–8.

We know that at the approach of the festival of the Pasch,—which recalled to the Hebrews the famous anniversary of the "passage" of the destroying angel[1]—they had to see that no trace of leaven was left in their houses; then, on the day of the feast, after having sacrificed the paschal lamb, they ate it with unleavened bread, that is to say bread made without yeast.[2]

All this was only a figure, a symbol[3] of the true Pasch, the Christian Pasch. "Purge out the old leaven"; "put off the old man,"[4] born in sin, with his evil desires which you have renounced by baptism; at that moment of baptismal regeneration, you participated in the death of Christ, Who caused sin to die in you[5]; you have become, and you must remain, through grace, a new paste, that is to say a "new creature,"[6] "a new man,"[7] after the example of Christ come forth glorious from the sepulchre.

Therefore, like the Jews, who, the Pasch having come, abstained from all leaven in order to eat the Paschal lamb, we, Christians, who would be partakers of the mystery of the Resurrection, who would unite ourselves to Christ, the Lamb Who was slain and rose again for us, we must henceforward live no longer in sin; we must keep ourselves from those evil desires which are like a leaven of malice and perversity: *Non ergo regnet peccatum in vestro mortali corpore;*[8] we must preserve within us the grace which will enable us to live in the truth and sincerity of the Divine law.

Such is St. Paul's doctrine that the Church reads to us on the very day of Easter, and that especially points out the first element of holiness to us: to renounce sin, and all human springs of action which can, like old leaven, corrupt our deeds; to live, in regard to all sin and all created things, in that spiritual liberty which appeared so vividly in the Risen Christ.

We ask this grace of Jesus Himself, in this strophe repeated in each of the paschal hymns.

> *Quaesumus auctor omnium*
> *In hoc paschali gaudio,*
> *Ab omni mortis impetu,*
> *Tuum defende populum.*[9]

---

1 Pasch signifies passage. Cf. Exod. xii, 26–27.   2 Ibid. xii, 8, 15.
3 I Cor. x, 6, 11.   4 Ephes. iv, 22; Col. iii, 9.   5 Cf. Rom. vi, 2 et seq.
6 II Cor. v, 17.   7 Ephes. iv, 24.
8 "Let not sin therefore reign in your mortal body," Rom. vi, 12.
9 Hymn at Vespers, Matins and Lauds. (Monastic Breviary.)

"We beseech Thee, the Author of all things, to defend Thy people from all attacks of death in these days full of Easter gladness." We ask Christ to preserve His people, this people "purchased with His own Blood,"[1] says St. Paul, that it may be pleasing to Himself, *Populum acceptabilem.*[2] To preserve it from what? From all the attacks of spiritual death, that is to say from all sin, from all that leads to sin, from all that tends to destroy or weaken within us the life of grace. It is then that we shall make part of that society that Christ wills to be without "spot or wrinkle," but "holy and without blemish": *Sine ruga, sine macula.*[3]

IV

The second element of holiness, which, moreover, gives its motive and value to the first, is the belonging to God, devotedness to God, which St. Paul calls living unto God: *Viventes Deo.*[4]

This life for God comprises an infinity of degrees. To begin with, it supposes that one is totally separated from all mortal sin; between mortal sin and the divine life, there is absolute incompatibility. Next there is separation from venial sin, from all natural springs of action, and detachment from all that is created. The more complete the separation is, the more we are spiritually free, and the more also the divine life develops and expands within us: in the measure that the soul is freed from what is earthly, she opens to what is divine, she savours heavenly things, she lives unto God.

In this happy state, the soul is not only free from all sin, but she no longer acts save under the inspiration of grace, and for a supernatural motive. And when this supernatural motive extends to all her actions, when the soul by a movement of love, habitual and steadfast, refers all to God, to the glory of Christ and that of His Father, then there is within her the plenitude of life, that is holiness: *Vivit Deo.*

You will notice that during Paschal time, the Church frequently speaks to us of life, not only because Christ, by His Resurrection, has vanquished death, but above all because He has reopened to souls the fountains of eternal life. It is in Christ that we find this life: *Ego sum vita.*[5] This is why, likewise frequently, the Church makes us read over again on these

---

1 Act. xx, 28.   2 Tit. ii. 14.   3 Ephes. v, 27.   4 Rom. vi, 11.
5 "I am the life," Joan. xiv, 6.

blessed days, the parable of the Vine: "I am the Vine," says Jesus, "you are the branches; abide in Me and I in you, for without Me you can do nothing."[1] We must abide in Christ and He in us, in order that we may bear much fruit.[2]

How is this accomplished?

By His grace, by the faith that we have in Him, and by the virtues whereof He is the Exemplar and which we imitate. When, having renounced sin, we die to ourselves, as the grain of wheat dies in the earth before producing fruitful ears,[3] when we no longer act save under the inspiration of the Holy Spirit and in conformity with the precepts and maxims of the Gospel of Jesus, then it is Christ's divine life that blossoms forth in our souls, it is Christ Who lives in us: *Vivo ego, jam non ego, vivit vero in me Christus.*[4]

Such is the ideal of perfection: *Viventes Deo in Christo Jesu.* We cannot attain it in a day; holiness, ingrafted in us at baptism, is only developed little by little, by successive stages. Let us try to act in such a way that each Easter, each day of this blessed season which extends from the Resurrection to Pentecost, may produce within us a more complete death to sin, to the creature, and a more vigorous and more abundant increase of the life of Christ.

Christ must reign in our hearts, and all within us must be subject to Him. Since the day of Christ's triumph, He gloriously lives and reigns in God, in the bosom of the Father: *Vivit et regnat Deus.* Christ only lives where He reigns, and He lives in us in the same degree as He reigns in our soul. He is King as He is High Priest. When Pilate asked Him if He was a King, Our Lord answered Him: *Tu dicis quia rex sum ego*[5]; "I am, but My kingdom is not of this world." "The kingdom of God is within you": *Regnum Dei intra vos est.*[6] This dominion of Christ must, day by day, be extended in our souls; it is this that we ask of God: *Adveniat regnum tuum!* Oh, may it come, Lord, that day when, truly, Thou wilt reign in us by Thy Christ!

And why has not that day already come? Because so many things in us, self-will, self-love, our natural activity, are not yet subject to Christ, because we have not yet done what the Father desires: *Omnia subjecisti*

---

1 Ibid. xv, 4–5.   2 Cf. Ibid. 5.   3 Ibid. xii, 25.   4 Gal. ii, 20.
5 "Thou sayest that I am a king," Joan. xviii, 37.   6 Luc. xvii, 21.

sub pedibus ejus,[1] we have not yet put all things beneath the feet of Christ. That is a part of the glory which the Father wills henceforth to give to His Son Jesus: *Exaltavit illum et donavit illi nomen...ut in nomine Jesu omne genu flectatur.*[2] The Father wills to glorify Christ, because Christ is His Son, because He humbled Himself; the Father wills that every knee should bend at the name of Jesus; all in creation is to be subject to Jesus; in heaven, upon earth, in hell; all, too, in each one of us: will, intelligence, imagination, energies.

Jesus came in us as King on the day of our baptism, but sin disputes this dominion with Him. When we destroy sin, infidelities, attachment to the creature; when we live by faith in Him, in His word, in His merits; when we seek to please Him in all things, then Christ is Master, then He reigns within us; as He reigns in the bosom of the Father, so He lives in us. He can say of us to the Father: "Behold this soul: I live and reign in her, O Father, that Thy name may be hallowed."

Such are the most profound aspects of the Paschal grace:—detachment from all that is human, earthly, created; the full donation of ourselves to God, through Christ. The Resurrection of the Word Incarnate becomes for us a mystery of life and of holiness. Christ being our Head, "God hath raised us up together" with Him: CON*resuscitavit nos.*[3] We ought then to seek to reproduce within ourselves the features that marked His Risen life.

St. Paul exhorts us to this with much insistency during these days. "If," says he, "you be risen with Christ," that is to say if you wish that Christ should make you partakers of the mystery of His Resurrection, you should enter into the dispositions of His Sacred Heart, if you wish to "eat the Pasch" with Him, and one day share His triumphant glory, "mind the things that are above, not the things that are upon the earth," love heavenly things that abide, detach yourself from things of earth which pass away: honours, pleasures, riches; *Si* CON*surrexistis cum Christo, quae sursum sunt quaerite...non quae super terram.*[4] "For you are dead; and your life is hid with Christ in God." And as "Christ rising again from the dead, dieth

---

1 "Thou hast subjected all things under his feet," Ps. viii, 8.
2 "He hath exalted him and hath given him a name...that in the name of Jesus every knee should bow," Philipp. ii, 9–10.
3 Ephes. ii, 6.   4 Col. iii, 1–2.

now no more" but lives for ever for His Father, so do you die to sin and live for God through the grace of Christ: *Ita et vos existimate, vos mortuos quidem esse peccato, viventes autem Deo in Christo Jesu.*[1]

V

You will perhaps now ask how we can strengthen this Paschal grace within us.

First of all by contemplating the mystery with great faith. See how when Christ Jesus, on appearing to His disciples, bids Thomas, the incredulous apostle, put His finger in the marks of His Wounds which He keeps, what does He say to him? "Be not faithless, but believing." And when the apostle adores Him as his God, Our Lord adds: *Beati qui non viderunt et crediderunt.*[2] "Because thou hast seen Me, Thomas, thou hast believed: blessed are they that have not seen, and have believed."

Faith places us in contact with Christ; if we contemplate this mystery with faith, Christ produces in us the grace which He gave to His disciples when, as their Risen Lord, He appeared to them. Jesus lives in our souls; and ever living, He unceasingly acts in us, according to the degree of our faith and in accordance with the grace proper to each of His mysteries. It is related in the life of St. Mary Magdalen of Pazzi that one Easter Day, when she was at table in the refectory, her countenance reflected such joy that a novice who was serving her could not refrain from asking her the reason. "It is the beauty of my Jesus," she replied, "which makes me so joyful; I see Him now in the heart of each one of my sisters." "Under what form?" asked the novice again. "I see Him in them all risen and glorious as the Church brings Him before us to-day," answered the Saint.

It is above all by Sacramental Communion that we now assimilate the fruits of this mystery.

What, indeed, do we receive in the Eucharist? We receive Christ, the Body and Blood of Christ. But if Communion supposes the immolation of Calvary and that of the Altar which reproduces it, it is however the glorified Flesh of the Saviour wherewith we communicate. We receive

---

1 Rom. vi, 9–11.   2 Joan. xx, 27–29.

290

Christ such as He is now, that is to say glorified in the highest heavens and possessing, in its fullest expansion, the glory of His Resurrection.

He Whom we thus really receive is the very Fount of holiness. He cannot fail to give us a share in the grace of His "holy" Resurrection; here, as in all things, it is of His fulness that we are all to receive.

Still in our days, Christ, ever living, repeats to each soul the words that He said to His disciples when, at the time of the Pasch, He was about to institute His Sacrament of love: "With desire, I have desired to eat *this pasch* with you."[1] Christ Jesus desires to effect in us the mystery of His Resurrection: He lives entirely for His Father above all that is earthly; He wills, for our joy, to draw us with Him into this divine current. If, after having received Him in Communion, we leave Him full power to act, He will give to our life, by the inspirations of His Spirit, that steadfast orientation towards the Father in which all holiness is summed up; so all our thoughts, all our aspirations, all our activity will refer to the glory of our Father in heaven.

It is You, O Divine Risen Lord, Who come to me; You Who after having expiated sin by Your sufferings, have vanquished death by Your triumph, Who, henceforward glorious, live only for Your Father. Come to me "to destroy the works of the devil," and to destroy sin and my infidelities, come to me to detach me more from all that is not You; come to make me a partaker of that superabundant perfect life which now overflows from Your Sacred Humanity; I will then sing, with You, a hymn of praise to Your Father Who upon this day has crowned You, as our Captain and our Head, with glory and honour!

These aspirations are expressed in one of the collects where the Church sums up, after the Communion, the graces which she implores of God for her children. "We beseech Thee, O Lord, that being purified from the stains of our past guilt, the participation in Thy august Sacrament may transform us into a new creature.[2]

The Church wills that this grace should remain in us, even when communion is over, even when the Paschal solemnities shall have come to an end. "Grant, we beseech Thee, Almighty God, that the virtue of the Paschal mystery may remain in our souls."[3] It is a permanent grace which gives

---

1 Luc. xxii, 15.   2 Postcommunion for Easter Wednesday.
3 Postcommunion for Easter Tuesday.

us the power, according to the expression of St. Paul, of being "renewed day by day,"[1] of increasing the life of Christ within us by bringing us to a closer and closer resemblance to the glorious traits of our Divine Model.

VI

In indicating the double aspect of the mystery of holiness that the Resurrection of Jesus ought to produce within our hearts, we have not exhausted the riches of the Paschal grace.

God is so magnificent in what He does for His Christ, that He wills that the mystery of His Son's Resurrection should extend not only to our souls but also to our bodies. We too shall rise again. That is a dogma of faith. We shall rise corporally, like Christ, with Christ. Could it be otherwise?

Christ, as I have often said, is our Head; we form with Him a mystical body. If Christ is risen,—and He is risen in His human nature,—it is necessary that we, His members, should share in the same glory. For it is not only in our soul, it is likewise in our body, it is in our whole being that we are members of Christ. The most intimate union binds us to Jesus. If then He is risen glorious, the faithful who, by grace, make part of His mystical body, will be united with Him even in His Resurrection.

Hear what St. Paul says on this subject: "Christ is risen from the dead, the firstfruits of them that sleep"; He represents the firstfruits of a harvest; after Him, the rest of the harvest is to follow. "By a man came death, and by a man the resurrection of the dead. And as in Adam all die, so also in Christ all shall be made alive."[2] God, he says more energetically still, "has raised us up together...through Jesus Christ": CON*resuscitavit nos...in Christo Jesu.*[3] How is this? It is that, by faith and grace, we are the living members of Christ, we share in His states, we are one with Him. And as grace is the principle of our glory, those who are, by grace, already saved in hope, are already also, in principle, risen in Christ.

This is our faith and our hope.

But now "our life is hidden with Christ in God"; we now live without

---

1 II Cor. iv, 16.   2 I Cor. xv, 20–22.   3 Ephes. ii, 6.

grace producing those effects of light and splendour which will have their fruition in glory; even as Christ, before His Resurrection, held back the glorious radiance of His Divinity and only allowed a reflection of it to be seen by the three disciples on the day of the Transfiguration on Thabor. Our inner life here below is only known to God; it is hidden from the eyes of men. Moreover, if we try to reproduce in our souls, by our spiritual liberty, the characteristics of the Risen Life of Jesus, it is a labour which is still wrought in a flesh wounded by sin, subject to the infirmities of time; we shall only attain this holy liberty at the cost of a struggle incessantly renewed and faithfully sustained. We too must suffer so as to enter into glory, as Christ said of Himself to the disciples of Emmaus, on the very day of His Resurrection: *Nonne haec oportuit pati Christum et ita intrare in gloriam suam?*[1] "We are the sons of God," says the Apostle, "and if sons, heirs also; heirs indeed of God, and joint heirs with Christ; yet so if we suffer with Him, that we may be also glorified with Him."[2]

May these thoughts of heaven sustain us during the days we have yet to pass here below. Yes, the time will come when there shall be no more mourning, nor crying, nor sorrow; God Himself will wipe away the tears of His servants[3] become the co-heirs of His Son; He will make them sit down at the eternal feast which He has prepared to celebrate the triumph of Jesus and of those whose Elder Brother Jesus is.

If, each year, we are faithful in sharing in Christ's sufferings during Lent and Holy Week, each year, too, the celebration of Easter, the contemplation of the glory of Jesus triumphant over death, makes us participate more fruitfully and more abundantly in the state of Our Risen Lord; it increases our detachment from all that is not God, and, by grace, faith and love, it makes the divine life grow within us. At the same time, it enlivens our hope: for, says St. Paul, when at the last day Christ, Who is our Life and our Head, shall appear, then we also, because we share in His life, "shall appear with Him in glory": *Cum Christus apparuerit vita vestra, tunc et vos apparebitis cum ipso in gloria.*[4]

This hope fills us with joy, and it is because the mystery of Easter, be-

---

1 "Ought not Christ to have suffered these things and so, to enter into his glory?" Luc. xxiv, 26.
2 Rom. viii, 17.   3 Apoc. xxi, 4.   4 Col. iii, 4.

ing a mystery of life, strengthens our hope, that it is also super-eminently a mystery of joy.

The Church shows this by multiplying, throughout Paschal time, the *Alleluia,*[1] the cry of gladness and felicity borrowed from the liturgy of Heaven. She had banished it during Lent in order to manifest her sadness and communicate in the sufferings of her Bridegroom. Now that Christ is risen, she rejoices with Him; she takes up again, with new fervour, this joyous acclamation wherein is summed up all the ardour of her feelings.

Never let us forget that we make only one with Christ Jesus. His triumph is ours; His glory is the principle of our joy. With the Church our Mother, let us, too, often repeat the *Alleluia* so as to manifest our joy to Christ in seeing Him triumphant over death, and to thank the Father for the glory that He gives to His Son. The *Alleluia* that the Church unweariedly repeats, during the fifty days of the Paschal season, is like the ever renewed echo of that prayer with which she ends Easter week: "Grant us, we beseech Thee, O Lord, ever to rejoice through these Paschal mysteries; that the continual work of our regeneration may ensure to us perpetual joy in heaven."[2]

---

1 "Praise God."   2 Secret for Easter Saturday.

...AND NOW, FATHER, GLORIFY THY SON

(Ascension)

SUMMARY.—I. The splendour of the triumph of Jesus in His Ascension to the right hand of the Father.—II. Chief reasons of this wonderful exaltation of Christ:—He is the Son of God; He humbled Himself in the ignominy of the Passion.—III. The grace that Christ gives to us in this mystery: we enter with Him into Heaven as members of His mystical body.—IV. Sense of profound joy to which this glorification of Jesus gives rise in us: *Tu esto nostrum gaudium.*—V. Why an unshaken confidence ought likewise to animate us in this solemnity: Christ enters into the Holy of Holies as supreme High-Priest and remains there as the one Mediator.—VI. We rely upon Christ, in order to be "kept from evil" in the midst of the sorrows and trials of this present life.

AFTER His Resurrection, Christ Jesus only remains forty days with His disciples. St. Leo says that these days did not pass in inaction: *Ii dies non otioso transiere decursu.*[1] By manifold apparitions to the Apostles, by His conversations with them, *Loquens de Regno Dei,*[2] Jesus fills their hearts with joy; He strengthens their faith in His triumph, in His Person, in His mission; He also gives them His last instructions[3] for the establishing and organising of the Church.

Now that the mission of His sojourn here below is fully terminated, the hour has come for Him to re-ascend to His Father. The Divine Giant

---

1 *Sermo I de Ascensione Domini,* c. ii.
2 "Speaking of the kingdom of God," Act. i, 3.   3 Ibid. 2.

has completely achieved His course upon earth: *Opus consummavi quod dedisti mihi.*[1] He is now about to taste in all their fulness the profound joys of a marvellous triumph; the ascension into Heaven gloriously consummates the earthly life of Jesus.

Of all the feasts of Our Lord, I venture to say, that in a certain sense, the Ascension is the greatest, because it is the supreme glorification of Christ Jesus. Holy Church calls this Ascension "admirable,"[2] and "glorious,"[3] and throughout the Divine Office of this feast, she makes us hymn the magnificence of this mystery.

Our Divine Saviour had asked of His Father to be glorified with that glory which He had, in His Divinity in the eternal splendours of Heaven: *Clarifica me, tu, Pater…claritate quam habui priusquam mundus esset apud te.*[4] The triumph of the Resurrection marked the dawn of this personal glorification of Jesus: *Haec est clarificatio Domini Nostri Jesu Christi, quae ab ejus resurrectione sumpsit exordium.*[5] The admirable Ascension establishes it in full noontide: *Assumptus est in caelum et sedet a dextris Dei.*[6] It is the divine glorification of Christ's Humanity above the highest heavens.

Let us, therefore, say a few words on this glorification, on its reasons as regards Jesus Himself, and on the special grace that it brings to us. The Church sums up these points in the collect of the Mass: *Concede, quaesumus, omnipotens Deus, ut qui hodierna die Unigenitum tuum Redemptorem nostrum ad caelos ascendisse credimus, ipsi quoque mente in caelestibus habitemus.* "Grant, we beseech Thee, Almighty God, that we who believe that Thy Only begotten Son, our Redeemer, this day ascended into heaven, may ourselves also dwell there in spirit."

This prayer first of all testifies to our faith in the mystery: in recalling the title "Only-begotten Son" and "Redeemer," given to Jesus, the Church shows forth the reasons for the celestial exaltation of her Bridegroom;— she finally denotes the grace therein contained for our souls.

---

1 "I have finished the work which thou gavest me to do," Joan. xvii, 4.
2 Litany of the Saints.   3 Secret of the Mass for the Ascension.
4 Joan xvii, 5.   5 S. Augustine, *Tractatus* in Joan. civ, 3.
6 "He was taken up into heaven and sitteth on the right hand of God," Marc. xvi, 19.

I

The mystery of Jesus Christ's Ascension is represented to us in a manner suitable to our nature: we contemplate the Sacred Humanity rising from the earth and ascending visibly towards the heavens.

For the last time Jesus assembles His disciples and leads them towards Bethany on the Mount of Olives. He gives them anew the mission of preaching to all the earth, while promising to be ever with them by His grace and the action of His Spirit.[1] Then having blessed them, He rises, by His own Divine power and that of His glorious soul, above the clouds, and disappears from their gaze.

But His material ascension, however real it is, however wonderful it appears to us, is at the same time the symbol of an ascension, of which the Apostles themselves did not see the term, an ascension more wonderful still, although incomprehensible for us. Our Saviour rises *super omnes caelos.*[2] He ascends "above all the Heavens," passing all the angelic choirs, staying only at the right hand of God: *Assumptus est in caelum, et sedet a dextris Dei.*

You know that this expression "at the right hand of God" is only figurative and must not be taken literally; God, being spirit, has in Him nothing that is corporal, but Holy Scriptures[3] and the Church[4] employ this expression to demonstrate the sublimity of the triumph granted to Christ in the sanctuary of the divinity.

In the same way, when we say that Jesus is "seated," we mean to signify that He has entered for ever into possession of that eternal repose merited for Him by His glorious combats. This repose, however, does not exclude the continual exercise of the omnipotence communicated to Him by the Father in order that He may rule, sanctify and judge all mankind.

St. Paul has celebrated this divine glorification of Jesus, in magnificent terms, in his Epistle to the Ephesians. "What is the exceeding greatness of (God's) power towards us, who believe, according to the operation of

---

1 He dwells also by the Real Presence in the Sacrament of the Eucharist.
2 Ephes. iv, 10.
3 Ps. cix, 1; Marc. xvi, 19; Ephes. i, 20, iv, 10; Col. iii, 1.
4 Apostles' Creed, Nicene Creed, and *Quicumque.*

the might of His power, which He wrought in Christ, raising Him up from the dead, and setting Him on His right hand in the heavenly places. Above all principality, and power, and virtue, and dominion, and every name that is named, not only in this world, but also in that which is to come. And He hath subjected all things under His feet, and hath made Him head over all the Church."[1]

Henceforward Christ Jesus is and remains for every soul the one source of salvation, of grace, of life, of benediction; henceforward, says the Apostle, His name has become so great, so resplendent, so glorious that every knee shall bow before it, in heaven, on earth, and in hell, and every tongue shall confess that Jesus lives and reigns "in the glory of God the Father."[2]

Consider how, in very truth, since that blessed hour, the countless multitudes of the elect in the Heavenly Jerusalem, of which the Lamb that was slain is the eternal light, cast their crowns at His feet, and fall down before Him; proclaiming in a chorus like the sound of many waters, that He is worthy of all honour and glory because their salvation and beatitude have their beginning and their end in Him.[3]

Since that hour, upon all the face of the earth, every day, during the holy action of the Mass, the praise and supplication of the Church ascend to Him Who alone can sustain her in her conflicts, because He is the one source of all strength and of all virtue: "Thou Who sittest at the right hand of the Father, have mercy on us. For Thou only art holy, Thou only art the Lord: Thou only O Jesus Christ with the Holy Ghost, art most high in the glory of God the Father": *Tu solus Altissimus, Jesu Christe... in gloria Dei Patris.*

Again since that hour, the princes of darkness, from whom the victorious Christ has snatched their prey for ever: *Captivam duxit captivitatem,*[4] are filled with terror at the very name of Jesus, and constrained to flee, and bow down their pride before the victorious sign of the cross.

Such is the splendour of the triumph into which the Humanity of Jesus entered for ever, on the day of His admirable ascension.

---

1 Ephes. i, 19–22.   2 Philipp. ii, 10–11.   3 Apoc. passim.
4 Ephes. iv, 8.

II

You will perhaps ask what are the reasons of this supreme exaltation of Jesus, of this incommensurable glory conferred upon His holy Humanity?

We can resume them all in two chief reasons: The first is that Jesus Christ is God's own Son; the second, that to redeem us, He chose to sound the abyss of humiliation.

Jesus is God and Man. As God, He fills heaven and earth with His divine presence; it is therefore as Man that He arose to the right hand of the Father. But the Humanity in Jesus is united to the Person of the Word; it is the Humanity of a God; in this quality it enjoys the right of Divine glory in the eternal splendours.

During Christ's mortal life,—except on the day of the Transfiguration,—this glory was veiled and hidden. The Word willed to unite Himself to a humanity feeble like our own, to a humanity subject to infirmity, suffering and death.

We have seen that from the dawn of His resurrection, Jesus entered into possession of this resplendent glory; His Humanity is henceforth glorious, and impassible. But it still remained here below, in a place of corruption where death reigns. To attain the summit, the full expansion of this glory, the Risen Jesus had need of an abode that responded fittingly to His new condition; He needed the heights of heaven, whence His glory and His power might henceforth radiate in their fulness upon the entire company of the elect.

As God-Man, Son of God, equal to His Father, Jesus has the right of sitting at His right hand, of sharing with Him the Divine glory, the infinite beatitude and almighty power of the sovereign Being.[1]

The second reason of this supreme glorification is its being a recompense for the humiliations that Jesus underwent out of love of His Father and charity for us.

I have often said that in entering into this world, Christ yielded Himself

---

1 If we consider the Humanity of Jesus as to its nature, this nature being created, "to sit at the right hand of God," evidently does not signify that it has equality with the Divine Being in His essential glory, but that it has a sublime and eminent participation in the infinite beatitude and power.

up entirely to the will of the Father. *Ecce venio ut faciam, Deus, voluntatem tuam.*[1] He accepted to accomplish to the full all the abasements that had been foretold, to drink to the dregs the bitter chalice of sufferings and of untold ignominies; He annihilated Himself even to the malediction of the Cross. And why was this? *Ut cognoscat mundus quia diligo Patrem.*[2] "That the world may know that I love the Father," His perfections, and His glory, His might and His good pleasure.

"For which cause," *Propter quod* (remark these words, borrowed from St. Paul, they show the reality of the motive) God has glorified His Son, and has exalted Him above all things: *Propter quod et Deus exaltavit illum.*[3]

After the combat, it is with joy that earthly princes reward the valiant captains who have defended their prerogatives, won the victory over the enemy, and by their conquests widened the boundaries of the kingdom.

Was it not this that took place in heaven on the day of the Ascension, though with an incomparable glory? With supreme fidelity, Jesus had accomplished the work that His Father had given Him to do: *Quae placita sunt ei facio semper....*[4] *Opus consummavi*[5]; abandoning Himself to the action of Divine justice, as a holy Victim, He had descended into an incomprehensible abyss of sorrows and humiliations. And now all was expiated, the price was paid and redemption accomplished, the powers of darkness were defeated, the perfections of the Father were acknowledged and His rights avenged, and the gates of the kingdom of heaven were opened to all the human race. If we may thus lisp about such mysteries, what joy for the Heavenly Father, to crown His Son after the victory gained over the prince of this world! What divine gladness to call the Sacred Humanity of Jesus to the enjoyment of the splendour, the beatitude and power of an eternal exaltation!

And what still further enhanced this divine gladness, was that Jesus, when about to consummate His sacrifice, has asked of His Father that glory which was to extend that of the Father: "Father, the hour is come: glorify Thy Son, that Thy Son may glorify Thee."[6]

Yea, Father, the hour is come. Thy justice has been satisfied by expi-

---

1 Hebr. x, 9; cf. Ps. xxxix, 8. 2 Joan. xiv, 31. 3 Philipp. ii, 9.
4 "I do always the things that please him," Joan. viii, 29.
5 "I have finished the work," Ibid. xvii, 4.
6 Ibid. xvii, 1. The Church gives us this text in the Mass for the Vigil of the Ascension.

ation; may it be so likewise by the glory that comes to Thy Son Jesus, because of the love that He has manifested to Thee in His sufferings. O Father, glorify Thy Son! Establish His reign in the hearts of those who love Him; bring under His sceptre the souls that have turned away from Him; draw to Him those who, sitting in darkness, do not yet know Him. Father, glorify Thy Son, so that in His turn, Thy Son may glorify Thee in manifesting to us Thy Divine Being, Thy perfections, Thy will! *Pater, clarifica Filium tuum ut Filius tuus clarificet te.*

The works of God are full of ineffable and secret harmonies which ravish faithful souls.

Where was it that the Passion of Jesus began? At the foot of the Mount of Olives. There, during three long hours, His blessed soul—foreseeing in the divine light, the sum of afflictions and outrages which were to constitute His sacrifice,—was a prey to sadness, weariness, fear and anguish. We shall never know what poignant agony was undergone by the Son of God in the Garden of Olives: Jesus suffered there in anticipation all the sorrows of His Passion: "Father, if it be possible, let this chalice pass from Me."[1]

And where was it that our Divine Saviour entered into the joys of His Ascension? Jesus, Eternal Wisdom, Who, let us not forget it, makes only one with His Father and the Holy Spirit, chose the summit of this same mountain that had witnessed His sorrowful abasements from whence to ascend to Heaven. There, in the same place where it fell upon Christ like a vengeful torrent, Divine Justice crowns Him with honour and glory[2]; there, where in the horror of darkness, were preluded mighty combats, now arises the radiant dawn of an incomparable triumph.

Is not the Church, our Mother, justified in extolling as "admirable" the Ascension of her Divine Head? *Per admirabilem ascensionem tuam.*

III

Such is the mystery of the Ascension of Jesus: it is the sublime glorification of Christ above every creature, at the right hand of God.

Jesus "came forth from the Father" *Exivi a Patre,* and He has returned

---

1 Matth. xxvi, 39.   2 Hebr. ii, 9.

to the Father, after having fulfilled His mission here below: *Et vado ad Patrem*.[1] He "hath rejoiced as a giant to run the way": *Exultavit ut gigas ad currendam viam*; He came forth from the highest heaven, from the sanctuary of the Divinity, *A summo caelo egressio ejus*; and He now reascends to the summit of all things, there to enjoy divine glory, beatitude and power: *Et occursus ejus usque ad summum ejus*.[2]

In that which, properly speaking, is divine, this triumph is the exclusive privilege of Christ, the God-Man, the Incarnate Word. Jesus alone, being the Son of God, Redeemer of the world, has a right to this infinite glory. This is why St. Paul exclaims: "To which of the Angels said (God) at any time: Sit on My right hand?"[3]

Our Lord Himself expressed the same thought in His conversation with Nicodemus. "No man hath ascended into heaven, but He that descended from heaven, the Son of man Who is in heaven": *Nemo ascendit in caelum, nisi qui descendit de caelo, Filius hominis qui est in caelo*.[4] Jesus is the Son of man by His Incarnation; but in becoming incarnate He remains the Son of God, Who is ever in heaven. Having come down from heaven, from the bosom of the Father, to take upon Himself our nature, Christ thither ascends as to His native abode; to Him alone, God's true Son, belongs the full right to ascend to the Father, and to share in the sublime honours of the Divinity. They are reserved for Him alone. *Nemo ascendit...nisi qui descendit*.

And as for ourselves, shall we not penetrate into the heavens? Are we to remain shut out from this sojourn of glory and beatitude? Have we not a part in the Ascension of Jesus? Certainly we have;—but, as you know, it is through Christ and in Christ that we enter into heaven.

How does this come to pass? Through baptism which makes us children of God. Our Lord revealed this in the same conversation with Nicodemus: *Nisi quis renatus fuerit ex aqua et Spiritu Sancto, non potest introire in regnum Dei*.[5] "Unless a man be born again of water and the Holy Ghost, he cannot enter into the Kingdom of God." It is as if He said: There is no means of entering into heaven if one is not born again of God; there is an eternal birth in the bosom of the Father; that is My birth; of full right, I

---

1 Joan. xvi, 28.   2 Ps. xviii, 6–7.   3 Hebr. i, 13.
4 Joan. iii, 13.   5 Ibid. iii, 5.

ascend into heaven, because I am God's own Son, begotten in holiness and splendour. But there is another category of children of God: those who are born of God by baptism: *Ex Deo nati sunt.*[1]

These are children of God, and in consequence, says St. Paul, His heirs. *Si filii et heredes*; "heirs of God and joint heirs with Christ," *Coheredes Christi,*[2] therefore partaking of His own eternal inheritance.

In making us God's children, baptism also makes us living members of the Mystical Body of which Christ is the head. St. Paul is so explicit upon this! *Vos estis corpus Christi, et membra de membro*[3]; "Now you are the body of Christ, and members of member"; and even more emphatically; "No man ever hated his own flesh, but nourisheth and cherisheth it...we are members of His body, of His flesh, and of His bones": *De carne ejus et de ossibus ejus.*[4]

Now the members share in the glory of the head, and the joy of a person reacts upon all his body: this is why we share in all the treasures that Christ possesses: His joys, His glory, His beatitude become ours.

Such is the marvel of Divine mercy. "God, (Who is rich in mercy) for His exceeding charity wherewith He loved us, even when we were dead in sins, hath quickened us together in Christ, (by Whose grace you are saved), and hath raised us up together, and hath made us sit together in the heavenly places, through Christ Jesus. That He might shew in the ages to come the abundant riches of His grace, in His bounty towards us in Christ Jesus."[5]

And as all that the Father does, the Son does likewise,[6] Christ Jesus takes our humanity up with Him to give it a place in His glory and beatitude. This is the great action of Jesus, the magnificent exploit of the Divine Giant: to re-open by His sufferings the gates of heaven to fallen humanity, and to transport it, in His train, into the splendours of heaven: *Unitam sibi fragilitatis nostrae substantiam, in gloriae tuae dextera collocav-*

---

1 Ibid. i, 13.   2 Rom. viii, 17.   3 I Cor. xii, 27.   4 Ephes. v, 30.
5 *Deus qui dives ut in misericordia, propter nimiam caritatem suam, qua dilexit nos, et cum essemus mortui peccatis, convivificavit nos in Christo Jesu: ut ostenderet in saeculis supervenientibus divitias gratiae suae in bonitate super nos in Christo Jesu.* Ephes. ii, 4–7.
6 Joan. v, 19.

it...*Est elevatus in caelum, ut nos divinitatis suae tribueret esse participes.*[2]

When Christ ascended into heaven, says St. Paul, a whole train of holy souls, a glorious conquest, entered therein with Him: *Captivam duxit captivitatem.*[3] But these souls of the just who escorted Jesus in His triumph are only the first-fruits of innumerable harvests. Unceasingly souls are ascending into heaven, until that day when the kingdom of Jesus shall have attained the measure of its fulness.

"Christ's Ascension is therefore also our own, upon the glory of the Head rests the hope of the body. On this holy day, we have received not only the assurance of entering into possession of eternal glory, but we have already entered into the heights of heaven with Christ Jesus."[4] "The wiles of the old enemy tore us away from the first sojourn of felicity, the earthly paradise; the Son of God, in incorporating us with Himself placed us at the right hand of His Father." *Quos inimicus primi habitaculi felicitate dejecit, eos sibi concorporatos Dei Filius ad dexteram Patris collocavit.*[5]

How well we understand the chorus of thanksgiving sung by the elect in praise of the Lamb slain for man! How well we understand those acclamations and adorations that they ceaselessly offer to Him Who, by indescribable torments, bought their unending beatitude!...

The hour of this glorification has not yet struck for us. But while awaiting our eternal union with the choir of the blessed, we should in mind and holy desires dwell in that heaven where Christ, our Head, lives and reigns for ever.

We are upon earth only as strangers and pilgrims seeking our country; as members of the city of saints and the household of God, we may, says St. Paul, already dwell in heaven by faith and hope.[6]

This is also the grace that the Church asks on this solemnity in the

---

1 "He established at the right hand of your glory the substance of our frail nature, united to himself," Communicantes for the Mass of the Ascension.

2 "He was taken up into heaven that he might make us partakers in His own Divinity," Preface from the Mass of the Ascension.

3 "He led captivity captive," Ephes. iv, 8.

4 *Christi ascensio nostra provectio est; et quo processit gloria capitis eo spes vocatur et corporis; hodie non solum paradisi possessores firmati sumus, sed etiam caelorum in Christo superna penetravimus.* S. Leo, *Sermo I De Ascensione Domini,* c. iv.

5 S. Leo, *Sermo I De Ascensione Domini,* c. iv.   6 Philipp. iii, 20.

collect already quoted: *Ipsi quoque mente in caelestibus habitemus.*[1]

In the Postcommunion of the same Mass, we ask that we may obtain the invisible effects of these mysteries in which we visibly participate: *Ut quae visibilibus mysteriis sumenda persepimus, invisibili consequamur effectu.*

By Communion, we are united to Jesus: in coming to us, Our Lord grants us to share, in hope, that glory of which He enjoys the reality: He gives us the very pledge of it: *Et futurae gloriae nobis pignus datur.*[2]

Let us say to Him: Draw us after You, great and almighty Victor: *Trahe nos post te.* Grant us to ascend into the heavens with You, there to dwell by faith, hope and charity! Grant that we may detach ourselves from all earthly things, which are only passing, so that we may only seek the joys that are true and abiding. Grant that in heart we may be where we know that Your Sacred Humanity has corporally ascended: *Ut illuc sequamur corde, ubi eum corpore ascendisse credimus.*[3]

IV

The Ascension of Jesus gives rise to manifold sentiments in the faithful soul that contemplates it. If Christ no longer merits, His Ascension has, however, the virtue of efficaciously producing the graces that it signifies or symbolises.

It strengthens our faith in the Divinity of Jesus; it increases our hope by the vision of the glory of our Head; by stirring us up to the observance of His commandments, on which our merits rest, and that are themselves the principle of our future beatitude, it still further enkindles our love. It engenders in us wonder at so marvellous a triumph, and gratitude for the share in it that Christ gives to us. Lifting up our souls towards heavenly realities, it quickens in us detachment from passing things: *Quae sursum sunt quaerite, ubi Christus est in dextera Dei sedens, non quae super terram.*[4] It gives us patience in adversity, for, says St. Paul, if we suffer with Christ,

---

1 "That we might also dwell in mind among heavenly things."
2 "And a pledge of future glory is given to us," Antiphon for the Feast of Corpus Christi, *O sacrum convivium.*
3 S. Gregory, *Homil. xxix in Evangel.* c. ii.
4 "Seek the things that are above, where Christ is sitting at the right hand of God...not the things that are upon the earth," Col. iii, 1–2.

we shall also share in His glory: *Si tamen compatimur ut et conglorificemur.*[1]

There are two dispositions upon which I would dwell with you a few instants, because, springing with special abundance from the contemplation of this mystery, they are singularly profitable for our souls: they are joy and confidence.

And first of all *why should we rejoice?*

Our Lord Himself said to His Apostles before leaving them: *Si diligeretis me, gauderetis utique quia vado ad Patrem,*[2] "because I go to the Father." To us too Christ repeats those words. If we love Him, we shall rejoice in His glorification; we shall rejoice in that, having finished His course, He ascends to His Father's right hand, to be there exalted to the highest heaven, there to taste, after His labours, sufferings, and death, eternal repose in incommensurable glory. Bliss, such as is incomprehensible to us, envelops and penetrates Him for ever in the bosom of the Divinity. Supreme power is given to Him over every creature.

How can we fail to rejoice in that justice is rendered in all fulness to Jesus, by His Father.

See how the Church invites us, in her liturgy, to celebrate with gladness this exaltation of her Bridegroom, our God and our Redeemer.

At times she urges all nations to let the fulness of their joy burst forth in repeated hymns. *Omnes gentes plaudite manibus*: "O clap your hands, all ye nations; shout unto God with the voice of joy!" *Jubilate Deo in voce exsultationis.* "God is ascended with jubilee, and the Lord with the sound of the trumpet. Sing praises to our God, sing ye: sing praises to our King, sing ye! God shall reign over the nations: God sitteth on His Holy throne": *Ascendit Deus in jubilo et Dominus in voce tubae.*[3] "Exalt the King of kings, and sing a hymn to God": *Exaltate Regem regum et hymnum dicite Deo.*[4]

At other times the Church calls upon the angelic powers: "Lift up your gates, O ye princes...and the King of glory shall enter in": *Attollite portas principes vestras, et introibit Rex gloriae.* Astonished, the Angels ask: "Who is this King of glory?" *Quis est iste Rex gloriae?* "It is the Lord strong and mighty, the Lord mighty in battle": *Dominus fortis et potens,*

---

1 Rom. viii, 17.　　2 Joan. xiv, 28.　　3 Ps. xlvi, 1, 6–7, 9.
4　4th Antiphon from Lauds of the Ascension.

Dominus potens in praelio. And the heavenly spirits repeat: "Who is this King of glory?" "It is the Lord of hosts, He is the King of glory": *Ipse est Rex gloriae!*[1]

And again, in language full of poetry borrowed from the Psalmist, she addresses Jesus Himself: "Be Thou exalted, O Lord, in Thy own strength; we will sing and praise Thy power": *Exaltare, Domine, in virtute tua: cantabimus et psallemus virtutes tuas.*[2] "For Thy magnificence is elevated above the heavens."[3] "Thou hast put on praise and beauty: and art clothed with light as with a garment; Who makest the clouds Thy chariot: Who walkest upon the wings of the winds": *Confessionem et decorem induisti, amictus lumine sicut vestimento.*[4]

Yes, let us rejoice! Those who love Jesus experience a deep and intense joy in contemplating Him in the mystery of His Ascension, in thanking the Father for having given such glory to His Son, and in felicitating Jesus in having been the object of it.

Let us rejoice yet again in that this triumph and this glorification of Jesus are likewise ours.

Ascendo ad Patrem meum et Patrem vestrum, Deum meum et Deum vestrum[5]; "I ascend to My Father and to your Father, to My God and your God." Jesus has but gone before us: He does not separate Himself from us, He does not separate us from Him. If He enters into His glorious Kingdom, it is to "go and prepare a place" for us: *Vado parare vobis locum*; He promises to come again one day to take us to Himself, so that, He says "where I am, you also may be."[6] Thus, we are already participants in the glory and bliss of Christ Jesus; we shall be there one day in reality. Did He not ask of His Father: *Volo, Pater, ut ubi sum ego, et illi sint mecum.*[7] What power in this prayer, and what sweetness in this promise!

Let us then give ourselves up to this intimate and wholly spiritual joy. Nothing will so much "dilate" our hearts, and make us run with more generosity in the way of the Lord's precepts: *Viam mandatorum tuorum cucurri, cum dilatasti cor meum.*[8] Often let us repeat to Christ Jesus during these holy days, the ardent aspirations of the hymn for this feast:

---

1 Ps. xxiii, 7–16. 2 Ibid. xx, 14. 3 Ibid. viii, 2. 4 Ibid. ciii, 1–3.
5 Joan. xx, 17. 6 Ibid. xiv, 2–3.
7 "Father I will that where I am, they also may be with me," Ibid. xvii, 24.
8 Ps. cxviii, 32.

Tu esto nostrum Gaudium
Qui es futurus praemium;
Sit nostra in te gloria
Per cuncta semper saecula.[1]

"Be Thou our joy, Thou Who wilt one day be our recompense; and grant that Thy glory may abide in us, for ever, and for ages of ages!"

V

With this deep joy we ought to combine unwavering *confidence*. This confidence especially rests on the almighty power of mediation that Christ has with His Father, not only as an invincible King entering into His triumph, but as a supreme High Priest interceding for us, after having offered to His Father an oblation of infinite worth. Now, it is on the day of His Ascension that Jesus, in a special manner began this unique mediation.

We have here a very interior aspect of the mystery on which it is highly useful to dwell for some instants. St. Paul, who has revealed it to us in his Epistle to the Hebrews, himself declares it to be ineffable: *Ininterpretabilis sermo.*[2]

I am, however, going to try, following the teaching of the great Apostle, to give you some idea of it. May the Holy Spirit grant us to understand how marvellous are the divine works.

St. Paul first of all recalls the rites of the most solemn sacrifice of the Old Covenant. Why does he recall them? Doubtless because he was speaking to the Jews. It was necessary to speak to them in a way they would understand. But there was a deeper reason. The Apostle discloses it himself. It was on account of the most close relation established by God between the ancient ceremonial and the sacrifice of Christ.

As we know, God's eternal foreknowledge embraces the whole series of centuries. Moreover, being Infinite Wisdom, God disposes all things with perfect measure and equilibrium. Now, He has willed that the principal events that have stood out in the history of the Chosen People, and the sacrifices He had prescribed to Israel should be so many unfinished types and obscure symbols of the magnificent realities that were to suc-

---

1 Hymn for Vespers and Lauds. (Monastic Breviary.) 2 Hebr. v, 11.

ceed them when the Incarnate Word appeared here below: *Haec omnia in figura contingebant illis...*[1] *Umbra futurorum.*[2]

Therefore the Apostle insists first of all upon the Jewish sacrifices. It is not for the pleasure of establishing a simple comparison to help his hearers to comprehend his exposition, but because the Old Covenant presaged, in outline, the splendours of the New Law laid down by Jesus Christ.

St. Paul also recalls what was the structure of the temple of Jerusalem of which God Himself had ordained all the details. There was, he says, a tabernacle called the Holy; the priests entered there at all times for the service of worship;—beyond the veil was a second tabernacle called the Holy of Holies, where stood the altar of incense and the ark of the Covenant.[3]

This "Holy of Holies" was the most august place upon earth. It was the centre towards which the worship and desire of Israel converged, towards which the hands of the entire Jewish people were raised. And why was this? Because it was there that God made His special dwelling; He had promised that His eyes and heart should be there always: *Erunt oculi mei et cor meum ibi, cunctis diebus*[4]; there He received homage, blessed the vows and heard the prayers of Israel; there He entered, so to speak, into contact with His people.

But this contact, as you likewise know, was only established by the intermediary of the high priest. So redoubtable indeed was the majesty of this tabernacle, that only the high priest of the Jews might enter there, and the entry was forbidden to any other under pain of death. The high priest entered the Holy of Holies clad in pontifical vestments, wearing upon his breast the mysterious "rational," composed of twelve precious stones, upon which were engraved the names of the twelve tribes of Israel; it was only in this symbolical manner that people had access into the Holy of Holies.

Moreover, the high priest himself might only cross the threshold of this holy tabernacle once a year; and, first of all, he had to immolate outside, two victims,—one for his own sins, the other for the sins of the people;—he sprinkled with their blood the propitiatory where reposed the divine majesty, while the levites and people filled the courts.

---

1 "All these things happened to them in figure," I Cor. x, 11.
2 "A shadow of things to come," Col. ii, 17.   3 Hebr. ix, 2–4.
4 III Reg. ix, 3.

This solemn sacrifice, by which the high priest of the Jewish religion offered to God, once a year, in the Holy of Holies, the homage of all His people, and the blood of victims for sin, constituted the supreme and most august act of his priesthood.

And yet, as St. Paul teaches, all this was but in figure: *Quae parabola est temporis instantis.*[1] And what imperfections in these symbols! This sacrifice was so lacking in power that it needed renewing each year; this high priest was so imperfect that he had no power to open the door of the sanctuary to the people whom he represented; and he himself might only enter there once a year, and under the protection, as it were, of the blood of the victims offered for his own sins.

Where then are the realities? Where is the one perfect sacrifice, which is to replace for ever these repeated and powerless offerings?

We find these realities,—and with what plenitude!—in Christ Jesus.

Christ, says St. Paul, is the supreme High Priest, but, "a High Priest, holy, innocent, undefiled, separated from sinners, and made higher than the heavens"[2]; He enters into a tabernacle not made by the hand of man: *Non hujus creationis*[3] but in the "heaven of heavens," in the sanctuary of the divinity: *Ad interiora velaminis*[4]; like the high priest, He enters therein bearing the blood of the victim. What victim? Was it the blood of animals, as under the ancient covenant? No, this blood is none other than "His own Blood": *Per proprium sanguinem,*[5] precious Blood, of infinite value, shed, "outside" that is to say upon the earth, and shed for sins, no longer for the sins of the people of Israel alone, but for the sins of all mankind;—He enters through the veil, that is to say, by His Sacred Humanity; it is through this veil that the way to heaven is henceforward open to us: *Initiavit nobis viam novam per velamen, id est carnem suam*[6]; finally, He does not only enter there once a year, but once for ever: *Semel*[7]; for His Sacrifice being perfect and of infinite value, it is unique, and suffices to procure for ever the perfection of those whom He wills to sanctify: *Una enim oblatione consummavit in sempiternum sanctificatos.*[8]

But—and it is above all in this that the divine work is admirable, and

---

1 "Which is a parable of the time present," Hebr. ix, 9.   2 Hebr. vii, 26.
3 Ibid. ix, 11; cf. Ibid. 24.   4 Ibid. vi, 19.   5 Ibid ix, 12.
6 Ibid. x, 20.   7 Ibid. ix, 12.   8 Ibid. x, 14.

that the reality surpasses the figure—Christ does not enter there alone. Our High Priest takes us with Him, not in a symbolical manner, but in reality, for we are His members, "the fulness of Him Who is filled all in all,"[1] as the Apostle says.

Before Him, none might enter into the heavens. This interdiction was symbolised by the rigorous prohibition to pass the veil of the Holy of Holies; the Holy Spirit Himself declares this, as St. Paul bears witness: *Hoc significante Spiritu sancto nondum propalatam esse sanctorum viam.*[2]

But Christ Jesus, by His death, has reconciled man to God; with His pierced Hands He has blotted out "the handwriting of the decree" of our expulsion[3]; and therefore it was that when He died, the veil of the Temple, as you know, was torn in twain. What did this prodigy signify? Not only that the Old Covenant with the Jewish people had ceased, that symbols had henceforward given place to a higher and more efficacious reality, but likewise that Christ had reopened to us the gates of heaven that we might enter into the eternal inheritance.

On the day of His Ascension, Christ, the supreme High Priest of the human race, took us with Him into heaven, by right and in hope.

Never forget that it is only through Him that we can enter there; no man can enter into the Holy of holies except with Him; no creature can enjoy eternal bliss except by following Jesus: it was His merits that won for us infinite beatitude. Throughout eternity, we shall say to Him: O Christ Jesus, it is through You, through Your Blood shed for us, that we are before the Face of God; it is Your sacrifice, Your immolation, that has gained for us each instant of our glory and beatitude: to You, O Lamb slain for us, be all honour, all praise, all thanksgiving!

Whilst awaiting that Christ Jesus will come to take us to Himself, as He promised, He is preparing us a place, and above all He aids us by His prayers. St. Paul tells us that He has entered into Heaven, "that He may appear now in the presence of God for us" *Ut appareat* NUNC *vultui Dei pro nobis.*[4] His priesthood is eternal. And what infinite power in His mediation!

He is there before His Father unceasingly presenting to Him His sacri-

---

1 Ephes. i, 23.   2 Hebr. ix, 8.   3 Col. ii, 14.   4 Hebr. ix, 24.

fice, recalled by the marks of His Wounds which He was willed to retain. He is there "always living to make intercession for us": *Semper vivens ad interpellandum pro nobis.*[1]

A High Priest Who is always heard, He repeats for us the sacerdotal prayer of the Last Supper: "Holy Father, keep them in Thy Name whom Thou hast given Me...that they may have My joy filled in themselves.... Father, I will that where I am, they also whom Thou hast given Me may be with Me; that they may see My glory which Thou hast given Me...that the love wherewith Thou hast loved Me, may be in them, and I in them."[2]

How can these sublime truths of our faith fail to give rise within us to an unshakable confidence? Souls of little faith, what can we fear? What is there we may not hope? Jesus is praying for us, always. As St. Paul says, if the blood of animal-victims purified the flesh of those who were sprinkled with it, "how much more shall the Blood of Christ, Who...offered Himself unspotted unto God, cleanse our conscience from dead works to serve the Living God?"[3]

Let us, then, have absolute confidence in the sacrifice, the merits and the prayer of our High Priest. He has entered to-day into the heavens; He inaugurates, with His triumph, His unceasing mediation; He is the beloved Son in Whom the Father is well pleased; how can He fail to be heard, after having manifested by His Sacrifice such love to His Father? *Exauditus est pro sua reverentia.*[4]

O Father, look upon Thy Son; look upon His Wounds: *Respice in faciem Christi tui;* and by Him, in Him, grant us to be one day where He is, so that also by Him, in Him and with Him, we may render Thee all honour and all glory!

VI

When you communicate during these holy days, let your souls give themselves up to these thoughts of joy and confidence.

---

1   Ibid. vii, 25. See above p. 86 and following pages concerning the oblation of Christ in Heaven.

2   Joan. xvii, 11, 13, 24, 26.   3   Hebr. ix, 13–14.

4   "He was heard for his reverence," Ibid, v, 7.

In uniting yourself with Jesus Christ you incorporate yourself with Him; He is in you, and you are in Him; you stand in the presence of the Father. Undoubtedly you do not behold Him; but by faith, you know yourself to be with Jesus in the bosom of the Father, in the sanctuary of the divinity. This is for us the grace of the Ascension: to share, in faith, in the ineffable intimacy that Christ Jesus has in Heaven with His Father.

It is related in the life of St. Gertrude, that one day, on the festival of the Ascension, when she received the Sacred Host from the hand of the priest, she heard Jesus say to her, "Behold Me: I come, not to bid thee farewell, but to take thee with Me to heaven, and present thee to My Father."[1] Leaning upon Jesus, the soul is powerful, because Christ makes her a partaker of all His riches and of all His treasures: *Quae est ista quae ascendit de deserto, deliciis affluens innixa super dilectum suum!*[2] In spite of our miseries and our weaknesses, never let us fear to approach God, by the grace of the Saviour, and with Him, we can be for ever in the bosom of our Father in heaven.

Let us, then, turn to Christ Jesus and lean upon Him, not only in prayer, but in all that we do. And we shall be strong. If without Him we can do nothing: *Sine me, nihil potestis facere*[3]; with Him, we can do all things: *Omnia possum in eo qui me confortat.*[4] We have in Him, Who is the source of our confidence, the most efficacious motive for fidelity and patience in the midst of the sadness, the disappointments, the trials, and the sufferings that we must undergo here below until the end of our exile.

When the mortal life of Jesus was drawing to its close, He made a touching prayer to His Father for the disciples whom He was about to leave: "Holy Father, when I was with them, I kept them in Thy name.... And now I come to Thee....I pray not that Thou shouldst take them out of the world, but that Thou shouldst keep them from evil": *Cum essem cum eis, ego servabam eos; nunc autem ad te venio; non rogo ut tollas eos de mundo, sed ut serves eos a malo.*[5]

What wholly divine solicitude is revealed in this prayer!

---

1 The Herald of Divine Love.
2 "Who is this that cometh up from the desert, flowing with delights, leaning upon her beloved?" Cant. viii, 5.
3 Joan. xv, 5.   4 Philipp. iv, 13.   5 Joan. xvii, 12–13, 15.

Our Lord says it for us all. And the Church, who always enters into the dispositions of her Spouse, is inspired by it in the Secret of the Mass for the Feast of the Ascension. "Receive, O Lord, the gifts which we offer Thee in memory of the glorious Ascension of Thy Son, vouchsafe to deliver us from the dangers of this present life, and bring us to everlasting life, through the same Jesus Christ our Lord."[1] Why is this prayer of Jesus repeated by the Church?

Because there are obstacles that hinder us from going to God; and these obstacles are all summed up in sin, which turns us away from God. Our Lord asks that we may be delivered from evil, that is to say from sin, which, in keeping us away from our Heavenly Father is the one true evil: *Ut serves eos a malo.* Left to ourselves, to our weakness, we cannot avoid these obstacles; but we can do so if we lean upon Christ. He ascends to-day to heaven, victorious over Satan and the world: *Confidite, ego vici mundum....*[2] *Princeps mundi hujus in me non habet quidquam.*[3] He enters, as an all-powerful High Priest, into the divine sanctuary: *Per hostiam suam apparuit.*[4] By Communion, Our Lord gives us a share in His power and His triumph. That is why we ought with such trust to seek our support in Him.

With Christ, offering for us His merits to His Father, there is no temptation that we cannot vanquish, no difficulty that we cannot overcome, no adversity that we cannot support, no senseless joy from which we cannot detach ourselves. Until we rejoin Jesus in Heaven, or rather until He takes us there Himself, since He has gone to prepare a place for us, let us live there, by faith in the boundless power of His prayer and of His mediation, by hope of one day partaking of His felicity, by the love that yields us up joyously and generously to the faithful and entire fulfilment of His will and good pleasure[5]: it is thus that we shall fully participate in the glorious Ascension of Jesus: *Ipse quoque mente in caelestibus habitemus.*

---

1 *Suscipe, Domine, munera quae pro Filii tui gloriosa ascensione deferimus; et concede propitius, ut a praesentibus periculis liberemur, et ad vitam perveniamus aeternam. Per eumdem D.N.J.C.*

2 Joan. xvi, 33.

3 "The prince of this world in me hath not any thing," Ibid. xiv, 30.

4 "He hath appeared by the sacrifice of himself," Hebr. ix, 26.

5 *Fac nos tibi semper et devotam quere voluntatem et majestati tuae sincero corde servire.* Collect for the Sunday within the Octave of the Ascension.

THE MISSION OF THE
HOLY SPIRIT

(Pentecost)

SUMMARY.—In what way the visible mission of the Holy Ghost enters into the cycle of the mysteries of Jesus.—I. What the Holy Spirit is in the Trinity.—II. The reasons why the descent of the Holy Spirit upon the disciples only took place after the Ascension.—III. The work of the Divine Paraclete in the souls of the Apostles; He fills them with truth, love, strength and consolation.—IV. The assembly of the Apostles in the cenacle represents the entire Church; wonderful and unceasing action of the Holy Spirit in the Church: Pentecost ever continues.—V. Operations of the Spirit in our souls; our duties towards Him.

I F Y O U loved Me," said Christ Jesus to His Apostles, "you would indeed be glad, because I go to the Father": *Si diligeretis me, gauderetis utique quia vado ad Patrem.*[1]

For those who love Christ, the Ascension is, indeed, an inexhaustible source of joy. It is the supreme glorification of Jesus to the highest heavens; it is the realisation of that prayer of Christ: "Glorify Thou Me, O Father, with Thyself, with the glory which I had, before the world was, with Thee": *Clarifica me, tu, Pater, apud temetipsum, claritate quam habui, priusquam mundus esset, apud te.*[2] We are full of gladness in contemplating Jesus, the Son of God, our Redeemer, our Head, sitting at the right hand of His Father, after having fulfilled here below, in the self-abasement of His Incarnation and the humiliations of His death, His mission of salvation.

---

1 Joan. xiv, 28.   2 Ibid. xvii, 5.

315

But Our Lord did not only say to His disciples that they ought to re-joice in His Ascension; He added that His Ascension would profit them. *Veritatem dico: expedit vobis ut ego vadam; si enim non abiero, Paracletus non veniet ad vos; si autem abiero, mittam eum ad vos.*[1] "I tell you the truth: it is expedient to you that I go: for if I go not, the Paraclete will not come to you; but if I go, I will send Him to you."

All the utterances of the Incarnate Word are, as He Himself says, "spirit and life": *Verba quae ego locutus sum vobis, spiritus et vita sunt.*[2] They are deep and solemn, sometimes mysterious; there are some that are difficult to understand, and can hardly be fathomed except in prayer. The word of Jesus which we have just quoted on the subject of His leaving the world is one of these utterances.

Expedit vobis ut ego vadam.[3] "It is expedient to you that I go." How can it be good for the Apostles that Jesus shall go? That He shall leave them, to ascend to His Father? Is He not for them the source of every good, of every grace? Is He not "The Way, the Truth and the Life"?[4] Did He not say: "No man cometh to the Father, but by Me"?[5] How then can it be useful to the disciples for Jesus to leave them?

Might they not have answered Him in all truth: O Divine Master, say not so; we need none other save You, You are sufficient for us: *Ad quem ibimus?*[6] With You have we not every grace? Abide then with us. *Mane nobiscum.*[7]

But the Divine Master's words are formal: "I tell you the truth": *Ver-itatem dico.* "It is expedient to you that I go for if I go not, the Paraclete will not come to you."

This is the mystery, and it is this mystery that we are about to contem-plate, as far as that is possible for us; for here all is supernatural, and faith alone can be our guide.

Although in this conference, there will be constantly question of the Holy Spirit, we shall see that the visible mission of this Spirit to the dis-ciples—the mission that constitutes the special object of the solemnity of Pentecost—belongs to Jesus, in His Divine nature, (as it belongs also to the Father), and that it enters on this account into the cycle of His mysteries.

---

1 Joan. xvi, 7.   2 Ibid. vi, 64.   3 Ibid. xvi, 7.   4 Ibid. xiv, 6.
5 Ibid.   6 "To whom shall we go?" Ibid. vi, 69.   7 Luc. xxiv, 29.

Christ Jesus *prayed* for this mission; He made it the object of a special demand. Our Lord said to His disciples at the Last Supper: "I will ask the Father, and He shall give you another Paraclete, that He may abide with you for ever."[1]

Besides, Jesus *promised* His apostles to send them this Consoler. "When the Paraclete cometh, whom I will send you from the Father, the Spirit of truth, Who proceedeth from the Father, He shall give testimony of Me.... If I go, I will send Him to you."[2]

He, moreover, *merited* this mission. By His prayer, as by His sacrifice, Christ Jesus obtained from the Father that the Spirit of truth, of love, of fortitude and of consolation should be given to them. We owe every grace to the prayer and immolation of the Saviour, as was wonderfully verified in the coming of this Spirit, so powerful and so full of goodness that Jesus Himself declares Him His equal, in Whom the Apostles were to find another Himself.

Finally, and above all, the sending of the Holy Spirit to the Apostles has no other end, as you know, than *to achieve the establishment of the Church*. Jesus had founded this Church upon Peter, but He left to the Holy Spirit (we shall presently see wherefore) the care of bringing it to perfection. Indeed, before His Ascension, being at table with His apostles, He told them "that they should not depart from Jerusalem, but should wait for the promise of the Father."[3] The coming of this Spirit was to serve for the glorification of Jesus; at the same time, the Spirit would fill them with power whereby they should render testimony to Jesus in the holy city, "in all Judea, and Samaria, and even to the uttermost parts of the earth."[4] These are Jesus Christ's own words.

Then, as you see, this mission of the Holy Spirit to the Apostles truly belongs to Jesus. This is so true that St. Paul calls the Holy Spirit, "the Spirit of Christ," the Spirit of Jesus.[5] This is why we can never go through the cycle of Christ's mysteries without contemplating this marvellous work which was wrought ten days after the Ascension.

Let us then implore the Holy Spirit Himself to make known to us what He is, in what His mission and work consists on the day of Pentecost. "Come, Spirit of Truth, enlighten our minds so that the fire of love

---

1 Joan. xiv, 16–17.   2 Ibid. xv, 26; xvi, 7.   3 Act. i, 4.
4 Ibid. 8.   5 Rom. viii, 9; cf. Act. xvi, 7 & I Petr. i, 11.

of which Thou art the infinite source may be enkindled in our hearts."

I

We can only understand the words of Jesus concerning the Holy Spirit if we first recall what Revelation teaches us of the life of this Spirit in the Holy Trinity. You already know this mystery[1]; but, in contemplating it anew, your faith will find an increase of joy. Let us then penetrate, with the deepest reverence, into the sanctuary of the divinity.

What does faith tell us? That there is in God, the Father, the Son, and the Holy Spirit: three distinct Persons in one and the same unity of nature.

As you know the Father proceeds from none; He is the Principle without principle, the first Principle of all intimate life in God, the first origin of all the ineffable communications in the Trinity. The Father, knowing Himself, begets by an infinite Word, a Son only-begotten and perfect, to Whom He communicates all that He is, except the personal property of being the Father: *Sicut enim Pater habet vitam in semetipso, sic dedit et Filio habere vitam in semetipso.*[2] The Son is equal in all things to the Father; He is the adequate expression, the perfect image of the Father; He possesses with the Father the same divine nature. The Father and the Son give Themselves the One to the Other with a perfect love, and it is from this gift of love from the Father to the Son, and from the Son to the Father, that proceeds, in a mysterious manner, the Holy Spirit, the third Person. The Holy Spirit terminates the cycle of the intimate operations in God, He is the final term of the divine communications in the adorable Trinity.

Between these distinct Persons, as you likewise know, there is neither superiority nor inferiority: it would be a grave error to believe that there is. These Divine Persons are equal in power, wisdom and goodness, because all Three equally possess, in an indivisible manner, one and the same Divine nature with all its infinite perfection. And therefore all our praise is addressed at the same time to the Father, the Son, and the Holy Spirit: *Gloria Patri et Filio et Spiritui Sancto.*

---

1 See conference: The Holy Spirit, the Spirit of Jesus in the volume *Christ, the Life of the Soul.*

2 "For as the Father hath life in himself, so he hath given to the Son also to have life in himself," Joan. v, 26.

However, if there is among them neither inequality nor dependence, there is an order of nature, of origin, marking these communications themselves. The "procession" of the Son presupposes, without there being, however, inequality of time, the Father, Who is the first principle; the "procession" of the Holy Spirit presupposes the Father and the Son, of Whom He is the mutual gift.

Jesus wills that all His disciples should be baptized "in the name of the Father, and of the Son, and of the Holy Ghost"[1]: that is the very language of the Incarnate Word; it contains a divine reality, the intimate comprehension of which baffles our understanding; but because it is the language of Jesus, we must inviolably respect the order between the Persons of the Trinity. And as we must hold intact, in our doctrine and our prayer, the unity of nature, so too we must confess the distinction of Persons, this distinction which is based upon the communications that they have between Themselves and Their mutual relations. There is, at the same time, equality and order; there is an identical perfection and distinction of properties.

These truths constitute an ineffable mystery concerning which we can but lisp. However Our Lord has revealed to us the existence of this mystery, and He made this revelation in His last discourse with His disciples on the eve of His death, that our "joy may be filled."[2] He Himself tells us that if we are His friends, it is because He has made known to us these secrets of God's innermost life,[3] while we await the enjoyment of them in eternal happiness. And why should He have revealed these secrets to us, if He, Infinite Wisdom, had not judged that this revelation would be profitable to us?

But again remark that not only by His word has God revealed this order of principle, of origin, which exists in the ineffable communications of the Persons among Themselves and upon which Their distinction is founded, He has also chosen to manifest it by His works.

Jesus tells us, in the Gospel, that eternal life is to know that the Father is the true God, and that Jesus Christ is He Whom the Father has sent.[4] He often says that He was "sent" by the Father.[5] This term "sent" frequently used by Christ Jesus marks the distinction of persons. It is the Father Who

---

1 Matth. xxviii, 19.   2 Joan. xv, 11.   3 Ibid., 15.   4 Ibid. xvii, 3.
5 Ibid. iii, 17; iv, 34; vi, 29; etc.

"sends"; it is the Son Who is "sent": the order of origin that exists from all eternity in heaven between the Father and the Son, is also manifested in time. For Christ tells us in the same place, in speaking of His Father: "I and the Father are One"[1]; and again He says addressing the Father: "All My things are Thine, and Thine are Mine."[2]

Jesus uses the same term "send" in speaking of the Holy Spirit. He says to the Apostles that His Father will send them the Holy Ghost: *Paracletus autem Spiritus Sanctus quem mittet Pater.*[3] He also says that He Himself will send Him: *Si autem abiero, mittam eum ad vos.*[4] As you see it is the Father and the Son Who send; it is thus Our Lord speaks of the Spirit, thereby denoting the order that exists in God in the "procession" of the Holy Ghost.

II

Jesus told His Apostles that after He had returned to heaven, He would send them the Holy Ghost.

In His Divine Nature, Jesus is, with the Father, the principle from which the Holy Spirit proceeds. The gift of the Holy Spirit to the Church and to souls is a priceless gift, since this Spirit is Divine Love in Person. But this gift, like every grace, was merited for us by Jesus. It is the fruit of His Passion. He purchased it by the sufferings He endured in His Sacred Humanity. Was it not therefore just that this grace should not be given to the world until that Humanity, whereby it had been merited, had been glorified? This exaltation of the Humanity in Jesus was not accomplished in its fulness, nor did it reach its fruition until the day of the Ascension. It was only then that the Sacred Humanity entered definitively into possession of the glory to which it is doubly entitled as being united to the Son of God, and as a victim offered to the Father thereby to merit every grace for souls. Seated at the right hand of the Father in the glory of heav-

---

1 Ibid. x, 30.
2 This applies to Christ considered as a Divine Person; for the Humanity of Jesus considered in itself, as nature, is created and consequently inferior; it is in this latter sense that Jesus says in another place: "My Father is greater than I," *Pater major me est.* Joan. xiv, 28.
3 Ibid. xiv, 26,   4 Ibid. xvi, 7.

en, the Humanity of the Incarnate Word was to be thus associated with the "sending" of the Holy Spirit by the Father and the Son.

We now understand the reason Our Lord Himself said to His Apostles: "It is expedient to you that I go; for if I go not, the Paraclete will not come to you, but if I go I will send Him to you." It is as if He said: I have merited this grace for you by My Passion; in order that it may be given you, it is first of all necessary that My Passion should be followed by My glory.

The Fathers of the Church[1] add another reason which relates to the disciples.

One day Jesus promised that living water should spring up in those that believed in Him. St. John the Evangelist, in relating this promise, adds: "Now this He said of the Spirit which they should receive, who believed in Him: for as yet the Spirit was not given, because Jesus was not yet glorified."[2] Faith was therefore the source, so to speak, of the coming of the Holy Spirit in us. Now as long as Christ Jesus lived upon earth, the faith of the disciples was imperfect. It would only be entire, it could only unfold in all fulness when the Ascension had taken the human presence of their Divine Master from their sight. "Because thou hast seen Me, Thomas, thou hast believed," said Jesus to Thomas after the resurrection, "blessed are they that have not seen and have believed!"[3]

"After the Ascension, the faith of the disciples, better instructed, went further and higher to seek Christ sitting near to the Father and equal to the Father."[4]

It is because the apostles' faith, after the Ascension, had become purer, more interior, more intense, more efficacious, that the "river of living water" sprang up in them with such impetuosity.

We know, indeed, how magnificently Jesus fulfilled His divine promise, how ten days after the Ascension, the Holy Spirit, sent by the Father and the Son, descended upon the apostles assembled in the Cenacle, with what abundance of graces and charismata this Spirit of truth and love was poured forth in the souls of the disciples.

---

1 Cf. S. Augustine, *Enarr.* in Psalm. cix; *Sermones cxliii* and *cclxiv;* S. Leo, *Sermo II de Ascensione.*

2 Joan. vii, 38–39.   3 Ibid. xx, 29.   4 S. Leo, *Sermo II de Ascens.* c. 4.

III

What indeed was the work of the Holy Spirit in the souls of the Apostles on the day of Pentecost?

To understand it well, I ought first of all to recall to you the Church's teaching upon the character of divine works. You know that in the domain of the supernatural life of grace, as well as in the works of the natural creation, all that God produces outside Himself, in time, is accomplished by the Father, the Son and the Holy Spirit, without distinction of persons. The three Persons then act in the unity of their divine nature. The distinction of Persons exists only in the incomprehensible communications that constitute the innermost life of God in Himself.

But in order to remind ourselves more easily of these revelations concerning the Divine Persons, the Church, in her language, attributes specially such or such action to one of the three Persons, on account of the affinity that exists between this action and the exclusive properties whereby this Person is distinguished from the others.

Thus the Father is the first principle, proceeding from none other, but from Whom proceed the Son and the Holy Spirit. Therefore the work which marks the origin of everything, the creation, is especially attributed to Him. Did the Father create alone? Certainly not. The Son and the Holy Spirit created at the same time as the Father, and in union with Him. But between the property, peculiar to the Father, of being the first principle in the divine communications and the work of the creation, there is an affinity, in virtue of which the Church can, without error of doctrine, attribute the creation to the Father.

The Son, the Word, is the infinite expression of the thought of the Father; He is considered especially as Wisdom. The works in which this perfection shines forth above all, as in that of the ordering of the world, are particularly attributed to Him. He is indeed that Wisdom which coming forth out of the mouth of the Most High "reacheth from end to end mightily, and ordereth all things sweetly." *O Sapientia, quae ex ore Altissimi prodiisti, attingens a fine usque ad finem fortiter suaviterque disponens omnia.*[1]

The Church applies the same law to the Holy Spirit. What is He in

---

1 Antiphon for December 17th. Cf. Eccl. xxiv, 5; Sap. viii, 1.

the Adorable Trinity? He is the ultimate term, the consummation of life in God; He closes the intimate cycle of the admirable operations of the Divine Life. And this is why, in order that we may remember this property which is personal to Him, the Church specially attributes to Him all that which is the work of grace, of sanctification, all that concerns the completion, the crowning-point, the consummation: He is the divine Artist, Who, by His last touches, brings the work to its sovereign perfection: *Dextrae Dei tu digitus.*[1] The work attributed to the Holy Spirit, in the Church as in souls, is to lead to its end, to its term, to its ultimate perfection, the incessant labour of holiness.

Let us now contemplate, for a few moments, the divine workings of this Spirit in the souls of the Apostles.

He fills them with *truth.* You will at once say: Had not Christ Jesus done this? Certainly He had. Did He not Himself declare: "I am the Truth."[2] He came into the world to bear testimony to the truth,[3] and you know, also from Himself, that He wholly accomplished His mission: *Opus consummavi.*[4]

Yes, but now that He has left His apostles, it is the Holy Spirit Who is about to become their interior Master. "He shall not speak of Himself," said Jesus, wishing to signify by this that the Holy Spirit,—proceeding from the Father and the Son, receiving from them divine life,—will give us the infinite truth that He receives by His ineffable procession. "He will teach you all things and bring all things to your mind, whatsoever I shall have said to you"; "He shall glorify Me; because He shall receive of Mine, and shall show it to you": *Ille me clarificabit.*[5]

There is yet more. The apostles had no need to trouble about what they should reply when the Jews delivered them up before the tribunals, and forebade them to preach the name of Jesus; it was the Holy Spirit Who would inspire their replies.[6] And thus they should bear witness to Jesus: *Accipietis virutem supervenientis Spiritus Sancti in vos, et eritis mihi testes... usque ad ultimum terrae.*[7]

---

1 "The finger of the right hand of God," Hymn, *Veni Creator,* Monastic Breviary.
2 Joan. xiv, 6.   3 Ibid. xviii, 37.   4 Ibid. xvii, 4.
5 Ibid. xiv, 26; xvi, 13–14.   6 Matth. x, 19–20; Marc. xiii, 11; Luc. xii.
7 "You shall receive the power of the Holy Ghost coming upon you, and you shall be

And as it is by the tongue, the organ of speech, that testimony is rendered, and whereby the preaching of the name of Jesus was to go forth "to the uttermost part of the earth," this Spirit, on the day of Pentecost, descends visibly upon the Apostles in the form of tongues.

But these are tongues of fire: And why? Because the Holy Spirit comes to fill the hearts of the apostles with *love*. He is personal Love in the life of God. He is, as it were, the breath, the aspiration of the infinite love whence we drew life. It is related in Genesis that "the Lord God formed man of the slime of the earth, and breathed into his face the breath of life": *Inspiravit spiraculum vitae.*[1] This vital breath was the symbol of the Spirit to Whom we owe the supernatural life. On the day of Pentecost, the Divine Spirit brought such an abundance of life to all the Church that to signify it "there came a sound from heaven, as of a mighty wind coming, and it filled the whole house where they were sitting."[2]

In descending upon them, the Holy Spirit pours forth in them His love which is Himself. It was needful that the apostles should be filled with love in order that in preaching the name of Jesus they should give birth to the love of their Master in the souls of the hearers; it was necessary that their testimony, dictated by the Spirit, should be so full of life as to attach the world to Jesus Christ.

Moreover this love, ardent as a flame, powerful as a tempestuous wind, is necessary to the Apostles in order that they may be able to meet the dangers foretold by Christ when they shall have to preach His Name: the Holy Spirit fills them with *fortitude*.

Look at St. Peter, the prince of the Apostles. On the eve of the Passion of Jesus, he promises to follow Him even to death; but that same night, at the voice of a servant, he denies his Divine Master; he swears that he knows not the man.[3]—See him now on the day of Pentecost. He announces Christ to thousands of Jews; he reproaches them freely for having crucified Him. He renders testimony to His Resurrection and earnestly exhorts them to "do penance, and be baptized."[4] It is no longer the

---

witnesses unto me...even to the uttermost part of the earth," Act. i, 8.

1 Gen. ii, 7.   2 Act. ii, 2.   3 Matth. xxvi, 74; Marc. xiv, 71.
4 Act. ii, 23–24, 38.

timid disciple who fears danger and follows afar off,[1] he is the witness who declares before all in firm and bold words, that Christ is the Son of God.

What power in Peter's words! The Apostle is no longer recognisable. The virtue of the Holy Spirit has changed him, the love that he bears towards his Master is henceforward strong and generous. Our Lord Himself had foretold this transformation when He said to His disciples before ascending into heaven: "Stay you in the city till you be endued with power from on high."[2]

Again, see this same Peter and the other apostles, a few days after the event. Notice how the Jews are moved by their words, by the miracles they work, and the conversions that they bring about in the name of Jesus. The chief priests and the Sadducees who brought about Christ's death, forbid His disciples to preach the Saviour. You know their reply: "If it be just in the sight of God, to hear you rather than God, judge ye. For we cannot but speak the things which we have seen and heard."[3]

What is it that makes them speak with such courage, they who, on the night of the Passion, forsook Jesus; who, during the days that followed the Resurrection, remained hidden with doors fast shut, "for fear of the Jews": *Propter metum Judaeorum?*[4] It is the Spirit of truth, the Spirit of love, the Spirit of fortitude.

It is because their love for Christ is strong that they deliver themselves up to torments, for the Jews, seeing that the apostles pay no heed to their prohibition, bring them before the council; but Peter declares in the name of all that they "ought to obey God, rather than men."[5]

You know what the Jews then did. To overcome this constancy, they scourged the apostles before releasing them. But note what the sacred writer adds. On going forth from the Council the apostles rejoiced "that they were accounted worthy to suffer reproach for the name of Jesus."[6] And whence came this joy in suffering, and humiliations? From the Holy Spirit, for He is not only the Spirit of fortitude, He is too the Spirit of *Consolation*. "I will ask the Father," says Jesus, "and He shall give you another Paraclete": *Rogabo Patrem, et alium Paracletum dabit vobis...Spiritum veritatis.*[7]

Is not Christ Jesus Himself already a Consoler? Certainly He is; did

---

1 Marc. xiv, 54.   2 Luc. xxiv, 49.   3 Act. iv, 18–20.
4 Joan. xx, 19,   5 Act. v, 29.   6 Ibid. 41.   7 Joan. xiv, 16–17.

He not say: "Come to Me, all ye that labour, and are burdened, and I will refresh you"?[1] Is He not, as St. Paul has revealed to us, a High Priest Who knows how to have compassion on our sufferings, because He has Himself passed through suffering?[2]

But this Divine Consoler was to disappear from the earthly eyes of the disciples; that is why He asked His Father to send them *another* Consoler, equal to Himself, God like Himself.

Because He is the Spirit of truth, this Consoler assuages the needs of our intelligence; because He is the Spirit of love, He satisfies the desires of our heart; because He is the Spirit of strength, He sustains us in our toils, trials and tears: the Holy Spirit is eminently the Consoler.

> *Consolator optime,*
> *Dulcis hospes animae,*
> *Dulce refrigerium!*[3]

Oh! Come and dwell in us, Father of the poor, Giver of heavenly gifts, Thou best Consoler, sweet Guest, and Refreshment full of sweetness for the soul.

IV

The Holy Spirit came for us; those assembled in the Cenacle represented all the Church. The Spirit comes that He may abide with her for ever. This is Christ's own promise: *Ut maneat vobiscum* IN AETERNUM.[4]

The Holy Ghost descended visibly upon the Apostles at Pentecost; from that day the Holy Church has been spreading over all the earth; she is the kingdom of Jesus; and it is the Holy Spirit Who, with the Father and the Son, governs His Kingdom. He completes in souls the work of holiness begun by the redemption. He is, in the Church, what the soul is to the body: the Spirit that animates and quickens it, the Spirit that safeguards unity, whilst His action produces manifold and diverse effects; He brings all Her vigour and all beauty.

---

1 Matth. xi, 28.   2 Hebr. iv, 15; v, 2.

3 "Best comforter, sweet visitor of the soul, sweet consolation!" Sequence *Veni Sancte Spiritus.*

4 Joan. xiv, 16.

See indeed, what abundance of grace and charismata inundate the Church on the morrow of Pentecost. We read in "The Acts of the Apostles," the book which is the history of the beginning of the Church, that the Holy Spirit came down visibly upon those who were baptised and filled them with marvellous graces. With what complacency St. Paul enumerates them. "There are diversities of graces, but the same Spirit...Who worketh all in all. And the manifestation of the Spirit is given unto every man unto profit. To one indeed by the Spirit, is given the word of wisdom: and to another, the word of knowledge...to another, faith in the same Spirit; to another, the grace of healing in one Spirit: to another, the working of miracles; to another, prophecy; to another, the discerning of spirits; to another diverse kinds of tongues." And the Apostle adds: "But all these things one and the same Spirit worketh, dividing to every one according as He will."[1]

It is the Holy Spirit, promised and sent by the Father and by Jesus, Who gave this plenitude and this intensity of supernatural life to the first Christians; dissimilar as they were, they had however, on account of the love that the Holy Spirit poured forth in them, "but one heart and one soul."[2]

Since then, the Holy Spirit abides in the Church in a permanent, indefectible manner, therein exercising an unceasing action of life and sanctification: *Apud vos manebit, et in vobis erit.*[3] He renders her infallible in the truth: "When He, the Spirit of truth, is come, He will teach you all truth"[4] and will guard you from all error. By His action a wonderful supernatural fruitfulness springs up in the Church; He plants and unfolds in virgins, martyrs and confessors, those heroic virtues which are among the marks of holiness. In a word He is the Spirit Who by His inspirations, works in souls, rendering the Church which Jesus acquired for Himself by His Precious Blood,—"holy, and without blemish," worthy of being presented by Christ to His Father, on the day of final triumph.

Historically, and as a visible mission Pentecost is doubtless ended, but the inward action of the Spirit is unceasing. Its virtue endures for ever, its grace remains. The Holy Spirit's mission in souls is henceforth invisible, but it is none the less fruitful.

---

1 I Cor. xii, 4 seq.   2 Act. iv, 32.
3 "He shall abide with you and shall be in you," Joan. xiv, 17.   4 Ibid. xvi, 13.

Look at the Church, on the day when she celebrates the Ascension. What is her prayer, after having hymned the glorification of her Divine Bridegroom and having rejoiced thereat with gladness? "O King of Glory, Lord of hosts, Who didst to-day ascend in triumph to the highest heavens, leave us not orphans, but send down upon us the Spirit of truth promised by the Father": *O Rex gloriae, Domine virtutum, qui triumphator hodie super omnes caelos ascendisti, ne derelinquas nos orphanos, sed mitte promissum Patris in nos, Spiritum veritatis.*[1] O most powerful High Priest, now that Thou art seated at the right hand of the Father, and dost enjoy in all fulness Thy victory and power, ask Thy Father as Thou didst promise, to send us another Comforter. By the sufferings of Thy Humanity, Thou didst merit this grace for us; the Father will hear Thee because He loves Thee; because Thou art His beloved Son, He will send with Thee the Spirit that He Himself promised when He said: "I will pour forth the Spirit of grace and of prayers upon all the inhabitants of Jerusalem." Send Him into our souls, *in nos,* that He may abide there for ever.

The Church prays as if Pentecost was to be renewed for us; she repeats the antiphon *Rex gloriae* each day during the octave of the Ascension; then, on the day of the solemnity of Pentecost, she multiplies the praises she offers to the Spirit in language full of magnificence and poetry: "Come, Holy Spirit, fill the hearts of Thy faithful and kindle in them the fire of Thy love.[2] Come, and from the height of heaven send down on us a ray of Thy light! O most blessed light, fill our inmost hearts with Thy radiance![3] Fount of living water, Fire of love, spiritual Unction, come! shed Thy light in our minds, pour forth Thy charity into our hearts, strengthen our weakness with Thy unfailing strength!..."[4]

If the Church, our Mother, places these desires in our souls and these prayers upon our lips, it is not only to recall to us the visible mission which took place on the day of Pentecost but in order that this mystery may be interiorly renewed within us all.

Let us repeat these ardent aspirations with the Church. Above all, let us beseech the Heavenly Father to send us this Spirit. Through sanctifying grace, we are His children; and, as such, our condition urges the Father

---

1 Antiphon from 2nd Vespers of the Ascension.
2 Versicle of the Alleluia of the Mass.   3 Sequence *Veni Sancte Spiritus.*
4 Hymn *Veni Creator.*

to pour down His gifts upon us. It is because He loves us as His children that He gives us His Son; Holy Communion is "the Bread of children": *Panis filiorum,*[1] again it is because we are His children that He sends us His Spirit, one of His most perfect gifts: *Donum Dei altissimi.*[2] Indeed what does St. Paul say? *Quoniam estis filii, misit Deus Spiritum Filii sui in corda vestra*[3]: "Because you are sons, God hath sent the Spirit of His Son within your hearts"; He is the Spirit of the Son, because He proceeds from the Son as from the Father, and He is sent by both the Father and the Son. This is why, in the Preface for Pentecost, the Church sings: "It is truly meet and just...that we always and in all places, give thanks to Thee, O holy Lord, Father Almighty, eternal God, through Christ Our Lord. Who, ascending above all the heavens, and sitting at Thy right hand, did this day send down upon the children of adoption the Holy Spirit Whom He had promised": *Promissum Spiritum Sanctum hodierna die in filios adoptionis effudit.*

So then, it is to all the children of adoption, to all those who are the brethren of Jesus by sanctifying grace that the Holy Spirit is given. And because this Gift is Divine and contains every most precious gift of life and of holiness, His effusion in us—an effusion which was manifested with such abundance on the day of Pentecost—"fills the whole world with overflowing joy": *Quapropter profusis gaudiis, totus in orbe terrarum mundus exsultat.*[4]

V

You may perhaps say: Have we not already received the Holy Spirit at Baptism, and yet more specially in the Sacrament of Confirmation?

Assuredly we have, but we can always receive Him more abundantly; we can always receive from Him clearer light, greater strength; He can always make deeper well-springs of consolation rise up in our souls, and enkindle within our hearts a more intense love.

And this fruitful working of the Spirit within us can be renewed not only during the holy days of Pentecost, but moreover each time that we receive a Sacrament, we receive an increase of grace, for He makes only

---

1 Sequence *Lauda Sion.*   2 Hymn *Veni Creator.*   3 Gal. iv, 6.
4 Preface of Pentecost.

one with the Father and the Son: *Ad eum veniemus et mansionem apud eum faciemus.*[1] The Holy Ghost comes to dwell within us; He remains in order to sanctify us, to guide all our supernatural activity. He enriches us, bestows upon us His gifts of wisdom and of understanding, of counsel and of fortitude, of knowledge, of piety, and of fear of the Lord which make us act as children of God: *Quicumque Spiritu Dei aguntur ii sunt filii Dei.*[2]

He dwells in us; Divine Guest, full of love and kindness, He makes His abode in our hearts that He may help and strengthen us; He will leave us only if we have the misfortune to drive Him from our souls by mortal in. To drive out this Spirit of love, by preferring the creature to Him in an absolute manner is what St. Paul calls "to quench the Spirit."[3] Moreover, let us follow the Apostle's counsel and not "grieve"[4] the Spirit; do not let us resist His inspirations, by any fully deliberate fault, however slight, by wilfully replying "no" to the good He suggests to us.

His action is extremely delicate, and when the soul resists Him deliberately and frequently, she forces Him little by little to be silent; then she comes to a standstill in the path of holiness, and even incurs great risk of leaving the way of salvation. What can such a soul do, without a master to guide her, without light to enlighten her, without strength to sustain her, without joy to transport her?

Let us be faithful to this Spirit Who comes, with the Father and the Son, to take up His abode in us. "Know ye not," says St. Paul again, "that you are the temple of God, and that the Spirit of God dwelleth in you?"[5] Each increase of grace is like a new reception of this Divine Guest, a new taking possession of our souls by Him, a new embrace of love.

And how beneficial are these workings in the faithful soul! He makes us "know the Father": *Per te sciamus da Patrem*[6]; and, by making Him known, He produces in the soul the gift of piety, the attitude of adoration and love which it ought ever to preserve towards the Heavenly Father. Listen to what St. Paul so explicitly says: "Likewise the Spirit also helpeth our infirmity. For we know not what we should pray for as we ought, but the

---

1 "We will come to him and make our abode with him," Joan. xiv, 23.
2 "Whosoever are led by the Spirit of God, they are the sons of God," Rom. viii, 14.
3 I Thess. v, 19.   4 Ephes. iv, 30.   5 I Cor. iii, 16.
6 Hymn *Veni Creator.*

Spirit Himself asketh for us with unspeakable groanings."[1] And what is this prayer? "You have received the spirit of adoption of sons, whereby we cry: Abba (Father)! For the Spirit Himself giveth testimony to our spirit, that we are the sons of God."[2]

He makes us also "know the Son": *Noscamus atque Filium*[3]; He manifests Jesus to us; He is this inward Master Who makes us penetrate into the meaning of His words, and His mysteries; "He shall glorify Me," says Jesus, "because He shall receive of Mine, and shall shew it to you": *Ille me clarificabit.*[4] By making divine knowledge abound in us, by keeping us in the presence of Jesus, by inspiring us ever to do what is pleasing to Him, He causes Christ to reign in us. By His infinitely delicate and sovereignly efficacious action, He forms Jesus in us. Is not that the substance of all holiness?

Let us, then, ask Him to enter into us and increase in us the abundance of His gifts. Fervent prayer is the condition of His indwelling in our souls.

Humility is another condition. Let us come before Him with the intimate conviction of our inward poverty; this disposition of soul is excellent in order to receive Him of Whom the Church sings: *Sine tuo numine, nihil est in homine, nihil est innoxium.*[5] "Without Thy help there is nothing in man that is not harmful to him." Let us borrow, moreover from the Church, these fervent aspirations: "Come, Spirit of love; come, Thou solace in sorrow, wash away our stains, bedew our dryness, heal our wounds; bend that which is stubborn in us, melt that which is frozen, rule our wandering steps":

> *Lava quod est sordidum,*
> *Riga quod est aridum,*
> *Sana quod est saucium;*
> *Flecte quod est rigidum,*
> *Fove quod est frigidum,*
> *Rege quod est devium.*[6]

Despite our miseries, let us invoke the Holy Spirit; on account of these very miseries, He will hear us.

---

1 Rom. viii, 26.   2 Ibid. 15, and 16.   3 Hymn *Veni Creator.*
4 Joan. xvi, 14.   5 Sequence *Veni Sancte Spiritus.*   6 Ibid.

And since He is one with the Father and the Son, let us say likewise to the Father: Father, send to us, in the name of Thy Son Jesus, the Spirit of love that He may fill us with the intimate sense of our divine filiation. And Thou, O Jesus, our High Priest, now sitting at Thy Father's right hand, intercede for us, so that this mission of the Spirit, Whom Thou didst promise to us and didst merit for us, may be abundant; that it may be an impetuous river making glad the city of souls; or rather, according to Thine own words; "a fountain of water, springing up unto life everlasting." *Hoc autem dicebat de Spiritu Sancto quem accepturi erant credentes in eum.*[1]

---

1 "He said this of the Holy Spirit which they should receive who believed in him," Joan. vii, 39.

IN MEI MEMORIAM

(Corpus Christi)

SUMMARY.—The Eucharist is a mystery of faith.—I. The Sacrifice of the Altar perpetuates the memory of Jesus.—II. The manna, figure of the Eucharistic sacrifice.—III. We find in this Sacrament the virtue of the mysteries of Jesus.— IV. How to participate in it by the Sacrifice of the Mass, Communion, and visits to the Blessed Sacrament. The profound reverence with which we ought to surround this mystery.—V. How, by faith, we are united to Christ in this Sacrament and, by Him, to the Father and the Holy Spirit.

ALL Christ's mysteries are essentially mysteries of faith; without faith we cannot accept nor contemplate any of them.

However the degree of light which enlightens our faith in each of them is different. At Bethlehem we only see a little babe in the manger; without faith, we should not recognize in Him the Son of God, the sovereign Master of all creatures; but we hear the voices of the angels of heaven celebrating the coming of this Saviour of the world; we see a marvellous star leading the Eastern Kings to His feet. At the baptism of Jesus, our eyes only behold a man who submits himself, like the other Jews, to the rite of penance; but the heavens open, the voice of the Eternal Father is heard declaring that this Man is the Son of His dilection, in Whom He is infinitely well pleased. Upon Thabor, in the mystery of the Transfiguration, faith is powerfully aided; the glory of the Divinity which penetrates the Humanity of Jesus visibly shines through upon it; the dazzled disciples fall upon their faces on the earth. The Divinity is, on the contrary, veiled when Christ dies upon the Cross, like the last of men in the midst of torments; and yet the Centurion cries out that Christ is the Son of God. Nature herself, by the convulsions she undergoes at this unique moment, renders solemn homage to her Creator. At the Resurrection, what do we see? Jesus is all resplendent with glory; but He proves at the same time to His Apostles that He is still Himself, Man as well as God: He allows Himself to be touched, He eats with them, He shows them the marks of His Wounds, so as to manifest to them that He is not only a spirit, but that He is the same Jesus with Whom they had lived for three years.

As you then see, if in each of Christ's mysteries, there is enough shadow to render our faith meritorious, there is also enough light to help our faith; in all, we see manifested the ineffable union of the Divinity with the Humanity.

But there is one mystery in which the Divinity and Humanity, far from being revealed, both disappear from our senses: this is the mystery of the Eucharist.

What is there upon the altar before the consecration? A little bread, a little wine. And after the consecration? For the senses, still bread and wine. Faith alone penetrates beneath these veils, even to the Divine Reality therein totally hidden. Without faith, we shall never see anything but bread and wine; we do not see God, He does not here reveal Himself as in the Gospel. We do not even see His Manhood:

> *In cruce latebat sola deitas,*
> *At hic latet simul et humanitas.*[1]

When Christ, during His earthly life, declared that He was the Son of God, He gave the proof that He was so. It was clear indeed that He was a man, but a man whose doctrine could only come from God: *Quem enim misit Deus, verba Dei loquitur*[2]; a man who wrought marvels that only God could work: *A saeculo non est auditum quia quis aperuit oculos caeci nati; nisi esset hic a Deo, non poterat facere quidquam.*[3] Nicodemus the

---

1 Hymn *Adoro Te.*
2 "For he whom God hath sent speaketh the words of God," Joan. iii, 34.
3 "From the beginning of the world it hath not been heard, that any man hath opened the eyes of one born blind. Unless this man were of God, he could not do anything," Ibid. ix, 32–33.

Pharisee, like the man born blind, confessed this likewise: *Scimus quia a Deo venisti; nemo enim potest haec signa facere, quae tu facis, nisi fuerit Deus cum eo*[1]: "Rabbi, we know that Thou art come a teacher from God: for no man can do these signs which Thou dost, unless God be with Him." Faith was necessary, but the miracles of Jesus and the sublimity of His doctrine helped the faith of the Jews, that of the simple as well as of the wise.

In the Eucharist, there is only room for pure faith, founded solely upon the words of Jesus: "This is My Body, this is My Blood": the Eucharist is above all a "mystery of faith," *Mysterium fidei*.[2]

That is why, in this mystery of the Eucharist, more than in any that we have contemplated up to now, we must only listen to Jesus; reason is so confounded before this mystery that those who, in this, do not listen to Christ can only say like the Jews when Our Lord announced the Eucharist: *Durus est hic sermo, et quis potest eum audire?* "This saying is hard, and who can hear it?"[3] Let us, on the contrary, go to Jesus as did the faithful apostles on this occasion, and say to Him with Peter: "Lord, to whom shall we go? Thou hast the words of eternal life. And we have believed and have known, that Thou art the Christ, the Son of God": *Domine, ad quem ibimus? Verba vitae aeternae habes. Et nos credidimus et cognovimus quia tu es Christus Filius Dei vivi.*[4]

Let us then question Our Lord on the subject of this mystery. Christ Jesus is Infallible Truth, Eternal Wisdom, Almighty Power. Shall He not perform that which He has promised?

I

When our Divine Saviour instituted this mystery in view of perpetuating the fruits of His Sacrifice, He said to His apostles: *Hoc facite in meam commemorationem,* "Do this for a commemoration of Me."[5] Thus, besides the primary object of renewing His immolation and making us participate in it by Communion, Christ desired to make of it, in addition a memorial. And in what way is this mystery a memorial? How does it bring the remembrance of Christ to our hearts?

The Eucharist preserves the remembrance of Jesus, first of all as being

---

1 Ibid. iii, 2. 2 Canon of the Mass. 3 Joan. vi, 61.
4 Ibid. 69–70. 5 Luc. xxii, 19; I Cor. xi, 24.

a sacrifice.

Certainly, as you know, there is only one sacrifice, total, and perfect, that has paid off and expiated everything, that has merited everything, and from which every grace flows: that is the sacrifice of Calvary; there is none other. *Una enim oblatione consummavit in sempiternum sanctificatos.*[1] "By one oblation," says St. Paul, "He hath perfected for ever them that are sanctified."

But in order that the merits of this sacrifice may be applied to every soul of every time, Christ willed that it should be renewed upon the altar. The altar is another Calvary where the immolation of the Cross is commemorated, represented and reproduced. Thus, wherever there is to be found a priest to consecrate the bread and wine, the remembrance of the Passion is kept. That which is offered and given upon the altar is the Body that was broken for us, the Blood which was shed for our salvation.[2] It is the same High Priest, Christ Jesus, Who still offers them by the ministry of His priests. Hence how can we fail to think of the Passion when we assist at the Sacrifice of the Mass, where all is identical, except the manner in which the oblation is accomplished?[3]

No Mass is celebrated, no Communion made without our being enabled to remember that Jesus delivered Himself up to death for the redemption of the world. "For," says St. Paul, "as often as you shall eat this bread, and drink the chalice, you shall shew the death of the Lord, until He come.": QUOTIESCUMQUE *enim manducabitis panem hunc et calicem bibetis, mortem Domini annuntiabitis donec veniat.*[4]

Thus is perpetuated, living and fruitful, until the end of time, the remembrance of Christ among those whom He came to redeem by His immolation.

The Eucharist is then truly the memorial that Christ has left to us of His Passion and His Death: it is the testament of His love. Wherever the bread and wine are offered, wherever the consecrated Host is found, there

---

1 Hebr. x, 14.   2 Cf. Matth. xxvi, 28; Marc. xiv, 24; Luc. xxii, 19–20.
3 *In divino hoc sacrificio quod in missa peragitur, idem ille Christus continetur et incruente immolatur, qui in ara crucis seipsum cruentum obtulit* (In this divine sacrifice which is accomplished in the mass, that same Christ is contained and immolated in an unbloody manner, who offered himself in a bloody manner on the altar of the cross). *Concil. Trid. Sess.* 22, cap. ii.
4 I Cor. xi, 26.

appears the remembrance of Christ's immolation: *Hoc facite in meam commemorationem.*

The Eucharist recalls to us above all the memory of the Passion of Jesus. It was on the eve of His death that He instituted it; He left it to us as the testament of His love.

But it does not exclude the other mysteries. See what the Church does. She is the Bride of Christ, none knows better than she the intentions of her Divine Head; in the organisation of the public worship which she renders to Him, she is guided by the Holy Spirit. Now what does she say? Directly after the Consecration, she first of all recalls the words of Jesus: *Haec quotiescumque feceritis, in Mei memoriam facietis:* "As often as ye do these things, ye shall do them in remembrance of Me." And at once she adds, to show how closely she enters into the sentiments of her Spouse: "Wherefore, O Lord, we Thy servants together with Thy holy people, in memory of the blessed Passion of the same Christ Our Lord, and of His Resurrection from hell, also of His glorious Ascension into Heaven offer into Thy most excellent Majesty...the holy bread of eternal life, and the chalice of everlasting salvation": *Unde et memores...tam beatae passionis nec non et ab inferis resurrectionis sed et in caelos gloriosae ascensionis.*[1] After the mention of "the Ascension to the right hand of the Father," the Greeks likewise add, "that of the second and glorious coming of Christ."[2]

So then, although the Eucharist recalls (in a direct manner, and in the first place) the Passion of Jesus, it does not exclude the remembrance of the glorious mysteries which are linked so closely to the Passion of which they are, in a sense, the crown.

Since it is the Body and Blood of Christ that we receive, the Eucharist supposes the Incarnation and the mysteries which are founded upon or flow from it. Christ is upon the altar with the divine life which never ceases, with His mortal life of which the historical form has doubtless ceased, but of which the substance and merits remain, with His glorious

---

1 A similar prayer is made after the Offertory: "Receive, O holy Trinity, this oblation, which we make to Thee, in memory of the Passion, Resurrection, and Ascension of Our Lord Jesus Christ." *Suscipe, sancta Trinitas, hanc oblationem quam tibi offerimus ob memoriam passionis, resurrectionis, et ascensionis Jesu Christi Domini nostri.*
2 Cf. D.E. Vandeur, *La sainte Messe, Notes sur la liturgie, 35e mille,* pp. 164 and 223–226.

life which shall have no end.[1]

All this, as you know, is really contained in the Sacred Host and given in Communion to our souls. In communicating Himself to us, Christ Jesus gives Himself in the substantial totality of His works and mysteries, as in the oneness of His Person. Yes, let us say, with the Psalmist who sings in prophecy the glory of the Eucharist, the Lord "hath made a remembrance of His wonderful works, being a merciful and gracious Lord, He hath given food to them that fear Him": *Memoriam fecit mirabilium suorum, misericors et miserator Dominus: escam dedit timentibus se.*[2]

The Eucharist is like the synthesis of the marvels of the love of the Incarnate Word towards us.

II

If we now consider the Eucharist as a Sacrament, we shall discover in it wonderful properties which only a God could invent.

I have often said after St. Paul, to whom this idea is dear, that the chief events in the history of the Jewish people under the old Law were symbols, sometimes hidden and obscure, sometimes apparent and luminous, of the realities that were to be the light of the New Testament established by Christ. Now, according to Our Lord's own words, one of the most characteristic figures of the Eucharist was the manna; with a special insistence, our Divine Saviour established comparisons between this food which came down from heaven to nourish the Hebrews in the desert, and the Eucharistic bread which He was to give to the world. Therefore it is to enter into the intentions of Christ if we study the figure and symbol the better to grasp the reality.

Now see in what terms the sacred writer, the instrument of the Holy Spirit, speaks to us of the manna. "Thou didst feed Thy people with the food of angels, and gavest them bread, from heaven prepared without labour, having in it all that is delicious, and the sweetness of every taste. For Thy sustenance shewed Thy sweetness to Thy children, and serving every man's will, it was turned to what every man liked": *Deserviens uniuscujusque voluntati, ad quod quisque volebat convertebatur.*[3]

---

1 Cf. Mgr Gay.   2 Ps. cx, 4–5.

3 *Angelorum esca nutrivisti populum tuum, et paratum panem de caelo praestitisti illis*

The Church in the office of the Blessed Sacrament applies these magnificent words to the Eucharist.[1] We are about to see with what truth and fulness they express the properties of the Eucharistic Bread; we shall see with how much more reason we can sing of the Sacred Host what the inspired author sings of the manna.

Like to manna, the Eucharist is a food, but a spiritual food. It is in the midst of a repast, under the form of food, that Our Lord chose to institute it. Christ Jesus gives Himself to us as the nourishment of our souls: "My Flesh is meat indeed: and My Blood is drink indeed": *Caro mea vere est cibus, et sanguis meus vere est potus.*[2]

Again like the manna, the Eucharist is bread come down from heaven. But the manna was only an imperfect figure; that is why Our Lord said to the Jews who recalled to Him the miracle of the desert: "Moses gave you bread from heaven, but My Father giveth you the *true* bread from heaven. For the bread of God is that which cometh down from heaven and giveth life to the world." This bread is given not only to one particular people—but to all mankind.

And as the Jews murmured at hearing Jesus call Himself "the Bread come down from heaven," He added: "I am the Bread of life. Your fathers did eat manna in the desert and are dead. This is the bread which cometh down from heaven; that if any man eat of it, he may not die. I am the living Bread which came down from heaven; if any man eat of this bread, he shall live for ever,"—for it places in our very bodies the germ of the resurrection.—"And the bread that I will give, is My Flesh, for the life of the world."[3]

In these words our Saviour Himself shows us how the Divine Eucharistic reality surpasses in plenitude, in its substance and fruits, the nourishment given of old to the Jewish people.

This bread from heaven gives us life by nourishing grace within us. It has in it all that is delicious and sweet: *Omne delectamentum in se habentem, et omnis saporis suavitatem.*

---

sine labore omne delectamentum in se habentem, et omnis saporis suavitatem. Substantia enim tua dulcedinem tuam, quam in filios habes, ostendebat: et deserviens uniuscujusque voluntati, ad quad quisque volebat, convertebatur. Sap. xvi, 20–21.

1 Canticles of 3rd Nocturn of Matins (Monastic Breviary); cf. 2nd Antiphon of Lauds.
2 Joan. vi, 56. 3 Ibid. 32–33, 48–52.

Nothing is so joyous as a feast; Holy Communion is the feast of the soul, that is to say, a source of deepest joys. Why should not Christ Jesus, Truth and Life, principle of all being and of all beatitude, fill our hearts with joy? Why, in making us drink from the chalice of His Divine Blood, should He not pour into our souls that spiritual gladness which excites charity and sustains fervour? See Him in the supper room, after He has instituted this Divine Sacrament. He speaks to His Apostles of His joy; He desires that this joy, His own joy, altogether divine, should become ours, and that our hearts should be filled with it: *Ut gaudium* MEUM *in vobis sit.*[1] It is one of the effects of the Eucharist when received with devotion to fill the soul with supernatural sweetness that renders it prompt and devoted in God's service.

Let us not forget, however, that this joy is above all spiritual. The Eucharist being eminently the "mystery of faith," it may happen that God permits that this altogether inward joy should not react upon the sensible part of our being. It may happen that very fervent souls remain in a state of great dryness and aridity after having received the Bread of life. Do not let them be astonished at this: above all never let them be discouraged; if they have brought all the good dispositions possible for receiving Christ, and still suffer from their powerlessness, let them be reassured and remain in peace. Christ, ever living, acts in silence, but sovereignly in the innermost depths of the soul in order to transform it into Himself; that is the most precious effect of this heavenly food: "He that eateth My flesh, and drinketh My Blood, abideth in Me, and I in him."[2]

What more is there to be said? This living Bread which gives life, this delicious food that brings joy is granted to us "without labour"; *sine labore.* That was one of the properties of the manna. How much more is this verified in the Eucharistic food!

"What indeed is required of us in order that we may sit down at the great King" and eat with profit the heavenly Bread? That we come to it clad in the "wedding garment,"[3] that is to say that we should be in a state of grace, and have a right intention.

Nothing more is required on our side. But for Jesus? Certainly it was

---

1 Joan. xv, 11. 2 Ibid. vi, 57. 3 Matth. xxii, 11.

not without labour that He prepared this feast for us. It needed the self abasements of the Incarnation, the humility and obscure labours of the hidden life, the fatigue of the apostolate, the conflicts with the Pharisees, the combats against the prince of darkness, finally, that which contains and crowns all, the sufferings of the Passion. It was only at the cost of His bloodstained immolation and untold sufferings that Christ Jesus merited for us this wonderful grace of being united so closely to Himself in that He nourishes us with His Sacred Body, and gives us His Precious Blood to drink.

Therefore it was that He instituted this Sacrament on the eve of His Passion as if to give us the most touching proof of the excess of His love for us: *Cum dilexisset suos...in finem dilexit.*[1] It is because it is communicated to us at such a price that this gift is full of the sweetness of the infinite love of Jesus Christ: *Dulcedinem tuam...ostendebat...*

These are some of the marvels figured by the manna and brought about, for the life and joy of our souls, by the wisdom and bounty of our God.

How is it possible not to "admire" these marvels of the Church? How can we fail to surround these sacred mysteries with all our reverence and adoration? *Tribue quaesumus, ita nos corporis et sanguinis tui sacra mysteria venerari!*[2]

III

Of all the properties that Holy Scripture attributes to the manna, there is one which is particularly remarkable. The manna was a food which accommodated itself to the taste and wishes of the one who partook of it: *Deserviens uniuscujusque voluntati, ad quod quisque volebat convertebatur.*

In the heavenly Bread, the Eucharist, we can also find, if I may thus express myself, the savour of all the mysteries of Christ, and the virtue of all His states. We are not here considering the Eucharist any longer as a memorial, but as source of grace, and this is a fruitful aspect of the Eucharistic mystery on which I wish to dwell with you for a few moments. If we allow it to penetrate our souls, we shall feel the love and desire for

---

1 "Having loved his own...he loved them unto the end," Joan. xiii, 1.
2 "Grant us, we beseech Thee, so to venerate the sacred mysteries of your Body and Blood," Collect for the Feast of Corpus Christi.

this Divine Food increase within us.

As we know, Our Lord gives Himself as food to preserve within us the divine life of grace; moreover, by means of the union that this Sacrament establishes between our souls and the Person of Jesus,—*in me manet et ego in illo,*[1]...by the charity that this union nourishes, Christ works this transformation that caused St. Paul to say: "I live, now not I but Christ liveth in me."[2] Such is the virtue proper to this Sacrament.

But this transformation holds for us many degrees and comprehends many stages. We cannot realise it all at once; it is only gradually that this transformation is wrought, in the measure that we enter deeper into the knowledge of Christ Jesus and of His states, since His life is our model and His perfection the example of our own.

The contemplation of the mysteries of Jesus constitutes one of the elements of this transfiguration; I have already said that when, by a living faith, we place ourselves in contact with Him, Christ produces in us, by the ever efficacious virtue of His holy Humanity united to the Word, that resemblance which is the sign of our predestination.

If that be true of the simple contemplation of His mysteries, how much deeper and more extensive will the action of Jesus be in this domain when He dwells in our souls by Sacramental Communion! This union is the greatest and most intimate that we can have here below with Christ, the union that takes place between the bread and the one who takes it. Christ gives Himself to be our Food, but, inversely to what takes place as to corporal food, it is we who are assimilated to Him. Christ becomes our life.

The first property of the manna was to nourish; the grace belonging to the Eucharist is likewise to maintain divine life in the soul, by making us participate in the life of Christ.

But like the manna which "was turned to what every man liked," so the life that Christ gives us by Communion, is all His life that passes into our souls to be the exemplar and the form of ours, to produce within us the divers affections of the Heart of Jesus, to make us imitate all the virtues He practised in His states, and to shed within us the special grace which He merited for us when living His mysteries.

Doubtless we must never forget that under the Eucharistic species is

---

1 "He abideth in me and I in him," Joan. vi, 57.   2 Gal. ii, 20.

found only the substance of the *glorious* body of Jesus, such as it is at present in heaven, and not such as it was, for example, in the crib of Bethlehem.

But when the Father looks upon His Son Jesus in the heavenly splendours, what does He behold in Him? He sees the One Who lived thirty three years upon earth for us, He beholds all the mysteries that this mortal life contained, the satisfactions and the merits whereof these mysteries were the source; He beholds the glory that this Son gave Him in living each of them. In each of them too He beholds ever the same Son in Whom He was well pleased, although now Christ Jesus sits at His right hand only in His glorious state.

In the same way, it is Jesus born of Mary Whom we receive, Jesus, Who dwelt at Nazareth, Who preached to the Jews of Palestine; it is the Good Samaritan; it is He Who healed the sick, delivered Magdalen from the devil, and raised Lazarus from the dead; it is He Who, wearied, slept in the ship; it is He Who was crushed by anguish; it is He Who was crucified upon Calvary; it is the glorious Jesus risen from the sepulchre, it is the mysterious Pilgrim of Emmaus, Who made Himself known "in the breaking of bread"[1]; it is He Who ascended to Heaven to the Father's right hand; it is the eternal High Priest, ever living, Who never ceases to pray for us.

All these states of the life of Jesus are, in substance, given to us in Communion, with their properties, their spirit, their merits and their virtue: under the diversity of states, and the variety of mysteries, is perpetuated the identity of the Person Who lived them and now lives eternally in Heaven.

When, therefore, we receive Christ at the Holy Table, we may contemplate Him and converse with Him in any of His mysteries; although He is now in His glorious state, we find in Him the One Who has lived for us and merited for us the grace that these mysteries contain; dwelling in us, Christ communicates this grace to us in order to effect little by little that transformation of our life into Him, which is the effect proper to the sacrament. It is enough, in order to understand this truth, to read the secrets and postcommunions of the Mass for the different feasts of our Saviour. The object of these prayers, which hold a special rank among those of the Eucharistic Sacrifice, are diversified according to the virtue of the mysteries celebrated.[2]

---

1 Luc. xxiv, 35.   2 See above, pp. 90–91.

We can, for example, unite ourselves to Jesus as living *in sinu Patris,*[1] equal to His Father, God like Him; the One Whom we adore within us, we adore as the Word co-eternal with the Father, the very Son of God, the object of His Father's good pleasure: Yes, I adore Thee within Me, O Divine Word; by the intimate union that I have at this moment with Thee, grant me to be also with Thee *in sinu Patris,* now by faith, later in the eternal reality, that I may live by the very life of God, which is Thy life.

We can adore Him, the Incarnate Word, as Our Lady did when He lived in her before being manifested to the world. Only in heaven shall we know with what reverence and love the Blessed Virgin inwardly adored the Son of God Who, through her, took our flesh.

Again we can adore Him within ourselves as we would have adored Him nineteen centuries ago in the stable-cave of Bethlehem with the shepherds and Magi; He then communicates to us the grace of imitating the special virtues of humility, poverty and detachment, that we contemplate in Him in this state of His hidden life.

If we desire, He will be within us the Agonising Saviour, Who, by His wonderful submission to His Father's good pleasure obtains for us the grace to bear our daily crosses; He will be the Divine Risen Lord Who grants us to detach ourselves from all that is earthly, to "live unto God"[2] more generously and fully; He will be in us the Victor Who gloriously ascends into heaven and draws us after Him that we may already dwell there by faith, hope and holy desire.

Christ thus contemplated and received, is Christ living His mysteries over again in us; this contemplation is the life of Christ being instilled into ours, and, with all its own beauties, its particular merits and special graces substituting itself for our life: *Deserviens uniuscujusque voluntati.*

IV

In what I have been saying, I have given you to understand that the most perfect participation in this divine mystery of the altar is Sacramental Communion.

But you know that Communion itself supposes sacrifice. That is why

---

1 "In the bosom of the Father," Joan. i, 18.   2 Rom. vi, 11.

we already associate ourselves with the mystery of the altar in assisting at the Sacrifice of the Mass.

We would have given anything to have been at the foot of the Cross with the Blessed Virgin, St. John and Magdalen. Now the oblation of the altar reproduces and renews the immolation of Calvary in order to perpetuate its remembrance, and apply its fruits.

During Holy Mass, we ought to unite ourselves to Christ, but to Christ immolated. He is, upon the altar, *Agnus tamquam occisus,*[1] the Lamb of-fered as a victim, and it is with His Sacrifice that Jesus wills to associate us. After the consecration, the priest with his hands joined together upon the altar—a gesture which signifies the union of the priest and all the faith-ful with Christ's Sacrifice—says this prayer: "We beseech Thee, almighty God, command that these things be carried to Thy sublime altar, in the sight of the Divine Majesty."

The Church here places in relation two altars: that of the earth and that of heaven,—not that there is a material altar in the sanctuary of heaven, but the Church wishes to point out there is but one sacrifice: the immola-tion which is accomplished mystically upon earth is one with the offering that Christ, our High Priest, makes of Himself in the bosom of the Father, to Whom he offers for us the satisfactions of His Passion.

"These things," of which the Church speaks, says Bossuet, are truly the Body and Blood of Jesus, but they are this Body and this Blood together with us all and with our desires and prayers, and all these compose one same oblation.[2]

Thus in this solemn moment, we are introduced *ad interiora velaminis,*[3] in the sanctuary of the Divinity, but we are brought there by Jesus and with Him; and there, before the Infinite Majesty, in presence of all the heavenly court, we are presented with Christ to the Father in order that the Father may fill us "with all heavenly benediction and grace": *Omni benedictione caelesti et gratia repleamur.*

Oh! if our faith were ardent, with what reverence we should assist at this Holy Sacrifice! with what care we should seek to cleanse ourselves

---

1 Cf. Apoc. v, 6.
2 *Explication de quelques difficultés sur les prières de la messe.*
3 "Within the veil," Hebr. vi, 19.

from every stain so as to be less unworthy to enter, in the train of our Divine Chief into the Holy of Holies, there to be, with Christ, a living victim! "It is then only," as St. Gregory so well says, "that Christ is our Victim, when we offer ourselves, in order to share, by our generosity and sacrifice, in His life of immolation": *Tunc ergo vere pro nobis hostia erit Deo, cum nos ipsos hostiam fecerimus.*[1]

The Eucharistic Sacrifice gives us the Sacrament. It is only by being united to the victim that one perfectly participates in the sacrifice. In the prayer which I have just explained, the Church beseeches that we "may be filled with all heavenly benediction and grace,"—but it is on condition that we participate in this sacrifice by the reception of the Body and Blood of Jesus: *Quotquot ex hac altaris participatione sacrosanctum Filii tui corpus et sanguinem sumpserimus.*

It is then only by Communion that we perfectly enter into the thoughts of Jesus, that we fully respond to the desires of His Heart on the day on which He instituted the Eucharist: "Take ye and eat"[2]; "Except you eat the flesh of the Son of man...you shall not have life in you."[3] Communion is the first of the Eucharistic duties.

But let us bring the best of dispositions to this Eucharistic banquet. Doubtless, as you know, this Divine Sacrament produces its fruits in the soul that receives it in the state of grace and with a right intention. However, the abundance of its fruits is measured by the degree of each one's fervour.

I have shown elsewhere[4] how these dispositions are summed up in faith, confidence, the utter surrender of ourselves to Christ and union with the members of His mystical Body. I need not return to this subject.

There is however one disposition on which I would here touch, because it is the one which the Church herself points out to us in the collect of the Blessed Sacrament: it is reverence. "Grant, we beseech Thee, so to venerate the sacred mysteries of Thy Body and Blood, that we may

---

1 "For then it shall truly be a sacrifice for us to God, when we make ourselves a sacrifice to him," Dialogues L. iv, c. 59.
2 Matth. xxvi, 26.   3 Joan. vi, 54.
4 In the conference on The Bread of life, § v and vi, of the volume *Christ, the Life of the Soul.*

constantly feel within us the fruit of Thy redemption": *Ita nos corporis et sanguinis tui sacra mysteria* VENERARI, *ut redemptionis tuae fructum in nobis jugiter sentiamus.*

The Church beseeches that we may venerate Christ in the Eucharist. There is a double reason for this.

First because Christ is God.

The Church speaks to us of "Sacred Mysteries." The word "mysteries" indicates that under the Eucharistic species is hidden a reality; in adding "sacred" she gives us to understand that this reality is holy and divine. Indeed He Who is hidden in the Eucharist is He Who, with the Father and the Holy Spirit, is the Infinite Being, the Almighty, the Principle of all things. If Our Lord appeared to us in the splendour of His glory, our gaze would not be able to bear this splendour. In order to give Himself to us He hides Himself, no longer under the infirmity of passible flesh, as in the mystery of the Incarnation, but under the species of bread and wine. Let us say to Him: "Lord Jesus, for love of us, in order to draw us to You, to become our Food, You veil your majesty. But You will lose nothing of our homage thereby. The more You hide your Divinity the more we wish to adore You, the more too we wish to cast ourselves at Your feet with profound reverence and ardent love."

Adoro te devote, latens Deitas,
Quae sub his figuris vere latitas.[1]

The second reason is that Christ Jesus has humbled Himself and delivered Himself up for us.

The Church reminds us that this wonderful Sacrament is the memorial above all others of the Passion of Jesus. Now, during His Sacred Passion, Christ underwent untold humiliations, He was plunged into nameless ignominies.

But, says St. Paul, it is because Christ emptied Himself of His glory because He descended into such depths of self-abasement, that the Father has exalted Him. He, "hath given him a name which is above all names: that in the name of Jesus every knee should bow...and that every tongue should confess that the Lord Jesus Christ is in the glory of God the Father."

---

1 "I devoutly adore you, hidden Deity, Who are truly hidden beneath these figures," Hymn *Adoro Te.*

Let us enter into this thought of the Eternal Father that the Apostle reveals to us. The more Christ has humbled Himself, the more ought we, like the Father, to exalt Him in this Sacrament which recalls His Passion; the more ought we to lavish our homage upon Him. Justice, as well as love, requires this of us.

Then, is it not "for us" that He thus delivered Himself? *Propter nos et propter nostram salutem.*[1] If He suffered it is for me; if He bore so many outrages on the part of the rough soldiery, it is for me; if He was scourged and crowned with thorns, if He died in the midst of unutterable torments, it is for me, it is to draw me to Him: *Dilexit me et tradidit semetipsum pro me.*[2] Never let us forget that each of the sorrowful scenes of the Passion was preordained by Wisdom and accepted by Love for our salvation.

O Christ Jesus, really present upon the altar, I cast myself down at Your feet; may all adoration be offered to You in the Sacrament which You left to us on the eve of Your Passion, as the testimony of the excess of Your love!

Again we show this "veneration" by going to visit Christ in the tabernacle. Would it not indeed be a failing in respect to neglect this Divine Guest Who awaits us? He dwells there, really present, He Who was present in the Crib, at Nazareth, upon the mountains of Judaea, in the supper-room, upon the Cross. It is this same Jesus Who said to the Samaritan woman: "If thou didst know the gift of God!" Thou who art athirst for light, peace, joy, happiness if thou didst know Who I am, thou wouldst ask of Me living water...that water of divine grace which becomes "a fountain of water springing *up* into life everlasting."[3]

He is there, really present, He Who said: "I am the Way, the Truth and the Life..."[4] he that followeth Me, walketh not in darkness...."[5] No man cometh to the Father but by Me...."[6] I am the Vine, you are the branches; he that abideth in Me, and I in him, the same beareth much fruit: for without Me you can do nothing...."[7] He that cometh to Me, I will not cast out...."[8] Come to Me all you that labour and are burdened, and I will refresh you...and you shall find rest to your souls."[9]

He is there, the same Christ who healed the lepers, stilled the tempest

---

1 "For us and for our salvation," Creed of the Mass.
2 "He loved me and delivered himself for me," Gal. ii, 20.   3 Joan. iv, 10, 14.
4 Ibid. xiv, 6.   5 Ibid. viii, 12.   6 Ibid. xiv, 6.   7 Ibid. xv, 5.
8 Ibid. vi, 37.   9 Matth. xi, 28–29.

and promised to the good thief a place in His Kingdom. We find there our Saviour, our Friend, our Elder Brother, in the fulness of His almighty power, in the ever fruitful virtue of His mysteries, the infinite superabundance of His merits, and the ineffable mercy of His love.

He awaits us in His tabernacle, not only in order to receive our homage, but to communicate His grace to us. If our faith in His work is not a mere sentiment, we shall go to Him, we shall put our soul in contact, by faith, with His Sacred Humanity. Be assured that "virtue goes out from Him,"[1] as of old, to fill us with light, peace and joy.

We can only hope "ever to feel within us the fruit of the Redemption" if this attitude of respect and reverence deeply penetrate our souls. This veneration should be such that it will make us enjoy the Divine Gift in all its fulness: *Ita venerari* UT *fructum jugiter sentiamus.*

V

But why you may ask, does the Church seem to sum up in this "veneration" all our dispositions towards this Divine Sacrament?

It is because this reverence is a homage of faith. The man who is without faith does not bend his knee before the Sacred Host. This reverence has its source and nourishment only in faith.

Now, as I have often said, the root of all justification and the fundamental condition of all progress in the supernatural life, is the first disposition for receiving the "fruit of the Redemption" of Christ.

What, in fact, is this fruit for our souls? In a word, it is to be born again to the divine life of grace, to become again partakers of the eternal adoption. We shall only attain to this by faith. Faith is the primal condition for becoming a child of God, and gathering, in its substance, this fruit of the Cross: *Quotquot autem receperunt eum, dedit eis potestatem filios Dei fieri,* HIS QUI CREDUNT IN NOMINE EJUS...*qui ex Deo nati sunt.*[2]

The reception of the Eucharist unites us first of all to Christ's Sacred Humanity, and this union is wrought by faith. When you believe that the Humanity of Jesus is the Humanity of the Son of God, the very Human-

---

1 Luc. vi, 19; viii, 46.

2 "But as many as received him, he gave them power to be made the sons of God, to them that believe in his name...Who are born of God." Joan. i, 12–13.

ity of the Word, and that in Him there is but one Divine Person; when, with all the strength and all the fulness of your faith, you adore this holy Humanity, through it you enter into contact with the Word; for it is the way that leads you to the Divinity.

When Christ Jesus gives Himself to us in Holy Communion, He asks us the question that He asked His apostles: *Quem dicunt homines esse Filium hominis?*[1] And we must answer with Peter: *Tu es Christus, Filius Dei vivi*: "Thou art Christ, the Son of the Living God."[2] I see only a fragment of bread, only a little wine, but Thou Who art the Word, Eternal Wisdom and Infinite Truth, Thou hast said: *Hoc est corpus meum, hic est sanguis meus*: "This is my Body; this is My Blood"; and because Thou hast said it, I believe that Thou art present under these humble appearances! Our senses tell us nothing, it is faith that makes us penetrate as far as the divine reality hidden under the Eucharistic veils: *Praestet fides supplementum sensuum defectui.*[3]

And Our Saviour says to us as to the Centurion: *Sicut credidisti, fiat tibi*: "As thou hast believed, so be it done to thee."[4] Since you believe that I am God, I give Myself to you with all the treasures of My Divinity to fill you with them, to transform you into Myself; I give Myself to you with the ineffable relations of My intimate life as God.

For we do not unite ourselves only to Christ. Christ is but one with the Father: *Ego et Pater unum sumus,* one in the unity of the Holy Spirit. Communion unites us at the same time with the Father and the Holy Spirit. Christ, the Word Incarnate, belongs altogether to His Father; when we communicate, He takes us, He unites us to His Father, as He Himself is united to Him; Jesus said to His Father at the Last Supper, after having instituted the Blessed Eucharist: "And not for them [My Apostles] only do I pray but for them also who through their word shall believe in Me; that they may be one, as Thou, Father, in Me, and I in Thee; that they also may be one in Us;...that they may be one, as We also are One: I in them, and Thou in Me": *Ego in eis et tu in me.*[5]

The Word unites us also to the Holy Spirit. In the Adorable Trinity, the Holy Spirit in the substantial Love of the Father and the Son. Christ gives Him to us, as He gave Him to the Apostles, in order to direct us

---

1 "Whom do men say that the Son of man is?" Matth. xvi, 13.   2 Matth. xvi. 16.
3 Hymn *Pange Lingua.*   4 Matth, viii, 13.   5 Joan. xvii, 20–23.

350

through Him; He communicates to us His Spirit of adoption, Who, first of all giving testimony to us that we are the children of God, helps us by His lights and inspirations to live as God's "dearly-beloved children."

What a sanctuary is the soul that has just received Holy Communion! The Eucharist first gives us Christ's Body and Blood; It gives us the Divinity of the Word indissolubly united to the Human Nature; through the Word, our soul is united to the Father and the Spirit, in the indivisibility of their uncreated nature. The Trinity dwells in us; our soul becomes the heaven whence are wrought the mysterious operations of the divine life. We can offer to the Father, the Son of His dilection that He may anew place in Him all His delight; we can offer this delight to Jesus so that the ineffable joys that He experienced at the moment of His Incarnation may be renewed within His blessed soul; we can pray the Holy Spirit to be the bond of love that unites us to the Father and the Son....

Only faith can comprehend these marvels, and plunge into these abysses: *Mysterium fidei.*

THE HEART OF CHRIST

(Feast of the Sacred Heart)

SUMMARY.—Love explains all the mysteries of Jesus; the faith that we ought to have in the fulness of this love; the Church sets it before us as the object of worship in the Feast of the Sacred Heart.—I. In what, speaking in a general manner, devotion to the Heart of Jesus consists; how deeply this devotion plunges its roots into the Christian dogma.—II. Its divers elements.—III. The contemplation of the benefits which we owe to the love of Jesus, symbolised by His Heart, is the source of the love that we ought to give Him in return. The double character of our love for Christ; it ought to be affective and effective; Our Lord is our Model in this.—IV. Precious advantage of devotion to the Sacred Heart; it makes us take, little by little, the attitude that should characterise our relations with God. Our spiritual life depends, in great part, on the idea that we habitually have of God; diversity of aspects under which souls may consider God.—V. Christ alone unveils to us the true attitude of the soul in face of God; devotion to the Heart of Jesus helps us to acquire this attitude.

ALL that we possess in the domain of grace comes to us from Christ Jesus. "Of His fulness we have all received": *De plenitudine ejus nos omnes accepimus.*[1] He has destroyed the wall of separation that hindered us from going to God; He has merited for us all graces in infinite abundance; being Divine Head of the mystical body, He has the power of communicating to us the spirit of His states and the virtue of His mysteries, so as to transform us into Himself.

---

1 Joan. i, 16.

When we consider these mysteries of Jesus, which of His perfections do we see especially shine out? It is love.

Love brought about the Incarnation: *Propter nos...descendit de caelis et incarnatus est*[1]; love caused Christ to be born in passible and weak flesh, inspired the obscurity of the hidden life, nourished the zeal of the public life. If Jesus delivers Himself up to death for us, it is because He yields to the excess of a measureless love[2]; if He rises again, it is "for our justification"[3]; if He ascends into heaven, it is to prepare a place[4] for us in that abode of blessedness; He sends the Paraclete so as not to leave us orphans[5]; He institutes the Sacrament of the Eucharist as a memorial of His love.[6] All these mysteries have their source in love.

It is necessary that our faith in this love of Christ Jesus should be living and constant. And why? Because it is one of the most powerful supports of our fidelity.

Look at St. Paul. Never did man labour and spend himself as he did for Christ. One day when his enemies attack the lawfulness of his mission, he is led, in self-defence, to give a brief outline of his works, his toils and sufferings. However well we know this sketch drawn from the life, it is always a joy to the soul to read again this page, unique in the annals of the apostolate: Often, says the great Apostle, was he brought nigh to death: "Of the Jews five times did I receive forty stripes, save one. Thrice was I beaten with rods, once I was stoned, thrice I suffered shipwreck, a night and a day I was in the depth of the sea. In journeying often, in perils of waters, in perils of robbers, in perils from my own nation, in perils in the city, in perils in the wilderness, in perils in the sea, in perils from false brethren. In labour and painfulness, in much watchings, in hunger and thirst, in fastings often, in cold and nakedness. Besides those things which are without: my daily instance, the solicitude for all the churches."[7] Elsewhere, he applies to himself the words of the Psalmist: "For Thy sake, we are put to death all the day long, we are accounted as sheep for the slaughter...." And yet he immediately adds: "but in all these things we overcome, because of Him that hath loved us": *Sed in his omnibus su-*

---

1 "For us...He came down from heaven and became incarnate," Creed of the Mass.
2 Joan. xiii, 1.   3 Rom. iv, 25.   4 Joan. xiv, 2; Hebr. vi, 20.
5 Joan. xiv, 18.   6 Luc. xxii, 19.   7 II Cor. xi, 23–28.

peramus.[1] And where does he find the secret of this victory? Ask of him how he endures everything, though "weary even of life"[2]; how, in all his trials, he remains united to Christ with such an unshaken firmness that neither "tribulation, or distress, or famine, or nakedness, or the sword" can separate him from Jesus?[3] He will reply: *Propter eum qui dilexit nos*[4]: "Because of Him Who hath loved us." What sustains, strengthens, animates and stimulates him is the deep conviction of the love that Christ bears towards him: *Dilexit me et tradidit semetipsum pro me.*[5]

And, indeed, that which makes this ardent conviction strong within him is the sense that he no longer lives for himself—he who blasphemed the name of God and persecuted the Christians[6]—but for Him Who loved him to the point of giving His life for him: *Caritas Christi urget nos....*[7] "The charity of Christ presseth us," he exclaims. Therefore, I will give myself up for Him, I will spend myself willingly, without reserve, without counting the cost; I will consume myself for the souls won by Him: *Libentissime impendam et superimpendar!*[8]

This conviction that Christ loves him truly gives the key to all the work of the great Apostle.

Nothing urges one to love like knowing and feeling oneself to be loved. "Every time that we think of Jesus Christ," says St. Teresa, "let us remember the love with which He has heaped His benefits upon us....Love calls forth love."[9]

But how are we to learn this love which is at the foundation of all the states of Jesus, which explains them, and sums up all the motives of these mysteries? Where are we to drink of this knowledge, so wholesome and so fruitful that St. Paul made it the object, of his prayer for his Christians?[10] In the contemplation of the mysteries of Jesus. If we study them with faith, the Holy Spirit, Who is Infinite Love, will disclose to us their depths, and lead us to the love which is the source of them.

There is one feast, which by its object brings to our mind, in a general manner, the love that the Incarnate Word has shown to us: it is the Feast

---

1 Rom. viii, 36–37. 2 II Cor. i, 8. 3 Rom. viii, 35. 4 Ibid. 37.
5 "He loved me and delivered himself for me," Gal. ii, 20.
6 Cf. Act. xxvi, 9–10; I Cor. xv, 9. 7 II Cor. v, 14.
8 Ibid. xii, 15. 9 *Life* written by herself. Chap. xxii. 10 Ephes. iii, 19.

of the Sacred Heart. It is with this feast that the Church, according to the revelation of Our Lord to St. Margaret Mary, closes, so to speak, the annual cycle of the solemnities of the Saviour; it is as if, arrived at the term of the contemplation of her Bridegroom's mysteries, there is nothing left for her to do but to celebrate the very love that inspired them all.

Following the example of the Church, I will, now that we have passed in review the chief mysteries of our Divine Head, say a few words about the devotion to the Sacred Heart, its object and its practice. We shall grasp once more this important truth that for us all is resumed in the practical knowledge of the mystery of Jesus.

I

The word "devotion" comes from the Latin word *devovere*: to devote or consecrate oneself to a person beloved. Devotion towards God is the highest expression of our love. "Thou shalt love the Lord thy God, with thy whole heart, and with thy whole soul, and with thy whole mind, and with thy whole strength": *Diliges Dominum Deum tuum ex* TOTO *corde tuo, et ex* TOTA *anima tua, et ex* TOTA *mente tua.*[1] This *totus* denotes devotion: to love God with *all oneself*, without reserving anything; to love Him constantly; to love Him to the point of giving oneself to His service with promptitude and ease, such is devotion in general; and, thus understood, devotion constitutes perfection: for it is the very flower of charity.[2]

Devotion to Jesus Christ is the devotion of all our being and all our activity to the Person of the Incarnate Word, abstraction made of such or such particular state of the Person of Jesus or of such or such special mystery of His life. By this devotion to Jesus Christ, we strive to know, to honour, to serve the Son of God manifesting Himself to us through His Sacred Humanity.

A particular devotion is either "devotedness" to God considered specially in one of His attributes or one of His perfections, as His holiness or mercy, or again to one of the three Divine Persons, or to Christ contemplated in one or other of his states. As we have seen in the course of these conferences, it is always the same Christ Jesus Whom we honour,

---

1 Marc. xii, 30.   2 Cf. S. Thom. IIa–IIae, q. 82, a. 1.

it is always His Adorable Person to Whom our homage is offered, but we consider His Person under some particular aspect or as manifested to us in some special mystery. Thus devotion to the Holy Childhood is devotion to the very Person of Christ especially contemplated in the mysteries of His Nativity and His life as a Youth at Nazareth; devotion to the Five Wounds is devotion to the Person of the Incarnate Word considered in His sufferings, sufferings which are themselves symbolised by the five wounds of which Christ willed to retain the glorious marks after His Resurrection. These devotions can then have a special, proper, immediate object, but they have always their term in Christ's own Person.[1]

Hence you comprehend what is to be understood by devotion to the Sacred Heart. It is, in a general manner, devotion to the Person of Jesus Himself, manifesting His love for us and shewing us His Heart as a symbol of this love. Whom do we then honour in this devotion? Christ Jesus Himself, in person. But what is the immediate, special, proper object of this devotion? The Heart of flesh of Jesus, the Heart which beats for us in the bosom of the God-Man; but we do not honour it apart from the human nature of Jesus, nor from the Person of the Eternal Word to Whom this human nature was united in the Incarnation. Is this all? No; there is yet this to be added; we honour this Heart as the symbol of the love of Jesus towards us.

Devotion to the Sacred Heart is then summed up in the worship of the Incarnate Word manifesting His love to us and showing us His Heart as the symbol of this love.

I have no need to justify to you this devotion which is familiar to you; it will not however be without some use to say a word on this subject.

You know that, according to certain Protestants, the Church is like a lifeless body; she received, they think, all her perfection from the outset, and ought there to rest stationary; all that has arisen later, either in dogmatic matters, or in the domain of piety, is only, in their eyes, superfluity and corruption.

For us, the Church is a living organism, which, like all living organisms, is to be developed and perfected. The deposit of revelation was sealed at

---

1   Thom. III q. 25, a. 1.

the death of the last apostle; since then, no writing is admitted as inspired, and the revelations of the saints do not enter into the official deposit of the truths of faith. But many truths contained in the official revelation were only so in germ; the opportunity was only given little by little, under the pressure of events and the guidance of the Holy Spirit, of coming to explicit definitions which fixed in a precise and determined formula what was hitherto only known in an implicit manner.

From the first instant of His Incarnation, Christ Jesus possessed in His blessed soul all the treasures of divine knowledge and wisdom. But it is only by degrees that these were to be revealed. As Christ increased in age, this knowledge and wisdom manifested themselves, and the virtues of which He contained in Himself the germ were seen to blossom.

Something analogous takes place for the Church, Christ's Mystical Body. For example, we find in the deposit of the Faith this magnificent revelation: "The Word was God...and the Word was made Flesh."[1] This revelation contains treasures that have only come to light by degrees; it is like a seed that has blossomed, and borne fruits of truth to increase our knowledge of Christ Jesus. On the occasion of heresies that have sprung up, the Church, guided by the Holy Spirit, has defined that in Jesus Christ there is only one divine Person, but two natures, distinct and perfect, two wills, two sources of activity; that the Virgin Mary is the Mother of God; that all the parts of the Sacred Humanity of Jesus are adorable on account of their union with the Divine Person of the Word. Are these new dogmas? No. It is the deposit of the faith explained, made explicit, and developed.

What we say of dogmas applies equally to devotions. In the course of centuries, devotions have risen up that the Church, under the guidance of the Holy Spirit, has admitted and made her own. These are not innovations, properly so called. They are effects that flow from the established dogmas and the Church's organic activity.

When the teaching Church approves of a devotion and confirms it with her sovereign authority, it ought to be our joy to accept this devotion; to act otherwise would not be to share the mind of the Church, *Sentire cum Ecclesia,* it would be no longer to enter into the thoughts of Christ Jesus; for He says to His apostles and to their successors: "He that heareth you,

---

1 I Joan. i, 14.

heareth Me; and he that despiseth you, despiseth Me."[1] Now, how shall we go to the Father if we do not hearken to Christ?

Relatively modern under the form that it actually bears, the devotion to the Sacred Heart has its dogmatic roots in the deposit of faith. It was contained in germ in the words of St. John: "The Word was made Flesh, and dwelt among us...having loved His own...He loved them unto the end."[2] What, in fact, is the Incarnation? It is the manifestation of God, it is God revealing Himself to us through the Humanity of Jesus: *Nova mentis nostrae oculis lux tuae claritatis infulsit*[3]; it is the manifestation of Divine love to the world: "God so loved the world as to give His Only-begotten Son"; and this Son Himself so loved men as to deliver Himself up for them: "Greater love than this no man hath, that a man lay down his life for his friends": *Majorem hac dilectionem nemo habet.*[4] All the devotion to the Sacred Heart is in germ in these words of Jesus. And in order to show that His love had attained the supreme degree, Christ Jesus willed that immediately after He had drawn His last breath on the Cross, His Heart should be pierced by the soldier's lance.

As we are about to see, the love that is symbolised by the heart in this devotion is first of all the created love of Jesus, but, as He is the Incarnate Word, the treasures of this created love manifest to us the marvels of the Divine love, of the Eternal Word.

You perceive what depths this devotion reaches in the deposit of the faith. Far from being an alteration or a corruption, it is an adaptation, at once simple and magnificent, of what St. John said concerning the Word-made-Flesh immolated for love of us.

II

If we now dwell in a few words upon the divers elements of the devotion we shall see how they are justified.

The proper and direct object of it is Christ's physical Heart. This Heart is, indeed, worthy of adoration. Why so? Because it forms part of His

---

1 Luc. x, 16.   2 Joan. i, 14; xiii, 1.
3 "The new light of thy glory hath shone on the eye of the soul," Preface of the Nativity.
4 Joan. xv, 13.

Human Nature, and because the Word has united Himself to a perfect nature: *Perfectus homo.*[1] The same adoration that we give to the Divine Person of the Word attains all that is personally united thereto, all that subsists in and by the Person of the Word. This is true of the whole Human Nature of Jesus, this is true of each of the parts that compose it. The Heart of Jesus is the Heart of a God.

But the Heart which we honour, which we adore in this Humanity united to the Person of the Word, serves here as a symbol of what? Of love. When God says to us in the Scriptures: "My son, give Me Thy heart,"[2] we understand that the heart here signifies love. You may say of someone: I esteem him, I respect him, but I cannot give him my heart. You mean by these words that friendship, intimacy and union are impossible.

In the devotion to the Sacred Heart of Jesus, we then honour the love that the Incarnate Word bears towards us.

Created love first of all. Christ Jesus is both God and Man; perfect God, perfect Man; that is the very mystery of the Incarnation. As "Son of Man," Christ has a Heart like ours, a Heart of flesh, a Heart that beats for us with the tenderest, the truest, the noblest, the most faithful love that ever was.

In his Epistle to the Ephesians, St. Paul told them that he earnestly besought God that they might be able to comprehend what is the breadth and length, and height and depth, of the mystery of Jesus, so much was he dazzled by the incommensurable riches that it contained. He might have said as much of the love of the Heart of Jesus for us; he did say so in fact when he declared that, this love "surpasseth all knowledge."[3]

And, indeed, we shall never exhaust the treasure of tenderness, of loveableness, of kindness and charity, of which the Heart of the Man-God is the burning furnace. We have only to open the Gospel and, on each page, we shall see shine out the goodness, the mercy, the condescension of Jesus towards men. I have tried, in pointing out some aspects of the public life of Christ, to show you how deeply human and infinitely delicate is this love.

This love of Christ is not a chimera, it is very real, for it is founded upon the reality of the Incarnation itself. The Blessed Virgin, St. John, Magdalen, Lazarus knew this well. It was not only a love of the will, but also a heartfelt love. When Christ Jesus said: "I have compassion on the

---

1 Creed of S. Athanasius. 2 Prov. xxiii, 26. 3 Ephes. iii, 14–19.

multitude,"[1] He really felt the fibres of His human Heart moved by pity; when He saw Martha and Mary weeping for the loss of their brother, He wept with them; truly human tears were wrung from His Heart. Therefore the Jews who witnessed this sight said to one another: "Behold how He loved him."[2]

Christ Jesus does not change. He was yesterday, He is to-day:—His Heart remains the most loving and most loveable that could be met with. St. Paul tells us explicitly that we ought to have full confidence in Jesus because He is a compassionate High Priest Who knows our sufferings, our miseries, our infirmities, having Himself espoused our weaknesses— saving sin. Doubtless, Christ Jesus can no longer suffer: *Mors illi ultra non dominabitur*[3]; but He remains the One Who was moved by compassion, Who suffered and redeemed men through love: *Dilexit me et tradidit semetipsum pro me.*

Whence came this human love of Jesus, this created love? From the Uncreated and Divine Love, from the love of the Eternal Word to which the human nature is indissolubly united. In Christ, although there are two perfect and distinct natures, keeping their specific energies and their proper operations, there is only one Divine Person. As I have said, the created love of Jesus is only a revelation of His uncreated love. Everything that the created love accomplishes is only in union with the uncreated love, and on account of it; Christ's Heart draws its human kindness from the Divine ocean.[4]

Upon Calvary, we see Him die a man like unto ourselves, One Who has been a prey to anguish, Who has suffered, Who has been crushed beneath the weight of torments, heavier than any man ever bore; we understand the love that this Man shows us. But this love which, by its excess, surpasses our knowledge, is the concrete and tangible expression of the Divine love. The Heart of Jesus pierced upon the Cross reveals to us Christ's human love; but beneath the veil of the humanity of Jesus is

---

1 Matth. xv, 32; Marc. viii, 2.   2 Joan. xi, 36.
3 "Death shall have no more dominion over him," Rom. vi, 9.
4 "In the Sacred Heart you will find the symbol and the sensible image of the infinite charity of Jesus Christ, of that charity which draws us to love Him in return." Leo. XIII, Bull *Annum sac.*, 25 M. 1899.

shown the ineffable and incomprehensible love of the Word.

What a wide perspective this devotion opens out to us! How powerful it is to attract the faithful soul! For it gives us the means of honouring what is the greatest, the highest, the most efficacious in Christ Jesus, the Incarnate Word: the love that He bears to the world, the love of which His Heart is the furnace....

III

Love is active: it is of its nature overflowing. In Jesus, love can but be for us an inexhaustible source of gifts.

In the collect for the Feast of the Sacred Heart, the Church invites us to call to mind the principal benefits that we owe to the love of Jesus Christ: *Praecipua in nos caritatis ejus beneficia recolimus.* This contemplation is one of the elements of devotion to the Sacred Heart. How can we pay honour to a love of which we do not know the manifestations?

This love, as we have said, is the human love of Jesus, the revelation of the uncreated love. To this uncreated love, which is common to the Father and the Holy Spirit, we owe everything. There is no gift which does not find its most profound principle in this love. Who drew beings out of nothing? Love. We sing in the hymn for the feast[1]: "The earth, the sea, the stars are the work of love":

> *Ille amor almus Artifex*
> *Terrae marisque et siderum.*

Yet more than the creation, the Incarnation is due to love. Love caused the Word to come down from the splendours of heaven in order to assume a mortal body:

> *Amor coegit te tuus*
> *Mortale corpus sumere.*

But the benefits which we ought especially to recall, are the redemption through the Passion, the institution of the Sacraments, above all of the Eucharist. It is to the human love of Jesus as well as to His uncreated love

---

1 Hymn for Vespers.

that we owe them.

We have seen, in contemplating these mysteries, what deep and ardent love they manifest. Our Lord Himself has said that there is no greater act of love for a man than to give his life for his friends. He Himself has gone as far as this; many virtues shine out in His blessed Passion, but love most of all. It needed nothing less than an excess of love to plunge voluntarily into the abysses of humiliation and opprobrium, of suffering and sorrow, in each phase of the Passion.

And in the same way as love wrought our redemption, so it was love that established the sacraments whereby the fruits of the sacrifice of Jesus are to be applied to every soul of good will.

St. Augustine[1] is pleased to recall the expression purposely chosen by the Evangelist concerning the wound made by the lance in the side of Jesus dead upon the Cross. The sacred writer does not say that the lance "struck," or "wounded," but that it "opened" the Saviour's side: *Latus ejus aperuit.*[2] It was the gate of life that was opened, says the great Doctor; from the pierced Heart of Jesus rivers of graces were to be poured out upon the world to sanctify the Church.

This contemplation of the benefits of Jesus towards us ought to become the source of our practical devotion to the Sacred Heart. Love alone can respond to love. Of what does our Saviour complain to St. Margaret Mary? Of the lack of love in return for His love. "Behold this Heart that has so loved men and which receives from them only ingratitude." It is then by love, by the gift of the heart that we should respond to Christ Jesus. "Who will not love in return the one Who loves him? Who being redeemed will not love his Redeemer?"

> *Quis non amantem redamet?*
> *Quis non redemptus diligat?*[3]

This love to be perfect must bear a twofold character.

There is affective love; it consists in the different feelings which move the heart towards a person loved: admiration, complacency, joy, thanksgiving. This love gives birth to praise. We rejoice in the perfections of the Heart of Jesus, we celebrate Its beauties, and grandeurs, we delight in the

---

1 Tract in Joan. cxx, 2.   2 Joan. xix, 34.
3 Hymn of Lauds for the Feast of the Sacred Heart.

magnificence of Its benefits: *Exultabunt labia mea cum cantavero tibi!*[1]

This affective love is necessary. In contemplating Christ in His love, the soul should give vent to her admiration, complacency, joy. Why so? Because we ought to love God with all our being; God wishes that our love towards Him should be conformable to our nature. Now our nature is not that of the Angels, ours is a human nature wherein the feelings have their part. Christ Jesus accepts this form of love, because it is based upon our nature, which He Himself created. See Him, at the time of His triumphal entry into Jerusalem, a few days before His Passion: "When He was now coming near the descent of Mount Olivet, the whole multitude of His disciples began with joy to praise God with a loud voice, for all the mighty works they had seen, saying: Blessed be the King Who cometh in the name of the Lord. Peace in heaven, and glory on high! And some of the Pharisees, from amongst the multitude, said to Him: Master, rebuke Thy disciples." And what does Our Lord answer? Does He silence these acclamations? On the contrary He replies to the Pharisees: "I say to you, that if these shall hold their peace, the stones will cry out.[2]

Christ Jesus is pleased with the praises that burst forth from the heart to the lips. Our love ought to break out in affections. Look at the saints. Francis, the Poor Man of Assisi, was so transported with love that he sang God's praises as he went along the roads.[3] Magdalen of Pazzi ran through the cloisters of the monastery, crying out: "O Love, O Love!"[4] Saint Theresa was thrilled with joy every time she chanted these words of the *Credo*: *Cujus regni non erit finis*: "And of His Kingdom there shall be no end."[5] Read her "Exclamations": you will there see how the affections of human nature burst forth in ardent praise from souls possessed by love.

Let us not fear to multiply our praises of the Heart of Jesus. The Litany of the Sacred Heart, acts of reparation and of consecration are so many expressions of this affective love, without which the human soul does not reach the perfection of its nature.

Of itself alone, this affective love is, however, insufficient. To have all its value, it must be manifested by deeds: *Probatio dilectionis, exhibitio*

---

1   "My lips shall greatly rejoice, when I shall sing to thee," Ps. lxx, 23.
2   Luc. xix, 37–40.   3   His life by Joergensen, Book ii, chap. i.
4   Her Life by Fr. Cepari, t. II, chap. xvi.   5   The Way of Perfection, chap. xxiii.

operis.[1] "If you love Me," said Jesus Himself, "keep My commandments":
Si diligitis me, mandata mea servate.[2] It is the one touchstone. You will
meet souls who abound in affections, who have the gift of tears,—and
yet do not trouble themselves to repress their bad inclinations, to destroy
their bad habits, to avoid occasions of sin; who give way as soon as temptation arises, or murmur directly contradiction and disappointments befall them. With them, affective love is full of illusions; it is a fire of straw
which quickly burns away into ashes.

If we truly love Christ Jesus, not only shall we rejoice in His glory, and
hymn His perfections with every impulse of our soul, not only shall we
be saddened at the injuries made to His Heart, and offer Him honour-
able amends,—but, above all, we shall strive to obey Him in all things,
we shall accept readily all the dispositions of His Providence towards us,
we shall work to extend His reign in souls, to procure His glory, we shall
gladly spend ourselves, we shall go so far, if necessary, as to "be spent,"
according to the beautiful words of St. Paul: *Libentissime impendam et
superimpendar!*[3] The Apostle is speaking of charity towards our neigh-
bours; applied to our love for Jesus, this formula wonderfully sums up
the practice of devotion to His Sacred Heart.

Let us gaze on our Divine Saviour; in this as in every virtue, He is our
best Model; we shall find in His Person two forms of love.

Consider the love that He bears towards His Father. Christ Jesus has
in His Heart the truest affective love with which a human heart can beat.
The Gospel one day shows us Christ's Heart, overflowing with enthusiasm
for the Father's unfathomable perfections, burst forth in praise before His
disciples. "At the same hour He rejoiced in the Holy Ghost, and said: I
confess to Thee, O Father, Lord of heaven and earth, because Thou hast
hidden these things from the wise and prudent, and hast revealed them
to little ones. Yea, Father, for so it hath seemed good in Thy sight...."[4]

See again at the Last Supper how His Sacred Heart is full of affection
for His Father and how this affection is expressed in an ineffable prayer.
And so as to show the whole world the sincerity and intensity, of this

---

1 "Love is proved by deeds," S. Gregory, *Homil. in Evang.* xxx, 1.
2 Joan. xiv, 15.   3 "I most gladly will spend and be spent," II Cor. xii, 15.
4 Luc. x, 21.

love, *Ut cognoscat mundus quia diligo Patrem,*[1] Jesus immediately goes to the Garden of Olives where He is to enter into the long series of humiliations and sorrows of His Passion.

This twofold character is found likewise in His love towards mankind. For three days, a multitude of people follow Him, drawn by the charm of His divine words and the splendour of His miracles. But this multitude, having nothing to eat, begins to be overcome with faintness. Jesus knows this. "I have compassion on the multitude," He says, "for behold they have now been with me three days, and have nothing to eat. And if I shall send them fasting to their home, they will faint in the way; for some of them came from afar off": *Misereor super turbam.* What a deep sense of compassion moves His human Heart! And you know how Jesus puts His pity into action: in His blessed Hands, the loaves are multiplied to satisfy the hunger of the four thousand who had followed Him.[2]

Above all, see Him at the tomb of Lazarus. Jesus weeps, He sheds tears, real human tears. Can there be a more touching, a more authentic manifestation of the feelings of His Heart? And at once He puts His power into the service of His love: "Lazarus, come forth."[3]

It is love that is revealed in the gift of self; love which, overflowing from the heart, takes possession of the whole being and of all its activities so as to consecrate them to the interests and glory of the beloved object.

What is to be the extent of this love that we ought to show to Jesus in return for His?

It must first of all include the essential and sovereign love which makes us regard Christ and His Will as the supreme good which we prefer to all things. Practically, this love is summed up in the state of sanctifying grace. Devotion, as we have said, means devotedness; but where is the devotedness of a soul that does not seek to safeguard within her at any price, by a watchful fidelity, the treasure of our Saviour's grace? a soul who in temptation hesitates between the will of Christ Jesus and the suggestions of His eternal enemy?

As you know, it is this love which gives to our life all its value and makes of it a perpetual homage, pleasing to Christ's Heart. Without this essen-

---

1 Joan. xiv, 31.   2 Marc. viii, 2–9.   3 Joan. xi, 43.

tial love, nothing is of any worth in God's sight. Hear in what expressive terms St. Paul has laid stress on this truth: "If I speak with the tongues of men, and of angels, and have not charity, I am become as sounding brass, or a tinkling cymbal. And if I should have prophecy and should know all mysteries and all knowledge, and if I should have all faith, so that I could remove mountains, and have not charity, I am nothing. And if I should distribute all my goods to feed the poor, and if I should deliver my body to be burned, and have not charity, it profiteth me nothing."[1] In other words, I cannot be pleasing to God if I have not in me this essential charity by which I attach myself to Him as to the Sovereign Good. It is too evident that there cannot be true devotion where that essential love does not exist.

Secondly, let us accustom ourselves to do all things, even the smallest, in order to please Christ Jesus. To work, to accept our pains and sufferings, to fulfil our duties of state out of love, so as to be agreeable to Our Lord, in union with the dispositions of His Heart when He lived here below like us, constitutes an excellent practice of devotion towards the Sacred Heart. All our life is thus referred to Him.

It is this, moreover, that gives to our life an increase of fruitfulness. As you know, every act of virtue, of humility, of obedience, of religion, done in a state of grace possesses its own merit, its special perfection, its particular splendour: but when this act is dominated by love, it gains a new efficacy and beauty; without losing anything of its own value, the merit of an act of love is added to it. The Psalmist sings to God, "the queen stood on Thy right hand, in gilded clothing: surrounded with variety": *Adstitit regina a dextris tuis in vestitu deaurato, circumdata varietate.*[2] The queen is the faithful soul in whom Christ reigns by His grace. She stands at the King's right hand, clad in a robe woven of gold which signifies love; the various colours symbolise the different virtues; each one of them keeps its own beauty, but love, which is the deep source of these virtues, enhances their splendour.

Love thus reigns as queen in our heart directing all its movements to the glory of God and of His Son Jesus.

1 Cor. xiii, 1–3.   2 Ps. xliv, 10.

IV

In the same way as the Holy Spirit does not call every soul to shine in an equal manner by the same virtues, so in the matter of private devotion, He leaves them a holy liberty which we ourselves ought carefully to respect. There are souls who feel urged to honour especially the mystery of the Childhood of Jesus; others are attracted by the charms of His Hidden Life; yet others cannot turn themselves away from the meditation of the Passion.

However, devotion to the Sacred Heart of Jesus is one of those which should be especially dear to us. And why? Because it honours Christ Jesus not only in one of His states or particular mysteries, but in the generality and totality of His love, of that love wherein all His mysteries find their deepest meaning. Although being a clearly defined devotion, devotion to the Heart of Jesus bears something that is universal. In honouring the Heart of Christ, it is no longer to Jesus as Infant, Youth, or Victim, that our homage is especially addressed. It is on the Person of Jesus in the plenitude of His love that we especially linger.

Moreover, the general practice of this devotion tends, at the last analysis, to render to Our Lord love for love: *Movet nos ad amandum mutuo*[1]; to penetrate all our activity with love in order to please Christ Jesus. The special exercises of the devotion to the Sacred Heart of Jesus are but so many means of expressing to our Divine Master this reciprocity of love.

Herein is a very precious effect of this devotion. For all Christian religion is summed up in the giving of ourselves, out of love, to Christ, and, through Him, to the Father and Their common Spirit. This point is of capital importance, and I want, before ending this conference, to consider it with you for some moments.

It is a truth, confirmed by the experience of souls, that our spiritual life depends, in great part, on the idea that we *habitually* have of God.

Between us and God there are fundamental relations, based upon our nature as creatures; there exist moral relations resulting from our attitude towards Him; and this attitude is, most often, conditioned by the idea that we have of God.

---

1 Leon. XIII, i, c.

If we form a false idea of God, our efforts to advance will often be vain and barren, because they will not be to the point; if we have an incomplete idea of Him, our spiritual life will be full of imperfections and shortcomings; if our idea of God is true,—as true as is possible here below to a creature living by faith,—our souls will expand safely in the light.

This habitual idea that we form of God is the key to our inner life, not only because it rules our conduct towards Him, but also because, in many cases, it determines God's attitude towards us: God treats us as we treat Him.

But, you will say, does not sanctifying grace make us God's children? Certainly it does; however, in practice, there are souls that do not *act* as the adopted children of the Eternal Father. It would seem as if their condition of children of God had only a nominal value for them; they do not understand that it is a fundamental state which requires to be constantly manifested by acts corresponding to it, and that all spiritual life ought to be the development of the spirit of divine adoption, the spirit we receive at baptism through the virtue of Christ Jesus.

Thus, you may meet with some who habitually consider God as the Israelites regarded Him. God revealed Himself to the Israelites amidst the thunders and lightnings of Sinai.[1] For this "stiff-necked people,"[2] inclined to infidelity and idolatry, God was only a Lord Who must be adored, a Master Who must be served, a Judge Who must be feared. The Israelites had received, as St. Paul says, "the spirit of bondage in fear": *Spiritum servitutis in timore.*[3] God appeared to them only in the splendour of His Majesty and the sovereignty of His power. You know that He treated them with rigorous justice: the earth opened to swallow up the guilty Hebrews[4]; those who touched the ark of the covenant when their functions did not give them the right to do so were struck dead.[5] Poisonous serpents destroyed the murmurers[6]; scarcely dared they pronounce the name of Jehovah; once a year, the High Priest entered alone, in awe and trembling, into the Holy of Holies, armed with the blood of the victims immolated for sin.[7] This was "the spirit of bondage."

There are souls that habitually live only in dispositions of purely servile

---

1 Exod. xix, 16 sq.   2 Deut. xxxi, 27.   3 Rom. viii, 15.
4 Num. xvi, 32.   5 II Reg. vi, 6–7.   6 Num. xxi, 5–6.
7 Levit. xvi, 11 sq.

fear; if they were not afraid of God's chastisement, they would not mind offending Him. They habitually regard God only as a master, and do not seek to please Him. They are like those servants Christ Jesus speaks of in the parable. A King, before going into a far country, calls his servants and confides to them some talents—pieces of money—which they are to trade with until his return. One of the servants lays up his talent in safety, keeping it without turning it to account. He says to the King on his return: "Lord, behold here is thy pound, which I have kept laid up in a napkin. For I feared thee, because thou art an austere man; thou takest up what thou didst not lay down, and thou reapest that which thou didst not sow." And what does the King answer? He takes the negligent servant at his word. "Out of thy own mouth I judge thee, thou wicked servant. Thou knewest that I was an austere man...why then didst thou not give my money into the bank?" And the King commands that the money which had been given to the servant shall be taken away from him.[1]

Such souls act with God only at a distance, they treat with Him only as with a great Lord, and God treats them in consequence according to this attitude. He does not give Himself fully to them; between them and God, personal intimacy cannot exist; in them, inward expansion is impossible.

Other souls, more numerous perhaps, habitually regard God as a great benefactor; they act as a rule only in view of the reward: *Propter retributionem.*[2] This working in view of the recompense is not a false idea. We see Christ Jesus compare His Father to a Master who rewards,—and with what magnificent liberality!—the faithful servant: "Enter into the joy of thy Lord."[3] He Himself tells us that He ascends into Heaven to prepare a place for us.[4]

But when, as happens with certain souls, this attitude is habitual to the point of becoming exclusive, besides being wanting in nobility, it does not fully respond to the spirit of the Gospel. Hope is a Christian virtue, it powerfully sustains the soul in the midst of adversity, trial and temptation; but it is not the most perfect of the theological virtues, which are the specific virtues of our condition as children of God. Which is then the most perfect virtue? Which is the one which carries the palm? It is,

1 Luc. xix, 12–13, 20–24. 2 Ps. cxviii, 112. 3 Matth. xxv, 21.
4 Joan. xiv, 2.

replies St. Paul, charity: *Nunc manent fides, spes, caritas, tria haec: major autem horum est caritas.*[1]

V

This is why,—without losing view of the fear of outraging God Who created us, although this must not be the fear of the slave who dreads punishment; without putting aside the thought of the reward which awaits us, if we are faithful,—we ought to seek to have habitually towards God that attitude, composed of filial confidence and love, which Christ Jesus revealed to us as being that of the New Covenant.

Christ, indeed, knows better than anyone what our relations with God ought to be, He knows the divine secrets. If we listen to Him we do not run any risk of going astray: He is Truth itself. Now, what attitude does He want us to have with God? Under what aspect does He want us to contemplate and adore Him? Undoubtedly, He teaches us that God is the Supreme Master Whom we must adore: "It is written: Thou shalt adore the Lord thy God, and Him only shalt thou serve."[2] But this God Whom we must adore is a Father; *Veri adoratores adorabunt Patrem in spiritu et veritate, nam et Pater tales quaerit qui adorent eum.*[3]

Is adoration the only disposition which we ought to have in our heart? Does it constitute the one attitude which we must have towards this Father Who is God? No, Christ Jesus adds thereto love, and a love that is full, perfect, without reserve or restriction. When Jesus was asked which was the greatest of the commandments what did He answer? "Thou shalt love"[4]: love of complacency towards this Lord of such great majesty, towards this God of such high perfection; love of benevolence which seeks to procure the glory of the One Who is the object of this love; love of reciprocity towards a God Who "hath first loved us."[5]

It is God's will that our relations with Him should be impregnated at

---

1 "Now there remain faith, hope, and charity, these three: but the greatest of these is charity," I Cor. xiii, 13.
2 Deut. vi, 13; Luc. iv, 8.
3 "The true adorers shall adore the Father in spirit and in truth. For the Father also seeketh such to adore him," Joan. iv, 23.
4 Marc. xii, 30. 5 I Joan. iv, 10.

371

the same time with filial reverence and profound love. Without reverence, love runs the risk of degenerating into a liberty of the wrong kind, a most dangerous want of restraint; without the love which lifts us up on its wings to our Father, the soul lives in error, and outrages the divine gift.

And so as to safeguard within us these two dispositions of reverence and love, which may seem contradictory, God communicates to us the Spirit of His Son Jesus, Who, by His gifts of fear and piety, harmonises within us, in the proportion that they require, the most intimate adoration and most tender love: *Quoniam estis filii, misit Deus spiritum Filii sui in corda vestra.*[1]

According to the teaching of Jesus Himself, this Spirit ought to govern and direct all our life: it is "the Spirit of adoption" of the New Covenant, which St. Paul contrasts with "the spirit of bondage" of the Old Law.

You will perhaps ask the reason of this difference? It is because, since the Incarnation, God sees all humanity in His Son Jesus; on account of Him, He envelops entire humanity in the same look of complacency of which His Son, our Elder Brother, is the object. This is why He wishes that like Him, with Him, through Him, we should live as his "most dear children": *Sicut filii carissimi.*[2]

You may say too: And how are we to love God Whom we do not see: *Deum nemo vidit unquam?*[3] It is true that here below the Divine light is inaccessible[4]; but God reveals Himself to us in His Son Jesus: *Ipse illuxit cordibus nostris...in facie Christi Jesu.*[5] The Incarnate Word is the authentic revelation of God and of His perfections; and the love that Christ shows us is but the manifestation of the love that God has for us.

The love of God indeed is in itself incomprehensible; it is completely beyond us; it has not entered into the mind of man to conceive what God is; His perfections are not distinct from His nature: the love of God is God Himself: *Deus caritas est.*[6]

How then shall we have a true idea of God's love? In seeing God as He manifests Himself to us under a tangible form. And what is this form? It

---

1 "Because you are sons, God hath sent the Spirit of his Son into your hearts," Gal. iv, 6.
2 Ephes. v, 1. 3 Joan. i, 18. 4 I Tim. vi, 16.
5 "He hath shined in our hearts...in the face of Christ Jesus," II Cor. iv, 6.
6 I Joan. iv, 8.

is the Humanity of Jesus. Christ is God, but God revealing Himself to us. The contemplation of the Sacred Humanity of Jesus is the surest way for arriving at the true knowledge of God. He that seeth Him, seeth the Father[1]; the love that the Incarnate Word shows us, reveals the Father's love towards us, for the Word and the Father are but One: *Ego et Pater unum sumus.*[2]

This order once established does not change. Christianity is the love of God manifested to the world through Christ, and all our religion ought to be resumed in contemplating this love in Christ, and in responding to the love of Christ so that we may thereby attain to God.

Such is the divine plan; such is the thought of God concerning us. If we do not adapt ourselves to it, there will be for us neither light nor truth; there will be neither security nor salvation.

Now, the essential attitude that this Divine plan requires of us is that of adopted children. We still remain beings drawn out of nothing, and before this Father of an incommensurable majesty[3] we ought to cast ourselves down in humblest reverence; but to these fundamental relations which arise from our conditions as creatures, are superposed, not to destroy but to crown them, relations infinitely higher, wider and more intimate which result from our divine adoption, that are all summed up in the service of God through love.

This fundamental attitude responding to the reality of our heavenly adoption is particularly furthered by devotion to the Heart of Jesus. In causing us to contemplate the human love of Christ for us, this devotion admits us into the secret of divine love; in inclining our souls to answer to it by a life whereof love is the motive power, it maintains in us those dispositions of filial piety which we ought to have towards the Father.

When we receive Our Lord in Holy Communion, we possess within us that Divine Heart which is a furnace of love. Let us ask Him earnestly that He will Himself grant us to understand this love, for, in this, one ray from on high is more efficacious than all human reasoning; let us ask Him to enkindle within us the love of His Person. "If, by Our Lord's grace," says St. Teresa, "His love is imprinted one day in our heart, all will

---

1 Cf. Joan. xiv, 9.   2 Joan. x. 30.   3 Hymn *Te Deum.*

become easy to us; very rapidly and without trouble we shall come by this means to the works of love."[1]

If this love for the Person of Jesus is in our heart, our activity will spring forth from it. We may meet with difficulties, be subject to great trials, undergo violent temptations; if we love Christ Jesus, these difficulties, these trials, these temptations will find us steadfast: *Aquae multae non potuerunt exstinguere caritatem.*[2] For when the love of Christ urges us we shall not wish any longer to live for ourselves, but for Him Who loved us and delivered Himself up for us: *Ut et qui vivunt, jam non sibi vivant sed ei qui pro ipsis mortuus est.*[3]

---

1 *Life* written by herself, chap. xxii.—"Begin to love the Person (of Christ): the love of the Person will make you love the doctrine, and the love of the doctrine will lead you gently and mightily to the practice. Do not neglect to study Jesus Christ and to meditate upon His mysteries; it is this that will inspire you to love Him; the desire to please Him will hence follow and this desire will bear fruit in good works." Bossuet, Meditations upon the Gospel. The Last Supper, 1st part, 89th, day.
2 "Many waters cannot quench charity," Cant. viii, 7.   3 II Cor. v, 15.

CHRIST THE CROWN OF
ALL THE SAINTS

(All Saints)

SUMMARY.—Christ is inseparable from His Mystical Body.—I. The
motives that we have for tending to perfection: the will of God and the
infinite price that Jesus paid for our perfection.—II. Fundamental character of our holiness: it is the supernatural realisation of the Divine plan
of our free predestination in Jesus Christ.—III. How Christ is for us the
source of all holiness in being the Way, the Truth, and the Life.—IV. Dispositions that we ought to have in our seeking after holiness: profound
humility and absolute confidence.—V. Practical conclusions: to honour
the Saints; to seek to imitate them, by remaining united to Jesus Christ;
not to allow ourselves to be cast down by our miseries and trials.—VI.
The end of the eternal plan for our holiness is to magnify the power of
the grace of Jesus: *In laudem gloriae gratiae suae.*

THE God and Father of Our Lord Jesus Christ...hath subjected
all things under His feet, and hath made Him Head over all
the Church which is His body, and the fulness of Him Who
is filled all in all."[1]

These words of St. Paul show us the mystery of Christ Jesus considered
in His Mystical Body which is the Church.

In all the preceding conferences, we have had the joy of contemplating the Person of Jesus Himself, His states, His abasements, His conflicts,
His greatness, His triumph; we have not been able to turn our gaze away

---

1 Ephes. i, 3, 22–23.

from this adorable Humanity which is for us the example of every virtue and the one source of every grace.

But all the mysteries of the God-Man tend to the establishment and sanctification of the Church: *Propter nos et propter nostram salutem.*[1] Christ came in order to form to Himself a society which might appear glorious before Him "not having spot or wrinkle or any such thing; but holy and without blemish."[2]

So close and intimate is the union contracted with the Church that He is the Vine and she forms the branches; that He is the Head and she forms the body; that He is the Bridegroom and she has the rank of Bride. United together they compose what St. Augustine so well calls the "Whole Christ."[3]

Christ and the Church are inseparable; one is not to be conceived of without the other. This is why, at the end of these conferences upon the Person of Jesus Christ and His mysteries, we must speak of this Church that St. Paul calls the "completing" of Christ, and without which the mystery of Christ does not attain its perfection.

Here below, as you know, this ineffable union is wrought by faith, grace and charity; it is consummated in the splendours of heaven and the Beatific Vision. Thus, having reached the end of the Liturgical cycle, the Church celebrates in one solemn feast—the feast of All Saints—the glory of the kingdom of Jesus. It joins together in the same praise the entire multitude of the company of the elect in order to exalt their triumph and their joy, and at the same time to urge us to follow their example so that we may share in their felicity.

For this company is one, as Christ is one. To time succeeds eternity; here below souls are formed to perfection, but the term is only to be found in this glorious company; moreover, our degree of beatitude is measured by the degree of charity attained at the hour when we leave this earth.

I will first point out the reasons we have for tending to this heavenly beatitude; we will afterwards see the means of coming to it.

---

1 "For us and for our salvation," Creed of the Mass.   2 Ephes. v, 27.
3 *De Unitate Eccles.* 4.

I

The first reason that we have for tending to holiness is "the will of God": *Haec est voluntas Dei, sanctificatio vestra.*[1] God not only wills that we should be saved, but that we should become saints. And why does God will this? Because He Himself is holy: *Sancti estote quoniam ego sanctus sum.*[2] God is holiness itself; we are His creatures; He wishes the creature to reflect His image;—still more, He wills that, being His children, we should be perfect as He, our Heavenly Father, is perfect.[3] Such is the very precept of Jesus.

God finds His glory in our holiness. Never let us forget this truth: each degree of holiness to which we attain, each sacrifice we make in order to acquire it, each virtue which is to adorn our souls will be a glory for God eternally.

We sing every day, and it seems to me that every day it is with more gladness: *Tu solus sanctus Jesus Christe*[4]: "Thou only art holy...O Jesus Christ." And that is why Jesus Christ is the great glory of God. Throughout all eternity He will give infinite glory to His Father, He will stand before the face of His Father, showing Him His five Wounds, the magnificent expression of the sovereign fidelity and perfect love with which He always did that which His Father required of Him: *Quae placita sunt ei facio semper.*[5]

It is the same with the Saints. They stand "before the throne of God,"[6] and unceasingly render Him glory. The burning zeal of the apostles, the testimony of the martyrs, the profound knowledge of the doctors, the dazzling purity of the virgins constitute so much pleasing homage to God.

In this "multitude which no man could number,"[7] each saint shines with a special splendour; and God will eternally look with complacency upon each saint's efforts, the conflicts, the victories which are so many trophies laid down at His feet to honour His infinite perfections and to acknowledge His rights.

It is, then, a lawful ambition for us to tend with all our strength to procure this glory which God derives from our holiness; we ought ardently

---

1 I Thes. iv, 3.   2 Levit. xi, 44; xix, 2.   3 Matth. v, 48.
4 Gloria of the Mass.   5 Joan. viii, 29.   6 Apoc. vii, 9.
7 Ibid.

to aspire to make a part of that blessed company in which God Himself takes His delight: this is truly a motive for us not to be contented with a mediocre perfection, but continually to have it in view to respond as fully as possible to God's desire: *Sancti estote quia ego sanctus sum.*

Another reason is that the higher our holiness, the more we exalt the price of the Blood of Jesus.

St. Paul tells us that Christ delivered Himself up to death and the death of the Cross in order to sanctify the Church. That was the aim of His sacrifice.

Now one of the sources of the most poignant distress for the Heart of Jesus during His agony in the Garden of Olives was the perspective of the unavailingness of His Blood for so many souls who were to refuse the Divine gift: *Quae utilitas in sanguine meo?*[1] Christ knew that a single drop of His Blood would have sufficed to purify whole worlds, and sanctify multitudes of souls; out of obedience to His Father He consented with unspeakable love to shed, to the last drop, that Blood which contained the infinite virtue of the Divinity. And yet it might well be asked: "What profit is there in this blood?"

The great ambition of the Heart of Christ is to glorify His Father; this is why He desires with so much vehemence, *quomodo coarctor,*[2] to give His life so as to bring to His Father innumerable souls who will bear much fruit of life and holiness: *In hoc clarificatus est Pater meus, ut fructum* PLURIMUM *afferatis.*[3]

But how many understand the ardour of the love of Jesus? how many respond to the desires of His Heart? So many souls do not observe the divine laws! Others keep the commandments; but very few yield themselves up to Jesus and the action of His Spirit with that fulness which leads to holiness.

Happy are those souls that give themselves up unreservedly to the divine good pleasure! United to Christ, Who is the Vine, they bear much fruit and glorify the heavenly Father; they proclaim, above all, the virtue of the Blood of Jesus.

What in fact is the song that is sung by the elect whom St. John shows us, in his Apocalypse, casting themselves down before the Lamb? "Thou

---

1 "What profit is there in my blood?" Ps. xxix, 10.   2 Luc. xii, 50.
3 Joan. xv, 8.

wast slain, and hast redeemed us to God in Thy Blood, out of every tribe, and tongue, and people, and nation....To Him that sitteth on the throne and to the Lamb, benediction, and honour, and glory, and power, for ever and ever."[1] The saints confess that they are the trophies of the Blood of the Lamb, trophies so much the more glorious in proportion to the greatness of their holiness.

Let us then endeavour with all the ardour of our souls to purify ourselves more and more in the Blood of Jesus, to bring forth those fruits of life and holiness that Christ Jesus merited for us by His Passion and Death. If we become saints, our hearts will thrill, throughout eternity, with the joy that we shall give to Christ in singing the triumph of His Precious Blood and the almighty power of His grace.

II

How are we to attain this holiness so pleasing to God, so glorious for Jesus, and, for our souls, this inexhaustible spring of eternal joy of which we cannot fathom the depths? For, says St. Paul, it has not entered into the heart of a man to conceive the beatitude that God has prepared for them that love Him.[2] What path is to be followed whereby to arrive at that blessed state where the soul will contemplate all truth and rejoice in the fulness of all good?

This question is of first importance, but before replying to it, I would first of all show what is the proper character of our holiness. We can, in fact, only choose our way in all security if we understand the end that is to be attained. If we well understood the character that, according to God's plan, our holiness is to assume, the path to be followed in order to come to it would no longer be a secret for us.

What then is this character? What is the essential quality that God requires of our perfection?

It is that this perfection be supernatural.

You are aware of this truth which I have set forth at length elsewhere; but it is so vital that it will not be without interest to return to it for some moments.

---

1 Apoc. v, 9, 13.   2 I Cor. ii, 9.

As I have often said, the dawn of the divine mercies towards us dates from the eternal choice that God, freely, and out of love, made of us: *Elegit nos...ante mundi constitutionem ut essemus sancti.*[1]

Let us consider this election for an instant.

You know that the Eternal Father has ever contemplated, and unceasingly contemplates His Word, His Son; in Him, He sees Himself, with His infinite perfections, for this single Word expresses in divine language all that God is. Our own thoughts are finite, bounded, paltry, and yet, in order to express them, we must have recourse to a great variety of words; with a single word, God expresses His thought which is infinite; He comprehends Himself in His Word.

In order to understand anything fully, St. Thomas somewhere says, it is necessary to know likewise the manifold imitations of which this thing is susceptible.[2] God, Who comprehends Himself perfectly, sees in His Word all the different manners in which creatures can reflect or reproduce His perfections. God did not throw things into space haphazard: He did not create with a blind strength. Being Infinite Intelligence, He made all things according to the plans conceived in His Eternal Wisdom. In contemplating His Word, God sees, with a single glance, the boundless multitude of possible beings; and, from all eternity, He decided to choose, out of this multitude, creatures which should realise in themselves and outwardly manifest, although in a limited degree, the infinite perfections of His Word.

In the present order of the divine dispensation, God foresaw that man, made by Him the king of the earthly creation, would not maintain himself at the height of his election and would err from the plan that his Creator had traced in order to unite him to Himself. Divine Wisdom was not taken unprepared; to bring back fallen man, the thought of God rested before all upon Him Whom St. Paul calls "the Firstborn of every creature": *Primogenitus omnis creaturae,*[3] and this is the Incarnate Word.

The Father contemplated His Incarnate Word, made flesh. He saw in this Humanity hypostatically united to His Word the sum, the complete synthesis of all created perfection; God revealed to us on Thabor that

---

1 "He chose us...before the foundation of the world, that we should be holy," Ephes. i, 4.
2 I, q. xiv, a. 5 and 6; q. xv, a. 2.   3 Col. i, 15.

this God-Man was the masterpiece of His designs and the object of all His complacency: *Hic est Filius meus dilectus in quo mihi bene complacui.*[1]

This Humanity of Christ expresses outwardly the Divine Word; it was freely chosen, out of love.

That is not all. God willed to give a train of followers to His Son: that is the unnumbered multitude of the saints. The saints are so many reproductions of the Word, under a less perfect form. The ideal for each one of us is in the Word; each of us ought to be for God a special interpretation of one of the infinite aspects of His Word. This is why we sing of each saint: "There is not found one like to him": *Non est inventus similis illi.*[2] There are not two saints who interpret and manifest Christ with the same perfection.

When we are in heaven, we shall contemplate, in the midst of unspeakable joy, the Blessed Trinity. We shall see the Word, the Son, proceeding from the Father as the archetype of all possible perfection; we shall see that the Sacred Humanity of Jesus interpreted in a universal manner the perfections of the Word to Whom it was united; we shall see that God has associated with Christ so many brethren who reproduce in themselves the divine perfections, manifested and made tangible here below in Christ Jesus. So that Christ is "the Firstborn amongst many brethren" who are to be like unto Him: *Ut ipse primogenitus in multis fratribus.*[3]

Never let us forget that God chose us in His Son Jesus: *Elegit nos in ipso.*[4] In that eternal decree, we find the source of our true greatness. When, by our holiness, we fulfil God's decree concerning us, we become for Him like a part of the glory that His Son Jesus is for Him: *Splendor gloriae.*[5] We are like the prolongation, the rays of this glory, when we strive, each one in his place, to interpret and to realise in ourselves the divine ideal, of which the Incarnate Word is the unique Exemplar.

Such is the Divine Plan; such is our predestination; that we should be conformed to the Incarnate Word, Son of God by nature, and our model of sanctity: *Praedestinavit (nos) conformes fieri imaginis Filii sui.*[6]

It is from this eternal decree, from this predestination full of love that

---

1 "This is my beloved Son, in whom I am well pleased," Matth. xvii, 5.
2 Office for Confessor Pontiff. 2nd Ant. of Lauds; cf. Eccli. xliv, 20.
3 Rom. viii, 29.   4 Ephes. i, 4.   5 Hebr. i, 3.   6 Rom. viii, 29.

for each one of us dates the series of all God's mercies. In order to carry out this plan, in order that His designs for us may be completed, God gives us grace, a mysterious participation in His nature; by grace we become, in His Son Jesus Who has merited it for us, the true adoptive children of God.

We have then not only the simple relation of creatures with God; we have not only to unite ourselves to Him by the homage and the duties of a natural religion based upon our condition of created beings. Without anything pertaining to these relations or duties being destroyed or diminished we enter into more intimate relations with God, those of children, which create in us special duties, towards a Father Who loves us: *Estote imitatores Dei sicut filii carissimi.*[1] Relations and duties wholly supernatural, because they exceed the exigences and rights of our nature, and because the grace of Jesus alone renders them possible.

You now understand what is the fundamental character of holiness for us.

We can only be saints if we are so according to the Divine plan: that is to say by the grace that we owe to Christ Jesus. That is the primordial condition. Therefore His grace is called sanctifying. This is so true that outside this grace even salvation is not possible. In the kingdom of the elect there are only souls that resemble Jesus; now the fundamental similitude which we must have with Him is only brought about by grace.

As you see, God has Himself determined the character of our holiness; to wish to give it another character is, as St. Paul says "to beat the air": *Aerem verberans*[2]; God Himself has traced the way that we must follow; not to take it is to err and finally be lost: *Ego sum via: nemo venit ad Patrem nisi per me*[3]; He Himself has laid the foundation of all perfection, outside of which we only build upon sand: *Fundamentum aliud nemo potest ponere praeter id quod positum est, quod est Christus Jesus.*[4]

This is true of salvation, this is true of holiness: holiness only draws its principle and finds its support in the grace of Christ Jesus.

---

1 "Be ye therefore followers of God, as most dear children," Ephes. v, 1–2.
2 I Cor. ix, 26.
3 "I am the way....No man cometh to the Father, but by me," Joan. xiv, 6.
4 "For other foundation no man can lay, but that which is laid: which is Christ Jesus," I Cor. iii, 11.

III

We must go to God *in His way*; we shall only be saints in the measure wherein we adapt ourselves to the divine plan. I have pointed out the broad outline of this magnificent plan; let us see more in detail how Christ Jesus is for us the source of all sanctity.

Let us suppose a soul who in an impulse of generosity, acting under the influence of the Holy Spirit, kneels before the Heavenly Father and says to Him: "O Father, I love Thee, I desire nothing so much as Thy glory; I wish during all eternity to glorify Thee by my holiness; what am I to do? show me what Thou dost expect of me." What would the Father answer? He would show His Son, Christ Jesus, and would say: "Behold My beloved Son, in Whom I am well pleased, hear ye Him." Then He would leave this soul at the feet of Jesus.

And what does Jesus say? *Ego sum via, et veritas, et vita*[1]: "I am the Way, the Truth and the Life." These three words have such a depth of meaning that I would like to meditate on them with you. They are words which ought to remain engraved in the depths of our hearts.

You desire to go to My Father? says Jesus. You wish to unite yourself to Him Who is the Fountainhead of all good, and the principle of all perfection? You do well; it is I Who have made this desire arise in your heart; but you can only bring it into effect by Me. *Ego sum via: nemo venit ad Patrem nisi per me.*

As you know, there is an infinite distance between the creature and the Creator; between the one who has only being in participation and He Who is the Being subsistent of Himself. Take the angel that is the highest in the heavenly hierarchies: between him and God there is an abyss that no created strength can cross.

But God has thrown a bridge across this abyss. Christ, the God-Man, binds man to God. The Word is made Flesh: in Him a human nature is united to the Divinity: the two natures, Divine and Human, are united in an embrace, so intimate, so indissoluble that there is only one Person, that of the Word, in which the human nature subsists. The abyss of separation is filled up.

---

1 Joan. xiv, 6.

Christ being God, being one with His Father, is the way that leads to God. If then we would go to God, let us strive to have boundless faith in the power that Jesus has to unite us to His Father. What indeed does Our Lord say? "Father I will that where I am, they also whom Thou hast given Me may be with Me": *Pater, volo ut ubi sum ego, et illi sint mecum.*[1] And where is Christ? "In the bosom of the Father."

When our faith is intense, and we give ourselves wholly to Jesus, He draws us with Him *In sinu Patris.*[2] For Jesus is at the same time the Way and the End. He is the Way by His Humanity, *via qua imus;* He is the End by His Divinity, *patria quo imus.*[3] It is this that makes the great security of this way: it is perfect, and contains in it the term itself.

It is an excellent thing in prayer to make acts of faith in the almighty power that Jesus has of leading us to His Father.

O Christ Jesus, I believe that You are true God and true Man, that You are the Divine Way, the Way of an infinite efficacy for making me bridge the gulf that separates me from God; I believe that Your sacred Humanity is perfect and so powerful that, despite my miseries, my shortcomings, my weaknesses, it can bring me thither where You are in the Father's bosom. Grant that I may listen to Your words, that I may follow Your example and never be separated from You!

It is a precious grace to have found the way that leads to the end; but it is needful too to walk therein in the light. This end is supernatural, above our created powers; therefore the light which must bathe our path with its brightness must likewise come to us from on high.

God is so magnificent that He will be Himself our light: in Heaven, our holiness will be to contemplate the infinite light, to derive from its splendour the source of all life and all joy: *In lumine tuo videbimus lumen.*[4]

Here below, this light is inaccessible to us on account of its brilliance, our sight is too feeble to bear it. And yet it is necessary for us in order to attain the end. Who will be our light? Christ Jesus. *Ego sum veritas*: "I am the Truth." He alone can reveal the infinite light to us. He is God come forth from God, Light arising from Light: *Deus de Deo, lumen de*

---

1 Joan. xvii, 24.   2 Joan. i, 18.
3 S. Augustine, *Sermo xcii,* c. 3; *Sermo cxxiii,* c. 3.
4 "In thy light we shall see light," Ps. xxxv, 10.

lumine....[1] Being true God, He is Light itself, without shadow of darkness: *Deus lux est, et tenebrae in eo non sunt ullae.*[2]

This light has come down into our valleys, tempering the infinite splendour of its beams beneath the veil of the Sacred Humanity. Our eyes, which are so feeble, can contemplate this divine light which is hidden and revealed at the same time under the weakness of passible flesh: *Illuxit in cordibus nostris...in facie Christi Jesu*[3]; it "enlighteneth every man that cometh into this world": *Lux vera quae illuminat omnem hominem.*[4]

Christ Jesus, the Eternal Word, teaches us to look upon God, He reveals Him to us. He says to us: I am the Truth; if you believe in Me, not only shall you learn to know the truth concerning all things, but you are in the truth: "He that followeth Me, walketh not in darkness, but shall have the light of life."[5]

Hence what have we to do so as to walk in the light? To be guided according to the words of Jesus, according to the maxims of His Gospel, to consider all things in the light of the words of the Incarnate Word. Jesus tells us, for example, that the blessed who possess His Kingdom are the poor in spirit, the meek, those that mourn, those that hunger and thirst after justice, the merciful, the clean of heart, the peacemakers, those that suffer persecution for justice' sake.[6] We must believe Him, unite ourselves to Him by an act of faith, lay down at His feet, in homage, the assent of our intelligence to His Word. We must strive to live in humility, gentleness, mercy, purity, to keep peace with all, to bear contradiction with patience and confidence.

If we thus live in faith, the Spirit of Christ will little by little take possession of our soul to guide it in all things, to direct its activity, according to the Gospel. The soul, putting aside the merely natural lights of self judgment, sees all things through the eyes of the Lord: *Erit tibi Dominus in lucem.*[7] Living in the Truth, the soul constantly advances in the Way; united to the Truth, she lives by the Spirit of Truth: the thoughts, affections, desires of Jesus become her thoughts, affections and desires; she does nothing that is not fully in accord with Christ's will. Is not this the

---

1 Creed of the Mass. 2 I Joan. i, 5.
3 "He hath shined in our hearts...in the face of Christ Jesus," II Cor. iv, 6.
4 Joan. i, 9. 5 Ibid. viii, 12. 6 Matth. v, 3–11.
7 "The Lord shall be unto thee for a light," Isa. lx, 19.

very foundation of all holiness?

It is not enough for us to have found the way, to walk in the light, we need besides the food that sustains us on our pilgrimage. Again it is Christ Who gives it to us: *Et vita.*

In God is infinite life: *Apud te est fons vitae.*[1] The torrent of this ineffable life has filled Christ's soul with the fulness of its power: *Sicut Pater habet vitam in semetipso, sic dedit et Filio habere vitam in semetipso.*[2]

The Son comes to give us a share in this Divine life: *Ego veni ut vitam habeant, et abundantius habeant.*[3] He tells us: "As I live by the Father, so He that eateth Me, the same shall live by Me": *Et qui manducat me, et ipse vivet propter me.*[4]

To live on this Divine life is holiness. Indeed to put away all that can destroy or diminish the supernatural life within us—sin, infidelity, attachment to creatures, purely natural views;—to develop the supernatural life by the virtues of faith, hope and charity which unite us to God, is for us, as I have said,[5] the double element of our holiness.

In being Himself the Life, Christ Jesus becomes our holiness, because He is the very source thereof: *Christus Jesus factus est nobis...sanctificatio.*[6] In giving Himself to us in Communion, He gives us His Humanity, His Divinity; He makes love active; He transforms us little by little unto Himself, so that we live no longer for ourselves, but by Him and for Him. He establishes between our desires and His desires, between our will and His will, such a likeness, such accordance, that it is no longer we who live, but He Who lives in us: *Vivo autem jam non ego, vivit vero in me Christus.*[7] No formula is more expressive than these words of the Apostle, to sum up all the work of holiness.

---

1 "For with thee is the fountain of life," Ps. xxxv, 10.
2 "For as the Father hath life in himself, so he hath given to the Son also to have life in himself," Joan. v, 26.
3 "I am come that they may have life and may have it more abundantly," Ibid. x, 10.
4 Ibid. vi, 58.   5 Cf. p. 287 & following.   6 Cf. I Cor. i, 30.
7 Gal. ii, 20.

IV

From this doctrine arise the sentiments that ought to animate us in seeking after holiness: a deep humility on account of our weakness, an absolute confidence in Christ Jesus. Our supernatural life oscillates between two poles: on the one hand we ought to have the intimate conviction of our powerlessness to attain perfection without God's help; on the other hand we ought to be filled with an unshaken hope of finding everything in the grace of Christ Jesus.

Because it is supernatural, because God—sovereignly Master of His designs and gifts—has placed it above the exigences and rights of our created nature, the holiness to which we are called is inaccessible without divine grace. Our Lord has told us: "Without Me you can do nothing," *Sine me* NIHIL, *potestis facere.*[1] St. Augustine[2] remarks that Christ Jesus did not say: "Without Me you cannot do great things," but: "Without me you can do nothing" which will bring you to eternal life. St. Paul has explained in detail this doctrine of our Divine Master: we are incapable of having "of ourselves," *quasi ex nobis,* a single thought that is of any value for heaven; in this domain all "our sufficiency is from God": *Sufficientia nostra ex Deo est.*[3] It is He Who gives us the power to will, and to bring all things to their supernatural end: *Deus est qui operatur in vobis et velle et perficere, pro bona voluntate.*[4] So, then, we cannot do anything for our holiness without divine grace.

Ought we therefore to be cast down? Quite the contrary. The intimate conviction of this powerlessness should neither lead us to discouragement, nor serve to excuse our idleness. If we cannot do anything without Christ, with Him we can do all things. *Omnia possum in eo qui me confortat*[5]: "I can do all things in Him Who strengtheneth me," St. Paul tells us again. Whatsoever be our trials, our difficulties, our weakness, we can, through Christ, reach the highest sanctity.

Why is this? Because in Him "are hid all the treasures of wisdom and knowledge"[6]; because, "in Him dwelleth all the fulness of the Godhead

---

1 Joan. xv, 5.   2 Tract. in Joan lxxxi, 3.   3 II Cor. iii, 5.
4 "For it is God who worketh in you, both to will and to accomplish, according to his good will," Philipp. ii, 13.
5 Ibid. iv, 13.   6 Col. ii, 3.

corporally"[1] and being our Head He has the power of making us partakers of this fulness of life and holiness,[2] so that nothing is wanting to us in any grace: *Ita ut nihil vobis desit in ulla gratia!*[3]

What assurance faith gives to us in these truths? Christ Jesus is ours, and in Him we find all. *Quomodo non etiam cum illo omnia nobis donavit?*[4] What then can prevent us from becoming saints? If at the last judgment God asks us: "Why have you not reached the height of your vocation? why have you not attained the holiness whereunto I called you?" We have no right to reply: "Lord, my weakness was too great, the difficulties insurmontable, the trials above my strength." God would answer us: "Of yourselves, it is but too true that you can do nothing, but I have given you My Son; in Him nothing has been lacking to you of that which was needful; His grace is all-powerful, and through Him you could have united yourself to the very source of life."

That is too true! A great genius, the greatest perhaps that the world has known, a man who had passed his youth in sin, who had emptied the cup of pleasure, whose mind was attracted by all the errors of his time, Augustine, overcome by grace, was converted and reached the highest sanctity. One day, as he himself relates, urged by grace, and held back by evil inclinations, he saw children, young girls, virgins shining with purity, widows venerable by their virtue; and he seemed to hear this gentle invitation given by a voice that said to him: *Tu non poteris quod isti, quod istae?*[5] "What these children, these maidens do, cannot you do; what they are, cannot you become?" And despite the ardour of the blood that beat in his veins, despite his strong passions and long habits of sin, Augustine yielded himself up to grace, and grace made of him, for all eternity, one of its most magnificent trophies.

When we celebrate the Feast of All Saints, we ought to repeat to ourselves the words that St. Augustine heard: *Cur non poteris quod isti, quod istae?* What reasons have we for not tending to holiness? Oh, I know well what each one is tempted to say: "I have such or such a difficulty, I have such or such a trial to contend with, I cannot become a saint." But be sure that all the saints have met with such difficulties, such trials, and

---

1 Ibid. 9.   2 Joan. i, 16.   3 I Cor. i, 7.
4 "How hath he not also, with him, given us all things?" Rom. viii, 32.
5 Confess. lib. viii, c. 11.

much greater ones than yours.

Thus then none can say, Holiness is not for me. What can make it impossible? God desires it for us: He wills us to be saints for His glory and our joy: *Haec est voluntas Dei, sanctificatio vestra.*[1] God does not mock us. When Our Lord says to us, "Be perfect,"[2] He knows all that He is asking of us, and that He requires nothing above our power when we rely upon His grace.

He who would attempt to arrive at perfection by his own strength, would commit the sin of Lucifer, who said: "I will exalt my throne above the stars of God....I will ascend above the height of the clouds, I will be like the Most High."[3] Satan was overthrown and cast down into the abyss.

As for us, what shall we say? what shall we do? We nourish the same ambition as this proud angel; we wish to reach the same height contemplated by him. But whilst he claimed to attain it of himself, we declare that without Christ Jesus we can do nothing. We say that it is with Christ and through Him that we can enter into the heavens. "O Christ Jesus, I have such faith in You that I believe You powerful enough to work this marvel of raising a finite creature, such as I am, not only up to the hierarchies of angels, but up to God Himself; it is by You alone that we can reach this divine height. I aspire, with all the energies of my soul, to that sublimity to which Your Father has predestined us. I long ardently, as You have asked for us, to be a partaker in Your own glory, to share the joy You have Yourself as Son of God. I aspire to this supreme felicity, but only through You; I desire that my eternity should be spent in singing Your praises, and in ceaselessly repeating with the elect: *Redemisti nos, Domine, in sanguine tuo.* Yes, Lord, it is You Who have saved us, it is Your Precious Blood shed for us that has opened to us the gates of Your Kingdom and prepared for us a place in the incomparable company of Your saints; to You be praise, honour, and glory for ever!"

A soul that lives ever with a like sense of humility and confidence gives great glory to Christ Jesus, because her whole life is the echo of the Saviour's own words: "Without me you can do nothing"; because she declares that He is the source of all salvation and all holiness, and refers all glory to Him.

---

1 "For this is the will of God, your sanctification," I Thess. iv, 3.

2 Matth. v, 48.   3 Isa. xiv, 13–14,

"O God," let us say with the Church, in the spirit of one of her most beautiful prayers, "O God, I believe that Thou art Almighty, that Thy grace is efficacious enough to raise me, miserable as I am, to a high degree of holiness; I believe that Thou art likewise infinite mercy, and that even though I have often left Thee, Thy love full of mercy never forsakes me. It is from Thee, O my God, Heavenly Father, that every perfect gift comes down; it is Thy grace that makes us Thy faithful servants pleasing to Thee by works worthy of Thy majesty and praise. Grant that, detached from myself, and from creatures, I may run without stumbling in the way of holiness, the way wherein Thy Son, like a giant goes before us; so that by Him and with Him, I may come to the happiness that Thou hast promised!"[1]

The saints lived on these truths; therefore they have reached the height where we contemplate them to-day.

The difference that exists between them and us does not arise from the greater number of difficulties that we have to overcome, but from the intensity of their faith in the word of Jesus Christ, and in the power of His grace, as besides from their greater generosity. We can, if we will, experience this for ourselves: Christ remains ever the same, as powerful, as magnificent in the distribution of His grace; the obstacles to the outpouring of His gifts only lie in ourselves.

Souls of little faith, why do we doubt God, our own God?

V

What practical conclusions are we to draw from these consoling truths of our faith?

First of all, we ought with all our hearts to celebrate the solemnities of the Saints. To honour the Saints is to declare that they are the realisation of a divine idea, masterpieces of the grace of Jesus. God places His delight in them, because they are the already glorious members of His beloved Son; they already make part of that resplendent kingdom won by Jesus

---

1 *Omnipotem et misericors Deus, de cujus munere venit ut tibi a fidelibus tuis digne et laudabiliter serviatur: tribue quaesumus nobis: ut ad promissiones tuas sine offensione curramus* (Almighty and merciful God, of whose gift it cometh that Thy faithful might serve Thee worthily and laudably: grant us, we beseech Thee, that we might run without stumbling toward your promises). Collect of the Mass for 12th Sunday after Pentecost.

for the glory of His Father: *Et fecisti nos Deo nostro regnum.*[1]

Next we ought to invoke them. Doubtless Christ Jesus is our one Mediator: "One God, and one mediator of God and men,"[2] says St. Paul; we have access to the Father only through Him. Christ, however,—not to diminish His mediation, but to extend it,—wills that the princes of the heavenly court should offer Him our prayers, which He Himself presents to His Father.

Moreover, the Saints have the most ardent longing for our welfare. In heaven they contemplate God, their will is ineffably united to that of God: therefore, like Him, they desire our sanctification. Thus, they form with us one mystical body; according to St. Paul's expression, "we are members one of another."[3] They have towards us an immense charity which they derive from their union with Jesus, the One Head of that company whereof they are the elect and among whom God has prepared our place.

To these relations of homage and prayer that unite us to the Saints we ought to add our efforts to resemble the Saints. Our hearts should be animated, not with vacillating desires which attain nothing, but with a firm and sincere longing for perfection, an efficacious will to respond fully to the merciful designs of our divine predestination in Jesus: *Secundum mensuram donationis Christi.*[4]

And what is needed for this? What means are to be employed in order to perfect so great a work, one so glorious for Christ and so fruitful for us?

To remain united to Jesus Christ. He Himself has told us that if we wish to bear abundant fruit, to reach great holiness, we must abide in Him as the branches are united to the vine;[5] And how are we to abide in Him? Firstly by sanctifying grace which makes us living members of His mystical body. Then by that upright intention, frequently renewed, that makes us seek in everything, in the vocation where Providence has placed us, the good pleasure of our Heavenly Father. This intention directs all our activity towards God's glory, in union with the thoughts, feelings, and will of the Heart of Jesus, our Master and our Model. *Quae placita sunt*

---

1 "And hast made us to our God a kingdom," Apoc. v, 10.

2 I Tim. ii, 5.   3 I Cor. xii, 12 sq.; Ephes. iv, 25; v, 30.

4 "According to the measure of the giving of Christ," Ephes. iv, 7.   5 Joan. xv, 5.

ei, facio semper.[1] "I do always the things that please Him." This formula, in which Jesus summed up all His relations with His Father excellently translates all the work of human holiness.

And our miseries, you may say? They ought in nowise to discourage us. Our miseries are very real; our weaknesses, our limitations, we know them well enough, but God knows them better than we do. And the sense of our frailty—recognised and avowed—honours God. And why so? Because there is in God one perfection wherein He wills to be eternally glorified, a perfection which is perhaps the key of all that befalls us here below: it is mercy. Mercy is love in the face of misery; if there was no misery, there would be no mercy. The angels declare God's holiness; but as for us, we shall be in heaven the living witnesses of the divine mercy; in crowning our works, God crowns the gift of His mercy: *Qui coronat te in misericordia et miserationibus,*[2] and it is this mercy that we shall exult during all eternity in the bosom of our beatitude: *Quoniam in aeternum misericordia ejus.*[3]

Let us no longer be discouraged by trials and disappointments. They will be so much the greater and deeper according as God calls us higher. Wherefore this law?

Because it is the way by which Jesus passed; and the more we wish to remain united to Him, the more we ought to resemble Him in the deepest and innermost of His mysteries. St. Paul, as you know, sums up all the inner life in the practical knowledge of Jesus, "Jesus Crucified."[4] And Our Lord Himself tells us that the Father, Who is the Divine Husbandman, purges the branch so that it may bear more fruit: *Purgabit eum ut fructum plus afferat.*[5] God has a powerful hand, and His purifying operations reach depths that only the saints know; by the temptations that He permits, by the adversities that He sends, by the desolations and terrible loneliness that He sometimes produces in the soul, He tries it so as to detach it from all that is created; He digs deeply into it so as to empty it of itself. He pursues it, He "persecutes it in order to possess it"[6]; He penetrates it to the marrow, He "breaks its bones," as Bossuet somewhere

---

1 Joan. viii, 29.   2 Ps. cii, 4.
3 "For his mercy endureth for ever," Ibid. cxxxv, 1 sq.
4 I Cor. ii, 2.   5 Joan. xv, 2.
6 Words of D. Pie de Hemptinne, See *Une Âme Bénédictine,* 4th edit., p. 95.

says, "so as to reign alone."

Happy the soul that thus yields itself into the hands of the eternal Husbandman. By His Spirit, all of fire and love, Who is the Finger of God[1] the Divine Artist engraves in it the features of Christ, so as to make it resemble the Son of His dilection according to the ineffable design of His wisdom and mercy.

For God places His glory in beatifying us. All the sufferings that He permits or sends are so many titles to heavenly glory and felicity. St. Paul confesses himself powerless to describe the splendour of glory and the heights of joy which crown the least of our sufferings borne with divine grace.[2]

This is why he so much encourages the faithful to struggle to obtain—not the corruptible crown of this passing world's glory and applause, but an incorruptible crown, and glory that has no end, an ineffable joy.[3]

Doubtless, in these moments full of the riches of grace, the soul is plunged in sorrow and suffering and aridity. But let us remain steadfast beneath the blows of the supreme High Priest! For God puts the unction of grace in the very bitterness of the cross. Look at St. Paul. No one ever lived in more intimate union with God, in Christ, than he: who then could separate him from Jesus?[4] And behold, how, by divine permission, Satan insults him, and overwhelms the Apostle's soul and body with his darts. In his anguish St. Paul thrice beseeches the Lord. And what does Christ answer? "My grace is sufficient for thee; for power is made perfect in infirmity": *Sufficit tibi gratia mea, nam virtus in infirmitate perficitur.*[5]

VI

We here touch,—and I cannot better end this conference than here,—on the reason underlying this surprising disposition of Providence which decrees that the work of our holiness should be wrought in weakness and trials.

"By grace you are saved through faith," said St. Paul, "not of works, that no man may glory."[6]

Who then merits all praise? To whom does the glory of our holiness

---

1 Hymn *Veni Creator.*   2 Rom. viii, 8; II Cor. iv, 17.   3 I Cor. ix, 25.
4 Rom. viii, 35.   5 II Cor. xii, 9.   6 Ephes. ii, 8, 9.

return? To Christ Jesus.

When the Apostle sets the divine plan before the faithful of Ephesus, he indicates in these words the supreme end: God has thus preordained all things "unto the praise of the glory of His grace": *In laudem gloriae gratiae suae.*[1]

Thus, "that He might shew in the years to come the abundant riches of His grace," God has predestined us to become the co-heirs of His Son: *Ut ostenderet abundantes divitias gratiae suae in bonitate super nos in Christo Jesu.*[2]

Here below, we owe all to Jesus; by His mysteries He has merited for us all the graces of justification, of forgiveness, of sanctification which we need: Christ is the very principle of our perfection. As the vine pours forth its nourishing sap into the branches so that they may bear fruit, so Christ Jesus ceaselessly pours forth His grace into all those who abide in Him. It is this grace that animates the Apostles and enlightens Doctors, sustains Martyrs, makes Confessors steadfast, and adorns Virgins with incomparable purity.

In Heaven likewise all the glory of the Saints is derived from this same grace; all the splendour of their triumph comes from this one source; it is because they are dyed with the blood of the Lamb that the garments of the elect shine so resplendently; and the degree of their holiness is measured by the degree of their likeness to the Divine Model.

Therefore, at the opening of this magnificent solemnity of all Saints, wherein the Church joins in the same praise all the elect, she invites us to adore Him Who being their Lord is at the same time their Crown: IPSE *est corona sanctorum omnium.*[3]

In heaven, we shall comprehend that all God's mercies took their rise on Calvary. The Blood of Jesus is the price of the heavenly happiness which we shall then for evermore enjoy. In the Heavenly Jerusalem, we shall be inebriated with divine gladness; but every instant of this joy will have been paid by the merits of the Blood of Christ Jesus. The river of beatitude which eternally flows in this city of God[4] has its source in the sacrifice of our divine High Priest. It will be an immense joy for us to acknowledge this and to sing our joy and praise and thanksgiving to Jesus.

---

1 Ephes. i, 6.   2 Ibid. ii, 7.   3 Invitatory of Matins.
4 Cf. Ps. xlv, 5.

Like the elect, we shall cast our crowns at His feet[1] to testify that we owe them to Him.

It is to this last end that all the mystery of Christ tends. God wills that His Son Jesus shall be for ever exalted, because He is His own Only-begotten Son, the object of His complacency; because this Son, although He was God, annihilated Himself so as to sanctify His Mystical Body: *Propter quod et Deus exaltavit illum.*[2]

Let us then enter with deep faith into these divine mysteries. When we celebrate the feasts of the Saints, we magnify the power of the grace that has raised them to these summits; nothing is more well-pleasing to God, because by this praise we unite ourselves with the most intimate of His designs which is to glorify His Son: *Clarificavi et iterum clarificabo.*[3] Let us ourselves seek to realise, with the help of this same grace, the design of God for each one of us; yet once more, it is in this perfect conformity that all holiness is summed up.

I have tried during these conferences to show to what a degree the Father unites us to His Son Jesus; I have sought to place before your eyes our Divine Model, at once so incomparable and so accessible; you have seen that Christ has lived each of His mysteries for us, that He unites us to each in the closest manner in order that, little by little, we may reproduce in ourselves, under the action of His Spirit, His ineffable features, and that we may become like unto Him, according to the decree of our predestination.

Never let us cease to contemplate this Model: Christ Jesus is God appearing and living amongst us so as to show us the way and lead us to life. For He has Himself said that eternal life consists in declaring with our lips as by our deeds, that His Father is the one God, that He is God with Him, but come into this world in our flesh in order to bring back humanity to God.

If during our life, we have faithfully followed Jesus; if each year, with faith and love, we have contemplated Him in the cycle of His mysteries, while seeking to imitate Him and remain united to Him, let us be as-

---

1 Cf. Apoc. iv, 10.   2 Philipp. ii, 9.
3 "I have both glorified it and will glorify it again," Joan. xii, 28.

sured that the constant prayer that He, as our one Mediator, offers for us to His Father will be answered. By His Spirit, He will imprint His living image upon our souls; the Father will recognise us at the last day as the members of the Son of His Love, and will make us co-heirs with Christ.

We shall enter into this fellowship that Christ, our Divine Head, has formed, altogether pure and resplendent, to Himself. On the day of the final triumph, He is, according to St. Paul's[1] words, to deliver up this kingdom to His Father as the wonderful trophy of His grace. May we all meet there for the greatest joy of our souls, and for the glory of our Heavenly Father! *In laudem gloriae gratiae suae.*

VERBUM MANENS APUD PATREM, VERITAS ET VITA;
INDUENS SE CARNE, FACTUS EST VIA.

S. Augustine *Tract. in Joan.* XXXIV, 9.

---

1   I Cor. xv, 24.

ANALYTICAL INDEX

Adam, subjected to trial 152;—by the first Adam came death; by the second resurrection, 292.

Adoption (divine). God predestines us to be conformed to His Son, 11;—He adopts us as His children and multiplies His heavenly favours for us, 44 sq.;—we only became God's children in Jesus Christ and through Him 46 sq.;—constitutes the greatness of the Christian and the sublimity of our religion, 49–50; permits us to appropriate the riches of Christ, 145–146; is conferred upon us by Baptism, 178–179;—how it is shown in the mystery of the Transfiguration, 236–237;—will attain its perfection in Heaven, 237;—gives us the right of sharing in Christ's glory, 301 sq.;—the Holy Spirit teaches us the attitude we ought to have towards our Father in Heaven, 330–331;—to act as children of God, 368;—to love God with a filial love full of reverence, 371–372;—by grace we are the adoptive children of God, 381–382.—*See* **Grace.**

Adoration, ought to be given to the Sacred Humanity of Jesus, 64–66;—rendered by Christ to His Father, 80–81;—of the Infant in the manger, 129–130; adoration of the Cross on Good Friday, 250–251.

Advent, why these weeks of preparation, 102 sq.;—our dispositions during Advent, our desires, our confidence, 105 sq.;—to remain united to the Blessed Virgin at this holy season, 109–110.

Agony of Jesus, 245–246, 248.

Alleluia, expresses the Joy of Paschal-tide, 294.

All Saints, why the Church celebrates this feast at the end of the liturgical cycle, 376.— *See* **Saints.**

Ambrose (St.). The bosom of God and the virginity of Mary, the dwelling-place of the Word, 105–106;—like the Magi, let us offer our gifts to God, 144–145.

Angels, were subjected to trial, 181.

Apparition of Christ to His Apostles in the Cenacle, 282.

Appropriation, its nature, its role, 322 sq.

Aridity after Holy Communion does not prevent Christ from acting in us, 340.

Ascension (The) is, in one sense, the greatest of the feasts of Our Lord, 296;—is represented to us in a manner conformed to our nature, 296;—Christ seated at the right hand of God, 297;—reasons for this exaltation, 299 sq.;—how the Father glorifies His Son, 299 sq.;—why Christ chose the Mount of Olives whence to ascend into Heaven, 308;—He only has the right to enter into Heaven, 302;—how He gives us

Christianity, sublimity of the Christian life, 52;—it is the love of God being manifested to the world, 373.—*See* **Divine Adoption.**

Church, Mystical Body of Christ, 11–12;—prolongation of the Incarnation, is for us the way, the truth and the life, 19;—God wishes that we should have recourse to her for light and direction, 142;—Christ chose Peter as the foundation of His Church, 213;—Christ loved the Church and delivered Himself up for her, 243 sq.;—He has sanctified her by His Sacrifice, 251–252, 257;—how, in her liturgy, she blends accents of triumph with her compassion in celebrating the sufferings of her Spouse, 258–259;—rejoices at the Ascension of Jesus, 306 sq.;—the Descent of the Holy Spirit completes the establishing of the Church, 317, 327;—with what insistence the Church calls down the Holy Spirit at Pentecost, 328;—a living organism which continues to develop, 357–358;—how she is united to Christ, 376.

Communion.—*See* **Eucharist.**

Condescension of Jesus towards sinners, 211 sq., 221.

Confidence in the ever active virtue of the Divinity of Jesus, 15–16;—in His Sacred Humanity, 65;—in the mediation of Christ, our High Priest, 83–84, 308; the confidence that ought to fill our souls during Advent, 107;—with which we ought to approach the Infant in the manger, 121;—confidence awakened in us by the promises contained in the 90th psalm, 190–191;—that we ought to have in Christ at hours of combat, 192;—its primary source in the Divine mercy, 212 sq.;—is increased by penitence, 211;—the beholding of Jesus upon the Cross, motive of confidence, 254.—*See* **Faith in the merits of Christ.**

Consolations, not to seek sensible consolations for themselves nor to cling to them, 240;—God sometimes permits us to be deprived of them after Holy Communion, 340.

Co-operation, *see* **Fidelity, Spiritual Life.**

Council of Trent, utility of the exterior rites of the Liturgy, 21, n. 2;—our salvation is a gift of the Divine mercy and a reward for our merits, 180, n. 1;—the Sacrifice of the Mass, the same as that of Calvary, 336, n. 3.

Creation, is the fruit of an eternal thought, 47.

Cross, adoration of the Cross on Good Friday, 250;—by the Cross, Christ destroyed sin and merited every grace, 251;—our cross is part of that of Jesus, 255, 268, 271;—Christ accepted the Cross for Himself and for His members, 267;—why He willed to be helped to carry His Cross, 271. —*See* **Way of the Cross, Sacrifice of Christ, Sufferings.**

David, Why he depicted beforehand an the traits of the Messias, 96–97.

Death, at the hour of death, Christ will come to our aid if we have remained with Him in His sufferings, 259–260;—to accept it in expiation for our sins, 266.

Dependence, as creatures, 43–44;—towards God, 63–64.

Detachment from creatures, fruit of the Paschal grace, 289.

Devil, could not tell if Christ was the Son of God, 183–184;—knew human nature, 185;—pursued Our Lord without intermission, 185;—tempts us, 186;—one of his most dangerous snares, 222–223.

Devotion, what it is, 356; to Jesus Christ, 357;—to the Sacred Heart (See Heart of Christ); to love the devotions approved by the Church, 359.

Holy Week, how the Church during these days, causes all the phases of the Passion of Jesus to be lived over again, 254;—she blends accents of triumph with her compassion, 258.

Humility, ought to make us lay down our activity at God's feet, 45;—draws Christ into us, 104;—Christ's humility cures us of our pride, 124, 266;—Christ humbled Himself in being baptized, 173;—to humble ourselves for our faults, 266;—Jesus touched the depths of humiliation, 277;—humility draws down the Holy Spirit into our souls, 331;—is born in us at the sight of our powerlessness, 387.

Hypostatic Union (The), gives infinite value to all the actions of Jesus, 59;—renders them infinitely pleasing to His Father, 61;—because of it the Sacred Humanity has no proper personality, 64;—safeguards the distinction of natures, 116;—gives infinite value to the expiation of Christ, 122;—makes of Christ the true Son of God, 150;—relations that result therefrom between Jesus and His Father, 199;—gives to Christ the right of sharing the Divine glory, 299, 301–302. —*See* **Incarnation.**

Incarnation, how through it the divine plan is carried into effect, 48;—masterpiece of wisdom and love, 66, 94;—through it Jesus possesses His priesthood, 74 sq.;—why God willed there should be such a long preparation for this mystery, 94;—promise after the fall of our first parents, 95;—summed up in an exchange between the Godhead and humanity, 149; renders God visible and passible, 120 sq.;—destroys sin and redeems the world, 122–123; from the time of His Incarnation Christ inaugurates His Sacrifice, 123;—is a revelation of the Divine light, 132;—accomplished at the moment of the Blessed Virgin's Fiat, 152.—*See* **Hypostatic Union.**

Infirmities.—*See* **Weaknesses. Miseries.**

Interior life, gives fruitfulness to exterior activity, 166;—hidden from the eyes of men, revealed in glory, 293.

Isaias. In what terms he speaks of the Messias to come, 97.

Jesus Christ, the knowledge of His mystery, source of all our spiritual life, 4 sq.;—reveals God and His perfections to us, 5, 10, 40, 60, 203;—in Him we have and can do all things, 4, 6, 107, 253, 291;—we ought to contemplate Him, 5;—His love for His Father, 8, 245;—for us Christ lived all His mysteries, 8;—He is our Example, 8, 122;—He is the Vine, we are the branches, 13;—of His fulness we receive every grace, 13;—all His riches are ours, 13;—the fruit of His mysteries and of His merits ever continues, 13;—merited for mankind of all times, 13, 103;—how He exercises His eternal Priesthood in heaven, 15, 84 sq., 308 sq.;—the reading of the Gospel teaches us to know Him, 18;—His mysteries are repeated for us in the Liturgy, 19;—in each of them Church produces in us the grace that He merited in living the mysteries, 20, 228;—to reproduce in ourselves the likeness of Christ is a supernatural task, 24;—His mysteries ought to be contemplated with faith, reverence and love, 24;—we ought to adore Him in His self-abasement as in His glory, 26, 347;—love is at the bottom of all His mysteries and explains them all, 26, 355;—Jesus reveals His Divinity to the soul that contemplates Him in His Humanity, 27;—He is the Incarnate Son of God, 34;—does not cease to declare that He receives all from His Father, 38;—through love for His

Manna, figure of the Eucharistic Sacrament, 341 sq.

Mary, Mother of God—*See* **Virgin Mary.**

Mary Magdalen (St.), At the house of Simon the Pharisee, 140, 211, 215;—why Jesus shows her so much condescension, 214;—how He intervenes in her favour, 216.

Mary Magdalen de Pazzi (St.). How she sees Christ one Easter day, 290;—her love for God, 364.

Marie d'Oignies (St.), How Our Lords showed Himself to her on different feasts, 88.

Mass, recalls and reproduces the Immolation of Calvary, 86, 254, 334;—how the priest is identified with Christ, 87;—why the Church does not celebrate any of the mysteries of Jesus without offering the Holy Sacrifice, 87 sq.;—let us offer Christ to His Father, 146, 159;—in Holy Mass we receive the same graces as if we had been at the foot of the Cross, 255;—to unite ourselves to the immolated Christ, 345;—the altar on earth put in relation with that of Heaven, 345, 346.

Maternal love. God has placed in the heart of mothers a spark of His love for us, 154.

Mechtilde (St.), What we should offer to God on the feast or the Epiphany, 145;— Christ joins our sufferings with His own, 367.

Mercier (Card.), Through Christ we go straight to God, 4, n. 8.

Mercy (Divine), first source of our confidence, 212;—is love faced by misery, 392;— how God wills to be glorified by the exercise of His mercy, 393.

Miracles of Jesus, He works them by His own authority, 197;—the water changed into wine at Cana, 204.

Miseries, the sight of our miseries ought not to discourage us, 107–108;—how Christ welcomes us with kindness, whatever be our miseries, 140, 206;—Christ supplies for our misery, 145;—the avowal of our misery draws down God's mercy 269;—does not hinder us from approaching God, 312;—to recognise them is an excellent disposition for receiving the Holy Spirit, 332.—*See* **Confidence, Weaknesses.**

Mission of the Holy Spirit.—*See* **Pentecost.**

Mortification.—*See* **Penance.**

Mysteries of Eucharist, are ours as much as they are His, 8;—how we are one with Christ in His mysteries, 11;—their virtue ever remains, 14;—represented by the Liturgy, 19;—how they are sources of grace for us and produce in us the grace proper to each of them, 21 sq., 228, 342;—what ought to be our dispositions in order to gather the fruits of Christ's mysteries, 24;—the contemplation of them "a fountain of living water," 27;—are never celebrated without the offering of the Sacrifice of the Mass, 87;—it is in participating in this Sacrifice that we obtain the grace of the mysteries with most abundance, 88;—these are mysteries of faith, and yet the light of the Divinity burns in them, 171, 333;—how all the mysteries of Christ are contained in the Eucharist, 337, 342;—the contemplation of them produces in us resemblance with Jesus, 342.

Name of Christ, the names given to the Incarnate Word declare His mission and characterize His work, 71;—the Church always addresses her prayers to God in the name of Jesus Christ, 86.

Nativity of Christ, with what splendour the Church celebrates this festival, 112;— "admirable exchange" between the Divinity and Humanity, 113, 125–126;—inmost grace

Pentecost, why this solemnity enters into the cycle of the mysteries of Jesus, 316;— reasons why the descent of the Holy Spirit takes place only after the Ascension, 321;—the Apostles are filled with truth, 323;—fortitude, 324;—consolation, 325;— the grace of Pentecost remains, 327.

Perfection. — *See* **Holiness, Spiritual Life.**

Peter (St.), Confesses Christ's Divinity, 197;—chosen by Jesus as the foundation of His Church, 213;—weeps over his sin, 214;—transformed by the virtues of the Holy Spirit, 325.

Pharisaism, what it is, 217;—how Our Saviour unmasks the Pharisees, 220 sq.;— different forms of pharisaism, 221.

Piety. — *See* **Spiritual Life.**

Pius X. Participation in the Sacred mysteries and in the prayer of the Church, source of the Christian spirit, 23, n. 4;—(Catechism published by his command), importance of the festivals of the Church for the inner life of Christians, 28, n. 1.

Postcommunions of the missal, are diversified in their object in accordance with the mysteries, 89, 344.

Poverty of Jesus in the crib, 125.

Prayer, during prayer, to adore, and listen to Jesus, 2–14.

Prayer of Christ, His sacerdotal prayer, 83;—how He intercedes for us in Heaven, 85;— He asks His Father to keeps us from evil, 314.

Presentation of Jesus in the Temple, why the Blessed Virgin accomplishes this ceremony, 156;—Christ comes into the Temple as a hidden God, 157;—glory that He gives to His Father by the oblation that He there makes of Himself, 158;—how the Virgin unites herself in this oblation, 159–160;—the prophecy of the old man Simeon, 159.

Priesthood (The) of Christ is a consequence of His Incarnation. 74 sq.;—how He exercises it in Heaven, 84, 312;—is continued here below, 87–88;—Christ gives a participation of it to priests, 88. —*See* **Sacrifice of Christ.**

Psalm XC, arouses our confidence, 181, 193.

Reason, is a light for mankind, 132.

Resurrection of Christ, why it is called "holy," 280;—the Risen Jesus no longer knows death nor any infirmity, 282;—He lives solely for His Father, 283;—the Paschal grace placed in us at baptism, 292;—meaning of the Epistle on Easter Sunday, 285;—the special grace belonging to this mystery, 292 sq.;—dogma of the resurrection of the dead, 292;—the Paschal Alleluia, 294.

Revelation, deposit of revelation sealed at the death of the last of the Apostles, 358;—the Church develops it and lays down its precise meaning, 358.

Reverence with which we ought to contemplate Christ's mysteries, 27;—that we ought to have towards the Sacrament of the Eucharist, 347;—ought to be allied to our filial love for God, 349.

Sacraments, channels whereby grace and divine life reach us, 252.

Sacred Heart. — *See* **Heart of Christ.**

THAT IN ALL THINGS GOD MAY BE GLORIFED.

S. Benedict, *Rule.*

About The Cenacle Press at Silverstream Priory

An apostolate of the Benedictine monastery of Silverstream Priory in Ireland, the mission of The Cenacle Press can be summed up in four words: *Quis ostendit nobis bona*—who will show us good things (Psalm 4:6)? In an age of confusion, ugliness, and sin, our aim is to show something of the Highest Good to every reader who picks up our books. More specifically, we believe that the treasury of the centuries-old Benedictine tradition and the beauty of holiness which has characterised so many of its followers through the ages has something beneficial, worthwhile, and encouraging in it for every believer.

cenaclepress.com

Also Available:

Blessed Columba Marmion OSB
Christ the Ideal of the Monk

Blessed Columba Marmion OSB
Words of Life on the Margin of the Missal

Dom Pius de Hemptinne OSB
*A Benedictine Soul: Biography, Letters, and Spiritual Writings
of Dom Pius de Hemptinne*

Robert Hugh Benson
The King's Achievement

Robert Hugh Benson
By What Authority

Robert Hugh Benson
The Friendship of Christ

Robert Hugh Benson
Confessions of a Convert

Dom Hubert Van Zeller OSB
Letters to A Soul

Dom Hubert Van Zeller OSB
We Work While the Light Lasts

Visit cenaclepress.com for our full catalogue.